The
ESSENTIAL
REFERENCE R

The
ESSENTIAL REFERENCE R

Mark Gardener

WILEY

John Wiley & Sons, Inc.

The Essential R Reference

Published by
John Wiley & Sons, Inc.
10475 Crosspoint Boulevard
Indianapolis, IN 46256
www.wiley.com

Published by John Wiley & Sons, Inc., Indianapolis, Indiana
Published simultaneously in Canada

ISBN: 978-1-118-39141-9
ISBN: 978-1-118-39140-2 (ebk)
ISBN: 978-1-118-39138-9 (ebk)
ISBN: 978-1-118-39139-6 (ebk)

Manufactured in the United States of America

10 9 8 7 6 5 4 3 2 1

For general information on our other products and services please contact our Customer Care Department within the United States at (877) 762-2974, outside the United States at (317) 572-3993 or fax (317) 572-4002.

Wiley publishes in a variety of print and electronic formats and by print-on-demand. Some material included with standard print versions of this book may not be included in e-books or in print-on-demand. If this book refers to media such as a CD or DVD that is not included in the version you purchased, you may download this material at http://booksupport.wiley.com. For more information about Wiley products, visit www.wiley.com.

Library of Congress Control Number: 2012948918

There's only one corner of the universe you can be certain of improving, and that's your own self.

—Aldous Huxley

ABOUT THE AUTHOR

Mark Gardener (http://www.gardenersown.co.uk) is an ecologist, lecturer, and writer working in the UK. He has a passion for the natural world and for learning new things. Originally he worked in optics, but returned to education in 1996 and eventually gained his doctorate in ecology and evolutionary biology. This work involved a lot of data analysis and he became interested in R as a tool to help in research. He is currently self-employed and runs courses in ecology, data analysis, and R for a variety of organizations. Mark lives in rural Devon with his wife Christine (a biochemist) and still enjoys the natural world and learning new things.

ABOUT THE TECHNICAL EDITOR

Richard Rowe started his professional life as a physicist, but switched fields to earn a PhD in insect behavior. He has taught data analysis courses, mainly to biologists, at Canterbury, then James Cook University, since 1982. He has worked with R since 1997 when a friend forced a very early copy onto him. The R system has exponentially improved over the past decade, and in light of the fact that Richard's individual capacity is more linear, he retired in 2011 but keeps his hand in data-analysis consultancies and master-class workshops regularly (the best way to learn is to teach). Based on life, his belief is that ecological and behavioral data is usually the dirtiest and most ill-behaved, and hence the most fun to explore for pattern. His other hobby is dragonfly biology.

CREDITS

ACKNOWLEDGMENTS

First of all my thanks go out to the R project team and the many authors and programmers who work tirelessly to make this a peerless program. I would also like to thank my wife, Christine, who has had to put up with me during this entire process, and in many senses became an R-widow! Thanks to Wiley, for helping this book become a reality, especially Carol Long and Victoria Swider. I couldn't have done it without you. Thanks also to Richard Rowe, the technical reviewer, who first brought my attention to R and its compelling (and rather addictive) power. Last but not least, thanks to the R community in general. I learned to use R largely by trial and error and using the vast wealth of knowledge that is in this community. I hope that this book is a worthwhile addition to the R knowledge base and that it will prove useful to all users of R.

— MARK GARDENER

CONTENTS

INTRODUCTION

R is rapidly becoming the *de facto* standard among professionals, and is used in every conceivable discipline from science and medicine to business and engineering. R is more than just a computer program; it is a statistical programming environment and language. R is free and open source and is, therefore, available to everyone with a computer.

R is a language with its own vocabulary and grammar. To make R work for you, you communicate with the computer using the language of R and tell it what to do. You accomplish this by typing commands directly into the program. This means that you need to know some of the words of the language and how to put them together to make a "sentence" that R understands. This book aims to help with this task by providing a "dictionary" of words that R understands.

The help system built into R is extensive, but it is arranged by command name; this makes it hard to use unless you know some command names to start with. That's where this book comes in handy; the command names (the vocabulary of R) are arranged by topic, so you can look up the kind of task that you require and find the correct R command for your needs.

I like to think of this book as a cross between a dictionary, a thesaurus, and a glossary, with a fair sprinkling of practical examples. Even though some may consider me an "R expert" at this point, I am still learning and still forgetting! I often have to refer to notes to remind me how to carry out a task in R. That is why I wrote this book—to help novice users learn more easily, and to provide more experienced users with a reference work they can delve into time and time again. I also learned a great deal more about R by writing about it, and I hope that you will find it an essential companion in your day-to-day conversations with R.

Who This Book Is For

This book is for anyone who needs to analyze any data, whatever their discipline or line of work. Whether you are in science, business, medicine, or engineering, you will have data to analyze and results to present. R is powerful and flexible and completely cross-platform. This means you can share data and results with anyone. R is backed by a huge project team, so being free does not mean being inferior!

Whether you are a student or an experienced programmer, this book is meant to be an essential reference. If you are completely new to R, this book will enable you to learn more quickly by providing an easy-to-use "dictionary." You may also consider reading my previous book,

Beginning R: The Statistical Programming Language, which provides a different learning environment by taking you from simple tasks to more complex ones in a linear fashion.

If you are already familiar with R, this book will help as a useful reference work that you can call upon time and time again. It is easy to forget the name of a command or the exact syntax of the command. In addition to jogging your memory, the examples in the book will help put the commands into context.

What This Book Covers

Each command listed in this book has an explanation of what the command does and how to use it—the "grammar," if you will. Related commands are also listed, as in a thesaurus, so if the word you are looking at is not quite what you need, you are likely to see the correct one nearby.

I can't pretend that this reference book covers every command in the R language, but it covers a lot (more than 400). I've also not covered some of the more obscure parameters (formally called "arguments" in R) for some of the commands. I called this book "Essential" because I believe it covers the essentials. I also hope that you will find it essential in your day-to-day use of R.

One of the weaknesses of the R help system is that some of the examples are hard to follow, so each command listed in this book is accompanied by various examples. These show you the command "in action" and hopefully help you to gain a better understanding of how the command works. The examples are written in R code and set out as if you had typed them into R yourself. And unlike the built-in help system in R, you get to see the results, too!

How This Book Is Structured

This book is not a conventional textbook; it is intended as a reference work that you can delve into at any point.

This book is organized in a topic-led, logical manner so that you can look for the kind of task that you want to carry out in R and find the command you need to carry out that task as easily as possible, even if you do not know the name of the command. The book is split into four grand themes:

- Theme 1: "Data"

- Theme 2: "Math and Statistics"

- Theme 3: "Graphics"

- Theme 4: "Utilities"

These are hopefully self-explanatory, with the exception perhaps of "Utilities"; this covers the commands that did not fit easily into one of the other themes, particularly those relating to the programming side of R.

You can use the table of contents to find your way to the topic that matches the task you want to undertake. If the command you need is not where you first look, there is a good chance that the command you did find will have a link to the appropriate topic or command (some commands have entries on more than one topic).

The index is also a helpful tool because it contains an alphabetical list of all the commands, so you can always find a specific command by its name there.

The following is a brief description of each of the four main themes:

Theme 1: "Data"—This theme is concerned with aspects of dealing with data. In particular:

- **Data types**—Different kinds of data and converting one kind of data into another kind.
- **Creating data**—Commands for making data items from the keyboard.
- **Importing data**—Getting data from sources on disk.
- **Saving data**—How to save your work.
- **Viewing data**—Seeing what data you have in R.
- **Summarizing data**—Ways of summarizing data objects. Some of these commands also appear in Theme 2, "Math and Statistics."
- **Distribution of data**—Looking at different data distributions and the commands associated with them, including random numbers.

Theme 2: "Math and Statistics"—This theme covers the commands that deal with math and statistical routines:

- **Mathematical operations**—Various kinds of math, including complex numbers, matrix math, and trigonometry.
- **Summary statistics**—Summarizing data; some of these commands are also in Theme 1, "Data."
- **Differences tests**—Statistical tests for differences in samples.
- **Correlations and associations**—Including covariance and goodness of fit tests.
- **Analysis of variance and linear modeling**—Many of the commands associated with ANOVA and linear modeling can be pressed into service for other analyses.
- **Miscellaneous Tests**—Non-linear modeling, cluster analysis, time series, and ordination.

Theme 3: "Graphics"—This theme covers the graphical aspects of the R language:

- **Making graphs**—How to create a wide variety of basic graphs.
- **Adding to graphs**—How to add various components to graphs, such as titles, additional points, and shapes.
- **Graphical parameters**—How to embellish and alter the appearance of graphs, including how to create multiple graphs in one window.

Theme 4: "Utilities"—This theme covers topics that do not fit easily into the other themes:

- **Installing R**—Notes on installing R and additional packages of R commands.
- **Using R**—Accessing the help system, history of previously typed commands, managing packages, and more.
- **Programming**—Commands that are used mostly in the production of custom functions and scripts. You can think of these as the "tools" of the programming language.

Each of the topics is also split into subtopics to help you navigate your way to the command(s) you need. Each command has an entry that is split into the following sections:

- **Command Name**—Name of the command and a brief description of what it does.

- **Common Usage**—Illustrates how the command looks with commonly used options. Use this section as a memory-jogger; if you need fine details you can look in the "Command Parameters" section.

- **Related Commands**—A list of related commands along with the page numbers or a link to their entries so you can easily cross-reference.

- **Command Parameters**—Details of commonly used parameters for the command along with an explanation of what they do.

- **Examples**—Examples of the command in action. The section is set out in code style as if you had typed the commands from the keyboard yourself. You also see the resulting output that R produces (including graphical output).

Some commands are relevant to more than one theme or section; those commands either have a cross-reference and/or have an entry in each applicable place.

What You Need to Use This Book

R is cross-platform technology and so whatever computer you use, you should be able to run the program. R is a huge, open-source project and is changing all the time. However, the basic commands have altered little, and you should find this book relevant for whatever version you are using. I wrote this book using Mac R version 2.12.1, Windows R version 2.14.2, and Linux R version 2.14.1.

Having said that, if your version of R is older than about 2009, I recommend getting a newer version.

Conventions

To help you get the most from the text and keep track of what's happening, we've used a number of conventions throughout the book.

R CODE

The commands you need to type into R and the output you get from R are shown in a monospace font. Each example that shows lines that are typed by the user begins with the > symbol, which mimics the R cursor like so:

```
> help()
```

Lines that begin with something other than the > symbol represent the output from R (but look out for typed lines that are long and spread over more than one line). In the following example the first line was typed by the user and the second line is the result:

```
> data1
 [1] 3 5 7 5 3 2 6 8 5 6 9
```

ANNOTATIONS

The hash symbol (#) is used as an annotation character in R (see the following example). Anything that follows is ignored by R until it encounters a new line character. The examples used throughout this book contain plenty of annotations to help guide you through the complexities and facilitate your understanding of the code lines.

```
## Some lines begin with hash symbols; that entire line is ignored by R.
## This allows you to see the commands in action with blow by blow notes.
> help(help) # This line has an annotation after the command
```

OPERATIONAL ASSIGNMENT

R uses two forms of "assignment." The original form (the form preferred by many programmers) uses a kind of arrow like so: <-. This is used to indicate an assignment that runs from right to left. For example:

```
> x <- 23
```

This assigns the value 23 to a variable named x. An alternative form of assignment is mathematical type of assignment, the equals sign (=):

```
> x = 23
```

In most cases the two are equivalent and which you use is entirely up to you. Most of the help examples found in R and on the Internet use the arrow (<-). Throughout this book I have tended to use the = operator (because that is what I am used to), unless <- is the only way to make the command work.

COMMAND PARAMETERS

Most R commands accept various parameters; you can think of them as additional instructions that make the command work in various ways. Some parameters have default values that are used if you do not explicitly indicate an alternative. These parameters are also "order specific." This means that you can specify the value you want the parameter to take without naming it as long as the values are in the correct order. An example should clarify this; the rnorm command generates random numbers from the normal distribution. The full command looks like this:

```
rnorm(n, mean = 0, sd = 1)
```

You supply n, the number of random values you want; mean, the mean of the values; and sd, the standard deviation. Both the mean and sd parameters have defaults, which are used if you do not specify them explicitly. You can run this command by typing any of the following:

```
> rnorm(n = 10, mean = 0, sd = 1)
> rnorm(10, 0, 1)
> rnorm(10)
```

These all produce the same result: ten values drawn randomly from a normally distributed set of values with a mean of zero and a standard deviation of one. The first line shows the full version of the command. The second line shows values for all the parameters, but unnamed. The third line shows only one value; this will be taken as n, with the other parameters having their default values.

This is useful for programming and using R because it means you can avoid a lot of typing. However, if you are trying to learn R it can be confusing because you might not remember what all the parameters are.

Some commands will also accept the name of the parameters in abbreviated form; others will not. In this book I have tried to use the full version of commands in the examples; I hope that this will help clarify matters.

CROSS-REFERENCES

You can find many cross-references in this book in addition to the commands listed in the "Related Commands" section of each command's entry. These cross-references look like this:

 The magnifying glass icon indicates a cross reference.

Cross references are used in the following instances:

- Relevant commands in the same section or a different section.

- Relevant sections in the same theme or in a different theme.

- An instance in which the command in question appears in another theme or section.

- An instance in which the command in question has related information in another theme.

Data Downloads

If you come across a command that has an example you would like to try on your own, you can follow along by manually typing the example into your own version of R. Some of these examples use sample data that is available for download at http://www.wiley.com/go/EssentialRReference. You will find all examples that require the data are accompanied by a download icon and note indicating the name of the file so you know it's available for download and can easily locate it in the download file. The download notes look like this:

 The download icon indicates an example that uses data you need to download.

Once at the site, simply locate the book's title and click the Download Code link on the book's detail page to obtain all the example data for the book.

There will only be one file to download and it is called Essential.RData. This one file contains the example data sets you need for the whole book; it contains very few because I have tried to make all data fairly simple and short so that you can type it directly. Once you have the file on your computer you can load it into R by one of several methods:

- For Windows or Mac you can drag the Essential.RData file icon onto the R program icon; this opens R if it is not already running and loads the data. If R is already open, the data is appended to anything you already have in R; otherwise, only the data in the file is loaded.

- If you have Windows or Macintosh you can also load the file using menu commands or use a command typed into R:

  - For Windows use File ➤ Load Workspace, or type the following command in R:

    ```
    > load(file.choose())
    ```

  - For Mac use Workspace ➤ Load Workspace File, or type the following command in R (same as in Windows):

    ```
    > load(file.choose())
    ```

- If you have Linux, you can use the load() command but you must specify the filename (in quotes) exactly. For example:

  ```
  > load("Essential.RData")
  ```

The Essential.RData file must be in your default working directory and if it is not, you must specify the location as part of the filename.

Ris an *object-oriented language*; that means that it deals with named objects. Most often these objects are the data that you are analyzing. This theme deals with making, getting, saving, examining, and manipulating data objects.

Topics in this Theme

COMMANDS IN THIS THEME:

case.names (p. 78) cbind (p. 33) character (p. 5) class (p. 79)

colMeans (p. 124) colnames (p. 80) colSums (p. 124) comment (p. 81)

cummax (p. 172) cummin (p. 172) cumprod (p. 172) cumsum (p. 172)

data (p. 46) data.frame (p. 6, 34) detach (p. 63) dget (p. 39)

dim (p. 83) dimnames (p. 84) dir (p. 64) dput (p. 52)

droplevels (p. 111) dump (p. 53) dxxxx (p. 148) ecdf (p. 152)

factor (p. 7) file.choose (p. 40) fivenum (p. 224) ftable (p. 138)

getwd (p. 65) gl (p. 23) head (p. 65) inherits (p. 18)

integer (p. 8) interaction (p. 24) IQR (p. 225) is (p. 19)

is.xxxx (p. 20) lapply (p. 126) length (p. 127) levels (p. 86)

list (p. 9) list.files (p. 64) load (p. 47) logical (p. 9)

ls (p. 67) ls.str (p. 87) lsf.str (p. 89) mad (p. 226)

margin.table (p. 140) matrix (p. 10) mean (p. 227) median (p. 228)

mode (p. 89) names (p. 90) NCOL (p. 92) ncol (p. 92)

nlevels (p. 93) NROW (p. 92) nrow (p. 92) numeric (p. 11)

objects (p. 67) order (p. 117) prop.table (p. 141) ptukey (p. 154)

pxxxx (p. 155) qtukey (p. 158) quantile (p. 229) qxxxx (p. 159)

range (p. 230) rank (p. 119) raw (p. 12) rbind (p. 36)

read.csv (p. 40) read.csv2 (p. 40) read.delim (p. 40) read.delim2 (p. 40)

read.spss (p. 48) read.table (p. 40) read.xls (p. 48) read.xlsx (p. 49)

relevel (p. 95) remove (p. 68) reorder (p. 96) resample (p. 112)

rep (p. 26) rm (p. 68) RNGkind (p. 161) row.names (p. 99)

rowMeans (p. 124) rownames (p. 100) rowsum (p. 130) rowSums (p. 124)

rxxxx (p. 162) sample (p. 113) sapply (p. 131) save (p. 59)

save.image (p. 59) scan (p. 43) sd (p. 132, 231) search (p. 69)

seq (p. 27) seq_along (p. 27) seq_len (p. 27) set.seed (p. 165)

setwd (p. 70) sort (p. 120) source (p. 45) storage.mode (p. 101)

str (p. 102) subset (p. 114) sum (p. 232) summary (p. 132)

sweep (p. 134) table (p. 12) tabulate (p. 144) tail (p. 71)

tapply (p. 135) ts (p. 13) typeof (p. 103) unclass (p. 104)

unlist (p. 105) var (p. 235) variable.names (p. 106) vector (p. 15)

View (p. 72) which (p. 116) with (p. 73) within (p. 37)

write (p. 55) write.csv (p. 57) write.csv2 (p. 57) write.table (p. 57)

xtabs (p. 144)

Data Types

R recognizes many kinds of data, and these data can be in one of several forms. This topic shows you the commands relating to the kinds of data and how to switch objects from one form to another.

WHAT'S IN THIS TOPIC:

- **Types of data** (p. 3)
    - The different types/forms of data objects
    - Creating blank data objects
- **Altering data types** (p. 16)
    - Switching data from one type to another
- **Testing data types** (p. 18)
    - How to tell what type an object is

TYPES OF DATA

Data can exist as different types and forms. These have different properties and can be coerced from one type/form into another.

COMMAND NAME

`array`

An `array` is a multidimensional object.

 SEE `drop` for reducing dimensions of arrays in Theme 2, "Math and Statistics: Matrix Math."

Common Usage

```
array(data = NA, dim = length(data), dimnames = NULL)
```

Related Commands

`as.array` (p. 16)
`is.array` (p. 20)
`dim` (p. 83)
`dimnames` (p. 84)
`drop` (p. 212)

Command Parameters

`data = NA`	A vector to be used to create the array. Other objects are coerced to form a vector before making the array.
`dim = length(data)`	The dimensions of the array as a vector. A vector of 2 sets row and column sizes, respectively.
`dimnames = NULL`	A list of names for each dimension of the array. The default, `NULL`, creates no names.

Examples

```
  ## Simple arrays
> array(1:12) # Simple 12-item vector
 [1]  1  2  3  4  5  6  7  8  9 10 11 12

> array(1:12, dim = 12) # Set length explicitly
 [1]  1  2  3  4  5  6  7  8  9 10 11 12

> array(1:12, dim = 6) # Can set length to shorter than data
[1] 1 2 3 4 5 6

> array(1:12, dim = 18) # Longer arrays recycle values to fill
 [1]  1  2  3  4  5  6  7  8  9 10 11 12  1  2  3  4  5  6

> array(1:24, dim = c(3, 4, 2)) # A 3-dimensional array
, , 1

     [,1] [,2] [,3] [,4]
[1,]    1    4    7   10
[2,]    2    5    8   11
[3,]    3    6    9   12


, , 2

     [,1] [,2] [,3] [,4]
[1,]   13   16   19   22
[2,]   14   17   20   23
[3,]   15   18   21   24


  ## Arrays with names
  ## A vector
> array(1:12, dim = 12, dimnames = list(LETTERS[1:12]))
 A  B  C  D  E  F  G  H  I  J  K  L
 1  2  3  4  5  6  7  8  9 10 11 12

  ## A matrix
> array(1:12, dim = c(3, 4), dimnames = list(letters[1:3], LETTERS[1:4]))
```

```
  A B C  D
a 1 4 7 10
b 2 5 8 11
c 3 6 9 12

  ## A 3D array (3 row by 4 column)*2
> array(1:24, dim = c(3, 4, 2), dimnames = list(letters[1:3], LETTERS[1:4],
  month.abb[1:2]))
, , Jan

  A B C  D
a 1 4 7 10
b 2 5 8 11
c 3 6 9 12

, , Feb

   A  B  C  D
a 13 16 19 22
b 14 17 20 23
c 15 18 21 24
```

COMMAND NAME

`character`

Data in text form (not numbers) is called `character` data. The command creates a blank data object containing empty text data items.

Common Usage

`character(length = 0)`

Related Commands

`as.character` (p. 16)
`is.character` (p. 20)
`numeric` (p. 11)
`integer` (p. 8)
`factor` (p. 7)
`data.frame` (p. 6, 34)
`matrix` (p. 10)
`list` (p. 9)
`table` (p. 12)

Command Parameters

`length = 0`   Sets the length of the new vector to be created. The default is 0.

```
   ## Make a 5-item vector containing blank entries
> (newchar = character(length = 5))
[1] "" "" "" "" ""
```

COMMAND NAME

```
data.frame
```

 SEE also data.frame in "Adding to Existing Data."

A data.frame is a two-dimensional, rectangular object that contains columns and rows. The columns can contain data of different types (some columns can be numbers and others text). The command makes a data frame from named objects.

Common Usage

```
data.frame(..., row.names = NULL,
          stringsAsFactors = default.stringsAsFactors())
```

Related Commands

matrix (p. 10)
list (p. 9)
table (p. 12)

Command Parameters

...	Items to be used in the construction of the data frame. Can be object names separated by commas.
row.names = NULL	Specifies which column will act as row names for the final data frame. Can be an integer or character string.
stringsAsFactors	A logical value, TRUE or FALSE. Should character values be converted to factor? Default is TRUE.

Examples

```
   ## Make some data
> abundance = c(12, 15, 17, 11, 15, 8, 9, 7, 9)
> cutting = c(rep("mow", 5), rep("unmow", 4))

   ## Make data frame with cutting as factor (the default)
> graze = data.frame(abundance, cutting)
```

```
  ## Make data frame with cutting as character data
> graze2 = data.frame(abundance, cutting, stringsAsFactors = FALSE)

  ## Make row names
> quadrat = c("Q1", "Q2", "Q3", "Q4", "Q5", "Q6", "Q7", "Q8", "Q9")

  ## Either command sets quadrat to be row names
> graze3 = data.frame(abundance, cutting, quadrat, row.names = 3)
> graze3 = data.frame(abundance, cutting, quadrat, row.names = "quadrat")
```

COMMAND NAME

factor

This command creates `factor` objects. These appear without quotation marks and are used in data analyses to indicate levels of a treatment variable.

 SEE subset for selecting sub-sets and droplevels for omitting unused levels.

Common Usage

```
factor(x = character(), levels, labels = levels)
```

Related Commands

as.factor (p. 16)
is.factor (p. 20)
character (p. 5)
numeric (p. 11)
gl (p. 23)
rep (p. 26)
interaction (p. 24)

Command Parameters

x = character()	A vector of data, usually simple integer values.
levels	Optional. A vector of values that the different levels of the factor could be. The default is to number them in alphabetical order.
labels = levels	Optional. A vector of labels for the different levels of the factor.

Examples

```
  ## Make an unnamed factor with 2 levels
> factor(c(rep(1, 5), rep(2, 4)))
[1] 1 1 1 1 1 2 2 2 2
Levels: 1 2
```

```
  ## Give the levels names
> factor(c(rep(1, 5), rep(2, 4)), labels = c("mow", "unmow"))
[1] mow    mow    mow    mow    mow    unmow unmow unmow unmow
Levels: mow unmow

  ## Same as previous
> factor(c(rep("mow", 5), c(rep("unmow", 4))))

  ## Change the order of the names of the levels
> factor(c(rep(1, 5), rep(2, 4)), labels = c("mow", "unmow"), levels = c(2,1))
[1] unmow unmow unmow unmow unmow mow    mow    mow    mow
Levels: mow unmow
```

COMMAND NAME

ftable

Creates a "flat" contingency table.

 SEE ftable in "Summary Tables."

COMMAND NAME

integer

Data objects that are numeric (not text) and contain no decimals are called integer objects. The command creates a vector containing the specified number of 0s.

Common Usage

integer(length = 0)

Related Commands

as.integer (p. 16)
is.integer (p. 20)
character (p. 5)
factor (p. 7)

Command Parameters

length = 0   Sets the number of items to be created in the new vector. The default is 0.

Examples

```
  ## Make a 6-item vector
> integer(length = 6)
[1] 0 0 0 0 0 0
```

COMMAND NAME

list

A list object is a collection of other R objects simply bundled together. A list can be composed of objects of differing types and lengths. The command makes a list from named objects.

Common Usage

list(...)

Related Commands

vector (p. 15)
as.list (p. 16)
is.list (p. 20)
unlist (p. 105)
data.frame (p. 6, 34)
matrix (p. 10)

Command Parameters

...   Objects to be bundled together as a list. Usually named objects are separated by commas.

Examples

```
  ## Create 3 vectors
> mow = c(12, 15, 17, 11, 15)
> unmow = c(8, 9, 7, 9)
> chars = LETTERS[1:5]

  ## Make list from vectors
> mylist = list(mow, unmow, chars) # elements are unnamed

  ## Make list and assign names
> mylist = list(mow = mow, unmow = unmow, chars = chars)
```

COMMAND NAME

logical

A logical value is either TRUE or FALSE. The command creates a vector of logical values (all set to FALSE).

Common Usage

logical(length = 0)

Related Commands

as.logical (p. 16)
is.logical (p. 20)
vector (p. 15)

`length = 0`   The length of the new vector. Defaults to 0.

Examples

```
## Make a 4-item vector containing logical results
> logical(length = 4)
[1] FALSE FALSE FALSE FALSE
```

COMMAND NAME

`matrix`

A `matrix` is a two-dimensional, rectangular object with rows and columns. A `matrix` can contain data of only one type (either all text or all numbers). The command creates a `matrix` object from data.

 SEE also `matrix` in "Adding to Existing Data."

Common Usage

```
matrix(data = NA, nrow = 1, ncol = 1, byrow = FALSE, dimnames = NULL)
```

Related Commands

`data.frame` (p. 6, 34)
`as.matrix` (p. 16)
`is.matrix` (p. 20)
`cbind` (p. 33)
`rbind` (p. 36)
`nrow` (p. 92)
`ncol` (p. 92)
`dimnames` (p. 84)
`colnames` (p. 80)
`rownames` (p. 100)
`dim` (p. 83)

Command Parameters

`data = NA`	The data to be used to make the matrix. Usually a vector of values (numbers or text).
`nrow = 1`	The number of rows into which to split the data. Defaults to 1.
`ncol = 1`	The number of columns into which to split the data. Defaults to 1.
`byrow = FALSE`	The new matrix is created from the data column-by-column by default. Use `byrow = TRUE` to fill up the matrix row-by-row.
`dimnames = NULL`	Sets names for the rows and columns. The default is `NULL`. To set names, use a `list` of two (rows, columns).

Examples

```
  ## Make some data
> values = 1:12 # A simple numeric vector (numbers 1 to 12)

  ## A matrix with 3 columns
> matrix(values, ncol = 3)
     [,1] [,2] [,3]
[1,]    1    5    9
[2,]    2    6   10
[3,]    3    7   11
[4,]    4    8   12

  # A matrix with 3 columns filled by row
> matrix(values, ncol = 3, byrow = TRUE)
     [,1] [,2] [,3]
[1,]    1    2    3
[2,]    4    5    6
[3,]    7    8    9
[4,]   10   11   12

  ## Make some labels
> rnam = LETTERS[1:4] # Uppercase letters A-D
> cnam = letters[1:3] # Lowercase letters a-c

  ## Set row and column names in new matrix
> matrix(values, ncol = 3, dimnames = list(rnam, cnam))
  a b  c
A 1 5  9
B 2 6 10
C 3 7 11
D 4 8 12
```

COMMAND NAME

```
numeric
```

Data that are numeric are numbers that may contain decimals (not integer values). The command creates a new vector of numbers (all 0).

Common Usage

```
numeric(length = 0)
```

Related Commands

as.numeric (p. 16)
is.numeric (p. 20)
integer (p. 8)
character (p. 5)
factor (p. 7)

Command Parameters

length = 0   Sets the number of items to be in the new vector. Defaults to 0.

Examples
```
  ## Make a 3-item vector
> numeric(length = 3)
[1] 0 0 0
```

COMMAND NAME

raw

Data that are raw contain raw bytes. The command creates a vector of given length with all elements 00.

Common Usage
```
raw(length = 0)
```

Related Commands
```
as.raw (p. 16)
is.raw (p. 20)
vector (p. 15)
```

Command Parameters

length = 0   Sets the length of the new vector. Defaults to 0.

Examples
```
  ## Make a 5-item vector
> raw(length = 5)
[1] 00 00 00 00 00
```

COMMAND NAME

table

The table command uses cross-classifying factors to build a contingency table of the counts at each combination of factor levels.

 SEE also table in "Summary Tables."

Related Commands

ftable (p. 138)
xtabs (p. 144)

COMMAND NAME

ts

A time-series object contains numeric data as well as information about the timing of the data. The command creates a time-series object with either a single or multiple series of data. The resulting object will have a `class` attribute "ts" and an additional "mts" attribute if it is a multiple series. There are dedicated `plot` and `print` methods for the "ts" class.

Common Usage

```
ts(data = NA, start = 1, end = numeric(0), frequency = 1, deltat = 1,
   ts.eps = getOption("ts.epd"), class = , names = )
```

Related Commands

as.ts (p. 16)
is.ts (p. 20)

Command Parameters

data = NA	The numeric data. The data can be a vector, a matrix, or a data frame. A vector produces a single time-series, whereas a data frame or a matrix produces multiple time-series in one object.
start = 1	The starting time. Either a single numeric value or two integers. If two values are given, the first is the starting time and the second is the period within that time (based on the frequency); e.g., start = c(1962, 2) would begin at Feb 1962 if frequency = 12 or 1962 Q2 if frequency = 4.
end = numeric(0)	The ending time, specified in a similar manner to start.
frequency = 1	The frequency of observation per unit time. Give either a frequency or deltat parameter.
deltat = 1	The fraction of the sampling period between successive observations (so 1/12 would be monthly data). Give either a frequency or deltat parameter.
ts.eps = getOption("ts.eps")	Sets the comparison tolerance. Frequencies are considered equal if their absolute difference is less than the value set by the ts.eps parameter.
names =	The names to use for the series of observations in a multiple-series object. This defaults to the column names of a data frame. You can use the colnames and rownames commands to set the names of columns (data series) or rows afterwards.

Examples

```
  ## A simple vector
> newvec = 25:45

## Make a single time-series for annual, quarterly, and monthly data

> ts(newvec, start = 1965) # annual
Time Series:
Start = 1965
End = 1985
Frequency = 1
 [1] 25 26 27 28 29 30 31 32 33 34 35 36 37 38 39 40 41 42 43 44 45

> ts(newvec, start = 1965, frequency = 4) # quarterly
     Qtr1 Qtr2 Qtr3 Qtr4
1965   25   26   27   28
1966   29   30   31   32
1967   33   34   35   36
1968   37   38   39   40
1969   41   42   43   44
1970   45

> ts(newvec, start = 1965, frequency = 12) # monthly
     Jan Feb Mar Apr May Jun Jul Aug Sep Oct Nov Dec
1965  25  26  27  28  29  30  31  32  33  34  35  36
1966  37  38  39  40  41  42  43  44  45

  ## Make a matrix
> mat = matrix(1:60, nrow = 12)

  ## Make a multiple time-series object, monthly data
> ts(mat, start = 1955, frequency = 12)
         Series 1 Series 2 Series 3 Series 4 Series 5
Jan 1955        1       13       25       37       49
Feb 1955        2       14       26       38       50
Mar 1955        3       15       27       39       51
Apr 1955        4       16       28       40       52
May 1955        5       17       29       41       53
Jun 1955        6       18       30       42       54
Jul 1955        7       19       31       43       55
Aug 1955        8       20       32       44       56
Sep 1955        9       21       33       45       57
Oct 1955       10       22       34       46       58
Nov 1955       11       23       35       47       59
Dec 1955       12       24       36       48       60
```

COMMAND NAME

`vector`

A `vector` is a one-dimensional data object that is composed of items of a single data type (all numbers or all text). The command creates a vector of given length of a particular type. Note that the `mode = "list"` parameter creates a list object. Note also that a `factor` cannot be a vector.

Common Usage

```
vector(mode = "logical", length = 0)
```

Related Commands

`as.vector` (p. 16)
`is.vector` (p. 20)
`matrix` (p. 10)
`data.frame` (p. 6, 34)

Command Parameters

`mode = "logical"` Sets the kind of data produced in the new vector. Options are `"logical"` (the default), `"integer"`, `"numeric"`, `"character"`, `"raw"` and `"list"`.

`length = 0` Sets the number of items to be in the new vector. Default is 0.

Examples

```
   ## New logical vector
> vector(mode = "logical", length = 3)
[1] FALSE FALSE FALSE

   ## New numeric vector
> vector(mode = "numeric", length = 3)
[1] 0 0 0

   ## New character vector
> vector(mode = "character", length = 3)
[1] "" "" ""

   ## New list object
> vector(mode = "list", length = 3)
[[1]]
NULL

[[2]]
NULL

[[3]]
NULL
```

COMMAND NAME

xtabs

This command carries out cross tabulation, creating a contingency table as a result.

 SEE also xtabs in "Summary Tables."

ALTERING DATA TYPES

Each type of data (for example, numeric, character) can potentially be switched to a different type, and similarly, each form (for example, data frame, matrix) of data object can be coerced to a new form. In general, a command of the form as.xxxx (where xxxx is the name of the required data type) is likely to be what you need.

COMMAND NAME

as.array
as.character
as.data.frame
as.factor
as.integer
as.list
as.logical
as.matrix
as.numeric
as.raw
as.table
as.ts
as.vector

These commands attempt to coerce an object into the specified form. This will not always succeed.

 SEE also as.data.frame.

Common Usage

as.character(x)

Related Commands

is.xxxx (p. 20)

Command Parameters

x   The object to be coerced to the new form.

Examples

```
   ## Make simple data vector
> sample = c(1.2, 2.4, 3.1, 4, 2.7)

   ## Make into integer values
> as.integer(sample)
[1] 1 2 3 4 2

   ## Make into characters
> as.character(sample)
[1] "1.2" "2.4" "3.1" "4"   "2.7"

   ## Make into list
> as.list(sample)
[[1]]
[1] 1.2

[[2]]
[1] 2.4

[[3]]
[1] 3.1

[[4]]
[1] 4

[[5]]
[1] 2.7

   ## Make a matrix of numbers
> matdata = matrix(1:12, ncol = 4)

   ## Coerce to a table
> as.table(matdata)
   A  B  C  D
A  1  4  7 10
B  2  5  8 11
C  3  6  9 12
```

COMMAND NAME

as.data.frame

This command attempts to convert an object into a data frame. For example, this can be useful for cross tabulation by converting a frequency table into a data table.

 SEE also xtabs in "Summarizing Data: Summary Tables."

TESTING DATA TYPES

You can determine what sort of data an object contains and also the form of the data object. Generally, a command of the form is.xxxx (where xxxx is the object type to test) is required. The result is a logical TRUE or FALSE.

COMMAND NAME

class

Returns the class attribute of an object.

 SEE class in "Data Object Properties."

COMMAND NAME

inherits

Tests the class attribute of an object. The return value can be a logical value or a number (0 or 1).

Common Usage

inherits(x, what, which = FALSE)

Related Commands

is (p. 19)
is.xxxx (p. 20)
class (p. 79)

Command Parameters

x	An R object.
what	A character vector giving class names to test. Can also be NULL.
which = FALSE	If which = FALSE (the default), a logical value is returned by the command. This value will be TRUE if any of the class names of the object match any of the class names in the what parameter. If which = TRUE, an integer vector is returned that is the same length as what. Each element of the returned vector indicates the position of the class matched by what; a 0 indicates no match.

Examples

```
   ## Make an object
> newmat = matrix(1:12, nrow = 3)

   ## See the current class
> class(newmat)
[1] "matrix"
```

```
  ## Test using inherits()
> inherits(newmat, what = "matrix")
[1] TRUE

> inherits(newmat, what = "data.frame")
[1] FALSE

> inherits(newmat, what = "matrix", which = TRUE)
[1] 1

> inherits(newmat, what = c("table", "matrix"), which = TRUE)
[1] 0 1

  ## Add an extra class to object
> class(newmat) = c("table", "matrix")
> class(newmat)
[1] "table"  "matrix"

  ## Test again
> inherits(newmat, what = "matrix")
[1] TRUE

> inherits(newmat, what = "data.frame")
[1] FALSE

> inherits(newmat, what = "matrix", which = TRUE)
[1] 2

> inherits(newmat, what = c("table", "matrix"), which = TRUE)
[1] 1 2

> inherits(newmat, what = c("table", "list", "matrix"), which = TRUE)
[1] 1 0 2
```

COMMAND NAME

is

Determines if an object holds a particular class attribute.

Common Usage

is(object, class2)

Related Commands

inherits (p. 18)
class (p. 79)
is.xxxx (p. 20)

Command Parameters

object An R object.

class2 The name of the class to test. If this name is in the class attribute of the object, TRUE is the result.

Examples

```
  ## Make an object
> newmat = matrix(1:12, nrow = 3)

> ## See the current class
> class(newmat)
[1] "matrix"

  ## Test using is()
> is(newmat, class2 = "matrix")
[1] TRUE

> is(newmat, class2 = "list")
[1] FALSE

  ## Add an extra class to object
> class(newmat) = c("table", "matrix")
> class(newmat)
[1] "table"  "matrix"

  ## Test again
> is(newmat, class2 = "matrix")
[1] TRUE

> is(newmat, class2 = "list")
[1] FALSE
```

COMMAND NAME

```
is.array
is.character
is.data.frame
is.factor
is.integer
is.list
is.logical
is.matrix
is.numeric
is.raw
is.table
is.ts
is.vector
```

These commands test an object and returns a logical value (TRUE or FALSE) as the result.

Common Usage

```
is.character(x)
```

Related Commands

as.xxxx (p. 16)

Command Parameters

x   The object to be tested. The result is a logical TRUE or FALSE.

Examples

```
  ## Make a numeric vector
> (sample = 1:5)
[1] 1 2 3 4 5

  ## Is object numeric?
> is.numeric(sample)
[1] TRUE

  ## Is object integer data?
> is.integer(sample)
[1] TRUE

  ## Is object a matrix?
> is.matrix(sample)
[1] FALSE

  ## Is object a factor?
> is.factor(sample)
[1] FALSE
```

Creating Data

Data can be created by typing in values from the keyboard, using the clipboard, or by importing from another file. This topic covers the commands used in creating (and modifying) data from the keyboard or clipboard.

WHAT'S IN THIS TOPIC:

- **Creating data from the keyboard** (p. 22)
    - Use the keyboard to make data objects
- **Creating data from the clipboard** (p. 29)
    - Use the clipboard to transfer data from other programs
- **Adding to existing data** (p. 29)
    - Add extra data to existing objects
    - Amend data in existing objects

CREATING DATA FROM THE KEYBOARD

Relatively small data sets can be typed in from the keyboard.

COMMAND NAME

c

This command is used whenever you need to combine items. The command combines several values/objects into a single object. Can be used to add to existing data.

 SEE also `data.frame` in "Adding to Existing Data."

Common Usage

c(...)

Related Commands

scan (p. 43)
read.table (p. 40)
dget (p. 39)
data (p. 43)
source (p. 45)
load (p. 47)

Command Parameters

...   Objects to be joined together (concatenated); names are separated by commas.

Examples

```
  ## Make a simple vector from numbers
> mow = c(12, 15, 17, 11, 15)

  ## Make text (character) vectors
> wday = c("Mon", "Tue", "Wed", "Thu", "Fri")
> week = c(wday, "Sat", "Sun")
```

COMMAND NAME

`cbind`

Adds a column to a matrix.

 SEE cbind in "Adding to Existing Data."

COMMAND NAME

`gl`

Generates factor levels. This command creates factor vectors by specifying the pattern of their levels.

Common Usage

`gl(n, k, length = n*k, labels = 1:n, ordered = FALSE)`

Related Commands

rep (p. 26)
seq (p. 27)
factor (p. 7)
levels (p. 86)
nlevels (p. 93)
interaction (p. 24)

Command Parameters

`n`	An integer giving the number of levels required.
`k`	An integer giving the number of replicates for each level.
`length = n*k`	An integer giving the desired length of the result.
`labels = 1:n`	An optional vector of labels for the factor levels that result.
`ordered = FALSE`	If `ordered = TRUE`, the result is ordered.

Examples

```
  ## Generate factor levels
> gl(n = 3, k = 1) # 3 levels, 1 of each
[1] 1 2 3
Levels: 1 2 3

> gl(n = 3, k = 3) # 3 levels, 3 of each
[1] 1 1 1 2 2 2 3 3 3
Levels: 1 2 3

> gl(n = 3, k = 3, labels = c("A", "B", "C")) # Use a label
[1] A A A B B B C C C
Levels: A B C

> gl(n = 3, k = 3, labels = c("Treat")) # All same label plus index
[1] Treat1 Treat1 Treat1 Treat2 Treat2 Treat2 Treat3 Treat3 Treat3
Levels: Treat1 Treat2 Treat3

> gl(n = 3, k = 1, length = 9) # Repeating pattern up to 9 total
[1] 1 2 3 1 2 3 1 2 3
Levels: 1 2 3

> gl(n = 2, k = 3, labels = c("Treat", "Ctrl")) # Unordered
[1] Treat Treat Treat Ctrl  Ctrl  Ctrl
Levels: Treat Ctrl

> gl(n = 2, k = 3, labels = c("Treat", "Ctrl"), ordered = TRUE) # Ordered
[1] Treat Treat Treat Ctrl  Ctrl  Ctrl
Levels: Treat < Ctrl

> gl(n = 3, k = 3, length = 8, labels = LETTERS[1:3], ordered = TRUE)
[1] A A A B B B C C
Levels: A < B < C
```

COMMAND NAME

```
interaction
```

This command creates a new `factor` variable using combinations of other factors to represent the interactions. The resulting `factor` is unordered. This can be useful in creating labels or generating graphs.

 SEE paste in Theme 4, "Utilities," for alternative ways to join items in label making.

Common Usage

```
interaction(..., drop = FALSE, sep = ".")
```

Related Commands

gl (p. 23)
factor (p. 7)
rep (p. 26)

Command Parameters

...	The factors to use in the interaction. Usually these are given separately but you can specify a list.
drop = FALSE	If drop = TRUE, any unused factor levels are dropped from the result.
sep = "."	The separator character to use when creating names for the levels. The names are made from the existing level names, joined by this character.

Examples

 USE the pw data in the Essential.RData file for these examples.

```
> load(file = "Essential.RData") # Load datafile

   ## Data has two factor variables
> summary(pw)
     height          plant      water
 Min.   : 5.00   sativa  :9   hi :6
 1st Qu.: 9.50   vulgaris:9   lo :6
 Median :16.00                mid:6
 Mean   :19.44
 3rd Qu.:30.25
 Max.   :44.00

   ## Make new factor using interaction
> int = interaction(pw$plant, pw$water, sep = "-")

   ## View the new factor
> int
 [1] vulgaris-lo  vulgaris-lo  vulgaris-lo  vulgaris-mid vulgaris-mid
 [6] vulgaris-mid vulgaris-hi  vulgaris-hi  vulgaris-hi  sativa-lo
[11] sativa-lo    sativa-lo    sativa-mid   sativa-mid   sativa-mid
[16] sativa-hi    sativa-hi    sativa-hi
6 Levels: sativa-hi vulgaris-hi sativa-lo vulgaris-lo ... vulgaris-mid

   ## Levels unordered so appear in alphabetical order
> levels(int)
[1] "sativa-hi"   "vulgaris-hi"  "sativa-lo"   "vulgaris-lo"  "sativa-mid"
[6] "vulgaris-mid"
```

COMMAND NAME

rep

Creates replicated elements. Can be used for creating factor levels where replication is unequal, for example.

Common Usage

```
rep(x, times, length.out, each)
```

Related Commands

seq (p. 27)
gl (p. 23)
factor (p. 7)
interaction (p. 24)

Command Parameters

x	A vector or other object suitable for replicating. Usually a vector, but lists, data frames, and matrix objects can also be replicated.
times	A vector giving the number of times to repeat. If times is an integer, the entire object is repeated the specified number of times. If times is a vector, it must be the same length as the original object. Then the individual elements of the vector specify the repeats for each element in the original.
length.out	The total length of the required result.
each	Specifies how many times each element of the original are to be repeated.

Examples

```
  ## Create vectors
> (newnum = 1:6) # create and display numeric vector
[1] 1 2 3 4 5 6
> (newchar = LETTERS[1:3]) # create and display character vector
[1] "A" "B" "C"

  ## Replicate vector
> rep(newnum) # Repeats only once
[1] 1 2 3 4 5 6

> rep(newnum, times = 2) # Entire vector repeated twice
 [1] 1 2 3 4 5 6 1 2 3 4 5 6

> rep(newnum, each = 2) # Each element of vector repeated twice
 [1] 1 1 2 2 3 3 4 4 5 5 6 6
```

```
> rep(newnum, each = 2, length.out = 11) # Max of 11 elements
 [1] 1 1 2 2 3 3 4 4 5 5 6

> rep(newchar, times = 2) # Repeat entire vector twice
[1] "A" "B" "C" "A" "B" "C"

> rep(newchar, times = c(1, 2, 3)) # Repeat 1st element x1, 2nd x2, 3rd x3
[1] "A" "B" "B" "C" "C" "C"

> rep(newnum, times = 1:6) # Repeat 1st element x1, 2nd x2, 3rd x3, 4th x4 etc.
 [1] 1 2 2 3 3 3 4 4 4 4 5 5 5 5 5 6 6 6 6 6 6

> rep(c("mow", "unmow"), times = c(5, 4)) # Create repeat "on the fly"
[1] "mow"   "mow"   "mow"   "mow"   "mow"   "unmow" "unmow" "unmow" "unmow"
```

COMMAND NAME

rbind

Adds a row to a matrix.

 SEE rbind in "Adding to Existing Data."

COMMAND NAME

seq
seq_along
seq_len

These commands generate regular sequences. The seq command is the most flexible. The seq_along command is used for index values and the seq_len command produces simple sequences up to the specified length.

Common Usage

```
seq(from = 1, to = 1, by = ((to - from)/(length.out - 1)),
    length.out = NULL, along.with = NULL)

seq_along(along.with)

seq_len(length.out)
```

Related Commands

rep (p. 26)
gl (p. 23)
factor (p. 7)

Command Parameters

`from = 1`	The starting value for the sequence.
`to = 1`	Then ending value for the sequence.
`by =`	The interval to use for the sequence. The default is essentially 1.
`length.out = NULL`	The required length of the sequence.
`along.with = NULL`	Take the required length from the length of this argument.

Examples

```
  ## Simple sequence
> seq(from = 1, to = 12)
 [1]  1  2  3  4  5  6  7  8  9 10 11 12


  ## Specify max end value and interval
> seq(from = 1, to = 24, by = 3)
[1]  1  4  7 10 13 16 19 22


  ## Specify interval and max no. items rather than max value
> seq(from = 1, by = 3, length.out = 6)
[1]  1  4  7 10 13 16


  ## seq_len creates simple sequences
> seq_len(length.out = 6)
[1] 1 2 3 4 5 6


> seq_len(length.out = 8)
[1] 1 2 3 4 5 6 7 8


  ## seq_along generates index values
> seq_along(along.with = 50:40)
 [1]  1  2  3  4  5  6  7  8  9 10 11


> seq_along(along.with = c(4, 5, 3, 2, 7, 8, 2))
[1] 1 2 3 4 5 6 7


  ## Use along.with to split seq into intervals
> seq(from = 1, to = 10, along.with = c(1,1,1,1))
[1]  1  4  7 10


> seq(from = 1, to = 10, along.with = c(1,1,1))
[1]  1.0  5.5 10.0
```

COMMAND NAME

scan

This command can read data items from the keyboard, clipboard, or text file.

SEE scan in "Importing Data" and scan in "Creating Data from the Clipboard."

CREATING DATA FROM THE CLIPBOARD

It is possible to use the clipboard to transfer data into R; the scan command is designed especially for this purpose.

COMMAND NAME

scan

This command can read data items from the keyboard, clipboard, or text file.

 SEE scan in "Importing Data."

ADDING TO EXISTING DATA

If you have an existing data object, you can append new data to it in various ways. You can also amend existing data in similar ways.

COMMAND NAME

$

Allows access to parts of certain objects (for example, list and data frame objects). The $ can access named parts of a list and columns of a data frame.

 SEE also $ in "Selecting and Sampling Data."

Common Usage

object$element

Related Commands

[] (p. 30)
c (p. 22)
cbind (p. 33)
rbind (p. 36)
data.frame (p. 6, 34)
unlist (p. 105)

Command Parameters

element   The $ provides access to named elements in a list or named columns in a data frame.

Examples

```
  ## Create 3 vectors
> mow = c(12, 15, 17, 11, 15)
> unmow = c(8, 9, 7, 9)
> chars = LETTERS[1:5]

  ## Make list
mylist = list(mow = mow, unmow = unmow)

## View an element
mylist$mow

## Add new element
> mylist$chars = chars

> ## Make new data frame
> mydf = data.frame(mow, chars)

> ## View column (n.b. this is a factor variable)
> mydf$chars
[1] A B C D E
Levels: A B C D E

> ## Make new vector
> newdat = 1:5

> ## Add to data frame
> mydf$extra = newdat
> mydf
  mow chars extra
1  12     A     1
2  15     B     2
3  17     C     3
4  11     D     4
5  15     E     5
```

COMMAND NAME

[]

Square brackets enable sub-setting of many objects. Components are given in the brackets; for vector or list objects a single component is given: `vector[element]`. For data frame or matrix objects two elements are required: `matrix[row, column]`. Other objects may have more dimensions. Sub-setting can extract elements or be used to add new elements to some objects (vectors and data frames).

 SEE also [] in "Selecting and Sampling Data."

Common Usage

```
object[elements]
```

Related Commands

$ (p. 109)
c (p. 22)
cbind (p. 33)
rbind (p. 36)
data.frame (p. 6, 34)

Command Parameters

elements   Named elements or index number. The number of elements required depends on the object. Vectors and list objects have one dimension. Matrix and data frame objects have two dimensions: [row, column]. More complicated tables may have three or more dimensions.

Examples

```
  ## Make a vector
> mow = c(12, 15, 17, 11)

  ## Add to vector
> mow[5] = 15
> mow
[1] 12 15 17 11 15

## Make another vector
unmow = c(8, 9, 7, 9, NA)

## Make vectors into data frame
> mydf = data.frame(mow, unmow)
> mydf
  mow unmow
1  12     8
2  15     9
3  17     7
4  11     9
5  15    NA

  ## Make new vector
> newdat = 6:1

  ## Add new column to data frame
> mydf[, 3] = newdat
```

```
> mydf
  mow unmow V3
1  12     8  6
2  15     9  5
3  17     7  4
4  11     9  3
5  15    NA  2
6  99    NA  1

  ## Give name to set column name
> mydf[, 'newdat'] = newdat
```

COMMAND NAME

c

Combines items. Used for many purposes including adding elements to existing data objects (mainly vector objects).

 SEE also "Creating Data from the Keyboard."

Common Usage

c(...)

Related Commands

$ (p. 109)
[] (p. 30)
cbind (p. 33)
rbind (p. 36)
data.frame (p. 6, 34)

Command Parameters

...   Objects to be combined.

Examples

```
  ## Make a vector
> mow = c(12, 15, 17, 11)
  ## Add to vector
> mow = c(mow, 9, 99)
> mow
[1] 12 15 17 11  9 99
```

```
  ## Make new vector
> unmow = c(8, 9, 7, 9)

  ## Add 1 vector to another
> newvec = c(mow, unmow)

  ## Make a data frame
> mydf = data.frame(col1 = 1:6, col2 = 7:12)

  ## Make vector
> newvec = c(13:18)

  ## Combine frame and vector (makes a list)
> newobj = c(mydf, newvec)
> class(newobj)
[1] "list"
```

COMMAND NAME

cbind

Binds together objects to form new objects column-by-column. Generally used to create new matrix objects or to add to existing matrix or data frame objects.

Common Usage

cbind(..., deparse.level = 1)

Related Commands

rbind (p. 36)
matrix (p. 10)
data.frame (p. 6, 34)
[] (p. 30)
$ (p. 109)

Command Parameters

...	Objects to be combined.
deparse.level = 1	Controls the construction of column labels (for matrix objects). If set to 1 (the default), names are created based on the names of the individual objects. If set to 0, no names are created.

Examples

```
  ## Make two vectors (numeric)
> col1 = 1:3
> col2 = 4:6
```

```
   ## Make matrix
> newmat = cbind(col1, col2)

   ## Make new vector
> col3 = 7:9

   ## Add vector to matrix
> cbind(newmat, col3)
     col1 col2 col3
[1,]   1    4    7
[2,]   2    5    8
[3,]   3    6    9

   ## Add vector to matrix without name
> cbind(col3, newmat, deparse.level = 0)
       col1 col2
[1,] 7    1    4
[2,] 8    2    5
[3,] 9    3    6

   ## Make data frame
> newdf = data.frame(col1, col2)

   ## Add column to data frame
> newobj = cbind(col3, newdf)
> class(newobj)
[1] "data.frame"
```

COMMAND NAME

`data.frame`

Used to construct a data frame from separate objects or to add to an existing data frame.

 SEE also "Types of Data."

Common Usage

```
data.frame(..., row.names = NULL,
           stringsAsFactors = default.stringsAsFactors())
```

Related Commands

$ (p. 109)
[] (p. 30)
c (p. 22)
cbind (p. 33)
rbind (p. 36)
matrix (p. 10)

Command Parameters

`...`	Items to be used in the construction of the data frame. Can be object names separated by commas.
`row.names = NULL`	Specifies which column will act as row names for the final data frame. Can be integer or character string.
`stringsAsFactors`	A logical value, TRUE or FALSE. Should character values be converted to factor? Default is TRUE.

Examples

```
  ## Make two vectors
> col1 = 1:3
> col2 = 4:6

  ## Make data frame
> newdf = data.frame(col1, col2)

  ## Make new vector
> col3 = 7:9

  ## Add vector to data frame
> data.frame(newdf, col3)
  col1 col2 col3
1   1    4    7
2   2    5    8
3   3    6    9
```

COMMAND NAME

`matrix`

A `matrix` is a two-dimensional, rectangular object with rows and columns. A matrix can contain data of only one type (all text or all numbers). The command creates a matrix object from data or adds to an existing matrix.

Common Usage

`matrix(data = NA, nrow = 1, ncol = 1, byrow = FALSE, dimnames = NULL)`

Related Commands

`data.frame` (p. 6, 34)
`cbind` (p. 33)
`rbind` (p. 36)

Command Parameters

`data = NA`	The data to be used to make the matrix. Usually a vector of values (numbers or text).
`nrow = 1`	The number of rows into which to split the data. Defaults to 1.
`ncol = 1`	The number of columns into which to split the data. Defaults to 1.
`byrow = FALSE`	The new matrix is created from the data column-by-column by default. Use `byrow = TRUE` to fill up the matrix row-by-row.
`dimnames = NULL`	Sets names for the rows and columns. The default is `NULL`. To set names, use a `list` of two (rows, columns).

Examples

```
  ## Make a matrix
> newmat = matrix(1:12, ncol = 6)
> newmat
     [,1] [,2] [,3] [,4] [,5] [,6]
[1,]    1    3    5    7    9   11
[2,]    2    4    6    8   10   12

  ## Make a new vector
> newvec = c(100, 101)


  ## Add to matrix
> matrix(c(newmat, newvec), nrow = 2)
     [,1] [,2] [,3] [,4] [,5] [,6] [,7]
[1,]    1    3    5    7    9   11  100
[2,]    2    4    6    8   10   12  101
```

COMMAND NAME

`rbind`

Binds together objects to form new objects row-by-row. Generally used to create new matrix objects or to add to existing matrix or data frame objects.

Common Usage

`rbind(..., deparse.level = 1)`

Related Commands

`cbind` (p. 33)
`matrix` (p. 10)
`data.frame` (p. 6, 34)
`c` (p. 22)
`[]` (p. 30)
`$` (p. 109)

Command Parameters

...   Objects to be combined.

`deparse.level = 1` Controls the construction of row labels (for matrix objects). If set to 1 (the default), names are created based on the names of the individual objects. If set to 0, no names are created.

Examples

```
  ## Make 3 vectors
> row1 = 1:3
> row2 = 4:6
> row3 = 7:9

  ## Make a matrix
> newmat = rbind(row1, row2)

  ## Add new row to matrix
> rbind(newmat, row3)
     [,1] [,2] [,3]
row1    1    2    3
row2    4    5    6
row3    7    8    9

  ## Make a data frame
> newdf = data.frame(col1 = c(1:3), col2 = c(4:6))

  ## Add row to data frame
> rbind(newdf, c(9, 9))
  col1 col2
1    1    4
2    2    5
3    3    6
4    9    9
```

COMMAND NAME

`within`

Objects may contain separate elements. For example, a data frame contains named columns. These elements are not visible in the search path and will not be listed as objects by the `ls` command. The `within` command allows an object to be opened up temporarily so that the object can be altered.

Common Usage

`within(data, expr)`

Related Commands

with (p. 73)
attach (p. 61)
$ (p. 109)

Command Parameters

data   An R object, usually a list or data frame.

expr   An expression to evaluate. The symbolic arrow <- should be used here in preference to = in creating expressions.

Examples

```
  ## Make objects
> newlist = list(Ltrs = letters[1:5], Nmbrs = 100:110)
> newdf = data.frame(col1 = 1:3, col2 = 4:6)


  ## Alter list object
> newlist # Original
$Ltrs
[1] "a" "b" "c" "d" "e"

$Nmbrs
 [1] 100 101 102 103 104 105 106 107 108 109 110


> within(newlist, lNmbrs <- log(Nmbrs)) # Make new item. N.B <-
$Ltrs
[1] "a" "b" "c" "d" "e"

$Nmbrs
 [1] 100 101 102 103 104 105 106 107 108 109 110

$lNmbrs
 [1] 4.605170 4.615121 4.624973 4.634729 4.644391 4.653960 4.663439 4.672829
 [9] 4.682131 4.691348 4.700480


  ## Alter data frame
> newdf # Original
  col1 col2
1    1    4
2    2    5
3    3    6


> within(newdf, col1 <- -col1) # Alter column. N.B <-
  col1 col2
1   -1    4
2   -2    5
3   -3    6
```

```
> within(newdf, col3 <- col1 + col2) # Make new column. N.B <-
  col1 col2 col3
1    1    4    5
2    2    5    7
3    3    6    9
```

Importing Data

Data can be imported to R from disk files. Usually these files are plain text (for example, CSV files), but it is possible to import data saved previously in R as a binary (data) file.

WHAT'S IN THIS TOPIC:

- **Importing data from text files** (p. 39)
  - Import data as plain text (e.g., TXT or CSV)
- **Importing data from data files** (p. 46)
  - Import data previously saved by R

IMPORTING DATA FROM TEXT FILES

Most programs can write data to disk in plain text format. The most commonly used format is CSV; that is, comma-separated variables. Excel, for example, is commonly used for data entry and storage and can write CSV files easily.

COMMAND NAME

dget

Gets a text file from disk that represents an R object (usually created using dput). The object is reconstructed to re-create the original object if possible.

Common Usage

dget(file)

Related Commands

dput (p. 52)
read.table (p. 40)
read.csv (p. 40)
scan (p. 43)
source (p. 45)

Command Parameters

file   The filename in quotes. Defaults to the current working directory unless specified explicitly. Can also link to URL. For Windows and Mac OS the filename can be replaced by file.choose(), which brings up a file browser.

Examples

```
  ## Make some objects to dput to disk
> mow = c(12, 15, 17, 11, 15)
> unmow = c(8, 9, 7, 9)
> newlist = list(mow = mow, unmow = unmow)
> newmat = matrix(1:12, nrow = 2)
> newdf = data.frame(col1 = 1:3, col2 = 4:6)

  ## Use dput to write disk files
> dput(mow, file = "dput_vector.txt", control = "all")
> dput(newlist, file = "dput_list.txt", control = "all")
> dput(newmat, file = "dput_matrix.txt", control = "all")
> dput(newdf, file = "dput_frame.txt", control = "all")

  ## Use dget to recall the objects from disk
> dget(file = "dput_vector.txt")
[1] 12 15 17 11 15

> dget(file = "dput_list.txt")
$mow
[1] 12 15 17 11 15

$unmow
[1] 8 9 7 9

> dget(file = "dput_matrix.txt")
     [,1] [,2] [,3] [,4] [,5] [,6]
[1,]    1    3    5    7    9   11
[2,]    2    4    6    8   10   12

> dget(file = "dput_frame.txt")
  col1 col2
1    1    4
2    2    5
3    3    6
```

COMMAND NAME

`file.choose`

Allows the user to select a file interactively. This command can be used whenever a `file` parameter is required (that is, whenever a filename is needed). The command opens a browser window for file selection. Note that this does not work on Linux OS.

COMMAND NAME

```
read.table
read.csv
read.csv2
read.delim
read.delim2
```

These commands read a plain text file from disk and creates a data frame. The basic `read.table` command enables many parameters to be specified. The `read.csv` command and the other variants have certain defaults permitting particular file types to be read more conveniently.

Common Usage

```
read.table(file, header = FALSE, sep = "", dec = ".", row.names, col.names,
           as.is = !stringsAsFactors, na.strings = "NA",
           fill = !blank.lines.skip, comment.char = "#",
           stringsAsFactors = default.stringsAsFactors())

read.csv(file, header = TRUE, sep = ",", dec = ".", fill = TRUE,
         comment.char = "", ...)

read.csv2(file, header = TRUE, sep = ",", dec = ";", fill = TRUE,
          comment.char = "", ...)

read.delim(file, header = TRUE, sep = "\t",  dec = ".", fill = TRUE,
           comment.char = "", ...)

read.delim2(file, header = TRUE, sep = "\t", dec = ";", fill = TRUE,
            comment.char = "", ...)
```

Related Commands

`dget` (p. 39)
`scan` (p. 43)
`source` (p. 45)
`write.table` (p. 57)
`write.csv` (p. 57)

Command Parameters

file	The filename in quotes. Defaults to the current working directory unless specified explicitly. Can also link to URL. For Windows and Mac OS the filename can be replaced by `file.choose()`, which brings up a file browser.
header	If `header` = `TRUE`, the column names are set to values in the first row of the file.
sep	The separator character used in the file. For `read.table` this is "", that is, simple white space. For `read.csv` the separator is a comma and for `read.delim` the separator is a tab character.
dec	The character representing decimal points.
row.names	Sets row names. If this is a single number, it represents the column in the file that contains the row names. This can also be a vector giving the actual row names explicitly.
col.names	A vector of explicit names.
as.is	By default, any character variables are converted to factor objects as the file is read. Columns can be kept "as is" by giving the number of the column in the parameter.

na.strings	Missing values are interpreted as NA items. This parameter also permits other characters to be interpreted as NA.
fill	If TRUE, blank fields are added if the rows have unequal length.
comment.char	Sets the comment character to use.
stringsAsFactors	If TRUE, character columns are converted to factor objects. This is overridden by the as.is parameter.
...	Additional commands to pass to the read.table command.

Examples

```
  ## Make a matrix with row and column names
> newmat = matrix(1:20, ncol = 5, dimnames = list(letters[1:4], LETTERS[1:5]))

  ## Write to disk as text with various headers and separators
  ## row & col names, separator = space
> write.table(newmat, file = "myfile.txt")

  ## col names but no row names, separator = comma
> write.table(newmat, file = "myfile.csv", row.names = FALSE, sep = ",")

  ## no row or col names, separator = tab
> write.table(newmat, file = "myfile.tsv", row.names = FALSE,
 col.names = FALSE, sep = "\t")

  ## Target file has columns with headers. Data separated by comma
> read.csv(file = "myfile.csv")
  A B  C  D  E
1 1 5  9 13 17
2 2 6 10 14 18
3 3 7 11 15 19
4 4 8 12 16 20

  ## Target file has columns with headers and first column are row names
  ## Data separated by space
> read.table(file = "myfile.txt", header = TRUE, row.names = 1)
  A B  C  D  E
a 1 5  9 13 17
b 2 6 10 14 18
c 3 7 11 15 19
d 4 8 12 16 20

  ## Target file is data only - no headers. Data separated by tab
> read.table(file = "myfile.tsv", header = FALSE, sep = "\t")
  V1 V2 V3 V4 V5
1  1  5  9 13 17
2  2  6 10 14 18
3  3  7 11 15 19
4  4  8 12 16 20
```

```
  ## Same as previous example
> read.delim(file = "myfile.tsv", header = FALSE)

  ## Same as previous example, target file has no headers.
  ## Row and column names added by read.table command
> read.table(file = "myfile.tsv", header = FALSE, sep = "\t",
 col.names = LETTERS[1:5], row.names = letters[1:4])
  A B  C  D  E
a 1 5  9 13 17
b 2 6 10 14 18
c 3 7 11 15 19
d 4 8 12 16 20
```

COMMAND NAME

scan

Reads data from keyboard, clipboard, or text file from disk (or URL). The command creates a vector or list. If a filename is not specified, the command waits for input from keyboard (including clipboard); otherwise, the filename is used as the target data to read.

Common Usage

```
scan(file = "", what = double(0), sep = "", dec = ".", skip = 0,
     na.strings = "NA", comment.char = "")
```

Related Commands

read.table (p. 57)
read.csv (p. 57)
dget (p. 39)
source (p. 45)

Command Parameters

file = ""	The filename in quotes. Defaults to the current working directory unless specified explicitly. Can also link to URL. For Windows and Mac OS the filename can be replaced by file.choose(), which brings up a file browser.
what = double(0)	The type of data to be read; the default is numeric data. Other options include logical, character, and list. If a list is required, each column in the file is assumed to be of one data type (see the following examples).
sep = ""	The character separating values; defaults to simple space. Use "\t" for tab character.
dec = "."	The decimal point character.

skip = 0	The number of lines to skip before reading data from the file.
na.strings	The character to be interpreted as missing values (and so assigned NA). Empty values are automatically considered as missing.
comment.char = ""	The comment character. Any lines beginning with this character are skipped. Default is "", which disables comment interpretation.

Examples

```
  ## Create new numerical vector from keyboard or clipboard
  ## Type data (or use clipboard) separated by spaces
  ## Enter on a blank line to finish
> newvec = scan()

  ## Same as previous but separate data with commas
> newvec = scan(sep = ",")

  ## Create character vector from keyboard (or clipboard)
  ## Items separated by spaces (the default)
> scan(what = "character")

  ## Make two vectors, 1st numbers 2nd text
> numvec = 1:20
> txtvec = month.abb

  ## Write vectors to disk
> cat(numvec, file = "numvec.txt") # space separator
> cat(numvec, file = "numvec.csv", sep = ",") # comma separator
> cat(txtvec, file = "txtvec.tsv", sep = "\t") # tab separator

  ## Read data from disk
> scan(file = "numvec.txt")
Read 20 items
 [1]  1  2  3  4  5  6  7  8  9 10 11 12 13 14 15 16 17 18 19 20

> scan(file = "numvec.csv", sep = ",")
Read 20 items
 [1]  1  2  3  4  5  6  7  8  9 10 11 12 13 14 15 16 17 18 19 20

> scan(file = "txtvec.tsv", what = "character", sep = "\t")
Read 12 items
 [1] "Jan" "Feb" "Mar" "Apr" "May" "Jun" "Jul" "Aug" "Sep" "Oct" "Nov" "Dec"

  ## Make a new matrix
> newmat = matrix(1:12, ncol = 3, dimnames = list(NULL, LETTERS[1:3]))

  ## Save to disk with header row
> write.csv(newmat, file = "myfile.csv", row.names = FALSE)
```

```
## Import as list (3 items, each a column in file)
## Skip original header and set data type to numbers
## Create list item names as part of list() parameter
> scan(file = "myfile.csv", sep = ",", what = list(no.1 = double(0),
no.2 = double(0), last = double(0)), skip = 1)
```

COMMAND NAME

source

Reads a text file and treats it as commands typed from the keyboard. Commonly used to run saved scripts, that is, lines of R commands.

 SEE also source command in Theme 4, "Programming: Saving and Running Scripts."

Common Usage

source(file)

Related Commands

scan (p. 43)
read.table (p. 40)
read.csv (p. 40)
dget (p. 39)
dump (p. 53)

Command Parameters

file   The filename in quotes. Defaults to the current working directory unless specified explicitly. Can also link to URL. For Windows and Mac OS the filename can be replaced by file.choose(), which brings up a file browser.

Examples

```
## Make a custom function/script
> myfunc = function(x) {
    tmp = seq_along(x)
    for(i in 1:length(tmp)) tmp[i] = median(x[1:i])
    print(tmp)
  }

## Write to disk and delete original
> dump(ls(pattern = "myfunc"), file = "myfunc.R")
> rm(myfunc)

## recall the script
> source("myfunc.R")
```

IMPORTING DATA FROM DATA FILES

R can read data that it previously saved (and so binary encoded) to disk. R can also read a variety of proprietary formats such as Excel, SPSS, and Minitab, but you will need to load additional packages to R to do this. In general, it is best to open the data in the proprietary program and save the data in CSV format before returning to R and using the `read.csv` command.

 SEE also "Importing Data from Text Files."

COMMAND NAME

`data`

The base distribution of R contains a `datasets` package, which contains example data. Other packages contain data sets. The `data` command can load a data set or show the available data. Data sets in loaded packages are available without any command, but the `data` command adds them to the search path.

Common Usage

```
data(..., list = character(0), package = NULL)
```

Related Commands

`load` (p. 47)
`source` (p. 45)
`read.table` (p. 40)
`package: foreign` (p. 48)
`package: gdata` (p. 48)
`package: xlsx` (p. 49)

Command Parameters

`...`	A sequence of names or character strings. These are data sets that will be loaded.
`list = character(0)`	A character vector specifying the names of the data sets to be loaded.
`package = NULL`	Specifies the name of the package(s) to look for the data. The default, `NULL`, searches all packages in the current search path. To search all packages, use `package = .packages(all.available = TRUE)`.

Examples

```
  ## Show available datasets
> data()

  ## Show datasets available in MASS package
> data(library = "MASS")
```

```
  ## Show all datasets across all packages (even those not loaded)
> data(package = .packages(all.available = TRUE))

  ## Load DNase dataset: three commands equivalent
> data(DNase)
> data("DNase")
> data(list = ("DNase"))

  ## Load Animals datast from MASS package
> data(Animals, package = "MASS")

  ## Effect of data() on search path
> ls(pattern = "^D") # look at objects
> data(DNase)         # load dataset
> ls(pattern = "^D") # look at objects again
> rm(DNase)           # remove dataset
> ls(pattern = "^D") # look at objects once more
```

COMMAND NAME

load

Reloads data that was saved from R in binary format (usually via the save command). The save command creates a binary file containing named R objects, which may be data, results, or custom functions. The load command reinstates the named objects, overwriting any identically named objects with no warning.

 SEE also load in Theme 4, "Programming: Saving and Running Scripts."

Common Usage

load(file)

Related Commands

save (p. 59)
save.image (p. 59)
source (p. 45)
scan (p. 43)
read.table (p. 40)
read.csv (p. 40)
dget (p. 39)

Command Parameters

file   The filename in quotes. Defaults to the current working directory unless specified explicitly. Can also link to URL. For Windows and Mac OS the filename can be replaced by file.choose(), which brings up a file browser.

```
  ## Create some objects
> newvec = c(1, 3, 5, 9)
> newmat = matrix(1:24, nrow = 3, dimnames = list(letters[1:3], LETTERS[1:8]))

  ## Save to disk
> save(newvec, newmat, file = "saved.RData") # Give the .RData extension

  ## List then Remove objects
> ls(pattern = "^new") # see the objects
[1] "newmat" "newvec"
> rm(newvec, newmat) # check that the objects are gone
> ls(pattern = "^new")
character(0)

  ## reload objects from disk
> load(file = "saved.RData")
> ls(pattern = "^new") # see that the objects are loaded
[1] "newmat" "newvec"
```

COMMAND NAME

package: foreign
read.spss

This command is available in the `foreign` package, which is not part of the base distribution of R. The command allows an SPSS file to be read into a data frame.

Common Usage

To get the package, use the following commands:

```
> install.packages("foreign")
> library(package)
```

Related Commands

package: gdata (p. 48)
package: xlsx (p. 49)
library (p. 487)
install.packages (p. 477)

COMMAND NAME

package: gdata
read.xls

This command is available in the `gdata` package, which is not part of the base distribution of R. The command allows a Microsoft Excel file to be read into a data frame.

Common Usage

To get the package, use the following command:

```
> install.packages("gdata")
> library(gdata)
```

Related Commands

package: foreign (p. 48)
package: gdata (p. 48)
library (p. 487)
install.packages (p. 477)

COMMAND NAME

package: xlsx
read.xlsx

This command is available in the xlsx package, which is not part of the base distribution of R. The command allows a Microsoft Excel file to be read into a data frame.

Common Usage

To get the package, use the following command:

```
> install.packages("xlsx")
```

Related Commands

package: gdata (p. 48)
package: foreign (p. 48)
library (p. 487)
install.packages (p. 477)

Saving Data

The R objects you create can be saved to disk. These objects might be data, results, or customized functions, for example. Objects can be saved as plain text files or binary encoded (therefore only readable by R). Most of the commands that allow you to save an object to a file will also permit the output to be routed to the computer screen.

WHAT'S IN THIS TOPIC:

- **Saving data as a text file to disk** (p. 50)
    - Save data items to disk file
    - Show data items on screen

- **Saving data as a data file to disk** (p. 59)
  - Save individual objects
  - Save the entire workspace to disk

SAVING DATA AS A TEXT FILE TO DISK

In some cases it is useful to save data to disk in plain text format. This can be useful if you are going to transfer the data to a spreadsheet for example.

COMMAND NAME

cat

This command outputs objects to screen or a file as text. The command is used more for handling simple messages to screen rather than for saving complicated objects to disk. The cat command can only save vectors or matrix objects to disk (the names are not preserved for matrix objects).

 SEE also Theme 4, "Utilities."

Common Usage

```
cat(..., file = "", sep = " ", fill = FALSE, labels = NULL, append = FALSE)
```

Related Commands

dput (p. 52)
dump (p. 53)
write (p. 55)
write.table (p. 57)
write.csv (p. 57)
save (p. 59)

Command Parameters

...	R objects. Only vectors and matrix objects can be output directly.
file = ""	The filename in quotes; if blank, the output goes to current device (usually the screen). Filename defaults to the current working directory unless specified explicitly. Can also link to URL. For Windows and Mac OS the filename can be replaced by file.choose(), which brings up a file browser.
sep = " "	The separator character(s) to be used between elements.
fill = FALSE	Sets the width of the display. Either a positive integer or a logical value; TRUE sets width to value of current device and FALSE sets no new lines unless specified with "\n".
labels = NULL	Sets the labels to use for beginning of new lines; ignored if fill = FALSE.
append = FALSE	If the output is a file, append = TRUE adds the result to the file, otherwise the file is overwritten.

Examples

```
  ## Make a matrix
> mat = matrix(1:24, nrow = 3, dimnames = list(letters[1:3], LETTERS[1:8]))

  ## Display matrix
> cat(mat) # plain
1 2 3 4 5 6 7 8 9 10 11 12 13 14 15 16 17 18 19 20 21 22 23 24

> cat(mat, fill = 40, sep = ".. ") # set width and separator
1.. 2.. 3.. 4.. 5.. 6.. 7.. 8.. 9..
10.. 11.. 12.. 13.. 14.. 15.. 16.. 17..
18.. 19.. 20.. 21.. 22.. 23.. 24

> cat(mat, fill = 40, labels = c("First", "Second", "Third")) # with row labels
First 1 2 3 4 5 6 7 8 9 10 11 12 13 14
Second 15 16 17 18 19 20 21 22 23 24

  ## Print a message and use some math (the mean of the matrix)
> cat("Mean = ", mean(mat))
Mean =  12.5

  ## Make a vector
> vec = month.abb[1:12]

  ## Display vector
> cat(vec) # Basic
Jan Feb Mar Apr May Jun Jul Aug Sep Oct Nov Dec

> cat(vec, fill = 18) # Set width
Jan Feb Mar Apr
May Jun Jul Aug
Sep Oct Nov Dec

  ## Add fancy row labels
> cat(newvec, fill = 18, labels = paste("Qtr", 1:4, sep = ""), sep = ".. ")
Qtr1 Jan.. Feb..
Qtr2 Mar.. Apr..
Qtr3 May.. Jun..
Qtr4 Jul.. Aug..
Qtr1 Sep.. Oct..
Qtr2 Nov.. Dec

  ## Create a text message with separate lines
> cat("A message", "\n", "Split into separate", "\n", "lines.", "\n")
A message
 Split into separate
 lines.
```

COMMAND NAME

dput

This command attempts to write an ASCII representation of an object. As part of this process the object is deparsed and certain attributes passed to the representation. This is not always entirely successful and the dget command cannot always completely reconstruct the object. The dump command may be more successful. The save command keeps all the attributes of the object, but the file is not ASCII.

Common Usage

```
dput(x, file = "", control = c("keepNA", keepInteger", "showAttributes"))
```

Related Commands

dget (p. 39)
cat (p. 509)
dump (p. 53)
write (p. 55)
write.table (p. 57)
write.csv (p. 57)
save (p. 59)

Command Parameters

x   An R object.

file = ""   The filename in quotes; if blank the output goes to current device (usually the screen). Filename defaults to the current working directory unless specified explicitly. Can also link to URL. For Windows and Mac OS the filename can be replaced by file.choose(), which brings up a file browser.

control =   Controls the deparsing process. Use control = "all" for the most complete deparsing. Other options are "keepNA", "keepInteger", "showAttributes", and "useSource".

Examples

```
  ## Make some objects to dput to disk
> mow = c(12, 15, 17, 11, 15)
> unmow = c(8, 9, 7, 9)
> newlist = list(mow = mow, unmow = unmow)
> newmat = matrix(1:12, nrow = 2)
> newdf = data.frame(col1 = 1:3, col2 = 4:6)

  ## Use dput to write disk files
> dput(mow, file = "dput_vector.txt", control = "all")
> dput(newlist, file = "dput_list.txt", control = "all")
```

```
> dput(newmat, file = "dput_matrix.txt", control = "all")
> dput(newdf, file = "dput_frame.txt", control = "all")

  ## Use dget to recall the objects from disk
> dget(file = "dput_vector.txt")
[1] 12 15 17 11 15

> dget(file = "dput_list.txt")
$mow
[1] 12 15 17 11 15

$unmow
[1] 8 9 7 9

> dget(file = "dput_matrix.txt")
     [,1] [,2] [,3] [,4] [,5] [,6]
[1,]    1    3    5    7    9   11
[2,]    2    4    6    8   10   12

> dget(file = "dput_frame.txt")
  col1 col2
1    1    4
2    2    5
3    3    6

## Make a matrix
> newmat = matrix(1:12, nrow = 2, dimnames = list(letters[1:2], LETTERS[1:6]))

  ## Examine effects of control (deparsing) options
> dput(newmat, control = "all") # keeps structure
structure(1:12, .Dim = c(2L, 6L),
\ .Dimnames = list(c("a", "b"), c("A", "B", "C", "D", "E", "F")))
> dput(newmat, control = "useSource") # loses structure
1:12
```

COMMAND NAME

dump

This command attempts to create text representations of R objects. Once saved to disk, the objects can usually be re-created using the source command.

 SEE also dump in Theme 4, "Programming: Saving and Running Scripts."

Common Usage

```
dump(list, file = "dumpdata.R", append = FALSE, control = "all")
```

Related Commands

cat (p. 509)
dput (p. 52)
write (p. 55)
write.table (p. 57)
write.csv (p. 57)
save (p. 59)

Command Parameters

list	A character vector containing the names of the R objects to be written.
file = "dumpdata.R"	The filename in quotes; if blank the output goes to current device (usually the screen). Filename defaults to the current working directory unless specified explicitly. Can also link to URL. For Windows and Mac OS the filename can be replaced by file.choose(), which brings up a file browser.
append = FALSE	If the output is a file, append = TRUE adds result to the file, otherwise the file is overwritten.
control = "all"	Controls the deparsing process. Use control = "all" for the most complete deparsing. Other options are "keepNA", "keepInteger", "showAttributes", and "useSource". Use control = NULL for simplest representation.

Examples

```
> ## Make some objects
> mow = c(12, 15, 17, 11, 15)
> unmow = c(8, 9, 7, 9)
> newlist = list(mow = mow, unmow = unmow)
> newmat = matrix(1:12, nrow = 2, dimnames = list(letters[1:2], LETTERS[1:6]))
> newdf = data.frame(col1 = 1:3, col2 = 4:6)

  ## Dump items (to screen)
> dump("newmat", file = "")
newmat <-
structure(1:12, .Dim = c(2L, 6L),
 .Dimnames = list(c("a", "b"), c("A", "B", "C", "D", "E", "F")))

> dump(c("mow", "unmow"), file = "") # multiple items
mow <-
c(12, 15, 17, 11, 15)
unmow <-
c(8, 9, 7, 9)

> dump("newlist", file = "")
newlist <-
structure(list(mow = c(12, 15, 17, 11, 15), unmow = c(8, 9, 7, 9)),
 .Names = c("mow", "unmow"))
```

```
## Different control options
> dump("newdf", file = "") # Default control = "all"
newdf <-
structure(list(col1 = 1:3, col2 = 4:6), .Names = c("col1", "col2"),
 row.names = c(NA, -3L), class = "data.frame")

> dump("newdf", file = "", control = NULL) # Compare to previous control
newdf <-
list(col1 = 1:3, col2 = 4:6)
```

COMMAND NAME

write

Writes data to a text file. The command is similar to the cat command and can handle only vector or matrix data.

Common Usage

```
write(x, file = "data", ncolumns = if(is.character(x)) 1 else 5,
      append = FALSE, sep = " ")
```

Related Commands

cat (p. 509)
dput (p. 52)
dump (p. 53)
write.table (p. 57)
write.csv (p. 57)
save (p. 59)

Command Parameters

x	The data to be written.
file = "data"	The filename in quotes; if blank, the output goes to the current device (usually the screen). Filename defaults to the current working directory unless specified explicitly. Can also link to URL. For Windows and Mac OS the filename can be replaced by file.choose(), which brings up a file browser.
ncolumns =	The number of columns to be created in the file. For character data the default is 1. For numerical data the default is 5.
append = FALSE	If the output is a file, append = TRUE adds result to the file, otherwise the file is overwritten.
sep = " "	The separator character to use between data items.

Examples

```
  ## Make some objects
> vecnum = 1:12 # simple numbers
> vectxt = month.abb[1:6] # Text (month names)
> mat = matrix(1:12, nrow = 2, dimnames = list(letters[1:2], LETTERS[1:6]))

  ## Use write on vectors
> write(vecnum, file = "") # default 5 columns
1 2 3 4 5
6 7 8 9 10
11 12

> write(vecnum, file = "", ncolumns = 6) # make 6 columns
1 2 3 4 5 6
7 8 9 10 11 12

> write(vectxt, file = "") # defaults to single column
Jan
Feb
Mar
Apr
May
Jun

> write(vectxt, file = "", ncol = 3) # set to 3 columns
Jan Feb Mar
Apr May Jun

  ## Use write on a matrix
> mat # original matrix
  A B C D  E  F
a 1 3 5 7  9 11
b 2 4 6 8 10 12

> write(mat, file = "") # default 5 columns
1 2 3 4 5
6 7 8 9 10
11 12

> write(mat, file = "", ncolumns = 6, sep = ",") # note data order
1,2,3,4,5,6
7,8,9,10,11,12

> write(t(mat), file = "", ncolumns = 6) # matrix transposed
1 3 5 7 9 11
2 4 6 8 10 12
```

COMMAND NAME

```
write.table
write.csv
write.csv2
```

Writes data to disk and converts it to a data frame.

Common Usage

```
write.table(x, file = "", append = FALSE, quote = TRUE, sep = " ",
            eol = "\n", na = "NA", dec = ".", row.names = TRUE,
            col.names = TRUE, qmethod = "escape")

write.csv(...)
write.csv2(...)
```

Related Commands

`read.table` (p. 40)
`read.csv` (p. 40)
`cat` (p. 509)
`dput` (p. 52)
`dump` (p. 53)
`write` (p. 55)
`save` (p. 59)

Command Parameters

`x`	The object to be written; ideally this is a data frame or matrix.
`file = ""`	The filename in quotes; if blank, the output goes to the current device (usually the screen). Filename defaults to the current working directory unless specified explicitly. Can also link to URL. For Windows and Mac OS the filename can be replaced by `file.choose()`, which brings up a file browser.
`append = FALSE`	If the output is a file, `append = TRUE` adds the result to the file, otherwise the file is overwritten.
`quote = TRUE`	Adds quote marks around text items if set to TRUE (the default).
`sep = " "`	The separator between items. For `write.csv` this is ","; for `write.csv2` this is ";".
`eol = "\n"`	Sets the character(s) to print at the end of each row. The default "\n" creates a newline only. Use "\r\n" for a Windows-style line end.
`na = "NA"`	Sets the character string to use for missing values in the data.
`dec = "."`	The decimal point character. For `write.csv2` this is ",".

row.names = TRUE	If set to FALSE, the first column is ignored. A separate vector of values can be given to use as row names.
col.names = TRUE	If set to FALSE, the first row is ignored. A separate vector of values can be given to use as column names. If col.names = NA, an extra column is added to accommodate row names (this is the default for write.csv and write.csv2).
qmethod = "escape"	Specifies how to deal with embedded double quote characters. The default "escape" produces a backslash and "double" doubles the quotes.

Examples

```
  ## Make data frames without and with row names
> dat = data.frame(col1 = 1:3, col2 = 4:6)
> datrn = dat # copy previous data frame
> rownames(datrn) = c("First", "Second", "Third") # add row names

  ## Default writes row names (not required here)
> write.table(dat, file = "")
"col1" "col2"
"1" 1 4
"2" 2 5
"3" 3 6

  ## Remove row names
> write.table(dat, file = "", row.names = FALSE)
"col1" "col2"
1 4
2 5
3 6

  ## With row names header is wrong
> write.table(datrn, file = "")
"col1" "col2"
"First" 1 4
"Second" 2 5
"Third" 3 6

  ## Add extra column to accommodate row names
> write.table(datrn, file = "", col.names = NA)
"" "col1" "col2"
"First" 1 4
"Second" 2 5
"Third" 3 6

  ## write.csv and write.csv2 add extra column
> write.csv(datrn, file = "")
```

```
"","col1","col2"
"First",1,4
"Second",2,5
"Third",3,6

  ## quote = FALSE removes quote marks
> write.table(datrn, file = "", col.names = NA, quote = FALSE, sep = ",")
,col1,col2
First,1,4
Second,2,5
Third,3,6
```

SAVING DATA AS A DATA FILE TO DISK

Any R object can be saved to disk as a binary-encoded file. The save command saves named objects to disk that can be recalled later using the load command (the data command can also work for some objects). The save.image command saves all the objects; that is, the current workspace.

COMMAND NAME

```
save
save.image
```

These commands save R objects to disk as binary encoded files. These can be recalled later using the load command. The save.image command is a convenience command that saves all objects in the current workspace (similar to what happens when quitting R).

 SEE also save in Theme 4, "Programming: Saving and Running Scripts."

Common Usage

```
save(..., list = character(0L), file = stop("'file' must be specified"),
    ascii = FALSE)

save.image(file = ".RData")
```

Related Commands

load (p. 47)
source (p. 45)
cat (p. 509)
dput (p. 52)
dump (p. 53)
write (p. 55)
write.table (p. 57)
write.csv (p. 57)

Command Parameters

`...`	Names of R objects (separated by commas) to be saved.
`list =`	A list can be given instead of explicit names; this allows the `ls` command to be used, for example.
`file =`	The filename in quotes; defaults to the current working directory unless specified explicitly. Can also link to URL. For Windows and Mac OS the filename can be replaced by `file.choose()`, which brings up a file browser. For `save.image` the default workspace file is used: `".RData"`.
`ascii = FALSE`	If set to `TRUE`, an ASCII representation is written to disk.

Examples

```
   ## Make some objects to save to disk
> mow = c(12, 15, 17, 11, 15)
> unmow = c(8, 9, 7, 9)
> newvec = month.abb[1:6]
> newlist = list(mow = mow, unmow = unmow)
> newmat = matrix(1:12, nrow = 2, dimnames = list(letters[1:2], LETTERS[1:6]))
> newdf = data.frame(col1 = 1:3, col2 = 4:6)

   ## View the objects beginning with "new" or ending with "mow"
> ls(pattern = "^new|mow$")

   ## Save entire workspace
> save.image(file = "my_ws.RData")

   ## Save some objects
> save(newvec, newlist, newmat, newdf, file = "my_stuff.RData")

   ## Save selected objects
> save(list = ls(pattern = "^new|mow$"), file = "my_ls.RData")

   ## Recall objects in files using load("filename") e.g.
> load("my_stuff.RData")
> load("my_ls.RData")
```

Viewing Data

R works with named objects. An object could be data, a result of an analysis, or a customized function. You need to be able to see which objects are available in the memory of R and on disk. You also need to be able to see what an individual object is and examine its properties. Finally, you need to be able to view an object and possibly select certain components from it.

 SEE "Data Types" for determining what is an individual object.

WHAT'S IN THIS TOPIC:

- **Listing data** (p. 61)
  - View objects in current workspace
  - View files on disk
  - View objects within other objects (i.e., object components)
- **Data object properties** (p. 74)
- **Selecting and sampling data** (p. 107)
- **Sorting and rearranging data** (p. 117)
  - Obtain an index for items in an object
  - Reorder the items in an object
  - Return the ranks of items in an object

LISTING DATA

You need to be able to see what data items you have in your R workspace and on disk. You also need to be able to view the objects themselves and look at the components that make up each object.

COMMAND NAME

attach

Objects can have multiple components, which will not appear separately and cannot be selected simply by typing their name. The attach command "opens" an object and allows the components to be available. Data objects that have the same names as the components can lead to confusion, so this command needs to be used with caution.

Common Usage

attach(what)

Related Commands

detach (p. 63)
with (p. 73)
$ (p. 109)

Command Parameters

what   An R object to be "opened" and made available on the search path. Usually this is a data frame or list.

Examples

```
  ## Make some objects containing components
  ## A data frame with two columns
> newdf = data.frame(col1 = 1:3, col2 = 4:6)
  ## A list with 2 components
> newlist = list(item1 = letters[1:5], item2 = 100:110)

  ## Look for components (not found)
> item1
Error: object 'item1' not found

> item2
Error: object 'item2' not found

> col1
Error: object 'col1' not found

  ## Attach objects to open and add to search() path
> attach(newlist)
> attach(newdf)

  ## Now components are found
> item1
[1] "a" "b" "c" "d" "e"

> item2
 [1] 100 101 102 103 104 105 106 107 108 109 110

> col1
[1] 1 2 3

  ## Components do not appear using ls() but are in search() path
> search()
 [1] ".GlobalEnv"        "newdf"             "newlist"
 [4] "tools:rstudio"     "package:stats"     "package:graphics"
 [7] "package:grDevices" "package:utils"     "package:datasets"
[10] "package:methods"   "Autoloads"         "package:base"

  ## "Close" objects and remove from search() path
> detach(newdf)
> detach(newlist)

> search()
 [1] ".GlobalEnv"        "tools:rstudio"     "package:stats"
 [4] "package:graphics"  "package:grDevices" "package:utils"
 [7] "package:datasets"  "package:methods"   "Autoloads"
[10] "package:base"
```

COMMAND NAME

`detach`

An object that has been added to the search path using the `attach` command should be removed from the search path. This tidies up and makes it less likely that a name conflict will occur. The `detach` command removes the object from the search path and makes its components invisible to the `ls` command and unavailable by simply typing the name. Also removes a library.

 SEE Theme 4, "Utilities" for managing packages of additional commands.

Common Usage

```
detach(name)
detach(package:name)
```

Related Commands

```
attach (p. 61)
library (p. 487)
```

Command Parameters

name   The name of the object or library/package that was attached to the search path.

Examples

```
   ## Make some objects containing components
> newdf = data.frame(col1 = 1:3, col2 = 4:6)
> newlist = list(item1 = letters[1:5], item2 = 100:110)

   ## Add objects to search() path
> attach(newdf)
> attach(newlist)

> ## Make MASS package available
> library(MASS)

Attaching package: 'MASS'

   ## Look at search() path
> search()
 [1] ".GlobalEnv"         "package:MASS"      "newlist"
 [4] "newdf"              "tools:rstudio"     "package:stats"
 [7] "package:graphics"   "package:grDevices" "package:utils"
[10] "package:datasets"   "package:methods"    "Autoloads"
[13] "package:base"
```

THEME 1: DATA

```
  ## Remove items from search() path
> detach(newdf)
> detach(newlist)
> detach(package:MASS) # note name convention: package:xxxx

## Check search() path
> search()
 [1] ".GlobalEnv"        "tools:rstudio"     "package:stats"
 [4] "package:graphics"  "package:grDevices" "package:utils"
 [7] "package:datasets"  "package:methods"   "Autoloads"
[10] "package:base"
```

COMMAND NAME

```
dir
list.files
```

View files in a directory or folder on disk.

Common Usage

```
dir(path = ".", pattern = NULL, all.files = FALSE, ignore.case = FALSE)

list.files(path = ".", pattern = NULL, all.files = FALSE, ignore.case = FALSE)
```

Related Commands

ls (p. 67)
search (p. 69)
file.choose (p. 40)
getwd (p. 65)
setwd (p. 70)

Command Parameters

path = "."	The path to use for the directory. The default is the current working directory. The path must be in quotes; ".." shows one level up from current working directory.
pattern = NULL	An optional regular expression for pattern matching. Only files matching the pattern are shown.
all.files = FALSE	If all.files = TRUE, invisible files are shown as well as visible ones.
ignore.case = FALSE	Used for pattern matching; if set to FALSE (the default), matching is case-insensitive.

Examples

```
## Show visible files in current working directory
> dir()

## Show invisible files
> dir(all.files = TRUE)

## Show all files in current directory beginning with letter d or D
> dir(pattern = "^d", ignore.case = TRUE)
```

COMMAND NAME

getwd

Gets the name of the current working directory.

Common Usage

getwd()

Related Commands

setwd (p. 70)
dir (p. 64)

Command Parameters

()   No instructions are required.

Examples

```
## Get the current working directory
> getwd()
[1] "/Users/markgardener"
```

COMMAND NAME

head

Shows the first few elements of an object.

Common Usage

head(x, n = 6L)

Related Commands

tail (p. 71)
str (p. 102)
names (p. 90)
summary (p. 132)

Command Parameters

x	The name of the object to view.
n = 6L	The number of elements of the object to view; defaults to 6.

Examples

```
## Look at the top few elements of the DNase data
> head(DNase)
  Run       conc density
1   1 0.04882812   0.017
2   1 0.04882812   0.018
3   1 0.19531250   0.121
4   1 0.19531250   0.124
5   1 0.39062500   0.206
6   1 0.39062500   0.215

> head(DNase, n= 3)
  Run       conc density
1   1 0.04882812   0.017
2   1 0.04882812   0.018
3   1 0.19531250   0.121

  ## Make a matrix
> newmat = matrix(1:100, nrow = 20, dimnames = list(letters[1:20],
  LETTERS[1:5]))

  ## Look at top 4 elements of matrix
> head(newmat, n = 4)
  A  B  C  D  E
a 1 21 41 61 81
b 2 22 42 62 82
c 3 23 43 63 83
d 4 24 44 64 84

  ## Show all except last 18 elements
> head(newmat, n = -18)
  A  B  C  D  E
a 1 21 41 61 81
b 2 22 42 62 82
```

COMMAND NAME

```
ls
objects
```

Shows (lists) the objects in the specified environment. Most commonly used to get a list of objects in the current workspace.

Common Usage

```
ls(name, pos = -1, pattern, all.names = FALSE)

objects(name, pos = -1, pattern, all.names = FALSE)
```

Related Commands

rm (p. 68)
search (p. 69)
ls.str (p. 87)
dir (p. 64)

Command Parameters

name	The name of the environment for which to give the listing. The default is to use the current environment; that is, name = ".GlobalEnv".
pos = -1	The position of the environment to use for the listing as given by the search command. The default pos = -1 and pos = 1 are equivalent and relate to the global environment (the workspace). Other positions will relate to various command packages.
pattern	An optional pattern to match using regular expressions.
all.names = FALSE	If set to TRUE, names beginning with a period are shown.

Examples

```
  ## list visible objects in workspace
> ls()

  ## list visible objects containing "data"
> ls(pattern = "data")

  ## list objects beginning with "d"
> ls(pattern = "^d")

  ## list objects beginning with "d" or "D"
> ls(pattern = "^d|^D")
```

```
  ## list objects ending with "vec"
> ls(pattern = "vec$")

  ## list objects beginning with "new" or ending with "vec"
> ls(pattern = "^new|vec$")

  ## list objects beginning with letters "d" or "n"
> ls(pattern = "^[dn]")
```

COMMAND NAME

```
rm
remove
```

Removes objects from a specified environment, usually the current workspace. There is no warning!

Common Usage

```
rm(..., list = character(0), pos = -1)

remove(..., list = character(0), pos = -1)
```

Related Commands

```
ls (p. 67)
detach (p. 63)
dir (p. 64)
search (p. 69)
```

Command Parameters

`...`	The objects to be removed.
`list = character(0)`	A character vector naming the objects to be removed.
`pos = -1`	The position of the environment from where the objects are to be removed. The default `pos = -1` and `pos = 1` are equivalent and relate to the global environment (the workspace). Other positions will relate to various command packages. The environment can also be specified as a character string.

Examples

```
  ## Make some objects
> newlist = list(Ltrs = letters[1:5], Nmbrs = 100:110)
> newmat = matrix(1:12, nrow = 3)
> newdf = data.frame(col1 = 1:3, col2 = 4:6)
> newvec = 1:6
```

```
  ## Attach newlist to search() path
> attach(newlist)

  ## List objects in workspace beginning with "new"
> ls(pattern = "^new")
[1] "newdf"   "newlist" "newmat"  "newvec"

  ## List objects in search() path pos = 2
> ls(pos = 2)
[1] "Ltrs"  "Nmbrs"

  ## Remove objects in workspace
> rm(newdf, newvec)
> rm(list = ls(pattern = "^new"))

  ## Remove object in search() path
> rm(Nmbrs, pos = 2)

> Ltrs # Object remains in search() path pos = 2
[1] "a" "b" "c" "d" "e"

> search() # Check search() path
 [1] ".GlobalEnv"         "newlist"            "tools:rstudio"
 [4] "package:stats"      "package:graphics"   "package:grDevices"
 [7] "package:utils"      "package:datasets"   "package:methods"
[10] "Autoloads"          "package:base"

  ## Tidy up
> detach(newlist) # Detach object
> Ltrs # Object is now gone
Error: object 'Ltrs' not found
```

COMMAND NAME

search

Shows the search path and objects contained on it. Includes packages and R objects that have been attached via the `attach` command.

Common Usage

search()

Related Commands

ls (p. 67)
objects (p. 67)
library (p. 487)
attach (p. 61)
detach (p. 63)

Command Parameters

() No instructions are required. The command returns the search path and objects on it.

Examples

```
## Basic search path
> search()
 [1] ".GlobalEnv"        "tools:rstudio"     "package:stats"
 [4] "package:graphics"  "package:grDevices" "package:utils"
 [7] "package:datasets"  "package:methods"   "Autoloads"
[10] "package:base"


## Load MASS package
> library(MASS)


## Search path shows new loaded package MASS
> search()
 [1] ".GlobalEnv"        "package:MASS"      "tools:rstudio"
 [4] "package:stats"     "package:graphics"  "package:grDevices"
 [7] "package:utils"     "package:datasets"  "package:methods"
[10] "Autoloads"         "package:base"
 ## Make a data frame
> newdf = data.frame(col1 = 1:3, col2 = 4:6)


## Add data frame to search path
> attach(newdf)


## Search path shows attached data frame
> search()
 [1] ".GlobalEnv"        "newdf"             "package:MASS"
 [4] "tools:rstudio"     "package:stats"     "package:graphics"
 [7] "package:grDevices" "package:utils"     "package:datasets"
[10] "package:methods"   "Autoloads"         "package:base"


## Detach data frame and unload package from search path
> detach(newdf)
> detach(package:MASS)
```

COMMAND NAME

setwd

Sets the working directory. Any operations that save a file to disk will use this directory unless their name includes the path explicitly.

Common Usage
```
setwd(dir)
```

Related Commands
getwd (p. 65)
dir (p. 64)
list.files (p. 64)
file.choose (p. 40)

Command Parameters

dir   A character string giving the directory to use as the working directory. The full path-name must be given using forward slash characters as required.

Examples
```
  ## Set working directory
> setwd("My Documents")
> setwd("My Documents/Data files")
```

COMMAND NAME
```
tail
```

Displays the last few elements of an object. This is usually a data frame, matrix, or list.

Common Usage
```
tail(x, n = 6L)
```

Related Commands
head (p. 65)
str (p. 102)
names (p. 90)
summary (p. 132)

Command Parameters

x   The name of the object to view.

n = 6L   The number of elements to display; defaults to the last 6.

```
## Show the last 6 elements of the DNase data frame
> tail(DNase)
    Run  conc density
171  11  3.125   0.994
172  11  3.125   0.980
173  11  6.250   1.421
174  11  6.250   1.385
175  11 12.500   1.715
176  11 12.500   1.721

## Show the last 2 elements of the data frame DNase
> tail(DNase, n = 2)
    Run conc density
175  11 12.5   1.715
176  11 12.5   1.721

## Show the last elements not including the final 174
> tail(DNase, n = -174)
    Run conc density
175  11 12.5   1.715
176  11 12.5   1.721
```

COMMAND NAME

View

Opens a spreadsheet-style viewer of a data object. The command coerces the object into a data frame and will fail if the object cannot be converted.

Common Usage

```
View(x)
```

Related Commands

str (p. 102)
head (p. 65)
tail (p. 71)

Command Parameters

x The object to be viewed. This will be coerced to a data frame and the command will fail if the object cannot be coerced.

Examples

```
## Make some objects
> newvec = month.abb[1:6] # Six month names, a character vector
```

```
> newdf = data.frame(col1 = 1:3, col2 = 4:6) # Numeric data frame
> newlist = list(item1 = letters[1:5], item2 = 100:110) # Simple list
> newmat = matrix(1:12, nrow = 4, dimnames = list(letters[1:4], LETTERS[1:3]))

  ## View items
> View(newvec)
> View(newmat)
> View(newdf)

> View(newlist) # Fails as list cannot be coerced to a data frame
Error in data.frame(item1 = c("a", "b", "c", "d", "e"), item2 = 100:110,  :
  arguments imply differing number of rows: 5, 11
```

COMMAND NAME

with

Allows an object to be temporarily placed in the search list. The result is that named components of the object are available for the duration of the command.

 SEE also with in "Selecting and Sampling Data."

Common Usage

with(x, expr)

Related Commands

$ (p. 109)
attach (p. 61)
detach (p. 63)
within (p. 37)

Command Parameters

x   An R object.

expr   An expression/command to evaluate.

Examples

```
> ## Make some objects containing components
> newdf = data.frame(col1 = 1:3, col2 = 4:6)
> newlist = list(item1 = letters[1:5], item2 = 100:110)
>
> ## Object components cannot be used "direct"
> col1
Error: object 'col1' not found
```

```
> item2
Error: object 'item2' not found
>
> ## Use with() to "open" objects temporarily
> with(newdf, col1)
[1] 1 2 3
> with(newlist, item1)
[1] "a" "b" "c" "d" "e"

> with(newlist, summary(item2))
   Min. 1st Qu.  Median    Mean 3rd Qu.    Max.
  100.0   102.5   105.0   105.0   107.5   110.0

> with(newdf, mean(col2, na.rm = TRUE))
[1] 5
```

DATA OBJECT PROPERTIES

Objects can be in various forms and it is useful to be able to see the form that an object is in. It is useful to be able to interrogate and alter various object properties, particularly names of components (rows and columns). Objects also have various attributes that may be used by routines to handle an object in a certain way.

 SEE "Summarizing Data" for statistical and tabular methods to view and summarize data.

 SEE "Distribution of Data" for methods to look at the shape (distribution) of numerical objects.

 SEE "Data Types" for the various object forms and for determining which form a given object is in.

COMMAND NAME

attr

Many R objects have attributes. These can dictate how an object is handled by a routine. The attr command gets and sets specific attributes for an object. Compare this to the attributes command, which gets or sets all attributes in one go. In general the class attribute is used to determine if a dedicated plot, print or summary command can be applied.

Common Usage

```
attr(x, which, exact = FALSE)

attr(x, which, exact = FALSE) <- value
```

Related Commands

attributes (p. 76)
class (p. 79)
names (p. 90)
row.names (p. 99)
dimnames (p. 84)
dim (p. 83)
levels (p. 86)

Command Parameters

x	An R object.
which	A character string specifying which single attribute to examine or set. Attributes include "class", "comment", "dim", "dimnames", "names", and "row.names". It is recommended that the "levels" attribute for a factor should be set via the levels command.
exact = FALSE	If exact = TRUE, the character string specified by which is matched exactly.
value	The new value of the attribute or NULL to remove it.

Examples

```
  ## Make an object
> newdf = data.frame(col1 = 1:3, col2 = 4:6)

  ## View all attributes
> attributes(newdf)
$names
[1] "col1" "col2"

$row.names
[1] 1 2 3

$class
[1] "data.frame"

  ## Query attribute
> attr(newdf, which = "names")
[1] "col1" "col2"

  ## Add attributes
> attr(newdf, which = "row.names") = c("First", "Second", "Third")
> attr(newdf, which = "comment") = "The data frame with amended attributes"

  ## View attributes again
> attributes(newdf)
$names
[1] "col1" "col2"
```

```
$row.names
[1] "First"  "Second" "Third"

$class
[1] "data.frame"

$comment
[1] "The data frame with amended attributes"

  ## Remove comment attribute
> attr(newdf, which = "comment") = NULL

 ## Alter an object by altering its attributes
> obj = 1:12 # A simple numeric vector
> attr(obj, which = "dim") = c(3, 4) # Set dimensions to 3 x 4 i.e. a matrix

> obj
     [,1] [,2] [,3] [,4]
[1,]    1    4    7   10
[2,]    2    5    8   11
[3,]    3    6    9   12

> class(obj)
[1] "matrix"

> attributes(obj) # Note that matrix object does not hold a class attribute
$dim
[1] 3 4
```

COMMAND NAME

attributes

Objects have various attributes that may be used by routines to handle an object in a certain way.
The attributes command gets or sets the attributes. Compare this to the attr command, which
gets or sets a single attribute.

Common Usage

```
attributes(x)

attributes() <- value
```

Related Commands

attr (p. 74)
class (p. 79)
comment (p. 81)
dimnames (p. 84)
names (p. 90)

Command Parameters

x   An R object.

value   A list of attributes (as characters).

Examples

```
  ## Make some objects
> newlist = list(Ltrs = letters[1:5], Nmbrs = 100:110)
> newmat = matrix(1:12, nrow = 3, dimnames = list(letters[1:3], LETTERS[1:4]))
> newdf = data.frame(col1 = 1:3, col2 = 4:6)
> newfac = gl(3,3, labels = c("hi", "mid", "lo"))

  ## View attributes
> attributes(newlist)
$names
[1] "Ltrs"  "Nmbrs"

> attributes(newmat)
$dim
[1] 3 4

$dimnames
$dimnames[[1]]
[1] "a" "b" "c"

$dimnames[[2]]
[1] "A" "B" "C" "D"

> attributes(newdf)
$names
[1] "col1" "col2"

$row.names
[1] 1 2 3

$class
[1] "data.frame"

> attributes(newfac)
$levels
[1] "hi"  "mid" "lo"

$class
[1] "factor"
```

```
  ## Remove all attributes
> attributes(newmat) = NULL
> newmat # Matrix has now become simple vector
 [1]  1  2  3  4  5  6  7  8  9 10 11 12

  ## Reinstate attributes to recreate matrix
> attributes(newmat) = list(dimnames = list(letters[1:3], LETTERS[1:4]),
 dim = c(3,4))
> newmat
  A B C  D
a 1 4 7 10
b 2 5 8 11
c 3 6 9 12
```

COMMAND NAME

case.names

Shows the case names for fitted models or the row names for data frames and matrix objects.

Common Usage

case.names(object)

Related Commands

rownames (p. 100)
row.names (p. 99)
names (p. 90)
dimnames (p. 84)
colnames (p. 80)
variable.names (p. 106)

Command Parameters

object   An object, typically a data frame, matrix, or fitted model result.

Examples

```
  ## Make some objects:
  ## A matrix
> newmat = matrix(1:12, nrow = 3, dimnames = list(letters[1:3], LETTERS[1:4]))
  ## A data frame

> newdf = data.frame(col1 = 1:3, col2 = 4:6, row.names = letters[1:3])

  ## A linear model result
> newlm = lm(col2 ~ col1, data = newdf)
```

```
  ## Get case names
> case.names(newmat)
[1] "a" "b" "c"


> case.names(newdf)
[1] "a" "b" "c"


> case.names(newlm)
[1] "a" "b" "c"
```

COMMAND NAME

`class`

Many R objects possess a `class` attribute. This attribute can be used by other routines for dedicated processes for that kind of object (for example `summary`, `print`). The `class` command can interrogate or set the class of an object.

Common Usage

```
class(x)

class(x) <- value
```

Related Commands

```
is (p. 19)
inherits (p. 18)
is.xxxx (p. 20)
as.xxxx (p. 16)
mode (p. 89)
storage.mode (p. 101)
typeof (p. 103)
```

Command Parameters

x   An object.

Examples

```
> ## Make some objects
> newdf = data.frame(col1 = 1:3, col2 = 4:6) # data frame
> newlist = list(item1 = letters[1:5], item2 = 100:110) # list
> newint = 1:10 # integer vector
> newnum = c(1.5, 2.3, 4.7) # numerical vector
> newchar = month.abb[1:6] # character vector
> newfac = gl(n = 3, k = 3, labels = c("hi", "mid", "lo")) # factor vector

> ## Examine class of objects
> class(newdf)
[1] "data.frame"
```

```
> class(newlist)
[1] "list"

> class(newint)
[1] "integer"

> class(newnum)
[1] "numeric"

> class(newchar)
[1] "character"

> class(newfac)
[1] "factor"

  ## Make matrix from data frame
> mat = as.matrix(newdf)

  ## Change class of object (objects can have multiple classes)
> class(mat) = c("matrix", "table", "special_object")
> class(mat)
[1] "matrix"          "table"          "special_object"
```

COMMAND NAME

colnames

Views or sets column names for matrix and data frame objects.

Common Usage

```
colnames(x)

colnames(x) <- value
```

Related Commands

variable.names (p. 106)
rownames (p. 100)
row.names (p. 99)
case.names (p. 79)
names (p. 90)
dimnames (p. 84)

Command Parameters

x   An object, usually a matrix or data frame.

value   The column names to set as some form of character.

Examples

```
  ## Make some objects
> newdf = data.frame(col1 = 1:3, col2 = 4:6)
> newlist = list(item1 = letters[1:5], item2 = 100:110)
> newmat = matrix(1:12, nrow = 3, dimnames = list(letters[1:3], LETTERS[1:4]))

  ## Examine column names
> colnames(newdf)
[1] "col1" "col2"

> colnames(newlist) # Fails as this is not a matrix/data frame
NULL

> colnames(newmat)
[1] "A" "B" "C" "D"

  ## Alter column names
  ## Make vector of names as characters
> newnames = c("First", "Second", "Third", "Fourth")
> colnames(newmat) = newnames
> newmat
  First Second Third Fourth
a    1      4     7     10
b    2      5     8     11
c    3      6     9     12

  ## Give new names directly
> colnames(newdf) = c("One", "Two")
> newdf
  One Two
1   1   4
2   2   5
3   3   6
```

COMMAND NAME

```
comment
```

Objects can be assigned a comment attribute; this can be useful to keep track of data items. The command can get or set comment attributes for objects. Note in the following examples that the hash character is used as a comment character in command lines.

Common Usage

```
comment(x)
```

```
comment(x) <- value
```

Related Commands

attributes (p. 76)
attr (p. 74)
class (p. 79)

Command Parameters

x   An R object.

value   A character vector that will form the comment. Setting this to NULL removes the
          comment.

Examples

```
   ## Make some objects
> newdf = data.frame(col1 = 1:3, col2 = 4:6)
> newnum = c(1.5, 2.3, 4.7)
> newfac = gl(3,3, labels = c("hi", "mid", "lo"))

   ## Assign comments to objects
> comment(newdf) = "A 2-col data frame with simple numeric variables"
> comment(newnum) = "Decimal values"
> comment(newfac) = "A 3-level factor variable with 3 replicates"

   ## View the comments
> comment(newdf)
[1] "A 2-col data frame with simple numeric variables"

> comment(newnum)
[1] "Decimal values"

> comment(newfac)
[1] "A 3-level factor variable with 3 replicates"

   ## Comments appear as attributes
> attributes(newdf)
$names
[1] "col1" "col2"

$row.names
[1] 1 2 3

$class
[1] "data.frame"

$comment
[1] "A 2-col data frame with simple numeric variables"
```

```
> attributes(newnum)
$comment
[1] "Decimal values"

> attributes(newfac)
$levels
[1] "hi"  "mid"  "lo"

$class
[1] "factor"

$comment
[1] "A 3-level factor variable with 3 replicates"

  ## Remove comments
> comment(newdf) = NULL
> comment(newnum) = NULL
> comment(newfac) = NULL
```

COMMAND NAME

`dim`

Objects can have several dimensions. This command gets or sets object dimensions. Vector objects are one-dimensional and the `dim` command returns `NULL`. For other multidimensional objects, the command returns a vector of values representing the rows, columns, and other dimensions.

Common Usage

```
dim(x)

dim(x) <- value
```

Related Commands

```
ncol (p. 92)
nrow (p. 92)
dimnames (p. 84)
attributes (p. 76)
matrix (p. 10)
```

Command Parameters

x   An R object.

value   The number of dimensions to set as a numerical vector.

```
   ## Make some objects
> newlist = list(Ltrs = letters[1:5], Nmbrs = 100:110)
> newmat = matrix(1:12, nrow = 3, dimnames = list(letters[1:3], LETTERS[1:4]))
> newdf = data.frame(col1 = 1:3, col2 = 4:6)
> newnum = c(1.5, 2.3, 4.7)
> newchar = month.abb[1:6]
> newfac = gl(3,3, labels = c("hi", "mid", "lo"))

   ## Get dimensions of objects
> dim(newlist) # Has none
NULL

> dim(newmat)  # Equates to rows, columns
[1] 3 4

> dim(newdf)   # Equates to rows, columns
[1] 3 2

> dim(newnum)  # Has none
NULL

> dim(newchar) # Has none
NULL

> dim(newfac)  # Has none
NULL

   ## Set dimensions of an object
> obj = 1:12 # A simple numerical vector
> dim(obj) = c(3, 4) # Set to 3 rows and 4 columns
> obj # Object is now a matrix
     [,1] [,2] [,3] [,4]
[1,]    1    4    7   10
[2,]    2    5    8   11
[3,]    3    6    9   12
```

COMMAND NAME

dimnames

Some objects can have multiple names; for matrix or data frame objects these names would be row and column names, for example. The command gets or sets the current names for all the dimensions of an object.

Common Usage

dimnames(x)

dimnames(x) <- value

Related Commands
names (p. 90)
rownames (p. 100)
colnames (p. 80)

Command Parameters

x   An R object.

Examples

```
  ## Make an object with row/col names
> newdf = data.frame(col1 = 1:3, col2 = 4:6, row.names = letters[1:3])

> ## Get the dimnames
> dimnames(newdf)
[[1]]
[1] "a" "b" "c"

[[2]]
[1] "col1" "col2"


  ## Make an object without names
> newmat = matrix(1:12, nrow = 3) # basic matrix

> ## View and then set names
> dimnames(newmat) # no names at present
NULL

> dimnames(newmat) = list(letters[1:3], LETTERS[1:4]) # set names

> dimnames(newmat) # view new names (note [[n]] label)
[[1]]
[1] "a" "b" "c"

[[2]]
[1] "A" "B" "C" "D"


  ## Set one name only
> dimnames(newdf)[[1]] = month.abb[1:3] # use abbreviated month names

  ## View the result via dimnames() command
> dimnames(newdf)
[[1]]
[1] "Jan" "Feb" "Mar"

[[2]]
[1] "col1" "col2"
```

```
  ## See the result applied to the data frame
> newdf
    col1 col2
Jan    1    4
Feb    2    5
Mar    3    6

  ## Cannot use dimnames() to set value to NULL
> dimnames(newdf)[[1]] = NULL
Error in `dimnames<-.data.frame`(`*tmp*`, value = list(c("col1", "col2" :
  invalid 'dimnames' given for data frame
```

COMMAND NAME

length

Gets or sets the number of items in an object.

 SEE length in "Summary Statistics."

COMMAND NAME

levels

Factor variables are a special kind of character object. They have a levels attribute, which is used in many kinds of analytical routines. The levels command allows access to the levels attribute and can get or set values for an object.

 SEE aov and lm for two analytical routine examples, analysis of variance and linear modeling, respectively.

Common Usage

levels(x)

levels(x) <- value

Related Commands

nlevels (p. 93)
relevel (p. 95)
reorder (p. 96)
attributes (p. 76)
attr (p. 74)
factor (p. 7)
gl (p. 23)
rep (p. 26)
seq (p. 27)
interaction (p. 24)

Command Parameters

x   An object, usually a factor.

value   The values for the levels required, usually a character vector or list.

Examples

```
   ## Make a factor
> newfac = gl(n = 3, k = 3, length = 9) # 3 levels, 3 replicates, 9 total
> newfac
[1] 1 1 1 2 2 2 3 3 3
Levels: 1 2 3


   ## Set levels
> levels(newfac) = letters[1:3] # Use a standard to make levels
> levels(newfac)                # View levels
[1] "a" "b" "c"
> newfac                        # View entire factor object
[1] a a a b b b c c c
Levels: a b c

> levels(newfac) = c("b", "c", "a") # Use a vector
> levels(newfac)
[1] "b" "c" "a"
> newfac
[1] b b b c c c a a a
Levels: b c a

> levels(newfac) = list(First = "a", Second = "b", Third = "c") # Use a list
> levels(newfac)
[1] "First"  "Second" "Third"
> newfac
[1] Second Second Second Third  Third  Third  First  First  First
Levels: First Second Third

> levels(newfac) = c("First", "First", "Third") # Combine levels
> levels(newfac)
[1] "First" "Third"
> newfac
[1] First First First Third Third Third First First First
Levels: First Third
```

COMMAND NAME

`ls.str`

Gives the structure of every object matching a pattern specified in the command. This can produce extensive displays if the workspace contains a lot of objects.

Common Usage

```
ls.str(pos = -1, name, all.names = FALSE, pattern)
```

Related Commands

str (p. 102)
ls (p. 67)
lsf.str (p. 89)
class (p. 79)

Command Parameters

pos = -1	The position of the environment to use for the listing as given by the search command. The default pos = -1 and pos = 1 are equivalent and relate to the global environment (the workspace). Other positions will relate to various command packages.
name	The name of the environment to give the listing for. The default is to use the current environment; that is, name = ".GlobalEnv".
all.names = FALSE	If set to TRUE, names beginning with a period are shown.
pattern	An optional pattern to match using regular expressions.

Examples

```
  ## Make some objects
> newmat = matrix(1:12, nrow = 3, dimnames = list(letters[1:3], LETTERS[1:4]))
> newdf = data.frame(col1 = 1:3, col2 = 4:6, row.names = letters[1:3])
> newvec = month.abb[1:6]

  ## View structure of all objects starting with "new"
> ls.str(pattern = "^new")
newdf : 'data.frame':    3 obs. of  2 variables:
$ col1: int  1 2 3
 $ col2: int  4 5 6
newmat :   int [1:3, 1:4] 1 2 3 4 5 6 7 8 9 10 ...
newvec :   chr [1:6] "Jan" "Feb" "Mar" "Apr" "May" "Jun"

  ## Make a list object
> newlist = list(item1 = letters[1:5], item2 = 100:110)

> ## Put list into search() path
> attach(newlist)

> ## View search() list
> search()
```

```
[1] ".GlobalEnv"          "newlist"           "tools:rstudio"  "package:stats"
[5] "package:graphics"  "package:grDevices" "package:utils"  "package:datasets"
[9] "package:methods"   "Autoloads"          "package:base"

  ## Look at structure of objects at specified position in search() path
> ls.str(pos = 2) # Shows individual elements of "newlist" object
item1 :  chr [1:5] "a" "b" "c" "d" "e"
item2 :  int [1:11] 100 101 102 103 104 105 106 107 108 109 ...

  ## Tidy up and remove "newlist" from search() path
> detach(newlist)
```

COMMAND NAME

lsf.str

Shows the custom functions (commands) available from the specified position of the search path.

 SEE ls.str in "Viewing Data."

Examples

```
  ## Create custom functions
> manning = function(radius, gradient, coeff) {(radius^(2/3) * gradient^0.5 / coeff)}
> cubrt = function(x) {x^(1/3)}

  ## Show custom functions
> lsf.str()
cubrt : function (x)
manning : function (radius, gradient, coeff)
```

COMMAND NAME

mode

The mode of an object is an attribute related to its type. The command can get the current mode or set a new one.

Common Usage

mode(x)

mode(x) <- value

Related Commands

storage.mode (p. 101)
typeof (p. 103)
class (p. 79)

Command Parameters

x   An R object.

value   A character string giving the mode of the object to set.

Examples

```
  ## Make some objects
> newlist = list(Ltrs = letters[1:5], Nmbrs = 100:110)
> newmat = matrix(1:12, nrow = 3, dimnames = list(letters[1:3], LETTERS[1:4]))
> newdf = data.frame(col1 = 1:3, col2 = 4:6)
> newint = 1:10 # Integer values
> newnum = c(1.5, 2.3, 4.7) # Numeric values
> newchar = month.abb[1:6] # Characters
> newfac = gl(3,3, labels = c("hi", "mid", "lo")) # A factor vector

  ## Get the modes
> mode(newlist)
[1] "list"

> mode(newmat)
[1] "numeric"

> mode(newdf)
[1] "list"

> mode(newint)
[1] "numeric"

> mode(newnum)
[1] "numeric"

> mode(newchar)
[1] "character"

> mode(newfac)
[1] "numeric"
```

COMMAND NAME

names

Many R objects have named components; these may be columns or list elements, for example. The names command views or sets the names.

Common Usage

```
names(x)

names(x) <- value
```

Related Commands

rownames (p. 100)
colnames (p. 80)
dimnames (p. 84)
row.names (p. 99)

Command Parameters

x   An R object.

value   A character vector of names; must be the same length as the object. Can be set to NULL.

Examples

```
   ## Make some objects without explicit names
> newlist = list(letters[1:5], 100:110)
> newmat = matrix(1:12, nrow = 3)
> newdf = data.frame(1:3, 4:6)
> newvec = 1:6

   ## View names of objects
> names(newlist) # No names
NULL

> names(newmat) # No names
NULL

> names(newdf) # Data frame has default names
[1] "X1.3" "X4.6"

> names(newvec) # No names
NULL

   ## Set names
> names(newlist) = c("Letters", "Numbers")
> names(newmat) = c("One", "Two", "Three", "Four") # Will not work!
> names(newdf) = c("One", "Two")
> names(newvec) = month[1:6] # Character names (months)

   ## View objects to see their names
> newlist # Names applied okay
$Letters
[1] "a" "b" "c" "d" "e"

$Numbers
 [1] 100 101 102 103 104 105 106 107 108 109 110
```

```
> newmat # Names not applied to matrix (use colnames or dimnames)
     [,1] [,2] [,3] [,4]
[1,]    1    4    7   10
[2,]    2    5    8   11
[3,]    3    6    9   12
attr(,"names")
 [1] "One"   "Two"   "Three" "Four"  NA      NA      NA      NA      NA      NA
[11] NA      NA

> newdf # Names applied okay
  One Two
1   1   4
2   2   5
3   3   6

> newvec # Names applied okay
Jan Feb Mar Apr May Jun
  1   2   3   4   5   6
```

COMMAND NAME

```
ncol
NCOL
nrow
NROW
```

These commands examine the number of rows or columns of an object. The ncol and nrow commands return the number of columns and rows, respectively, of multidimensional objects; that is, data frames, matrix objects, and arrays. The NCOL and NROW commands do the same thing but will additionally return a result for list, vector, and factor objects.

 SEE also nrow in "Data Object Properties."

Common Usage

```
ncol(x)
nrow(x)
NCOL(x)
NROW(x)
```

Related Commands

dim (p. 83)
matrix (p. 10)
attributes (p. 76)

Command Parameters

x   An R object.

Examples

```
  ## Make some objects
> newlist = list(Ltrs = letters[1:5], Nmbrs = 100:110)
> newdf = data.frame(col1 = 1:3, col2 = 4:6)
> newnum = c(1.5, 2.3, 4.7)
> newarr = array(1:12, dim = c(2, 3, 2),
 dimnames = list(letters[1:2], LETTERS[1:3], c("One", "Two")))

  ## Examine data frame
> nrow(newdf) # 3 rows in data frame
[1] 3


> ncol(newdf) # 4 columns in data frame
[1] 2


  ## Examine vector
> nrow(newnum) # Has none
NULL


> NROW(newnum) # Gives length of vector
[1] 3


  ## Examine list
> nrow(newlist) # Has none
NULL


> NROW(newlist) # Shows two elements
[1] 2


  ## Examine array
> nrow(newarr) # 2 rows in array
[1] 2


> ncol(newarr) # 3 columns in array
[1] 3
```

COMMAND NAME

`nlevels`

Factor objects are a special kind of character object that contain a `levels` attribute. This is used in many analytical routines. The `nlevels` command returns the number of levels that an object possesses.

 SEE aov and lm for two analytical routine examples, ANOVA and linear modeling, respectively, in Theme 2, "Math and Statistics."

Common Usage

```
nlevels(x)
```

Related Commands

```
levels (p. 86)
factor (p. 7)
gl (p. 23)
attributes (p. 76)
relevel (p. 95)
```

Command Parameters

x   An R object.

Examples

```
  ## Make objects
> newfac = gl(n = 4, k = 3) # A simple factor object
> newvec = c("First", "Second", "Third") # A character vector
> fac2 = factor(newvec) # Make factor from character vector

> ## View number of levels
> nlevels(newfac)
[1] 4

> newfac
 [1] 1 1 1 2 2 2 3 3 3 4 4 4
Levels: 1 2 3 4

> nlevels(newvec) # Zero because no levels (not a factor)
[1] 0

> newvec
[1] "First"  "Second" "Third"

> nlevels(fac2) # Now object has levels because it is a factor
[1] 3

> fac2
[1] First  Second Third
Levels: First Second Third
```

COMMAND NAME

```
nrow
NROW
```

These commands examine the number of rows of an object.

SEE ncol in "Viewing Object Properties."

COMMAND NAME

relevel

Factor objects are a special kind of character object that contain a levels attribute. This is used in many analytical routines. The relevel command takes one level and replaces it at the front of the list. This is useful because some analytical routines take the first level as a reference.

 SEE aov and lm for two analytical routine examples, ANOVA and linear modeling, respectively, in Theme 2, "Math and Statistics."

Common Usage

relevel(x, ref)

Related Commands

reorder (p. 96)
levels (p. 86)
nlevels (p. 93)
factor (p. 7)
gl (p. 23)

Command Parameters

x   An unordered factor. If the factor is ordered, it will be unordered after the relevel process.

ref   The level to move to the head of the list.

Examples

```
  ## Make factor
> newfac = gl(n = 4, k = 3, labels = letters[1:4]) # 4 levels, 3 replicates
> newfac
 [1] a a a b b b c c c d d d
Levels: a b c d

  ## Alter level order
> relevel(newfac, ref = "c") # Pull out "c" and move to front
 [1] a a a b b b c c c d d d
Levels: c a b d

> relevel(newfac, ref = "b") # Pull out "b" and move to front
 [1] a a a b b b c c c d d d
Levels: b a c d
```

COMMAND NAME

`reorder`

This command reorders the levels of a factor. Factor objects are a special kind of character object that contain a `levels` attribute. This is used in many analytical routines. Character columns in data frames are usually factors. The `reorder` command alters the order that the levels are in based on values from another variable, usually another column in the data frame or a separate numeric vector.

 SEE `aov` and `lm` for two analytical routine examples, ANOVA and linear modeling, respectively, in Theme 2, "Math and Statistics."

Common Usage

```
reorder(x, X, FUN = mean, ...)
```

Related Commands

`relevel` (p. 95)
`levels` (p. 86)
`nlevels` (p. 93)
`factor` (p. 7)
`gl` (p. 23)

Command Parameters

x	A factor object. If the object is not a factor it will be coerced to be one.
X	A vector of the same length as x, the factor object. These values are used to determine the order of the levels.
FUN = mean	A function to apply to the subsets of X (as determined by x, the factor). This determines the final order of the levels. The default is the `mean`.
...	Other parameters; e.g., for `mean`, `na.rm = TRUE`.

Examples

```
  ## Make factor
> newfac = gl(n = 4, k = 4, labels = letters[1:4]) # 4 levels, 4 replicates
> newfac
 [1] a a a a b b b b c c c c d d d d
Levels: a b c d

  ## Make a numeric vector
> newvec = c(1:4, 4:7, 6:9, 2:5)
> newvec
 [1] 1 2 3 4 4 5 6 7 6 7 8 9 2 3 4 5

  ## Reorder levels
> reorder(newfac, newvec, FUN = mean)
 [1] a a a a b b b b c c c c d d d d
attr(,"scores")
```

```
    a    b   c   d
2.5 5.5 7.5 3.5
Levels: a d b c

> reorder(newfac, newvec, FUN = median)
 [1] a a a a b b b b c c c c d d d d
attr(,"scores")
    a    b   c   d
2.5 5.5 7.5 3.5
Levels: a d b c

> reorder(newfac, newvec, FUN = sum)
 [1] a a a a b b b b c c c c d d d d
attr(,"scores")
 a   b   c   d
10  22  30  14
Levels: a d b c
```

```
  ## Practical application for graphing (see Figures 1-1 and 1-2)
> boxplot(newvec ~ newfac) # Boxes ordered by plain level
  ## Give the graph some titles
> title(main = "Unorderd levels", xlab = "Levels of factor",
ylab = "Value axis")
  ## Makes Figure 1-1
```

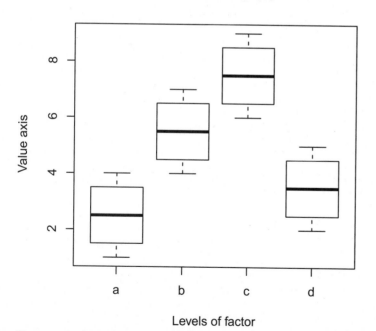

Figure 1-1: Boxplot using unordered factor

```
> boxplot(newvec ~ reorder(newfac, newvec, FUN = median)) # Reordered by median

  ## Give the graph some titles
> title(main = "Orderd levels (by median)", xlab = "Levels of factor",
 ylab = "Value axis")
  ## Makes Figure 1-2
```

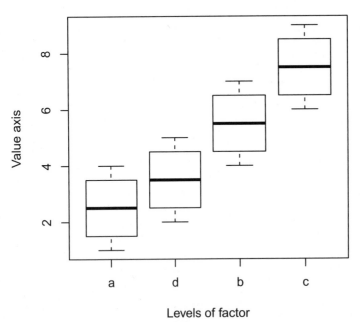

Figure 1-2: Boxplot using factor ordered by median (using the reorder command)

```
  ## Make frame using data from previous example
  ## vec = Numeric vector, fac = Factor, simple alphabetical labels
> newdf = data.frame(vec = c(1:4, 4:7, 6:9, 2:5),
 fac = gl(n = 4, k = 4, labels = letters[1:4]))

  ## Reorder the factor using the mean
  ## na.rm = TRUE not strictly needed as no NA
> with(newdf, reorder(x = fac, X = vec, FUN = mean, na.rm = TRUE))
 [1] a a a a b b b b c c c c d d d d
attr(,"scores")
  a   b   c   d
2.5 5.5 7.5 3.5
Levels: a d b c
```

COMMAND NAME

`row.names`

Gets or sets row names for data frame objects.

Common Usage

```
row.names(x)
```

```
row.names(x) <- value
```

Related Commands

rownames (p. 100)
colnames (p. 80)
names (p. 90)
dimnames (p. 84)
case.names (p. 78)
variable.names (p. 106)

Command Parameters

x   A data frame object.

value   The row names to set as some form of character.

Examples

```
  ## A simple data frame
> newdf = data.frame(col1 = 1:3, col2 = 4:6)

  ## Examine row names
> row.names(newdf)
[1] "1" "2" "3"

  ## Set row names (using month names)
> row.names(newdf) = month.name[1:3]

> ## View result
> newdf
        col1 col2
January     1    4
February    2    5
March       3    6

  ## Reset names to NULL
> row.names(newdf) = NULL # Produces simple index values
```

```
> newdf
  col1 col2
1    1    4
2    2    5
3    3    6
```

COMMAND NAME

rownames

Views or sets row names for matrix and data frame objects.

Common Usage

rownames(x)

rownames(x) <- value

Related Commands

row.names (p. 99)
colnames (p. 80)
case.names (p. 78)
names (p. 90)
dimnames (p. 84)
variable.names (p. 106)

Command Parameters

x   An R object, usually a data frame or matrix.

value   The column names to set as some form of character.

Examples

```
  ## Make some objects
> newdf = data.frame(col1 = 1:3, col2 = 4:6)
> newlist = list(item1 = letters[1:5], item2 = 100:110)
> newmat = matrix(1:12, nrow = 3, dimnames = list(letters[1:3], LETTERS[1:4]))

  ## Examine row names
> rownames(newdf)
[1] "1" "2" "3"

> rownames(newlist) # Fails - not a matrix or data frame
NULL

> rownames(newmat)
[1] "a" "b" "c"
```

```
  ## Set row names
> rownames(newdf) = LETTERS[1:3] # Use uppercase letters
> rownames(newdf) = c("First", "Second", "Third") # Set explicitly
```

COMMAND NAME

storage.mode

The storage.mode of an object is an attribute related to how it is stored in the R environment. The class, mode, and storage.mode attributes are all related to the type of object. The storage.mode command can get current values or set new ones.

Common Usage

```
storage.mode(x)
```

```
storage.mode(x) <- value
```

Related Commands

mode (p. 89)
typeof (p. 103)
class (p. 79)

Command Parameters

x   An R object.

value   A character string giving the new storage mode to assign to the object.

Examples

```
  ## Make some objects
> newlist = list(Ltrs = letters[1:5], Nmbrs = 100:110)
> newmat = matrix(1:12, nrow = 3, dimnames = list(letters[1:3], LETTERS[1:4]))
> newdf = data.frame(col1 = 1:3, col2 = 4:6)
> newint = 1:10
> newnum = c(1.5, 2.3, 4.7)
> newchar = month.abb[1:6]
> newfac = gl(3,3, labels = c("hi", "mid", "lo"))

  ## Get the storage modes
> storage.mode(newlist)
[1] "list"

> storage.mode(newmat)
[1] "integer"

> storage.mode(newdf)
[1] "list"
```

```
> storage.mode(newint)
[1] "integer"

> storage.mode(newnum)
[1] "double"

> storage.mode(newchar)
[1] "character"

> storage.mode(newfac)
[1] "integer"
```

COMMAND NAME

str

Displays the structure of an R object.

Common Usage

str(object)

Related Commands

class (p. 79)
ls.str (p. 87)
dput (p. 52)

Command Parameters

object   An R object.

Examples

```
  ## Make some objects
> newlist = list(Ltrs = letters[1:5], Nmbrs = 100:110)
> newmat = matrix(1:12, nrow = 3, dimnames = list(letters[1:3], LETTERS[1:4]))
> newdf = data.frame(col1 = 1:3, col2 = 4:6)
> newvec = 1:6

  ## Look at object structure
> str(newdf)
'data.frame': 3 obs. of  2 variables:
$ col1: int  1 2 3
 $ col2: int  4 5 6
```

```
> str(newlist)
List of 2
 $ Ltrs : chr [1:5] "a" "b" "c" "d" ...
 $ Nmbrs: int [1:11] 100 101 102 103 104 105 106 107 108 109 ...

> str(newmat)
 int [1:3, 1:4] 1 2 3 4 5 6 7 8 9 10 ...
 - attr(*, "dimnames")=List of 2
  ..$ : chr [1:3] "a" "b" "c"
  ..$ : chr [1:4] "A" "B" "C" "D"

> str(newvec)
 int [1:6] 1 2 3 4 5 6
```

COMMAND NAME

`typeof`

Determines the type (R internal storage mode) of an object. The command returns a character string giving the type. Usually the `typeof` command gives the same result as the `storage.mode` command, but not the `mode` command.

Common Usage

`typeof(x)`

Related Commands

`mode` (p. 89)
`storage.mode` (p. 101)
`class` (p. 79)

Command Parameters

x   An R object.

Examples

```
  ## Make some objects
> newlist = list(Ltrs = letters[1:5], Nmbrs = 100:110)
> newmat = matrix(1:12, nrow = 3, dimnames = list(letters[1:3], LETTERS[1:4]))
> newdf = data.frame(col1 = 1:3, col2 = 4:6)
> newint = 1:10
> newnum = c(1.5, 2.3, 4.7)
> newchar = month.abb[1:6]
> newfac = gl(3,3, labels = c("hi", "mid", "lo"))

  ## Get the types
> typeof(newlist)
[1] "list"
```

```
> typeof(newmat)
[1] "integer"

> typeof(newdf)
[1] "list"

> typeof(newint)
[1] "integer"

> typeof(newnum)
[1] "double"

> typeof(newchar)
[1] "character"

> typeof(newfac)
[1] "integer"
```

COMMAND NAME

unclass

R stores various types of objects and many have a class attribute. This is used by some commands to handle the object in a particular manner. The unclass command returns a copy of the object with the class attribute removed.

Common Usage

unclass(object)

Related Commands

class (p. 79)
inherits (p. 18)
is (p. 19)
is.xxxx (p. 20)
unlist (p. 104)

Command Parameters

object   An R object.

Examples

```
  ## Make some objects
> newlist = list(Ltrs = letters[1:5], Nmbrs = 100:110)
> newmat = matrix(1:12, nrow = 3, dimnames = list(letters[1:3], LETTERS[1:4]))
> newdf = data.frame(col1 = 1:3, col2 = 4:6)
> newvec = 1:6
```

```
  ## Return copy of objects with class attribute removed
> unclass(newlist) # Not much affected
$Ltrs
[1] "a" "b" "c" "d" "e"

$Nmbrs
 [1] 100 101 102 103 104 105 106 107 108 109 110

> unclass(newmat) # Not much affected
  A B C  D
a 1 4 7 10
b 2 5 8 11
c 3 6 9 12

> unclass(newvec) # Not much affected
[1] 1 2 3 4 5 6

> unclass(newdf) # Is affected
$col1
[1] 1 2 3

$col2
[1] 4 5 6

attr(,"row.names")
[1] 1 2 3

  ## Unclass makes data frame act like list
> mydf = unclass(newdf)
> class(mydf)
[1] "list"
```

COMMAND NAME

`unlist`

This command takes a list object and simplifies it to produce a vector object. This can produce a more readable output.

Common usage

`unlist(x, use.names = TRUE)`

Related commands

list (p. 9)
as.list (p. 16)
unclass (p. 104)
c (p. 22)

Command parameters

`x`	A list object.
`use.names = TRUE`	By default the names of the list elements are preserved as names in the resulting vector. If `use.names = FALSE` the resulting vector is unnamed.

Examples

```
   ## Create three vectors
> mow = c(12, 15, 17, 11, 15)
> unmow = c(8, 9, 7, 9)
> chars = LETTERS[1:5]

   ## Make lists
> l1 = list(mow = mow, unmow = unmow) # All elements numeric
> l2 = list(mow = mow, unmow = unmow, chars = chars) # Mix of numeric and text

> unlist(l1)
  mow1   mow2   mow3   mow4   mow5 unmow1 unmow2 unmow3 unmow4
    12     15     17     11     15      8      9      7      9

> unlist(l1, use.names = FALSE)
[1] 12 15 17 11 15  8  9  7  9

> unlist(l2)
  mow1   mow2   mow3   mow4   mow5 unmow1 unmow2 unmow3 unmow4 chars1 chars2
  "12"   "15"   "17"   "11"   "15"    "8"    "9"    "7"    "9"    "A"    "B"
chars3 chars4 chars5
   "C"    "D"    "E"
```

COMMAND NAME

`variable.names`

Shows the variable names for fitted models or the column names for data frames and matrix objects.

Common Usage

`variable.names(object)`

Related Commands

`case.names` (p. 78)
`colnames` (p. 80)
`names` (p. 90)
`dimnames` (p. 84)
`rownames` (p. 100)
`row.names` (p. 99)

Command Parameters

object   An R object, usually a fitted model result but can be a matrix or data frame.

Examples

```
  ## Make some objects:
  ## A matrix
> newmat = matrix(1:12, nrow = 3, dimnames = list(letters[1:3], LETTERS[1:4]))

  ## A data frame
> newdf = data.frame(col1 = 1:3, col2 = 4:6, row.names = letters[1:3])

  ## A linear model result
> newlm = lm(col2 ~ col1, data = newdf)

> ## Examine variable names
> variable.names(newmat)
[1] "A" "B" "C" "D"

> variable.names(newdf)
[1] "col1" "col2"

> variable.names(newlm)
[1] "(Intercept)" "col1"
```

SELECTING AND SAMPLING DATA

Data objects exist in a variety of forms, and often you will want to extract only a part of an existing object. This part may be a single column of a data frame or an item from a list. You may also want to extract values that correspond to some particular value.

COMMAND NAME

[]

The square brackets enable you to select/extract parts of an object. For vector objects that have a single dimension, a single value is required. For matrix and data frame objects that are two-dimensional, two values (row, column) are needed.

Common Usage

```
x[i]
x[i, j, ...]
```

Related Commands

$ (p. 109)
with (p. 73)
attach (p. 61)
which (p. 116)

Command Parameters

x   An R object.

i, j   Indices used to specify elements.

...   Other commands (including indices).

Examples

```
  ## Make some objects
> newlist = list(Ltrs = letters[1:5], Nmbrs = 100:110)
> newdf = data.frame(col1 = 1:3, col2 = 4:6)
> newnum = c(1.5, 2.3, 4.7)
> newarr = array(1:12, dim = c(2, 3, 2),
 dimnames = list(letters[1:2], LETTERS[1:3], c("One", "Two")))

  ## Extract some elements of objects
> newlist[2] # 2nd element of list
$Nmbrs
 [1] 100 101 102 103 104 105 106 107 108 109 110


> newdf[2:3, 1:2] # rows 2-3 and columns 1-2 of data frame
  col1 col2
2    2    5
3    3    6

> newdf[1:2,] # rows 1-2 and all columns of data frame
  col1 col2
1    1    4
2    2    5

> newnum[-2] # all except 2nd item of vector
[1] 1.5 4.7

> newarr[, c(1, 3), 2] # all rows and columns 1&3 for 2nd part of array
  A  C
a 7 11
b 8 12

  ## Replace or add to object
> newnum[4] = 9.9 # Add new item to end
> newnum[2] = 7.7 # Replace 2nd item
> newnum # View modified vector
[1] 1.5 7.7 4.7 9.9

> newdf[, 3] = 7:9 # Add unnamed column to data frame
> newdf[, "col3"] = 10:12 # Add named column to data frame
```

```
> newdf # View modifications
  col1 col2 V3 col3
1   1    4  7   10
2   2    5  8   11
3   3    6  9   12
```

COMMAND NAME

$

Objects can have several elements; for example, columns of a data frame or list items. The $ enables you to select elements within an object and either extract them or alter the values. You can also use the $ to add an element to an existing object. The $ can only be used for list and data frame objects (that is, ones with a `names` attribute).

Common Usage

```
x$name
x$name <- value
```

Related Commands

[] (p. 30)
with (p. 73)
attach (p. 61)

Command Parameters

x   An R object, usually a list or data frame.

name   A character string or name.

value A value to assign to the selected element.

Examples

```
  ## Make some objects
> newlist = list(Ltrs = letters[1:5], Nmbrs = 100:110) # List
> newdf = data.frame(col1 = 1:3, col2 = 4:6) # Data frame
> newlm = lm(col1 ~ col2, data = newdf) # Linear model result

  ## Check names
> names(newlist)
[1] "Ltrs"  "Nmbrs"

> names(newdf)
[1] "col1" "col2"

> names(newlm) # Result object is a form of list
[1] "coefficients" "residuals"    "effects"      "rank"
[5] "fitted.values" "assign"      "qr"           "df.residual"
[9] "xlevels"       "call"        "terms"        "model"
```

```
  ## View named elements
> newlist$Ltrs
[1] "a" "b" "c" "d" "e"

> newdf$col2
[1] 4 5 6

> newlm$coefficients
(Intercept)          col2
         -3             1

  ## Add elements
> newdf$col3 = 7:9 # Add new column to data frame
> newdf # View result
  col1 col2 col3
1    1    4    7
2    2    5    8
3    3    6    9

> newlist$Mnth = month.abb[1:3] # Add new item to list
> newlist # View result
$Ltrs
[1] "a" "b" "c" "d" "e"

$Nmbrs
 [1] 100 101 102 103 104 105 106 107 108 109 110

$Mnth
[1] "Jan" "Feb" "Mar"

  ## Replace elements
> newdf$col2 = c(100, 101, 102) # Replace whole column
> newdf # View result
  col1 col2 col3
1    1  100    7
2    2  101    8
3    3  102    9

> newlist$Ltrs[3] = "z" # Replace single item using []
> newlist # View result
$Ltrs
[1] "a" "b" "z" "d" "e"

$Nmbrs
 [1] 100 101 102 103 104 105 106 107 108 109 110

$Mnth
[1] "Jan" "Feb" "Mar"
```

COMMAND NAME

droplevels

This command will drop unused levels of factors from the object specified. Usually this will be a data frame that contains multiple columns, including factors. The subset command is used to create a subset of a dataset but this does not drop the levels from the original. The unused levels will thus appear in graphs and tables, for example (albeit with zero count, see the following examples).

 SEE drop for dropping array dimensions, and drop1 for dropping model terms in Theme 2, "Math and Statistics."

Common Usage

droplevels(x, except, ...)

Related Commands

subset (p. 114)
factor (p. 7)
gl (p. 23)
rep (p. 26)

Command Parameters

x   An object from which unused levels are to be dropped. Usually this is a data frame that contains columns of factors but you can also specify a single factor object.

except   Columns for which the levels should not be dropped. These are specified as a vector of column numbers or the names (in quotes) of the variables.

...   Other arguments from other methods can be used if appropriate.

Examples

```
  ## Use InsectSprays data from R datasets
> data(InsectSprays) # Make sure data is ready

  ## Look at InsectSprays dataset
> str(InsectSprays) # View data structure
'data.frame': 72 obs. of  2 variables:
 $ count: num  10 7 20 14 14 12 10 23 17 20 ...
 $ spray: Factor w/ 6 levels "A","B","C","D",..: 1 1 1 1 1 1 1 1 1 1 ...

> levels(InsectSprays$spray) # View levels of spray factor
[1] "A" "B" "C" "D" "E" "F"
```

```
> table(InsectSprays$spray) # View levels of spray as table of replicates

 A  B  C  D  E  F
12 12 12 12 12 12

  ## Make a subset without spray "C"
> ISs = subset(InsectSprays, spray != "C") # Subset and lose spray "C"

> levels(ISs$spray) # View levels, spray "C" is sill present
[1] "A" "B" "C" "D" "E" "F"
> table(ISs$spray) # View as table, spray "C" has no data

 A  B  C  D  E  F
12 12  0 12 12 12

  ## Drop the unused levels
> ISd = droplevels(ISs) # Drop unused levels
> table(ISd$spray) # Spray "C" now not present

 A  B  D  E  F
12 12 12 12 12
```

COMMAND NAME

resample

Takes random samples and permutations. This is a custom function that you must create in order to use. It overcomes a computational quirk in the sample command where an unexpected result occurs when a conditional sample is used (see the following examples).

Common Usage

Create the custom function like so:

```
resample <- function(x, ...) x[sample(length(x), ...)]
```

Use the new function exactly like the sample command:

```
resample(x, size, replace = FALSE)
```

Related Commands

sample (p. 113)
set.seed (p. 165)
function (p. 495)

Command Parameters

x	A vector of values.
size	The number of items to choose.
replace = FALSE	If replace = TRUE, items can be selected more than once (that is, re-placed).

Examples

```
  ## Make a vector
> newvec = 1:10

  ## Conditional selection
  ## sample() command has a quirk!
> sample(newvec[newvec > 8]) # This is fine
[1] 10  9

> sample(newvec[newvec > 9]) # This is wrong!
  [1]  3  5  4 10  2  7  8  1  9  6

> sample(newvec[newvec > 10]) # This is fine
integer(0)

  ## Create custom function
> resample <- function(x, ...) x[sample(length(x), ...)]

  ## Try conditional selection again
> resample(newvec[newvec > 8]) # Fine, same as before
[1]  9 10

> resample(newvec[newvec > 9]) # This is now correct
[1] 10

> resample(newvec[newvec > 10]) # Fine, same as before
integer(0)
```

COMMAND NAME

`sample`

Takes random samples and permutations. The `sample` command takes a sample of specified size from a specified object using replacement or not (as you specify). Due to the computational process used, some results can be unexpected when conditional sampling is used.

 SEE also `resample` for a robust alternative.

Common Usage

```
sample(x, size, replace = FALSE)
```

Related Commands

`resample` (p. 112)
`runif` (p. 163)
`set.seed` (p. 165)

Command Parameters

`x`	A vector of values.
`size`	The number of items to choose.
`replace = FALSE`	If `replace = TRUE`, items can be selected more than once (that is, re-placed).

Examples

```
  ## Make some vector samples
> newnum = 1:10
> newchar = month.abb[1:12]

  ## Sampling: effects of replacement
> set.seed(4) # Set random number seed
> sample(newchar, size = 4, replace = TRUE) # With replacement
[1] "Aug" "Jan" "Apr" "Apr"

> set.seed(4) # Set random number seed
> sample(newchar, size = 4) # Without replacement (the default)
[1] "Aug" "Jan" "Mar" "Oct"

  ## Sample: matching an expression
> set.seed(3) # Set random number seed
> sample(newnum[newnum > 5], size = 2) # Get 2 items larger than 5
[1] 6 9

> set.seed(3) # Set random number seed
> sample(newnum[newnum > 5]) # Get all items larger than 5
[1]  6  9  7 10  8

> set.seed(3) # Set random number seed
> sample(newnum  > 5) # Logical result
 [1] FALSE  TRUE FALSE FALSE  TRUE  TRUE FALSE FALSE  TRUE  TRUE

> set.seed(3) # Set random number seed
> sample(newnum == 5) # Logical result, N.B. double ==
 [1] FALSE FALSE FALSE FALSE FALSE FALSE FALSE  TRUE FALSE FALSE
```

COMMAND NAME

`subset`

This command extracts subsets of data objects (vectors, data frames, and matrix objects), which meet certain conditions. Note that `subset` is used as a parameter within many commands and can use a special syntax (see the following examples).

Common Usage

```
subset(x, subset, select)

command(subset = group %in% c("a", "b", ...))
```

Related Commands

which (p. 116)
droplevels (p. 111)

Command Parameters

x   An object. Can be a vector, matrix, or, more commonly, a data frame.

subset   An expression indicating which items to keep. When used as a parameter the syntax
             can be of the form subset = group %in% c("a", "b", ...) for example.

select   An expression indicating which columns to select from a data frame.

Examples

```
  ## Make a data frame: val = numeric, fac = 4-level factor
> newdf = data.frame(val = 1:12, fac = gl(n = 4, k = 3, labels = LETTERS[1:4]))

  ## Generate some subsets
> subset(newdf, subset = val > 5) # All columns shown as default
   val fac
6    6   B
7    7   C
8    8   C
9    9   C
10  10   D
11  11   D
12  12   D

> subset(newdf, subset = val > 5, select = c(fac, val)) # Columns in new order
   fac val
6    B   6
7    C   7
8    C   8
9    C   9
10   D  10
11   D  11
12   D  12

> subset(newdf, subset = fac == "C", select = c(fac, val))
  fac val
7   C   7
8   C   8
9   C   9

> subset(newdf, subset = val > 5 & fac == "D") # Two subsets 1 AND 2
   val fac
10  10   D
11  11   D
12  12   D
```

```
   ## Alternative syntax, often encountered when subset used as a parameter
> subset(newdf, subset = fac %in% "D")
   val fac
10  10   D
11  11   D
12  12   D
```

COMMAND NAME

which

Returns an index value for an expression. In other words, you can get an index value for the position of items in a vector or array that match certain conditions.

 SEE also which in "Sorting and Rearranging Data."

Common Usage

```
which(x. array.ind = FALSE)
```

Related Commands

[] (p. 30)
$ (p. 109)
sort (p. 120)
order (p. 117)
rank (p. 119)

Command Parameters

x   An R object, usually a vector, matrix, or array.

array.ind = FALSE   If array.ind = TRUE, the result is shown as an array.

Examples

```
   ## Make objects
> newnum = 10:1 # Descending values
> newchar = month.abb[1:12] # Characters (month names)
> newarr = array(1:12, dim = c(2, 3, 2),
 dimnames = list(letters[1:2], LETTERS[1:3], c("One", "Two"))) # A 3D array

   ## Get index values
> which(newchar == "Apr") # How far along the sequence is "Apr"?
[1] 4
> newchar
 [1] "Jan" "Feb" "Mar" "Apr" "May" "Jun" "Jul" "Aug" "Sep" "Oct" "Nov" "Dec"
```

```
> which(newnum == 5) # Which item(s) equal 5?
[1] 6
> newnum
 [1] 10  9  8  7  6  5  4  3  2  1

> which(newnum > 5) # Which items are greater than 5?
[1] 1 2 3 4 5

> which(newarr > 5) # Which items in array are greater than 5?
[1]  6  7  8  9 10 11 12

> which(newarr > 5, arr.ind = TRUE) # Shows result as an array
  dim1 dim2 dim3
b    2    3    1
a    1    1    2
b    2    1    2
a    1    2    2
b    2    2    2
a    1    3    2
b    2    3    2
```

COMMAND NAME

`with`

Allows an object to be temporarily placed in the search list. The result is that named components of the object are available for the duration of the command.

 SEE "Viewing Data: Listing Data."

SORTING AND REARRANGING DATA

Data within an object is usually unsorted; that is, it is arranged in the order in which the values were entered. For this reason, it can be useful to have an index for the order in which the items lie. It can also be useful to rearrange data into a new order.

COMMAND NAME

`order`

Returns the order in which items of a vector are arranged. In other words, you get an index value for the order of items. The command can use additional vectors to act as tie-breakers. This command can help to rearrange data frames and matrix objects by creating an index that can be used with the [] to specify a new row (or column) arrangement.

Common Usage

```
order(..., na.last = TRUE, decreasing = FALSE)
```

Related Commands

rank (p. 119)
sort (p. 120)
which (p. 116)

Command Parameters

...	R objects (vectors); all must be of the same length. The first named item is ordered and subsequent items are used to resolve ties.
na.last = TRUE	Controls treatment of NA items. If TRUE, NA items are placed at the end, if FALSE they are placed at the beginning, and if NA they are omitted.
decreasing = FALSE	If decreasing = TRUE, the items are ordered in descending fashion.

Examples

```
  ## Make objects
> newvec = c(3, 4, NA, 7, 1, 6, 5, 5, 2) # Vector containing NA
> tv1 = 1:9 # Vector of ascending values
> tv2 = 9:1 # Vector of descending values

  ## Get index for order of items
> order(newvec) # Default, ascending with NA last
[1] 5 9 1 2 7 8 6 4 3

> order(newvec, na.last = FALSE) # Ascending with NA first
[1] 3 5 9 1 2 7 8 6 4

> order(newvec, na.last = NA) # Ascending NA omitted
[1] 5 9 1 2 7 8 6 4

> order(newvec, na.last = NA, decreasing = TRUE) # Decreasing with NA omitted
[1] 4 6 7 8 2 1 9 5

  ## Effects of using a tie-breaker
> tv1 ; tv2 # view tie-breaker vectors
[1] 1 2 3 4 5 6 7 8 9
[1] 9 8 7 6 5 4 3 2 1

> order(newvec, tv1) # Same order as before (7, 8)
[1] 5 9 1 2 7 8 6 4 3

> order(newvec, tv2) # Different order (8, 7)
[1] 5 9 1 2 8 7 6 4 3
```

COMMAND NAME

rank

Gives the ranks of the values in a vector. The default method produces values that are used in a wide range on non-parametric statistical tests.

 SEE Theme 2, "Math and Statistics."

Common Usage

```
rank(x, na.last = TRUE, ties.method = "average")
```

Related Commands

order (p. 117)
sort (p. 120)
which (p. 116)

Command Parameters

x	A vector of values.
na.last = TRUE	Sets how NA items are handled. If na.last = TRUE, NA items are put last; if FALSE they are put first; and if na.last = NA they are omitted.
ties.method = "average"	Sets the method to determine how to deal with tied values. The default, "average", uses the mean. Alternatives are "first", "random", "max", and "min". The method name can be abbreviated (but must be in quotes).

Examples

```
  ## Make a vector
> newvec = c(3, 4, NA, 7, 1, 6, 5, 5, 2) # Vector containing NA

  ## Rank vector
> rank(newvec) # Using default (NA placed last, "average" method)
[1] 3.0 4.0 9.0 8.0 1.0 7.0 5.5 5.5 2.0

> rank(newvec, na.last = NA, ties.method = "average") # Remove NA
[1] 3.0 4.0 8.0 1.0 7.0 5.5 5.5 2.0

> rank(newvec, na.last = FALSE, ties.method = "max") # NA 1st, "max" method
[1] 4 5 1 9 2 8 7 7 3

> rank(newvec, na.last = FALSE, ties.method = "min") # NA 1st, "min" method
[1] 4 5 1 9 2 8 6 6 3
```

COMMAND NAME

sort

Rearranges data into a new order.

Common Usage

```
sort(x, decreasing = FALSE, na.last = NA)
```

Related Commands

order (p. 117)
rank (p. 119)
which (p. 116)

Command Parameters

x	A vector.
decreasing = FALSE	If set to TRUE, the vector is sorted in descending order.
na.last = NA	Sets how to deal with NA items. If na.last = NA (the default), NA items are omitted. If set to TRUE, they are placed last and if FALSE, they are placed first.

Examples

```
  ## Make a vector
> newvec = c(3, 4, NA, 7, 1, 6, 5, 5, 2) # Vector containing NA

> ## Sort vector
> sort(newvec) # The defaults, ascending order with NA omitted
[1] 1 2 3 4 5 5 6 7

> sort(newvec, na.last = TRUE) # Place NA last
[1]  1  2  3  4  5  5  6  7 NA

> sort(newvec, na.last = FALSE, decreasing = TRUE) # NA 1st, descending order
[1] NA  7  6  5  5  4  3  2  1
```

COMMAND NAME

which

Returns an index value for an expression. In other words, you can get an index value for the position of items in a vector or array that match certain conditions.

 SEE "Selecting and Sampling Data."

Summarizing Data

The more complicated and large an object is (large meaning lots of values), the more important it is to summarize the object in a more compact and meaningful manner.

 SEE also Theme 2, "Math and Statistics."

 SEE "Distribution of Data" to look at the shape (distribution) of data objects.

 SEE "Data Object Properties" to look at the general properties of data objects.

WHAT'S IN THIS TOPIC:

- **Summary statistics** (p. 121)
    - Averages and statistics for simple objects (vectors)
    - Summarizing complicated objects (e.g., data frames or lists)
- **Summary tables** (p. 136)
    - Summary statistics for table and table-like objects
    - Contingency tables
    - Cross tabulation

SUMMARY STATISTICS

It is important to be able to summarize data in a compact and meaningful manner. R provides various commands to carry out summary statistics as well as methods for dealing with complicated objects, such as data frames, with columns containing numerical and factor data.

COMMAND NAME

addmargins

Carries out a summary command on a table, array, or matrix object. You can specify the command and which margins to use.

 SEE addmargins in "Summary Tables."

COMMAND NAME

aggregate

Computes summary statistics on complicated objects based on grouping variables. The command accepts input in two different ways (see the following common usage). The `formula` input is a convenient way to carry out summaries on data frames.

Common Usage

```
aggregate(x, by, FUN, ...)

aggregate(formula, data, FUN, ..., subset, na.action = na.omit)
```

Related Commands

`tapply` (p. 135)
`apply` (p. 123)
`lapply` (p. 126)
`sapply` (p. 131)

Command Parameters

x	An R object.
by	A list of grouping elements, each the same length as the variable(s) in x.
FUN	The function to compute as a summary statistic.
...	Other relevant parameters; e.g., `na.omit = TRUE`.
formula	A formula specifying the variable to summarize on the left and the grouping variables on the right; e.g., y ~ x + z.
subset	An optional vector specifying a subset to use.
na.action = na.omit	For the formula method, NA items are omitted by default.

Examples

```
   ## Make some objects
> vec = 1:16 # Simple numeric vector
> fac1 = gl(n = 4, k = 4, labels = LETTERS[1:4]) # Factor 4 levels
> fac2 = gl(n = 2, k = 8, labels = c("First", "Second")) # Factor 2 levels
> newdf = data.frame(resp = vec, pr1 = fac1, pr2 = fac2) # Data frame

   ## Summarize
> aggregate(vec, by = list(fac1), FUN = max) # For one grouping
  Group.1  x
1      A   4
2      B   8
3      C  12
4      D  16
```

```
> aggregate(vec, by = list(fac1, fac2), FUN = median) # 2 grouping variables
  Group.1 Group.2    x
1       A   First  2.5
2       B   First  6.5
3       C  Second 10.5
4       D  Second 14.5

> aggregate(resp ~ pr1 + pr2, data = newdf, FUN = sum) # Formula method
  pr1    pr2 resp
1   A  First   10
2   B  First   26
3   C Second   42
4   D Second   58
```

COMMAND NAME

apply

Applies a function over the margins of an array or matrix.

Common Usage

apply(X, MARGIN, FUN, ...)

Related Commands

aggregate (p. 122)
tapply (p. 135)
lapply (p. 126)
sapply (p. 131)

Command Parameters

X   An array or matrix.

MARGIN   The margin over which the summary function is to be applied; e.g., MARGIN = 1
           summarizes rows, 2 summarizes columns.

FUN   The function to apply to the data.

...   Other relevant parameters as accepted by FUN; e.g., na.rm = TRUE.

Examples

```
  ## Make objects
> newarr = array(1:12, dim = c(2, 3, 2),
 dimnames = list(letters[1:2], LETTERS[1:3], c("One", "Two"))) # A 3D array
> newmat = matrix(1:24, nrow = 3, dimnames = list(letters[1:3], LETTERS[1:8]))
> newmat[5] = NA # Make one element a missing value, NA

  ## Summarize
> apply(newarr, MARGIN = 1, FUN = sum) # Sum for dimension 1 of array
 a  b
36 42
```

```
> apply(newarr, MARGIN = c(2, 3), FUN = sum) # Sum for 2 dimensions of array
  One Two
A   3  15
B   7  19
C  11  23

> apply(newmat, MARGIN = 2, FUN = median) # Median for columns of matrix
 A  B  C  D  E  F  G  H
 2 NA  8 11 14 17 20 23

> apply(newmat, MARGIN = 2, FUN = median, na.rm = TRUE) # Omit NA items
 A  B  C  D  E  F  G  H
 2  5  8 11 14 17 20 23
```

COMMAND NAME

colMeans
colSums
rowMeans
rowSums

Simple column (or row) sums or means for `array` or `matrix` objects. These are equivalent to the `apply` command with `FUN = mean` or `FUN = sum`, but are computationally more efficient. Compare to the `rowsum` command, which uses a grouping variable.

 SEE also `colSums`, `rowMeans`, and `rowSums` in "Summary Statistics."

Common Usage

```
colMeans(x, na.rm = FALSE, dims = 1)
colSums(x, na.rm = FALSE, dims = 1)
rowMeans(x, na.rm = FALSE, dims = 1)
rowSums(x, na.rm = FALSE, dims = 1)
```

Related Commands

apply (p. 123)
rowsum (p. 130)
aggregate (p. 122)

Command Parameters

x	An array of two or more dimensions or a data frame.
na.rm = FALSE	If na.rm = TRUE, NA items are omitted.
dims = 1	An integer value stating how many dimensions to calculate over. This must be at least one less than the total number of dimensions. The row and col commands treat this value differently (see the following examples).

Examples

```
  ## Make objects
> newarr = array(1:12, dim = c(2, 3, 2),
  dimnames = list(letters[1:2], LETTERS[1:3], c("One", "Two"))) # A 3D array
> newmat = matrix(1:24, nrow = 3, dimnames = list(letters[1:3], LETTERS[1:8]))
> newmat[5] = NA # Make one element a missing value, NA

  ## Summarize
> colMeans(newmat) # Default, NA items not omitted
 A  B  C  D  E  F  G  H
 2 NA  8 11 14 17 20 23

> colMeans(newmat, na.rm = TRUE) # Omit NA item
 A  B  C  D  E  F  G  H
 2  5  8 11 14 17 20 23

> colSums(newarr, dims = 1) # For cols one dimension at a time
  One Two
A   3  15
B   7  19
C  11  23

> colSums(newarr, dims = 2) # For cols dimensions combined
One Two
 21  57

> rowSums(newarr, dims = 1) # For rows dimensions combined
 a  b
36 42

> rowSums(newarr, dims = 2) # For rows one dimension at a time
   A  B  C
a  8 12 16
b 10 14 18
```

COMMAND NAME

colSums

Simple column sums for array or matrix objects.

 SEE colMeans.

COMMAND NAME

```
cummax
cummin
cumprod
cumsum
```

These commands provide functions for carrying out cumulative operations. The commands return values for cumulative maxima, minima, product, and sum. If used with the `seq_along` command, they can provide cumulative values for other functions.

 SEE Theme 2, "Math and Statistics."

COMMAND NAME

```
fivenum
```

This command produces Tukey's five-number summary for the input data. The values returned are minimum, lower-hinge, median, upper-hinge, and maximum.

 SEE Theme 2, "Math and Statistics."

COMMAND NAME

```
IQR
```

Calculates the inter-quartile range.

 SEE Theme 2, "Math and Statistics."

COMMAND NAME

```
lapply
```

Applies a function to elements of a list. The result is also a list.

 SEE also `sapply`, which produces a vector or matrix as a result.

Common Usage

```
lapply(X, FUN, ...)
```

Related Commands

```
sapply (p. 131)
apply (p. 123)
tapply (p. 135)
aggregate (p. 122)
```

Command Parameters

x   A list object.

FUN   The function to apply to each element of the list.

...   Other parameters relevant to the FUN applied; e.g., na.rm = TRUE.

Examples

```
  ## Make a list
> newlist = list(num = 1:10, vec = c(2:5, 4:5, 6:8, NA, 9, 12, 17), lg = log(1:5))

  ## Summarize
> lapply(newlist, FUN = mean, na.rm = TRUE)
$num
[1] 5.5

$vec
[1] 6.833333

$lg
[1] 0.9574983
```

COMMAND NAME

length

Determines how many elements are in an object. The command can get or set the number of elements.

 SEE also "Data Object Properties."

Common Usage

```
length(x)

length(x) <- value
```

Related Commands

summary (p. 132)

Command Parameters

x   An R object, usually a vector, list, or factor, but other objects may be specified.

value   The value to set for the length of the specified object.

Examples

```
  ## Make some objects
> newmat = matrix(1:12, nrow = 3) # A matrix
> newlist = list(num = 1:10, ltr = letters[1:6], vec = c(3, 4, NA, 7)) # A list
> newdf = data.frame(col1 = 1:3, col2 = 4:6, col3 = 5:3) # A data frame
> newfac = gl(n = 4, k = 3) # A factor
> newchar = month.abb[1:12] # Character vector
> newnum = 4:12 # Numerical vector

  ## Get Lengths
> length(newmat) # The number of items in the matrix
[1] 12

> length(newlist) # How many elements
[1] 3

> length(newdf) # Number of columns
[1] 3

> length(newfac) # Number of items (not number of different factors)
[1] 12

> length(newchar) # How many items
[1] 12

> length(newnum) # How many items
[1] 9

  ## Alter lengths
> length(newnum) = 12
> newnum # Object is padded with NA
 [1]  4  5  6  7  8  9 10 11 12 NA NA NA

> length(newnum) = 6
> newnum # Object is truncated
[1] 4 5 6 7 8 9
```

COMMAND NAME

mad

This command calculates the median absolute deviation for a numeric vector. It also adjusts (by default) by a factor for asymptotically normal consistency.

 SEE Theme 2, "Math and Statistics."

COMMAND NAME

`margin.table`

Produces `sum` values for margins of a contingency table, array, or matrix.

 SEE `margin.table` in "Summary Tables." The `margin.table` command is a simplified version of the `apply` command.

COMMAND NAME

`mean`

Calculates the mean value for the specified data.

 SEE Theme 2, "Math and Statistics."

COMMAND NAME

`median`

This command calculates the median value for an object.

 SEE Theme 2, "Math and Statistics."

COMMAND NAME

`prop.table`

This command expresses table entries as a fraction of the marginal total.

 SEE `prop.table` in "Summary Tables."

COMMAND NAME

`quantile`

Returns quantiles for a sample corresponding to given probabilities. The default settings produce five quartile values.

 SEE Theme 2, "Math and Statistics."

COMMAND NAME

range

Gives the range for a given sample; that is, a vector containing the minimum and maximum values.

 SEE Theme 2, "Math and Statistics."

COMMAND NAME

rowMeans

Simple row means for array or matrix objects.

 SEE colMeans in "Summary Statistics."

COMMAND NAME

rowsum

This command sums columns of a matrix or data frame based on a grouping variable. The column sums are computed across rows of a matrix for each level of a grouping variable. Contrast this to the colSums command, which produces a simple sum of each column.

Common Usage

```
rowsum(x, group, reorder = TRUE, na.rm = TRUE)
```

Related Commands

tapply (p. 135)
aggregate (p. 122)
apply (p. 123)
colSums (p. 124)
rowSums (p. 124)

Command Parameters

x	An R object; usually a data frame, matrix, table, or array.
reorder = TRUE	If reorder = FALSE, the result is in the order in which the groups were encountered.
na.rm = FALSE	If na.rm = TRUE, NA items are omitted.

Examples

```
  ## Make objects
> newdf = data.frame(col1 = 1:6, col2 = 8:3, col3 = 6:1) # Numeric 3 columns
```

```
> newchar = c("C", "C", "B", "B", "A", "A") # Grouping vector
> newdf # View original data frame
  col1 col2 col3
1    1    8    6
2    2    7    5
3    3    6    4
4    4    5    3
5    5    4    2
6    6    3    1

  ## Row sums by group
> rowsum(newdf, group = newchar) # Groups are re-ordered
  col1 col2 col3
A   11    7    3
B    7   11    7
C    3   15   11

> rowsum(newdf, group = newchar, reorder = FALSE) # Keep original group order
  col1 col2 col3
C    3   15   11
B    7   11    7
A   11    7    3
```

COMMAND NAME

rowSums

Simple row sums for array or matrix objects.

 SEE colMeans in "Summary Statistics."

COMMAND NAME

sapply

Applies a function to elements of a list (or a vector). The result is a matrix.

 SEE also the lapply command, which produces a list as a result.

Common Usage

sapply(X, FUN, ...,)

Related Commands

tapply (p. 135)
apply (p. 123)

Command Parameters

X   A list or vector object.

FUN   The function to apply to the elements of the object.

...   Other parameters relevant to the FUN used.

Examples

```
  ## Make a list
> newlist = list(num = 1:10, vec = c(2:5, 4:5, 6:8, NA, 9, 12, 17), lg = log(1:5))

  ## Summarize
> sapply(newlist, FUN = mean, na.rm = TRUE)
     num        vec         lg
5.5000000 6.8333333 0.9574983
```

COMMAND NAME

sd

Calculates standard deviation for vector, matrix, and data frame objects. If the data is a matrix or data frame, the standard deviation is calculated for each column.

 SEE Theme 2, "Math and Statistics."

COMMAND NAME

sum

This command returns the sum of the values present.

 SEE Theme 2, "Math and Statistics."

COMMAND NAME

summary

Summarizes an object. This command is very general and the result depends on the class of the object being examined. Some results objects will have a special class and possibly a dedicated summary routine to display them.

 SEE also aov and lm in Theme 2, "Math and Statistics."

Common Usage

```
summary(object, maxsum = 7, digits = max(3, getOption("digits")-3)
```

Related Commands

str (p. 102)
attributes (p. 76)
class (p. 79)

Command Parameters

object   An R object.

maxsum = 7   An integer value indicating the maximum number of levels of a factor to show.
             For a data frame this defaults to 7, but for a factor object the default is 100.

digits =   The number of digits to display for numeric variables.

Examples

```
## Make objects
> newnum = c(2:5, 4:5, 6:8, 9, NA, 17) # Numeric vector
> newfac = factor(c(rep("A", 3), rep("B", 3), rep("C", 3), rep("D", 2)))
> newdf = data.frame(response = na.omit(newnum), predictor = newfac)
> newchar = month.abb[1:12]
> newlist = list(Ltr = letters[1:10], Nmbr = 1:12)

## Summary
> summary(newnum)
   Min. 1st Qu.  Median    Mean 3rd Qu.    Max.    NA's
  2.000   4.000   5.000   6.364   7.500  17.000   1.000

> summary(newfac)
A B C D
3 3 3 2

> summary(newdf)
    response         predictor
 Min.   : 2.000    A:3
 1st Qu.: 4.000    B:3
 Median : 5.000    C:3
 Mean   : 6.364    D:2
 3rd Qu.: 7.500
 Max.   :17.000

> summary(newchar)
   Length     Class      Mode
       12 character character

> summary(newlist)
     Length Class  Mode
Ltr  10     -none- character
Nmbr 12     -none- numeric
```

COMMAND NAME

sweep

This command examines an array object and uses a second array with a mathematical operator to sweep out a summary statistic. The result is a new array. The command is particularly useful for comparing items in an array to some other value.

Common Usage

```
sweep(x, MARGIN, STATS, FUN = "-", ...)
```

Related Commands

apply (p. 123)

Command Parameters

x   An R object; usually an array, table or matrix.

MARGIN   The margin of the array that corresponds to the STATS being swept out. For a matrix, 1 is the rows and 2 is the columns; c(1, 2) gives both.

STATS   The summary statistic that is to be swept out.

FUN   The function used to carry out the sweep; this is applied like so: x FUN STATS.

...   Optional parameters that may be required by FUN.

Examples

```
  ## Make matrix (3 row x 4 col)
> set.seed(5) # Set seed for random numbers
> matdat = round(runif(24, 1, 25)) # Make 24 random values btwn 1 and 25
> newmat = matrix(matdat, nrow = 3,
 dimnames = list(letters[1:3], LETTERS[1:8])) # Make matrix
> newmat # The final matrix
   A  B  C  D  E  F  G  H
a  6  8 14  4  9  6 14 18
b 17  4 20  8 14 10 21  6
c 23 18 24 13  7 22 22  6

  ## Array summaries
  ## Get medians for columns
> matmed = apply(newmat, MARGIN = 2, FUN = median)
> matmed # View the result (a matrix of column medians)
 A  B  C  D  E  F  G  H
17  8 20  8  9 10 21  6
```

```
## Subtract col medians from original matrix
> sweep(newmat, MARGIN = 2, FUN = "-", STATS = matmed)
    A  B  C  D  E   F  G  H
a -11  0 -6 -4  0  -4 -7 12
b   0 -4  0  0  5   0  0  0
c   6 10  4  5 -2  12  1  0

## Multiply each element by itself (same as newmat^2)
> sweep(newmat, MARGIN = c(1,2), FUN = "*", STATS = newmat)
    A    B    C    D    E    F    G    H
a  36   64  196   16   81   36  196  324
b 289   16  400   64  196  100  441   36
c 529  324  576  169   49  484  484   36
```

COMMAND NAME

`tapply`

This command enables you to apply a summary function to a vector based on the levels of another vector. You can also use it to make one column (or several) of a data frame a grouping variable to summarize another column.

Common Usage

```
tapply(X, INDEX, FUN = NULL, ...)
```

Related Commands

aggregate (p. 122)
apply (p. 123)
lapply (p. 126)
sapply (p. 131)

Command Parameters

X   An R object; usually a vector.

INDEX   A list of factors, each the same length as X, which act as grouping levels for the function applied in FUN.

FUN   The function to be applied; if NULL is used, the result is a simple index.

...   Additional parameters that are relevant to the FUN applied.

Examples

```
## Make objects
> newnum = c(2:5, 4:5, 6:8, 9, 17) # Numeric vector
> fac1 = factor(c(rep("A", 3), rep("B", 3), rep("C", 3), rep("D", 2))) # Factor
> fac2 = gl(n = 2, k = 1, length = 11, labels = month.abb[1:2]) # Factor
> newdf = data.frame(response = newnum, pred1 = fac1, pred2 = fac2)
```

```
  ## Use tapply to summarize by group/level
> tapply(newnum, INDEX = fac1, FUN = NULL) # Gives index
 [1] 1 1 1 2 2 2 3 3 3 4 4

> tapply(newnum, INDEX = fac1, FUN = sum) # Sum for each level of INDEX
 A  B  C  D
 9 14 21 26

> tapply(newnum, INDEX = list(fac1, fac2), FUN = median) # Use 2 INDEX vars
   Jan Feb
A   3   3
B   4   5
C   7   7
D  17   9

  ## Use on a data frame
> with(newdf, tapply(response, INDEX = pred1, FUN = median))
 A  B  C  D
 3  5  7 13
```

COMMAND NAME

var

This command calculates the variance of numeric vectors.

 SEE Theme 2, "Math and Statistics."

SUMMARY TABLES

One way to summarize data is to create a contingency table, which shows the frequency of observations at each combination of levels of the variables. R has a range of commands related to the creation and examination of tables; these commands carry out tasks such as making contingency tables, applying summary commands on rows or columns, and cross tabulating.

 SEE also "Summarizing Data."

COMMAND NAME

addmargins

Carries out a summary command on a table, array, or matrix object. You can specify the command and which margins to use.

Common Usage

```
addmargins(A, margin = seq_along(dim(A)), FUN = sum, quiet = FALSE)
```

Related Commands

table (p. 12)
ftable (p. 138)
margin.table (p. 140)
apply (p. 123)

Command Parameters

A	An array, table, or matrix object.
margin =	The margin to use; the default uses all the dimensions of the object. The result is placed in the margin specified, so margin = 1 produces a row of results, but doesn't give the results of the row (see the following examples).
FUN = sum	The function to use for the summary. The default produces the sum.
quiet = FALSE	If several margins are specified explicitly, the command produces a message showing the order in which they were processed. You can suppress the message using quiet = TRUE.

Examples

```
  ## Make a matrix
> set.seed(5) # Set random number seed
> matdat = round(runif(n = 24, min = 0, max = 10), 0) # Make 24 random numbers
  ## Now make the matrix (3 rows x 8 columns)
> newmat = matrix(matdat, nrow = 3,
 dimnames = list(letters[1:3], LETTERS[1:8]))

  ## Default: sums for rows, columns and all
> addmargins(newmat)
    A  B  C D  E  F  G  H Sum
a   2  3  5 1  3  2  6  7  29
b   7  1  8 3  6  4  8  2  39
c   9  7 10 5  3  9  9  2  54
Sum 18 11 23 9 12 15 23 11 122

  ## A row of median values (margin = 1)
> addmargins(newmat, margin = 1, FUN = median)
       A B  C D E F G H
a      2 3  5 1 3 2 6 7
b      7 1  8 3 6 4 8 2
c      9 7 10 5 3 9 9 2
median 7 3  8 3 3 4 8 2

  ## A column of Std deviations (margin = 2)
> addmargins(newmat, margin = 2, FUN = sd)
  A B  C D E F G H        sd
a 2 3  5 1 3 2 6 7 2.133910
b 7 1  8 3 6 4 8 2 2.748376
c 9 7 10 5 3 9 9 2 3.058945
```

```
  ## Two different functions (one for each margin)
> addmargins(newmat, FUN = list(SUM = sum, Std.Dev. = sd))
Margins computed over dimensions
in the following order:
1:
2:
      A  B  C D  E  F  G  H Std.Dev.
a     2  3  5 1  3  2  6  7 2.133910
b     7  1  8 3  6  4  8  2 2.748376
c     9  7 10 5  3  9  9  2 3.058945
SUM 18 11 23 9 12 15 23 11 5.522681
```

COMMAND NAME

ftable

Creates contingency tables using cross-classifying factors to show the frequency of observations at each combination of variables. If a contingency table is created using multiple cross-classifying (grouping) variables, the result is an array with multiple dimensions. The ftable command creates "flat" tables, which are simpler. These tables have a class attribute "ftable".

Common Usage

```
ftable(..., row.vars = NULL, col.vars = NULL)
```

Related Commands

table (p. 12)
xtabs (p. 144)

Command Parameters

...	R objects to be tabulated. These can be one or more vectors or a factor, matrix, array, or data frame.
row.vars = NULL	If the object has named items (e.g., columns of a data frame), the names or column numbers can be specified as the row items in the final flat table. Otherwise, the order in which the items are specified in ... determines the final outcome.
col.vars = NULL	If the object has named items (e.g., columns of a data frame), the names or column numbers can be specified as the column items in the final flat table. Otherwise, the order in which the items are specified in ... determines the final outcome.

Examples

```
   ## Make objects
> newnum = c(1:3, 2:4, 2:3, 4:3) # Numeric vector
> fac1 = factor(c(rep("A", 3), rep("B", 4), rep("C", 3))) # Factor
> fac2 = gl(n = 2, k = 1, length = 10, labels = month.abb[1:2]) # Factor
> newdf = data.frame(Nmbr = newnum, Fct1 = fac1, Fct2 = fac2) # Data frame

   ## Flat table
> ftable(newdf) # Use entire data frame
         Fct2 Jan Feb
Nmbr Fct1
1    A         1   0
     B         0   0
     C         0   0
2    A         0   1
     B         1   1
     C         0   0
3    A         1   0
     B         1   0
     C         0   2
4    A         0   0
     B         0   1
     C         1   0


> ftable(fac1, fac2, newnum) # Change order of items
         newnum 1 2 3 4
fac1 fac2
A    Jan         1 0 1 0
     Feb         0 1 0 0
B    Jan         0 1 1 0
     Feb         0 1 0 1
C    Jan         0 0 0 1
     Feb         0 0 2 0


> ftable(Nmbr ~ Fct2, data = newdf) # Use formula to select from data frame
     Nmbr 1 2 3 4
Fct2
Jan       1 1 2 1
Feb       0 2 2 1


> ftable(newdf, row.vars = 1, col.vars = 2:3) # Specify rows/cols to use
     Fct1    A       B       C
     Fct2 Jan Feb Jan Feb Jan Feb
Nmbr
1         1   0   0   0   0   0
2         0   1   1   1   0   0
3         1   0   1   0   0   2
4         0   0   0   1   1   0
```

COMMAND NAME

`margin.table`

Produces `sum` values for margins of a contingency table, array, or matrix. The `margin.table` command is a simplified version of the `apply` command.

 SEE also "Summarizing Data."

Common Usage

```
margin.table(x, margin = NULL)
```

Related Commands

`apply` (p. 123)
`prop.table` (p. 141)
`addmargins` (p. 121)

Command Parameters

x   An R object, usually an array, table, or matrix.

margin = NULL   The margin to use for the summation; e.g., `margin = 1` gives row sums, `margin = 2` gives column sums.

Examples

```
  ## Make matrix and array
  ## Matrix (3 rows x 8 columns)
> newmat = matrix(1:24, nrow = 3, dimnames = list(letters[1:3], LETTERS[1:8]))
> newarr = array(1:12, dim = c(2, 3, 2),
  dimnames = list(letters[1:2], LETTERS[1:3], c("One", "Two"))) # A 3D array

  ## Margin sums for matrix
> margin.table(newmat, margin = NULL) # Sum of entire matrix
[1] 300

> margin.table(newmat, margin = 1) # Row sums
  a   b   c
 92 100 108

> margin.table(newmat, margin = 2) # Column sums
 A  B  C  D  E  F  G  H
 6 15 24 33 42 51 60 69

  ## Margin sums for array
> margin.table(newarr, margin = NULL) # Entire
[1] 78
```

```
> margin.table(newarr, margin = 1) # Rows
 a  b
36 42


> margin.table(newarr, margin = 2) # Columns
 A  B  C
18 26 34


> margin.table(newarr, margin = 3) # Dimension 3
One Two
 21  57
```

COMMAND NAME

`prop.table`

This command expresses table entries as a fraction of the marginal total. The command is a simplified form of the `sweep` command.

Common Usage

```
prop.table(x, margin = NULL)
```

Related Commands

`margin.table` (p. 140)
`sweep` (p. 134)

Command Parameters

`x`	A table, matrix, or array object.
`margin = NULL`	An index or vector of indices specifying the margin to use.

Examples

```
 ## Make matrix and array
 ## Matrix (3 rows x 4 columns)
> newmat = matrix(1:12, nrow = 3, dimnames = list(letters[1:3], LETTERS[1:4]))
> newarr = array(1:12, dim = c(2, 3, 2),
 dimnames = list(letters[1:2], LETTERS[1:3], c("One", "Two"))) # A 3D array


 ## Fractions of margins for matrix (2-dimensions)
> prop.table(newmat, margin = 1) # Rows sum to 1
          A         B         C         D
a 0.04545455 0.1818182 0.3181818 0.4545455
b 0.07692308 0.1923077 0.3076923 0.4230769
c 0.10000000 0.2000000 0.3000000 0.4000000
```

```
> prop.table(newmat, margin = 2) # Columns sum to 1
          A         B         C         D
a 0.1666667 0.2666667 0.2916667 0.3030303
b 0.3333333 0.3333333 0.3333333 0.3333333
c 0.5000000 0.4000000 0.3750000 0.3636364

> prop.table(newmat, margin = NULL) # Entire result sums to 1
           A          B          C          D
a 0.01282051 0.05128205 0.08974359 0.1282051
b 0.02564103 0.06410256 0.10256410 0.1410256
c 0.03846154 0.07692308 0.11538462 0.1538462

  ## Fractions of margins for array (3-dimensions)
> prop.table(newarr, margin = 3) # Table "One" sums to 1, Table "Two" sums to 1
, , One

           A         B         C
a 0.04761905 0.1428571 0.2380952
b 0.09523810 0.1904762 0.2857143

, , Two

          A         B         C
a 0.1228070 0.1578947 0.1929825
b 0.1403509 0.1754386 0.2105263

> prop.table(newarr, margin = c(1, 2)) # Can specify more than one dimension
, , One

      A         B         C
a 0.125 0.2500000 0.3125000
b 0.200 0.2857143 0.3333333

, , Two

      A         B         C
a 0.875 0.7500000 0.6875000
b 0.800 0.7142857 0.6666667
```

COMMAND NAME

table

This command uses cross-classifying variables to create a contingency table showing the frequency of observations at each combination of the variables. The resulting table has a special class attribute "table". The command is based on the tabulate command.

Common Usage

```
table(..., dnn = list.names(...))
```

Related Commands

```
is.table (p. 20)
as.table (p. 16)
ftable (p. 138)
xtabs (p. 144)
margin.table (p. 140)
prop.table (p. 141)
addmargins (p. 121)
tabulate (p. 144)
```

Command Parameters

`...`	R objects to be tabulated. These can be one or more vectors or a factor, matrix, array, or data frame.
`dnn = list.names(...)`	The names to be given to the dimensions in the result.

Examples

```
  ## Make objects
> newnum = c(1:3, 2:4, 2:3, 5, 6, 5) # Numeric vector
> fac1 = factor(c(rep("A", 3), rep("B", 3), rep("C", 3), rep("D", 2))) # Factor
> fac2 = gl(n = 2, k = 1, length = 11, labels = month.abb[1:2]) # Factor
> newdf = data.frame(Nmbr = newnum, Fct1 = fac1, Fct2 = fac2) # Data frame

  ## Make tables
> table(newnum) # Simple contingency table
newnum
1 2 3 4 5 6
1 3 3 1 2 1


> table(fac1) # Table for factor
fac1
A B C D
3 3 3 2


> table(fac2, dnn = "Table Factor") # Assign new name for dimension label
Table Factor
Jan Feb
  6   5
  ## Look at data frame (use columns 1,2 only)
> table(newdf[,1:2], dnn = list("Number var","Factor var")) # Set new names
          Factor var
Number var A B C D
         1 1 0 0 0
         2 1 1 1 0
         3 1 1 1 0
         4 0 1 0 0
         5 0 0 1 1
         6 0 0 0 1
```

COMMAND NAME

tabulate

Creates simple frequency tables for vectors or factor objects. This command is the basis for the table command.

Common Usage

```
tabulate(bin, nbins = max(1, bin, na.rm = TRUE))
```

Related Commands

table (p. 12)
factor (p. 7)

Command Parameters

bin   A vector of integers. If this is a factor, it is converted to integer values.

nbins   The number of bins to produce in the output. The default is the maximum number of items in the vector or the levels of the factor.

Examples

```
   ## Make objects
> fac1 = factor(c(rep("A", 3), rep("B", 4), rep("C", 3))) # Factor
> newvec = c(1, 2, 3, 3, 2.1, 4, 3, 3, 2, NA, 3.2, 5)

   ## Tabulate
> tabulate(fac1)
[1] 3 4 3

> tabulate(newvec) # NA items ignored. Items truncated to integer
[1] 1 3 5 1 1

> tabulate(newvec, nbins = 10) # Extra bins added
 [1] 1 3 5 1 1 0 0 0 0 0

> tabulate(newvec, nbins = 3) # Fewer bins means data truncated/ignored
[1] 1 3 5
```

COMMAND NAME

xtabs

Creates a cross-tabulation contingency table showing the frequencies of observation of a variable cross-tabulated against one or more grouping variables. The result has two class attributes, "xtabs" and "table". An "xtabs" object can be converted back to a frequency data frame using the as.data.frame command.

Common Usage

```
xtabs(formula = ~., data = parent.frame(), subset, drop.unused.levels = FALSE)
```

Related Commands

table (p. 12)
ftable (p. 138)
as.data.frame (p. 16)

Command Parameters

formula	A formula of the form y ~ x + z. It gives the variables to use for the cross tabulation.
data	The name of the data object where the variables in formula are found.
subset	A subset of variables to use (see: the following examples).
drop.unused.levels	If FALSE (the default), unused levels are shown with frequency 0.

Examples

```
  ## Make objects
> newnum = c(1:3, 2:4, 2:3, 4:3) # Numeric vector
> fac1 = factor(c(rep("A", 3), rep("B", 4), rep("C", 3))) # Factor
> fac2 = gl(n = 2, k = 1, length = 10, labels = month.abb[1:2]) # Factor
> newdf = data.frame(Freq = newnum, Fct1 = fac1, Fct2 = fac2) # Data frame

  ## Cross-tab everything
> xtabs(Freq ~ Fct1 + Fct2, data = newdf)
    Fct2
Fct1 Jan Feb
   A   4   2
   B   5   6
   C   4   6

  ## Use a subset (N.B. the unused levels show as 0 by default)
> xtabs(Freq ~ Fct1 + Fct2, data = newdf, subset = Fct2 %in% "Jan")
    Fct2
Fct1 Jan Feb
   A   4   0
   B   5   0
   C   4   0

  ## Do not show unused levels
> xtabs(Freq ~ Fct1 + Fct2, data = newdf, subset = Fct2 %in% "Jan",
 drop.unused.levels = TRUE)
    Fct2
Fct1 Jan
   A   4
   B   5
   C   4
```

```
   ## Use vectors rather than data frame
> xtabs(newnum ~ fac2 + fac1)
     fac1
fac2  A B C
  Jan 4 5 4
  Feb 2 6 6
```

Distribution of Data

Numerical data can fall into a variety of different probability distribution types. The normal distribution, for example, is only one of many distributions that R can deal with (see Table 1-1). In general, R has commands that deal with these distributions in terms of density, cumulative distribution, quantile, and random variate generation.

WHAT'S IN THIS TOPIC:

- **Density functions** (p. 148)

  - Density/mass functions for many probability distributions

- **Probability functions** (p. 152)

  - Cumulative distribution functions for many probability distributions

  - The empirical cumulative distribution function

  - The Studentized Range (Tukey)

- **Quantile functions** (p. 158)

  - Quantile functions for many probability distributions

  - The Studentized Range (Tukey)

- **Random numbers** (p. 161)

  - Random numbers from many probability distributions

  - Random number algorithms and control

 SEE Theme 3, "Graphics" for graphical methods of looking at data distribution.

 SEE Theme 2, "Math and Statistics: Tests of Distribution" for statistical tests of distribution.

SEE `family` in Theme 2, "Math and Statistics" for distribution families used in linear modeling.

The commands for distributions fall into four main groups:

- Density/mass functions
- Cumulative distribution functions
- Quantile functions
- Random variate generation

The R commands for these four groups of functions are generally named `dxxxx`, `pxxxx`, `qxxxx`, and `rxxxx`, respectively, where `xxxx` is the (abbreviated) name of the distribution (see Table 1-1). Commands for cumulative distribution, quantile, and random number generation begin with `p`, `q`, and `r`, respectively, rather than `d`.

TABLE 1-1:   **Distribution types in R and the related density command**

Distribution	Command	Distribution	Command
beta	dbeta	binomial	dbinom
Cauchy	dcauchy	chi-squared	dchisq
exponential	dexp	F	df
gamma	dgamma	geometric	dgeom
hypergeometric	dhyper	log-normal	dlnorm
multinomial	dmultinom	negative binomial	dnbinom
normal	dnorm	Poisson	dpois
Wilcoxon sign rank	dsignrank	Student's t	dt
uniform	dunif	Weibull	dweibull
Wilcoxon rank sum	dwilcox		

In addition to those listed in Table 1-1, R has commands to deal with the Studentized range: `ptukey` and `qtukey`.

DENSITY FUNCTIONS

The density/mass functions associated with these distributions are named dxxxx, where xxxx is the (abbreviated) name of the distribution. The distributions that R can deal with are listed previously in Table 1-1.

COMMAND NAME

dxxxx

Density/mass functions for various probability distributions (see Table 1-1). The individual commands are shown here:

dbeta
dbinom
dcauchy
dchisq
dexp
df
dgamma
dgeom
dhyper
dlnorm
dmultinom
dnbinom
dnorm
dpois
dsignrank
dt
dunif
dweibull
dwilcox

These commands provide access to the density computations for the various distributions. See the following examples for details of commonly used distributions.

Common Usage

```
dbeta(x, shape1, shape2, ncp, log = FALSE)
dbinom(x, size, prob, log = FALSE)
dcauchy(x, location = 0, scale = 1, log = FALSE)
dchisq(x, df, ncp = 0, log = FALSE)
dexp(x, rate = 1, log = FALSE)
df(x, df1, df2, ncp, log = FALSE)
dgamma(x, shape, rate = 1, scale = 1/rate, log = FALSE)
dgeom(x, prob, log = FALSE)
dhyper(x, m, n, k, log = FALSE)
dlnormal(x, meanlog = 0, sdlog = 1, log = FALSE)
dmultinom(x, size = NULL, prob, log = FALSE)
dnbinom(x, size, prob, mu, log = FALSE)
dnorm(x, mean = 0, sd = 1, log = FALSE)
dpois(x, lambda, log = FALSE)
```

```
dsignrank(x, n, log = FALSE)
dt(x, df, ncp, log = FALSE)
dunif(x, min = 0, max = 1, log = FALSE)
dweibull(x, shape, scale = 1, log = FALSE)
dwilcox(x, m, n, log = FALSE)
```

Related Commands

pxxxx (p. 155)
qxxxx (p. 159)
rxxxx (p. 162)
set.seed (p. 165)

Command Parameters

x	A vector of quantiles.
log = FALSE	If TRUE the probabilities are given as log(p).
Other parameters	Each distribution has its own set of parameters.

Examples

The built-in R help entries for each distribution give details about the various commands. Following are some detailed examples on some of the more commonly used distributions.

BINOMIAL DISTRIBUTION

The binomial distribution requires size (the number of trials) and prob, the probability of success for each trial:

```
  ## Binomial density
> dbinom(0:5, size = 5, prob = 0.4)
[1] 0.07776 0.25920 0.34560 0.23040 0.07680 0.01024
```

CHI-SQUARED DISTRIBUTION

The chi-squared distribution requires df (the degrees of freedom) and ncp, a non-centrality parameter (default ncp = 0):

```
  ## The chi-squared density for different degrees of freedom
> dchisq(1:5, df = 1)
[1] 0.24197072 0.10377687 0.05139344 0.02699548 0.01464498

> dchisq(1:5, df = 5)
[1] 0.08065691 0.13836917 0.15418033 0.14397591 0.12204152

  ## Use density to draw chi-squared distribution (see Figure 1-3)
> dcc = function(x) dchisq(x, df = 5) # Chi-Squared density
> curve(dcc, from = 0, to = 30) # Draw curve of chi-squared
> title(main = "Chi-squared distribution density function")
```

Chi−squared distribution density function

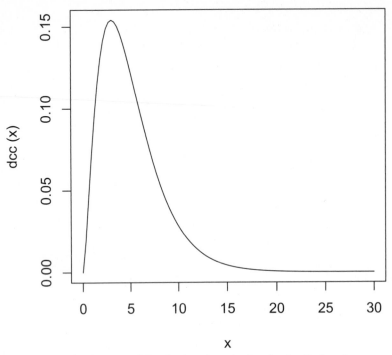

Figure 1-3: The chi-squared distribution plotted using the density function

F DISTRIBUTION

The F distribution requires degrees of freedom for numerator and denominator, df1 and df2, as well as ncp, a non-centrality parameter (if omitted, the central F is assumed):

```
  ## The F distribution density effects of df
> df(1:5, df1 = 1, df2 = 5)
[1] 0.21967980 0.09782160 0.05350733 0.03254516 0.02122066

> df(1:5, df1 = 2, df2 = 5)
[1] 0.30800082 0.12780453 0.06331704 0.03528526 0.02138334

> df(1:5, df1 = 1, df2 = 10)
[1] 0.23036199 0.10093894 0.05306663 0.03057288 0.01871043
```

NORMAL DISTRIBUTION

The normal distribution requires the mean (default mean = 0) and sd (standard deviation, default sd = 1):

```
  ## Normal distribution density
> dnorm(1:5, mean = 0, sd = 1)
[1] 2.419707e-01 5.399097e-02 4.431848e-03 1.338302e-04 1.486720e-06
```

```
> dnorm(1:5, mean = 5, sd = 1.5)
[1] 0.007597324 0.035993978 0.109340050 0.212965337 0.265961520


  ## Use density function to draw distribution (see Figure 1-4)
> curve(dnorm, from = -4, to = 4) # Draw density function
> title(main = "Normal distribution density function") # Add title
```

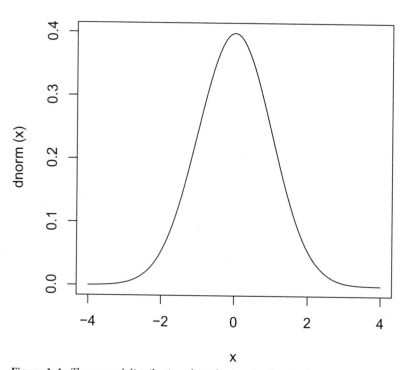

Figure 1-4: The normal distribution plotted using the density function

POISSON DISTRIBUTION

The Poisson distribution requires `lambda`, a (non-negative) mean value.

```
  ## Poisson density for values 0-5
> dpois(0:5, lambda = 1, log = FALSE)
[1] 0.367879441 0.367879441 0.183939721 0.061313240 0.015328310 0.003065662

> dpois(0:5, lambda = 1, log = TRUE)
[1] -1.000000 -1.000000 -1.693147 -2.791759 -4.178054 -5.787492
```

STUDENT'S T DISTRIBUTION

The t distribution requires the degrees of freedom, df, and ncp, a non-centrality parameter (if omitted, the central t is assumed).

```
  ## Student's t distribution, effects of degrees of freedom
> dt(1:5, df = 5)
[1] 0.219679797 0.065090310 0.017292579 0.005123727 0.001757438

> dt(1:5, df = 15)
[1] 0.234124773 0.059207732 0.009135184 0.001179000 0.000153436

> dt(1:5, df = Inf) # Set df to infinity
[1] 2.419707e-01 5.399097e-02 4.431848e-03 1.338302e-04 1.486720e-06
```

PROBABILITY FUNCTIONS

The cumulative probability functions associated with these distributions are named pxxxx, where xxxx is the (abbreviated) name of the distribution. The distributions that R can deal with are listed in Table 1-1. The Studentized range is covered by the ptukey command.

 SEE also the empirical cumulative distribution function, ecdf.

COMMAND NAME

ecdf

This command creates a custom cumulative distribution. A vector of values is used as the basis for the custom distribution. The resulting object has special attributes, namely a class "ecdf". Dedicated summary and plot commands also exist for objects of the class "ecdf" (see the following examples).

Common Usage

ecdf(x)

Related Commands

pxxxx (p. 155)
ptukey (p. 154)

Command Parameters

x   A vector of values.

Examples

```
## Make a cumulative distribution
> myd = c(1,2,4,8,16,32,64,128,150,100,70,50,30,20,10,5,2,1) # Values
> myecdf = ecdf(myd) # Make a custom cumulative distribution

> Fn = myecdf # Make a primitive function
> Fn(myd) # Gives percentiles for myd
 [1] 0.1111111 0.2222222 0.2777778 0.3888889 0.5000000 0.6666667 0.7777778 0.9444444
 [9] 1.0000000 0.8888889 0.8333333 0.7222222 0.6111111 0.5555556 0.4444444 0.3333333
[17] 0.2222222 0.1111111

> class(myecdf) # Object holds several classes
[1] "ecdf"     "stepfun"  "function"

> ## Dedicated commands for class "ecdf"
> summary(myecdf) # Summary command
Empirical CDF:       16 unique values with summary
  Min. 1st Qu.  Median   Mean 3rd Qu.   Max.
  1.00    7.25   25.00  43.12   65.50 150.00

> plot(myecdf, verticals = TRUE, do.points = TRUE) # Plot (see Figure 1-5)
```

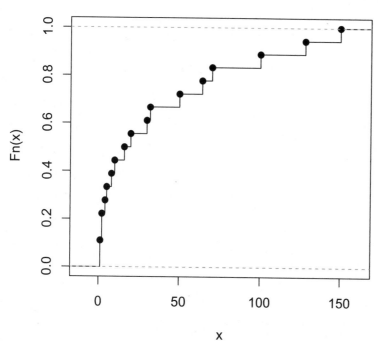

ecdf(myd)

Figure 1-5: Plotting an "ecdf" object, a custom cumulative distribution

COMMAND NAME

ptukey

The cumulative distribution of the Studentized range (often called Q). The Q statistic is often used in post-hoc analyses; for example, Tukey's Honest Significant Difference.

 SEE also TukeyHSD in Theme 2, "Math and Statistics."

Common Usage

ptukey(q, nmeans, df, lower.tail = TRUE, log.p = FALSE)

Related Commands

qtukey (p. 158)
pxxxx (p. 155)
TukeyHSD (p. 298)

Command Parameters

q	A vector of quantiles.
nmeans	The number of groups.
df	The degrees of freedom; for post-hoc pairwise comparisons this is Inf.
lower.tail = TRUE	If TRUE (default), probabilities are given as P[X ≤ x]; if FALSE, P[X > x].
log.p = FALSE	If TRUE, probabilities are given as log(p).

Examples

```
  ## Some values for Q
> vec = seq(from = 3, to = 3.5, by = 0.1)
> vec # Show values
[1] 3.0 3.1 3.2 3.3 3.4 3.5

  ## Calculate probs for 3 grps, pairwise comparison
> ptukey(vec, nmeans = 3, df = Inf, lower.tail = FALSE)
[1] 0.08554257 0.07252045 0.06116000 0.05131091 0.04282463 0.03555704
```

COMMAND NAME

pxxxx

Cumulative probability functions for various probability distributions (see Table 1-1). The individual commands are shown here:

```
pbeta
pbinom
pcauchy
pchisq
pexp
pf
pgamma
pgeom
phyper
plnorm
pmultinom
pnbinom
pnorm
ppois
psignrank
pt
punif
pweibull
pwilcox
```

These commands provide access to the cumulative probability computations for the various distributions. See the following examples for details of commonly used distributions.

Common Usage

```
pbeta(q, shape1, shape2, ncp, lower.tail = TRUE, log.p = FALSE)
pbinom(q, size, prob, lower.tail = TRUE, log.p = FALSE)
pcauchy(q, location = 0, scale = 1, lower.tail = TRUE, log.p = FALSE)
pchisq(q, df, ncp = 0, lower.tail = TRUE, log.p = FALSE)
pexp(q, rate = 1, lower.tail = TRUE, log.p = FALSE)
pf(q, df1, df2, ncp, lower.tail = TRUE, log.p = FALSE)
pgamma(q, shape, rate = 1, scale = 1/rate, lower.tail = TRUE, log.p = FALSE)
pgeom(q, prob, lower.tail = TRUE, log.p = FALSE)
phyper(q, m, n, k, lower.tail = TRUE, log.p = FALSE)
plnormal(q, meanlog = 0, sdlog = 1, lower.tail = TRUE, log.p = FALSE)
pmultinom(q, size = NULL, prob, lower.tail = TRUE, log.p = FALSE)
pnbinom(q, size, prob, mu, lower.tail = TRUE, log.p = FALSE)
pnorm(q, mean = 0, sd = 1, lower.tail = TRUE, log.p = FALSE)
ppois(q, lambda, lower.tail = TRUE, log.p = FALSE)
psignrank(q, n, lower.tail = TRUE, log.p = FALSE)
pt(q, df, ncp, lower.tail = TRUE, log.p = FALSE)
punif(q, min = 0, max = 1, lower.tail = TRUE, log.p = FALSE)
pweibull(q, shape, scale = 1, lower.tail = TRUE, log.p = FALSE)
pwilcox(q, m, n, lower.tail = TRUE, log.p = FALSE)
```

Related Commands

pxxxx (p. 155)
qxxxx (p. 159)
rxxxx (p. 162)
set.seed (p. 165)
ecdf (p. 152)
ptukey (p. 154)

Command Parameters

q	A vector of quantiles.
lower.tail = TRUE	If TRUE, probabilities are P[X ≤ x]. If FALSE, P[X > x].
log.p = FALSE	If TRUE, the probabilities are given as log(p).
Other parameters	Each distribution has its own set of parameters.

Examples

The built-in R help entries for each distribution give details about the various commands. Following are some detailed examples on some of the more commonly used distributions.

BINOMIAL DISTRIBUTION

The binomial distribution requires size (the number of trials) and prob, the probability of success for each trial:

```
  ## Binomial cumulative distribution
> pbinom(0:5, size = 5, prob = 0.4)
[1] 0.07776 0.33696 0.68256 0.91296 0.98976 1.00000
```

CHI-SQUARED DISTRIBUTION

The chi-squared distribution requires df (the degrees of freedom) and ncp, a non-centrality parameter (default ncp = 0):

```
  ## The chi-squared cumulative distribution for different degrees of freedom
> pchisq(1:10, df = 1)
 [1] 0.6826895 0.8427008 0.9167355 0.9544997 0.9746527 0.9856941 0.9918490
 [8] 0.9953223 0.9973002 0.9984346 0.9990889 0.9994680 0.9996885 0.9998172
[15] 0.9998925 0.9999367 0.9999626 0.9999779 0.9999869 0.9999923

> pchisq(1:20, df = 10)
 [1] 0.0001721156 0.0036598468 0.0185759362 0.0526530173 0.1088219811
 [6] 0.1847367555 0.2745550467 0.3711630648 0.4678964236 0.5595067149
[11] 0.6424819976 0.7149434997 0.7763281832 0.8270083921 0.8679381437
[16] 0.9003675995 0.9256360202 0.9450363585 0.9597373177 0.9707473119
```

F DISTRIBUTION

The F distribution requires degrees of freedom for numerator and denominator, df1 and df2, as well as ncp, a non-centrality parameter (if omitted, the central F is assumed):

```
## The F cumulative probability distribution effects of df
> pf(1:10, df1 = 1, df2 = 5)
[1] 0.6367825 0.7835628 0.8561892 0.8980605 0.9244132 0.9420272 0.9543409
[8] 0.9632574 0.9699008 0.974969

> pf(1:10, df1 = 1, df2 = 10)
[1] 0.6591069 0.8123301 0.8860626 0.9266120 0.9506678 0.9657123 0.9755090
[8] 0.9820999 0.9866563 0.9898804
```

NORMAL DISTRIBUTION

The normal distribution requires the mean (default mean = 0) and sd (standard deviation, default sd = 1):

```
## Normal cumulative distribution
> pnorm(0:5, mean = 0, sd = 1.5)
[1] 0.5000000 0.7475075 0.9087888 0.9772499 0.9961696 0.9995709

> pnorm(0:5, mean = 0, sd = 1.5, lower.tail = FALSE)
[1] 0.5000000000 0.2524925375 0.0912112197 0.0227501319 0.0038303806 0.0004290603
```

POISSON DISTRIBUTION

The Poisson distribution requires lambda, a (non-negative) mean value:

```
## Poisson cumulative probability, effects of lambda
> ppois(0:5, lambda = 1)
[1] 0.3678794 0.7357589 0.9196986 0.9810118 0.9963402 0.9994058
> ppois(0:11, lambda = 5)
[1] 0.006737947 0.040427682 0.124652019 0.265025915 0.440493285 0.615960655
[7] 0.762183463 0.866628326 0.931906365 0.968171943 0.986304731 0.994546908
```

STUDENT'S T DISTRIBUTION

The t distribution requires the degrees of freedom, df, and ncp, a non-centrality parameter (if omitted, the central t is assumed):

```
## Student's t cumulative probability
> pt(-1:5, df = 5, lower.tail = TRUE)
[1] 0.1816087 0.5000000 0.8183913 0.9490303 0.9849504 0.9948383 0.9979476

> pt(-1:5, df = 5, lower.tail = FALSE)
[1] 0.818391266 0.500000000 0.181608734 0.050969739 0.015049624 0.005161708
[7] 0.002052358
```

QUANTILE FUNCTIONS

The quantile probability functions associated with these distributions are named qxxxx, where xxxx is the (abbreviated) name of the distribution. The distributions that R can deal with are listed in Table 1-1. The Studentized range is covered by the qtukey command.

COMMAND NAME

qtukey

Calculates quantiles for probabilities of the Studentized range (often called Q). The Q statistic is often used in post-hoc analyses; for example, Tukey's Honest Significant Difference.

 SEE also TukeyHSD in Theme 2, "Math and Statistics."

Common Usage

```
qtukey(p, nmeans, df, lower.tail = TRUE, log.p = FALSE)
```

Related Commands

ptukey (p. 154)
qxxxx (p. 159)
TukeyHSD (p. 298)

Command Parameters

p	A vector of probabilities.
nmeans	The number of groups.
df	The degrees of freedom; for post-hoc pairwise comparisons this is Inf.
lower.tail = TRUE	If TRUE (default), probabilities are given as P[X ≤ x]; if FALSE, P[X > x].
log.p = FALSE	If TRUE, probabilities are given as log(p).

Examples

```
## Calculate critical values of Q for pairwise comparisons (groups 2-6)
> qtukey(0.95, nmeans = 2:6, df = Inf)
[1] 2.771808 3.314493 3.633160 3.857656 4.030092

> qtukey(0.99, nmeans = 2:6, df = Inf)
[1] 3.642773 4.120303 4.402801 4.602821 4.757047
```

COMMAND NAME

qxxxx

Quantile functions for various probability distributions (see Table 1-1). The individual commands are shown here:

qbeta
qbinom
qcauchy
qchisq
qexp
qf
qgamma
qgeom
qhyper
qlnorm
qmultinom
qnbinom
qnorm
qpois
qsignrank
qt
qunif
qweibull
qwilcox

These commands provide access to the quantile computations for the various distributions. See the following examples for details of commonly used distributions.

Common Usage

```
qbeta(p, shape1, shape2, ncp, lower.tail = TRUE, log.p = FALSE)
qbinom(p, size, prob, lower.tail = TRUE, log.p = FALSE)
qcauchy(p, location = 0, scale = 1, lower.tail = TRUE, log.p = FALSE)
qchisq(p, df, ncp = 0, lower.tail = TRUE, log.p = FALSE)
qexp(p, rate = 1, lower.tail = TRUE, log.p = FALSE)
qf(p, df1, df2, ncp, lower.tail = TRUE, log.p = FALSE)
qgamma(p, shape, rate = 1, scale = 1/rate, lower.tail = TRUE, log.p = FALSE)
qgeom(p, prob, lower.tail = TRUE, log.p = FALSE)
qhyper(p, m, n, k, lower.tail = TRUE, log.p = FALSE)
qlnormal(p, meanlog = 0, sdlog = 1, lower.tail = TRUE, log.p = FALSE)
qmultinom(pq, size = NULL, prob, lower.tail = TRUE, log.p = FALSE)
qnbinom(p, size, prob, mu, lower.tail = TRUE, log.p = FALSE)
qnorm(p, mean = 0, sd = 1, lower.tail = TRUE, log.p = FALSE)
qpois(p, lambda, lower.tail = TRUE, log.p = FALSE)
qsignrank(p, n, lower.tail = TRUE, log.p = FALSE)
qt(p, df, ncp, lower.tail = TRUE, log.p = FALSE)
qunif(p, min = 0, max = 1, lower.tail = TRUE, log.p = FALSE)
qweibull(p, shape, scale = 1, lower.tail = TRUE, log.p = FALSE)
qwilcox(p, m, n, lower.tail = TRUE, log.p = FALSE)
```

Related Commands

qtukey (p. 158)
pxxxx (p. 155)
dxxxx (p. 148)
rxxxx (p. 162)
set.seed (p. 165)

Command Parameters

p	A vector of probabilities.
lower.tail = TRUE	If TRUE, probabilities are P[X ≤ x]. If FALSE, P[X > x].
log.p = FALSE	If TRUE, the probabilities are given as log(p).

Examples

The built-in R help entries for each distribution give details about the various commands. Following are some detailed examples on some of the more commonly used distributions.

BINOMIAL DISTRIBUTION

The binomial distribution requires size (the number of trials) and prob, the probability of success for each trial:

```
## Binomial distribution, quantile function
> qbinom(c(0.3, 0.50, 0.9, 0.95, 0.99), size = 5, prob = 0.4)
[1] 1 2 3 4 5
```

CHI-SQUARED DISTRIBUTION

The chi-squared distribution requires df (the degrees of freedom) and ncp, a non-centrality parameter (default ncp = 0):

```
## Critical values for chi-squared at 95% for df = 1-5
> qchisq(0.95, df = 1:5)
[1]  3.841459  5.991465  7.814728  9.487729 11.070498
```

F DISTRIBUTION

The F distribution requires degrees of freedom for numerator and denominator, df1 and df2, as well as ncp, a non-centrality parameter (if omitted, the central F is assumed):

```
## Critical values for F at 95%
 > qf(0.95, df1 = 1, df2 = c(3, 5, 7, 9))
[1] 10.127964  6.607891  5.591448  5.117355
```

NORMAL DISTRIBUTION

The normal distribution requires the mean (default mean = 0) and sd (standard deviation, default sd = 1):

```
  ## Critical values for various probabilities for the normal distribution
> qnorm(c(0.95, 0.98, 0.99, 0.999), mean = 0, sd = 1)
[1] 1.644854 2.053749 2.326348 3.090232
```

POISSON DISTRIBUTION

The Poisson distribution requires lambda, a (non-negative) mean value:

```
  ## Poisson distribution critical values
> qpois(0.95, lambda = 1:5)
[1] 3 5 6 8 9

> qpois(0.99, lambda = 1:5)
[1]  4  6  8  9 11
```

STUDENT'S T DISTRIBUTION

The t distribution requires the degrees of freedom, df, and ncp, a non-centrality parameter (if omitted, the central t is assumed):

```
  ## Critical values for 95% (two-tailed) t distribution
 > qt(0.975, df = c(1, 3, 5, 10, Inf))
[1] 12.706205  3.182446  2.570582  2.228139  1.959964
```

RANDOM NUMBERS

Random variates can be generated for many distribution types. The random variate functions associated with these distributions are named rxxxx, where xxxx is the (abbreviated) name of the distribution. The distributions that R can deal with are listed in Table 1-1. Control over random number generation is also provided by set.seed and RNGkind commands.

COMMAND NAME

RNGkind

Controls the way random numbers are generated. There are two kinds of generators; the first is the "regular" one and the second sets the generator for Normal generation. The RNGkind command can get or set the values that determine the algorithms used in generating random numbers.

Common Usage

```
RNGkind(kind = NULL, normal.kind = NULL)
```

Related Commands

set.seed (p. 165)
rxxxx (p. 162)

Command Parameters

kind = NULL — A character string specifying the kind of generator to use. If NULL, the value is unchanged. If "default" is specified, the default is used: "Mersenne-Twister". If both kind and normal.kind are omitted or set to NULL, the current settings are displayed.

normal.kind = NULL — A character string specifying the kind of Normal generator to use. If NULL, the value is unchanged. If "default" is specified, the default is used: "Inversion". If both kind and normal.kind are omitted or set to NULL, the current settings are displayed.

Examples

```
  ## Random Number Generators
> RNGkind() # See current generators
[1] "Mersenne-Twister" "Inversion"


  ## Set to new generators
> RNGkind(kind = "Super-Duper", normal.kind = "Box-Muller")
> RNGkind() # Check to see current generators
[1] "Super-Duper" "Box-Muller"


  ## Set new generator but leave Normal generator "as is"
> RNGkind(kind = "Wichmann-Hill", normal.kind = NULL)
> RNGkind() # Check generators
[1] "Wichmann-Hill" "Box-Muller"


  ## Reset R default generators
> RNGkind(kind = "default", normal.kind = "default")
> RNGkind() # Check generators
[1] "Mersenne-Twister" "Inversion"
```

COMMAND NAME

rxxxx

Random number generation functions for various probability distributions (see Table 1-1). The individual commands are shown here:

rbeta
rbinom
rcauchy
rchisq
rexp
rf
rgamma
rgeom
rhyper
rlnorm
rmultinom

```
rnbinom
rnorm
rpois
rsignrank
rt
runif
rweibull
rwilcox
```

These commands provide access to random variate generation for the various distributions. See the following examples for details of commonly used distributions. The `runif` command produces random numbers for the uniform distribution, that is, regular numbers.

Common Usage

```
rbeta(n, shape1, shape2, ncp)
rbinom(n, size, prob)
rcauchy(n, location = 0, scale = 1)
chisq(n, df, ncp = 0)
rexp(n, rate = 1)
rf(n, df1, df2, ncp)
rgamma(n, shape, rate = 1, scale = 1/rate
rgeom(n, prob)
rhyper(nn, m, n, k)
rlnormal(n, meanlog = 0, sdlog = 1)
rmultinom(n, size = NULL, prob)
rnbinom(n, size, prob, mu)
rnorm(n, mean = 0, sd = 1)
rpois(n, lambda)
rsignrank(nn, n)
rt(n, df, ncp)
runif(n, min = 0, max = 1)
rweibull(n, shape, scale = 1)
rwilcox(x, m, n)
```

Related Commands

`set.seed` (p. 165)
`RNGkind` (p. 161)
`dxxxx` (p. 148)
`pxxxx` (p. 155)
`qxxxx` (p. 159)

Command Parameters

n   The number of random numbers to generate. For `rhyper` and `rsignrank` the parameter is `nn`, because `n` refers to something else (# black balls or # in sample, respectively).

Other parameters   Each distribution has its own set of parameters.

Examples

The built-in R help entries for each distribution give details about the various commands. Following are some detailed examples on some of the more commonly used distributions.

BINOMIAL DISTRIBUTION

The binomial distribution requires `size` (the number of trials) and `prob`, the probability of success for each trial:

```
  ## Random numbers from the binomial distribution
> set.seed(5) # Set random number seed
> rbinom(10, size = 5, prob = 0.4)
 [1] 1 3 4 1 1 3 2 3 4 1
```

CHI-SQUARED DISTRIBUTION

The chi-squared distribution requires `df` (the degrees of freedom) and `ncp`, a non-centrality parameter (default `ncp = 0`):

```
  ## Random variates from the chi-squared distribution
set.seed(5) # Set random number seed
> rchisq(5, df = 1)
[1] 0.11237767 3.25084859 0.03070214 0.78143200 4.54600483

> set.seed(5) # Set random number seed again
> rchisq(5, df = 5)
[1]   1.975221  2.550650   4.200854 10.305201  2.476468
```

NORMAL DISTRIBUTION

The normal distribution requires the `mean` (default `mean = 0`) and `sd` (standard deviation, default `sd = 1`):

```
  ## Random numbers from the normal distribution
> set.seed(5) # Set the random number seed
> rnorm(5, mean = 0, sd = 1)
[1] -0.84085548  1.38435934 -1.25549186  0.07014277  1.71144087

> set.seed(5) # Set the random number seed
> rnorm(5, mean = 5, sd = 1)
[1] 4.159145 6.384359 3.744508 5.070143 6.711441
```

POISSON DISTRIBUTION

The Poisson distribution requires `lambda`, a (non-negative) mean value:

```
  ## Random values from the Poisson distribution
> set.seed(5) # Set the random number seed
> rpois(5, lambda = 1)
 [1] 0 1 2 0 0
```

```
> set.seed(5) # Set the random number seed
> rpois(5, lambda = 5)
[1] 3 6 8 4 2
```

UNIFORM DISTRIBUTION

This is what you would think of as "regular" numbers. The command requires `min` and `max` parameters, which set the minimum and maximum values for the random values:

```
  ## Random values from the uniform distribution
> set.seed(5) # Set the random number seed
> runif(5, min = 0, max = 100)
[1] 20.02145 68.52186 91.68758 28.43995 10.46501

> set.seed(5) # Set the random number seed
> runif(5, min = 1, max = 9)
[1] 2.601716 6.481749 8.335006 3.275196 1.837201
```

COMMAND NAME

`set.seed`

Sets the random number seed. Think of this as setting the starting point for the generation of random numbers. If you set this to a particular value, you will get the same results each time you run a command that generates random values; this is useful for testing and teaching purposes.

Common Usage

`set.seed(seed, kind = NULL, normal.kind = NULL)`

Related Commands

RNGkind (p. 161)
rxxxx (p. 162)

Command Parameters

seed	A single value (an integer), which sets the starting point for the random seed generator.
kind = NULL	Sets the random number generator to one of the options. If NULL, the currently set option is used (see: RNGkind). If "default" is used, the default setting is used, which is "Mersenne-Twister".
normal.kind = NULL	Sets the method of Normal generation. If NULL, the current setting is used (see: RNGkind). If "default", the default setting is used, which is "Inversion".

Examples

```
  ## Random numbers
> set.seed(1) # Start with a seed value
> runif(5) # Five values from uniform distribution
[1] 0.2655087 0.3721239 0.5728534 0.9082078 0.2016819

> set.seed(10) # Use a new seed
> runif(5) # Five new random values
[1] 0.50747820 0.30676851 0.42690767 0.69310208 0.08513597

> set.seed(1) # Set seed to earlier value
> runif(5) # Five more values, match the earlier result
[1] 0.2655087 0.3721239 0.5728534 0.9082078 0.2016819

> set.seed(1, kind = "Super-Duper") # Use the "Super-Duper" generator
> runif(5) # Five more values
[1] 0.3714075 0.4789723 0.9636913 0.6902364 0.6959049

> RNGkind() # Check to see what generators are set
[1] "Super-Duper" "Inversion"

> set.seed(1) # Start seed again, sets to current generator
> runif(5) # Five more values
[1] 0.3714075 0.4789723 0.9636913 0.6902364 0.6959049

> set.seed(1, kind = "default") # Set seed, uses default "Mersenne-Twister"
> runif(5) # Five more values, match earlier result
[1] 0.2655087 0.3721239 0.5728534 0.9082078 0.2016819
```

THEME 2: MATH AND STATISTICS

R is a powerful statistical environment and can be used for many analytical tasks. This theme deals with various aspects of mathematical operations and statistical tests.

Topics in this Theme

COMMANDS IN THIS THEME:

Conj (p. 197)   confint (p. 305)   contrasts (p. 286)   contr.xxxx (p. 286)

cor (p. 267)   cor.test (p. 269)   cos (p. 202)   cosh (p. 202)

cov2cor (p. 272)   cov (p. 271)   crossprod (p. 208)   cummax (p. 223)

cummin (p. 223)   cumprod (p. 223)   cumsum (p. 223)   cutree (p. 318)

density (p. 235)   det (p. 209)   determinant (p. 209)   diag (p. 211)

diff (p. 173)   diffinv (p. 174)   dist (p. 319)   drop (p. 212)

drop1 (p. 306)   effects (p. 289)   eigen (p. 213)   exp (p. 175)

expm1 (p. 175)   factorial (p. 176)   family (p. 307)   fisher.test (p. 278)

fitted (p. 309)   fitted.values (p. 309)   fivenum (p. 224)   fligner.test (p. 254)

floor (p. 176)   formula (p. 290)   forwardsolve (p. 206)   friedman.test (p. 255)

glm (p. 310)   hclust (p. 321)   Im (p. 312)   interaction.plot (p. 291)

IQR (p. 225)   is.complex (p. 199)   isTRUE (p. 191)   kmeans (p. 322)

kruskal.test (p. 258)   ks.test (p. 237)   length (p. 226)   lfactorial (p. 176)

lm (p. 312)   loess (p. 333)   log (p. 177)   log10 (p. 177)

log1p (p. 177)   log2 (p. 177)   Logic (p. 192)   lower.tri (p. 215)

lowess (p. 335)   mad (p. 226)   manova (p. 292)   matmult (p. 216)

%*% (p. 216)   %o% (p. 218)   max (p. 178)   mean (p. 227)

median (p. 228)   min (p. 179)   Mod (p. 200)   model.tables (p. 294)

mood.test (p. 259)   nlm (p. 337)   nls (p. 338)   oneway.test (p. 242)

optim (p. 340)   optimise (p. 341)   optimize (p. 341)   outer (p. 218)

p.adjust (p. 244)   pairwise.t.test (p. 245)   pairwise.wilcox.test (p. 261)   pi (p. 203)

pmax (p. 178)   pmin (p. 179)   polyroot (p. 342)   power.anova.test (p. 295)

power.prop.test (p. 280)   power.t.test (p. 247)   PP.test (p. 332)   prcomp (p. 326)

princomp (p. 329)   prod (p. 180)   prop.test (p. 281)   qqline (p. 411)

qqnorm (p. 385)   qqplot (p. 387)   qr (p. 219)   quade.test (p. 263)

quantile (p. 229)   range (p. 230)   Re (p. 201)   replications (p. 297)

resid (p. 314)   residuals (p. 314)   round (p. 182)   sd (p. 231)

shapiro.test (p. 239)   sign (p. 183)   signif (p. 184)   sin (p. 203)

sinh (p. 203)   solve (p. 220)   sqrt (p. 185)   SSlogis (p. 343)

step (p. 315)   sum (p. 186, 232)   summary (p. 132, 233, 522)   svd (p. 221)

t.test (p. 248)   tan (p. 204)   tanh (p. 204)   tcrossprod (p. 208)

trunc (p. 187)   TukeyHSD (p. 298)   uniroot (p. 344)   upper.tri (p. 222)

var (p. 273)   var.test (p. 251)   wilcox.test (p. 265)

Mathematical Operations

You can think of R as a powerful calculator; many commands relate to various aspects of math.

What's In This Topic:

Math

R uses a wide range of commands that carry out many different mathematical operations.

COMMAND NAME

abs

This command returns the absolute magnitude of a numeric value (that is, ignores the sign). If it is used on a logical object the command produces 1 or 0 for TRUE or FALSE, respectively.

Common Usage

abs(x)

Related Commands

sign (p. 183)
round (p. 182)
trunc (p. 187)
signif (p. 184)
floor (p. 176)
ceiling (p. 171)

   x   An R object, usually a vector. The object can be numeric or logical.

Examples

```
## Make a numeric vector containing positive and negative values
> xx = seq(from = -5.2, to = 5.2, by = 1)
> xx
 [1] -5.2 -4.2 -3.2 -2.2 -1.2 -0.2  0.8  1.8  2.8  3.8  4.8

## Get the absolute values
> abs(xx)
 [1] 5.2 4.2 3.2 2.2 1.2 0.2 0.8 1.8 2.8 3.8 4.8

## Make a vector of logicals
> logic = c(TRUE, TRUE, FALSE, TRUE, FALSE)
> logic
[1]  TRUE  TRUE FALSE  TRUE FALSE

## Get a numeric representation of the logicals
> abs(logic)
[1] 1 1 0 1 0
```

COMMAND NAME

```
Arith
+ - * ^ %% %/% /
```

Arithmetical operators are the general symbols used to define math operations. The +, -, *, and / are used for addition, subtraction, multiplication, and division. The ^ is used to raise a number to a power. The %% and %/% are for modulo and integer division. `Arith` is not a command but using `help(Arith)` will bring up an R help entry.

Common Usage

```
x + y
x - y
x * y
x / y
x ^ y
x %% y
x %/% y
```

Command Parameters

   x, y   Numeric or complex objects (or objects that can be coerced into one or the other).

Examples

```
  ## Make a simple vector of numbers (integers)
> x = -1:12

  ## Addition
> x + 1
 [1]  0  1  2  3  4  5  6  7  8  9 10 11 12 13

  ## Compare regular and Modulo division
> x / 2
 [1] -0.5  0.0  0.5  1.0  1.5  2.0  2.5  3.0  3.5  4.0  4.5  5.0  5.5  6.0
> x %% 2
 [1] 1 0 1 0 1 0 1 0 1 0 1 0 1 0

  ## Compare regular and integer division
> x / 5
 [1] -0.2  0.0  0.2  0.4  0.6  0.8  1.0  1.2  1.4  1.6  1.8  2.0  2.2  2.4
> x %/% 5
 [1] -1  0  0  0  0  0  1  1  1  1  1  2  2  2

  ## Make a simple vector of numbers
> x = 1:6

  ## Use exponent
> 2 ^ x
[1]  2  4  8 16 32 64
```

COMMAND NAME

ceiling

This command rounds up a value to the nearest integer.

Common Usage

ceiling(x)

Related Commands

floor (p. 176)
round (p. 182)
trunc (p. 187)
abs (p. 169)

Command Parameters

x   A vector of numeric values.

```
## Make some simple numeric values
> xx = seq(from = -2, to = 2, by = 0.3)
> xx
 [1] -2.0 -1.7 -1.4 -1.1 -0.8 -0.5 -0.2  0.1  0.4  0.7  1.0  1.3  1.6  1.9

## Round up to the nearest integer
> ceiling(xx)
 [1] -2 -1 -1 -1  0  0  0  1  1  1  1  2  2  2
```

COMMAND NAME

cummax
cummin
cumprod
cumsum

Cumulative values. For a vector of values these commands produce cumulative maximum, minimum, product, and sum, respectively.

 SEE also cummax, cummin, cumprod, and cumsum in "Simple Summary Stats."

Common Usage

cummax(x)
cummin(x)
cumprod(x)
cumsum(x)

Related Commands

max (p. 178)
min (p. 179)
sum (p. 186, 232)
prod (p. 180)

Command Parameters

x   A numeric object. For cumprod or cumsum this can contain complex numbers.

Examples

```
## Cumulative product
> cumprod(1:9)
 [1]      1      2      6     24    120    720   5040  40320 362880
```

```
  ## Make a vector of numbers
> xx = c(3:1, 2:0, 4:2)
> xx
[1] 3 2 1 2 1 0 4 3 2

  ## Some cumulative values
> cummax(xx)
[1] 3 3 3 3 3 3 4 4 4

> cummin(x)
[1] 3 2 1 1 1 0 0 0 0

> cumprod(xx)
[1]   3   6   6  12  12   0   0   0   0

> cumsum(xx)
[1]   3   5   6   8   9   9  13  16  18
```

COMMAND NAME

diff

Returns lagged differences for an object. The basic command works on vector or matrix objects as well as time series (ts) objects.

Common Usage

```
diff(x, lag = 1, differences = 1)
```

Related Commands

diffinv (p. 174)

Command Parameters

x	A numeric vector, matrix, or time series object.
lag = 1	The lag between items in the difference calculation.
differences = 1	If this is set to a value greater than 1, the difference calculation is carried out successively the specified number of times.

Examples

```
  ## Create some values
> xx = cumsum(cumsum(1:10))
> xx
 [1]   1   4  10  20  35  56  84 120 165 220

  ## Differences between successive items
> diff(xx, lag = 1)
[1]   3   6  10  15  21  28  36  45  55
```

```
  ## Increase the lag
> diff(xx, lag = 2)
[1]   9  16  25  36  49  64  81 100

  ## Second order differences
> diff(xx, lag = 1, differences = 2)
[1]   3  4  5  6  7  8  9 10

  ## Also second order differences (same as previous example)
> diff(diff(xx))
```

COMMAND NAME

diffinv

This command carries out discrete integration, that is, it computes the inverse function of the lagged differences. The basic command works on vector or matrix objects as well as time series (ts) objects.

Common Usage

diffinv(x, lag = 1, differences = 1, xi)

Related Commands

diff (p. 173)

Command Parameters

x	A numeric vector, matrix, or time series object.
lag = 1	The lag between items in the difference calculation.
differences = 1	An integer value giving the order of the difference.
xi	The initial values for the integrals; zeros are used if missing. This can be a numeric vector, matrix, or time series.

Examples

```
  xx = cumsum(cumsum(1:10)) # Original data
> xx
  [1]    1    4   10   20   35   56   84  120  165  220

> dx = diff(xx, lag = 1) # Compute lagged differences
```

```
> dx
[1]   3   6 10 15 21 28 36 45 55
> d2 = 3:10

  ## Discrete Integration
> diffinv(dx, xi = 1) # First order
 [1]    1    4   10   20   35   56   84 120 165 220

> diffinv(d2, lag = 1, differences = 2, xi = c(1, 4)) # Second order
 [1]    1    4   10   20   35   56   84 120 165 220
```

COMMAND NAME

exp
expm1

Computes the exponential function. The `expm1` command computes `exp(x) -1`.

Common Usage

exp(x)
expm1(x)

Related Commands

log (p. 177)
log10 (p. 177)
log2 (p. 177)

Command Parameters

x   A numeric vector.

Examples

```
  ## Create some values using logarithms
> xx = log(c(2, 3, 12, 21, 105))

## Produce the exponentials
> exp(xx)
[1]   2   3  12  21 105

  ## The value of e, the natural logarithm
> exp(1)
[1] 2.718282
```

COMMAND NAME

```
factorial
lfactorial
```

Computes the factorial, that is, x!. The lfactorial command returns the natural log of the factorial.

Common Usage

```
factorial(x)
lfactorial(x)
```

Related Commands

cumprod (p. 223)

Command Parameters

x   A numeric R object.

Examples

```
> factorial(6)
[1] 720

> cumprod(1:6)
[1]   1   2   6  24 120 720

> lfactorial(6)
[1] 6.579251

> log(720)
[1] 6.579251
```

COMMAND NAME

```
floor
```

This command rounds values down to the nearest integer value.

Common Usage

```
floor(x)
```

Related Commands

ceiling (p. 171)
round (p. 182)
trunc (p. 187)
abs (p. 169)
as.integer (p. 16)

Command Parameters

x   A numeric vector.

Examples

```
  ## Make a vector of values
> xx = seq(from = -2, to = 2, by = 0.3)
> xx
 [1] -2.0 -1.7 -1.4 -1.1 -0.8 -0.5 -0.2  0.1  0.4  0.7  1.0  1.3  1.6  1.9

  ## Round down to nearest integer
> floor(xx)
 [1] -2 -2 -2 -2 -1 -1 -1  0  0  0  1  1  1  1
```

COMMAND NAME

```
log
log10
log2
log1p(x)
```

These commands compute logarithms. Natural logarithms are used by default but any base can be specified (see the following examples). The `log10` and `log2` commands are convenience commands for bases 10 and 2, respectively. The `log1p` command computes the natural log of a value + 1, that is, $\log(1 + x)$.

Common Usage

```
log(x, base = exp(1))
log10(x)
log2(x)
log1p(x)
```

Related Commands

exp (p. 175)

Command Parameters

x   A numeric or complex vector.

base = exp(1)   The base for the logarithm; the natural log is the default.

Examples

```
  ## Logs to base 10
> log10(c(1, 10, 100, 1000))
[1] 0 1 2 3

> log(c(1, 10, 100, 1000), base = 10) # Same as previous
[1] 0 1 2 3

  ## Logs to base 2
> log2(c(2, 4, 8, 16, 32))
[1] 1 2 3 4 5

> log(c(2, 4, 8, 16, 32), base = 2) # Same as previous
[1] 1 2 3 4 5

  ## Natural logs
> log(0.2)
[1] -1.609438
> log(1.2) # Add +1 to previous value
[1] 0.1823216
> log1p(0.2) # Same as adding +1 to value
[1] 0.1823216

  ## An exotic logarithm, base Pi (~3.142)
> log(c(1, 2, 4, 8), base = pi)
[1] 0.0000000 0.6055116 1.2110231 1.8165347
```

COMMAND NAME

max
pmax

The max command returns the maximum value in a numerical vector or object. The pmax command returns the parallel maxima by comparing two or more objects.

 SEE also max and pmax in "Simple Summary Stats."

Common Usage

```
max(..., na.rm = FALSE)
pmax(..., na.rm = FALSE)
```

Related Commands

min (p. 179)
cummax (p. 223)
range (p. 230)
pmin (p. 179)

Command Parameters

. . .	Vector(s) of values. These can be numeric or character (see the following examples).
na.rm = FALSE	By default, NA items are not omitted.

Examples

```
## Make some numeric vectors
> xx = c(3, 3, 5, 8, 4)
> yy = c(2, 3, 6, 5, 3)
> zz = c(4, 2, 4, 7, 4)

## Get maxima
> max(yy)
[1] 6
> max(zz)
[1] 7

## Parallel maxima
> pmax(yy, zz)
[1] 4 3 6 7 4

> pmax(xx, yy, zz)
[1] 4 3 6 8 4

## Make character data
> pp = c("a", "f", "h", "q", "r")
> qq = c("d", "e", "x", "c", "s")

## Maxima
> max(pp) # Max of single vector
[1] "r"
> pmax(pp, qq) # Parallel maxima
[1] "d" "f" "x" "q" "s"
```

COMMAND NAME

```
min
pmin
```

The min command returns the minimum value in a vector or object (which can be numeric or character). The pmin command returns the parallel minima by comparing two objects.

 SEE also min and pmin in "Simple Summary Stats."

Common Usage

```
min(..., na.rm = FALSE)
pmin(..., na.rm = FALSE)
```

Related Commands

max (p. 178)
range (p. 230)
cummin (p. 223)

Command Parameters

...	Vector(s) of values. These can be numeric or character (see the following examples).
na.rm = FALSE	By default, NA items are not omitted.

Examples

```
  ## Make some numeric vectors
> yy = c(2, 3, 6, 5, 3)
> zz = c(4, 2, 4, 7, 4)

  ## Get minima
> min(yy)
[1] 2
> min(zz)
[1] 2

  ## Parallel minima
> pmin(yy, zz)
[1] 2 2 4 5 3

  ## Make character data
> pp = c("a", "f", "h", "q", "r")
> qq = c("d", "e", "x", "c", "s")

  ## Minima
> min(pp) # Min of single vector
[1] "a"
> pmin(pp, qq) # Parallel minima
1] "a" "e" "h" "c" "r"
```

COMMAND NAME

prod

Returns the product of all the values specified.

Common Usage

```
prod(..., na.rm = FALSE)
```

Related Commands

sum (p. 186)
cumprod (p. 223)
cumsum (p. 223)
factorial (p. 176)

Command Parameters

...	Vector(s) of values.
na.rm = FALSE	By default, NA items are not omitted.

Examples

```
  ## Make some numbers
> zz = c(4, 2, 4, 7, 4)

  ## Product
> prod(zz)
[1] 896

> 4 * 2 * 4 * 7 * 4 # Same as prod(zz)
[1] 896
```

COMMAND NAME

range

Gives the range for a given sample; that is, a vector containing the minimum and maximum values.

 SEE also range in "Simple Summary Stats."

Common Usage

```
range(..., na.rm = FALSE)
```

Related Commands

IQR (p. 225)
max (p. 178)
min (p. 179)

Command Parameters

...   Vector(s) of values.

`na.rm = FALSE`   By default, `NA` items are not omitted.

Examples

```
  ## Make objects
> newvec = c(2:5, 4:5, 6:8, 9, 12, 17) # numeric vector
> vec = c(11, 15, 99, 45) # numeric vector

  ## Range
> range(newvec) # A vector containing min and max of the object
 [1] 2 17

> range(newvec, vec) # The range for the two named objects combined
 [1] 2 99
```

COMMAND NAME

round

Rounds numeric values to a specified number of decimal places.

Common Usage

```
round(x, digits = 0)
```

Related Commands

`signif` (p. 184)
`trunc` (p. 187)
`floor` (p. 176)
`ceiling` (p. 171)
`as.integer` (p. 16)
`abs` (p. 169)

Command Parameters

x   A numeric object, usually a vector or matrix.

`digits = 0`   The number of decimal places to show; defaults to 0.

Examples

```
  ## Make some numbers
> xx = log(2:6)
> xx
[1] 0.6931472 1.0986123 1.3862944 1.6094379 1.7917595
```

```
  ## Basic rounding
> round(xx) # Default 0 digits
[1] 1 1 1 2 2

> round(xx, digits = 2) # Two digits
[1] 0.69 1.10 1.39 1.61 1.79

  ## Effects of 0.5 (rounds to even digit)
  ## Make some values
> vv = 0.5 + -4:4
> vv
[1] -3.5 -2.5 -1.5 -0.5  0.5  1.5  2.5  3.5  4.5

> round(vv) # Use 0 digits
[1] -4 -2 -2  0  0  2  2  4  4

 ## Add a tiny amount to each value for rounding
> round(vv + sign(vv) * 1e-10)
[1] -4 -3 -2 -1  1  2  3  4  5
```

COMMAND NAME

sign

This command returns the sign of elements in a vector. If negative an item is assigned a value of –1; if positive, +1; and if zero, 0.

Common Usage

sign(x)

Related Commands

abs (p. 169)

Command Parameters

x   An R object, usually a vector or matrix object.

Examples

```
  ## Make some values
> xx = -3:3
> xx
[1] -3 -2 -1  0  1  2  3
```

```
  ## Return the signs of the values
> sign(xx)
[1] -1 -1 -1  0  1  1  1

  ## Make a matrix
> mat = matrix(c(2, 3, -2, -6, -2, 5, 0, 7, -5), ncol = 3)
> mat
     [,1] [,2] [,3]
[1,]    2   -6    0
[2,]    3   -2    7
[3,]   -2    5   -5

  ## Return absolute values
> abs(mat)
     [,1] [,2] [,3]
[1,]    2    6    0
[2,]    3    2    7
[3,]    2    5    5
```

COMMAND NAME

signif

This command returns a value rounded to the specified number of significant figures.

Common Usage

signif(x, digits = 6)

Related Commands

round (p. 182)
ceiling (p. 171)
floor (p. 176)
trunc (p. 187)
abs (p. 169)

Command Parameters

x   A numeric object, usually a vector or matrix (can be complex numbers).

digits = 6   The number of digits to use; defaults to 6.

Examples

```
  ## Make some numbers
> xx = log(2:6)
> xx
[1] 0.6931472 1.0986123 1.3862944 1.6094379 1.7917595
```

```
   ## Show 3 digits
> signif(xx, digits = 3)
[1] 0.693 1.100 1.390 1.610 1.790


   ## Make some large numbers
> yy = 2^(12:20)
> yy
[1]    4096    8192   16384   32768   65536  131072  262144  524288 1048576


   ## Show 3 digits
> signif(yy, digits = 3)
[1]    4100    8190   16400   32800   65500  131000  262000  524000 1050000


   ## Display 3 digits
> signif(c(3.1683564e+1, 235467, 0.1134597898), digits = 3)
[1] 3.17e+01 2.35e+05 1.13e-01


   ## Small values displayed to 3 digits
> signif(0.0000000000012345678, digits=3)
[1] 1.23e-12


> signif(1.2345678e-12, digits=3)
[1] 1.23e-12
```

COMMAND NAME

sqrt

Determines the square root of a numerical object, that is, sqrt(2) is the same as 2^0.5.

Common Usage

sqrt(x)

Related Commands

abs (p. 169)
Arith: ^0.5 (p. 170)

Command Parameters

x   A numerical R object, usually a vector or matrix object (can contain complex numbers).

Examples

```
> sqrt(1:9)
[1] 1.000000 1.414214 1.732051 2.000000 2.236068 2.449490 2.645751 2.828427
[9] 3.000000
```

COMMAND NAME

sum

This command returns the sum of all the items specified.

 SEE also sum in "Simple Summary Stats."

Common Usage

```
sum(..., na.rm = FALSE)
```

Related Commands

cumsum (p. 223)
colSums (p. 125)
prod (p. 180)

Command Parameters

...	Numeric R object(s). Usually a vector or matrix, but complex and logical objects can also be specified.
na.rm = FALSE	If na.rm = TRUE, then NA items are omitted.

Examples

```
  ## Make some values
> xx = 1:9
> xx
[1] 1 2 3 4 5 6 7 8 9

  ## Determine the sum
> sum(xx)
[1] 45

  ## Make more values
> yy = c(2, 3, 6, 5, 3)
> yy
[1] 2 3 6 5 3

  ## Determine sums
> sum(yy) ## Just sum of yy
[1] 19

> sum(xx, yy) # Sum of xx and yy together
[1] 64
```

```
   ## Make a logical vector
> logic = c(TRUE, TRUE, FALSE, TRUE, FALSE)

   ## Sum the logical (total of TRUE items)
> sum(logic)
[1] 3
```

COMMAND NAME

trunc

Creates integer values by truncating items at the decimal point.

Common Usage

trunc(x)

Related Commands

as.integer (p. 16)
round (p. 182)
signif (p. 184)

Command Parameters

x   A numeric vector.

Examples

```
   ## Make some numbers
> xx = 0.5 + -2:4
> xx
[1] -1.5 -0.5  0.5  1.5  2.5  3.5  4.5

   ## Truncate to integer
> trunc(xx)
[1] -1  0  0  1  2  3  4

   ## Round values to 0 decimal
> round(xx)
[1] -2  0  0  2  2  4  4
```

LOGIC

Many R commands produce logical values (that is, TRUE or FALSE). Logical operators and comparisons (relational operators) are used in many commands to make decisions and to produce results that match logical criteria.

COMMAND NAME

all

This command returns a logical value TRUE if all the values specified are TRUE.

 SEE also Theme 4, "Conditional Control."

Common Usage

```
all(..., na, rm = FALSE)
```

Related Commands

any (p. 189)

Command Parameters

...   Logical vectors or an expression that returns a logical result.

na.rm = FALSE   If na.rm = TRUE, then NA items are omitted.

Examples

```
   ## A vector of values
> yy = c(2, 3, 6, 5, 3)

   ## Test all items in vector to a condition
> all(yy < 5)
[1] FALSE

> all(yy >= 2)
[1] TRUE
```

COMMAND NAME

all.equal

Tests to see if two objects are (nearly) equal. The result is a logical TRUE or FALSE.

Common Usage

```
all.equal(target, current, tolerance = .Machine$double.eps ^ 0.5)
```

Related Commands

Comparison (p. 190)
isTRUE (p. 191)
Logic (p. 192)

Command Parameters

target   An R object to be compared to the current.

current   An R object to be compared to the target.

tolerance   A numerical value to be considered as different. The value must be ≥ 0. If the tolerance is set to 0, the actual difference is shown. The default tolerance equates to around 1.49e-08.

Examples

```
  ## Some simple values
> x1 = 0.5 - 0.3
> x2 = 0.3 - 0.1

  ## Are objects the same?
> x1 == x2
[1] FALSE

  ## Set tolerance to 0 to show actual difference
> all.equal(x1, x2, tolerance = 0)
[1] "Mean relative difference: 1.387779e-16"

  ## Use default tolerance
> all.equal(x1, x2)
[1] TRUE

  ## Wrap command in isTRUE() for logical test
> isTRUE(all.equal(x1, x2))
[1] TRUE

> isTRUE(all.equal(x1, x2, tolerance = 0))
[1] FALSE

  ## Make some character vectors
> pp = c("a", "f", "h", "q", "r")
> qq = c("d", "e", "x", "c", "s")

  ## Test for equality
> all.equal(pp, qq)
[1] "5 string mismatches"
```

COMMAND NAME

any

This command returns a logical value TRUE if any of the values specified are TRUE.

 SEE also Theme 4, "Conditional Control."

Common Usage

```
any(..., na.rm = FALSE)
```

Related Commands

all (p. 188)

Command Parameters

...	Logical vectors or an expression that returns a logical result.
na.rm = FALSE	If na.rm = TRUE, then NA items are omitted.

Examples

```
  ## Make some values to test
> yy = c(2, 3, 6, 5, 3)

  ## Test if any element matches a condition
> any(yy == 3)
[1] TRUE

> any(yy > 6)
[1] FALSE
```

COMMAND NAME

Comparison
< > <= >= == !=

These symbols allow the representation of comparisons; they are relational operators. The < and > symbols represent "less than" and "greater than," respectively. The <= and >= symbols represent "less than or equal to" and "greater than or equal to," respectively. The == and != symbols represent "equal to" and "not equal to," respectively. The results are a logical, either TRUE or FALSE. Comparison is not a command but using help(Comparison) will bring up an R help entry.

Common Usage

```
x < y
x > y
x <= y
x >= y
x == y
x != y
```

Related Commands

all.equal (p. 188)
Logic (p. 192)
isTRUE (p. 191)

Command Parameters

x, y   R objects or values.

Examples

```
  ## Make some numbers
> zz = c(4, 2, 4, 7, 4)
> zz
[1] 4 2 4 7 4

  ## Logic tests
> zz == 4 # Shows which are equal to 4
[1]  TRUE FALSE  TRUE FALSE  TRUE

> zz <= 4 # Shows which are equal or less than 4
[1]  TRUE  TRUE  TRUE FALSE  TRUE

> zz != 4 # Shows which are not equal to 4
[1] FALSE  TRUE FALSE  TRUE FALSE

  ## Use braces to return values
> zz[zz != 4] # Shows items that are not equal to 4
[1] 2 7

  ## Beware of rounding errors
  ## Create some values
> xx = seq(from = -1, to = , by = 0.3)
> xx
[1] -1.0 -0.7 -0.4 -0.1  0.2  0.5  0.8

> xx == 0.2 # Nothing is TRUE because of precision
[1] FALSE FALSE FALSE FALSE FALSE FALSE FALSE

> round(xx, digits = 1) == 0.2 # Use rounding get TRUE result
[1] FALSE FALSE FALSE FALSE  TRUE FALSE FALSE
```

COMMAND NAME

isTRUE

This command tests to see if an object or result is TRUE. It is useful as a wrapper for other commands where a single non-logical result could occur, for example, the all.equal command.

Common Usage

isTRUE(x)

Related Commands

all.equal (p. 188)
Comparison (p. 190)
Logic (p. 192)

Command Parameters

x   An R object.

Examples

```
  ## Simple values to compare
> x1 = 0.5 - 0.3
> x2 = 0.3 - 0.1

  ## Comparisons
> x1 == x2 # Gives FALSE because of precision
[1] FALSE

> isTRUE(all.equal(x1, x2)) # Gives a TRUE result
[1] TRUE

> all.equal(x1, x2, tolerance = 0) # Gives a non-logical result
[1] "Mean relative difference: 1.387779e-16"

> isTRUE(all.equal(x1, x2, tolerance = 0)) # Gives a logical result
[1] FALSE
```

COMMAND NAME

```
Logic
! & && | || xor
```

These symbols are used to define logical operators and so define comparisons. The ! symbol indicates logical NOT. The & and && symbols indicate logical AND. The | and || symbols indicate logical OR. The xor symbol indicates exclusive OR. The single symbols & and | perform element-wise comparisons. The longer && and || evaluate left to right, examining only the first element of each vector. Logic is not a command but typing help(Logic) will bring up a help entry.

Common Usage

```
! x
x & y
x && y
x | y
x || y
xor(x, y)
```

Related Commands

Comparison (p. 190)

Command Parameters

x, y   R objects for comparison.

Examples

```
  ## Make vectors to compare
> yy = c(2, 3, 6, 5, 3)
> zz = c(4, 2, 4, 7, 4)
> yy ; zz
[1] 2 3 6 5 3
[1] 4 2 4 7 4

  ## Comparisons
> yy > 2 & zz > 4 # One condition AND another
[1] FALSE FALSE FALSE  TRUE FALSE

> yy > 3 | zz > 4 One condition OR another
[1] FALSE FALSE  TRUE  TRUE FALSE

> ! yy > 3 Test for items NOT greater than 3
[1]  TRUE  TRUE FALSE FALSE  TRUE

  ## Contrast single and double operators
> yy == 2 | zz > 3 # Multiple result
[1]  TRUE FALSE  TRUE  TRUE  TRUE

> yy == 2 || zz > 3 # Single result (1st element from previous)
[1] TRUE

> yy > 2 | zz > 4 # Multiple result
[1] FALSE  TRUE  TRUE  TRUE  TRUE

> yy > 2 || zz > 4 # Single result (1st element from previous)
[1] FALSE
```

COMPLEX NUMBERS

Complex numbers can be dealt with by many commands. However, several commands are designed to create, test, and extract elements of complex numbers. In addition, complex numbers hold a class attribute "complex".

COMMAND NAME

Arg

Returns the argument of an imaginary number.

Common Usage

Arg(z)

Related Commands

as.complex (p. 195)
complex (p. 195)
Conj (p. 197)
Im (p. 198)
is.complex (p. 199)
Mod (p. 200)
Re (p. 201)

Command Parameters

z   A complex number or an R object that holds a class attribute "complex".

Examples

```
  ## Make some complex numbers
> z0 = complex(real = 1:8, imaginary = 8:1)
> z1 = complex(real = 4, imaginary = 3)
> z2 = complex(real = 4, imaginary = 3, argument = 2)
> z3 = complex(real = 4, imaginary = 3, modulus = 4, argument = 2)

> z0 ; z1 ; z2; z3
[1] 1+8i 2+7i 3+6i 4+5i 5+4i 6+3i 7+2i 8+1i
[1] 4+3i
[1] -0.4161468+0.9092974i
[1] -1.664587+3.63719i

  ## Display the arguments
> Arg(z0)
[1] 1.4464413 1.2924967 1.1071487 0.8960554 0.6747409 0.4636476 0.2782997
[8] 0.1243550

> Arg(z1)
[1] 0.6435011

> Arg(z2)
[1] 2
```

COMMAND NAME

as.complex

Attempts to coerce an object to a complex object, that is, one holding a class attribute "complex".

Common Usage

as.complex(z)

Related Commands

as.xxxx (p. 16)
is.complex (p. 199)
Arg (p. 194)
complex (p. 195)
Conj (p. 197)
Im (p. 198)
Mod (p. 200)
Re (p. 201)

Command Parameters

z   An R object.

Examples

```
  ## Make a character vector
> zz = c("3+2i", "4+2i")
> zz
[1] "3+2i" "4+2i"

> class(zz) # Check the class
[1] "character"

  ## Make character vector into complex
> zz = as.complex(zz)

> zz
[1] 3+2i 4+2i

> class(zz)
[1] "complex"
```

COMMAND NAME

complex

Creates a complex number or vector of numbers. The command can also be used to create a blank vector containing a certain number of items.

Common Usage

```
complex(length.out = 0, real = numeric(), imaginary = numeric(),
        modulus = 1, argument = 0)
```

Related Commands

as.complex (p. 195)
is.complex (p. 199)
Arg (p. 194)
Conj (p. 197)
Im (p. 198)
Mod (p. 200)
Re (p. 201)

Command Parameters

length.out = 0   The number of elements to create. Used to limit a sequence or to create a blank vector of complex numbers.

real = numeric()   The real part of the number(s).

imaginary = numeric()   The imaginary part of the number(s).

modulus = 1   The modulus of the complex number(s).

argument = 0   The argument of the complex number(s).

Examples

```
   ## A blank complex vector
> zz = complex(length.out = 3)
> zz
[1] 0+0i 0+0i 0+0i

   ## Some complex numbers as vectors
> z0 = complex(real = 1:8, imaginary = 8:1)
> z1 = complex(real = 4, imaginary = 3)
> z2 = complex(real = 4, imaginary = 3, argument = 2)
> z3 = complex(real = 4, imaginary = 3, modulus = 4, argument = 2)

> z0 ; z1 ; z2; z3
[1] 1+8i 2+7i 3+6i 4+5i 5+4i 6+3i 7+2i 8+1i
[1] 4+3i
[1] -0.4161468+0.9092974i
[1] -1.664587+3.63719i
```

COMMAND NAME

Conj

Displays the complex conjugate for a complex number.

Common Usage

Conj(z)

Related Commands

Arg (p. 194)
as.complex (p. 195)
complex (p. 195)
Im (p. 198)
is.complex (p. 199)
Mod (p. 200)
Re (p. 201)

Command Parameters

z   A complex number or an R object that holds a class attribute "complex".

Examples

```
   ## Make some complex numbers
> z0 = complex(real = 1:8, imaginary = 8:1)
> z1 = complex(real = 4, imaginary = 3)
> z2 = complex(real = 4, imaginary = 3, argument = 2)
> z3 = complex(real = 4, imaginary = 3, modulus = 4, argument = 2)

> z0 ; z1 ; z2; z3
[1] 1+8i 2+7i 3+6i 4+5i 5+4i 6+3i 7+2i 8+1i
[1] 4+3i
[1] -0.4161468+0.9092974i
[1] -1.664587+3.63719i

   ## The complex conjugates
> Conj(z0)
[1] 1-8i 2-7i 3-6i 4-5i 5-4i 6-3i 7-2i 8-1i

> Conj(z1)
[1] 4-3i

> Conj(z2)
[1] -0.4161468-0.9092974i

> Conj(z3)
[1] -1.664587-3.63719i
```

COMMAND NAME

`Im`

Shows the imaginary part of a complex number.

Common Usage

`Im(z)`

Related Commands

`Arg` (p. 194)
`as.complex` (p. 195)
`complex` (p. 195)
`Conj` (p. 197)
`is.complex` (p. 199)
`Mod` (p. 200)
`Re` (p. 201)

Command Parameters

z   A complex number or an R object that holds a `class` attribute `"complex"`.

Examples

```
   ## Make some complex numbers
> z0 = complex(real = 1:8, imaginary = 8:1)
> z1 = complex(real = 4, imaginary = 3)
> z2 = complex(real = 4, imaginary = 3, argument = 2)
> z3 = complex(real = 4, imaginary = 3, modulus = 4, argument = 2)

> z0 ; z1 ; z2; z3
[1] 1+8i 2+7i 3+6i 4+5i 5+4i 6+3i 7+2i 8+1i
[1] 4+3i
[1] -0.4161468+0.9092974i
[1] -1.664587+3.63719i

   ## Show the imaginary part of the numbers
> Im(z0)
[1] 8 7 6 5 4 3 2 1

> Im(z1)
[1] 3

> Im(z2)
[1] 0.9092974

> Im(z3)
[1] 3.63719
```

COMMAND NAME

is.complex

Tests to see if an object is a complex object (does it have a class attribute "complex"?). The result is a logical, TRUE or FALSE.

Common Usage

is.complex(z)

Related Commands

is.xxxx (p. 20)
Arg (p. 194)
as.complex (p. 195)
complex (p. 195)
Conj (p. 197)
Im (p. 198)
Mod (p. 200)
Re (p. 201)

Command Parameters

z   A complex number or an R object that holds a class attribute "complex".

Examples

```
  ## Make some objects
> zz = c(3+2i, "2+4i") # Mixed so ends up as character
> z0 = c(3+2i, 4+2i) # Complex
> z1 = complex(real = 4, imaginary = 3) # Complex

> zz ; z0 ; z1
[1] "3+2i" "2+4i"
[1] 3+2i 4+2i
[1] 4+3i

  ## Test objects
> is.complex(zz)
[1] FALSE

> is.complex(z0)
[1] TRUE

> is.complex(z1)
[1] TRUE
```

COMMAND NAME

Mod

Shows the modulus of a complex number.

Common Usage

```
Mod(z)
```

Related Commands

Arg (p. 194)
as.complex (p. 195)
complex (p. 195)
Conj (p. 197)
Im (p. 198)
is.complex (p. 199)
Re (p. 201)

Command Parameters

z   A complex number or an R object that holds a class attribute "complex".

Examples

```
  ## Make some complex numbers
> z0 = complex(real = 1:8, imaginary = 8:1)
> z1 = complex(real = 4, imaginary = 3)
> z2 = complex(real = 4, imaginary = 3, argument = 2)
> z3 = complex(real = 4, imaginary = 3, modulus = 4, argument = 2)

> z0 ; z1 ; z2; z3
[1] 1+8i 2+7i 3+6i 4+5i 5+4i 6+3i 7+2i 8+1i
[1] 4+3i
[1] -0.4161468+0.9092974i
[1] -1.664587+3.63719i

  ## The modulus
> Mod(z0)
[1] 8.062258 7.280110 6.708204 6.403124 6.403124 6.708204 7.280110 8.062258

> Mod(z1)
[1] 5

> Mod(z2)
[1] 1

> Mod(z3)
[1] 4
```

COMMAND NAME

Re

Shows the real part of complex numbers.

Common Usage

```
Re(z)
```

Related Commands

Arg (p. 194)
as.complex (p. 195)
complex (p. 195)
Conj (p. 197)
Im (p. 198)
is.complex (p. 199)
Mod (p. 200)

Command Parameters

z A complex number or an R object that holds a class attribute "complex".

Examples

```
  ## Make some complex numbers
> z0 = complex(real = 1:8, imaginary = 8:1)
> z1 = complex(real = 4, imaginary = 3)
> z2 = complex(real = 4, imaginary = 3, argument = 2)
> z3 = complex(real = 4, imaginary = 3, modulus = 4, argument = 2)

> z0 ; z1 ; z2; z3
[1] 1+8i 2+7i 3+6i 4+5i 5+4i 6+3i 7+2i 8+1i
[1] 4+3i
[1] -0.4161468+0.9092974i
[1] -1.664587+3.63719i

  ## Show the real parts
> Re(z0)
[1] 1 2 3 4 5 6 7 8

> Re(z1)
[1] 4

> Re(z2)
[1] -0.4161468

> Re(z3)
[1] -1.664587
```

TRIGONOMETRY

R contains various basic trigonometric commands and hyperbolic functions as well as `pi`, the constant π.

COMMAND NAME

cos
acos
cosh
acosh

These commands deal with the cosine. The commands calculate the cosine, arc-cosine, and hyperbolic equivalents. Angles are in radians (a right angle is π / 2 radians).

Common Usage

```
cos(x)
acos(x)
cosh(x)
acosh(x)
```

Related Commands

sin (p. 203)
tan (p. 204)
pi (p. 203)

Command Parameters

x   A numeric value to evaluate. Can be numeric vectors or complex objects. Angles are in radians.

Examples

```
> cos(45) # In radians
[1] 0.525322

> cos(45 * pi/180) # Convert 45 degrees to radians
[1] 0.7071068

> acos(1/2) * 180/pi # To get result in degrees
[1] 60

> acos(sqrt(3)/2) * 180/pi # To get result in degrees
[1] 30

> cosh(0.5) # Hyperbolic function
[1] 1.127626
```

COMMAND NAME

pi

The numeric constant π; this is approximately 3.142.

 SEE also Theme 4, "Constants."

Common Usage

pi

Related Commands

cos (p. 202)
sin (p. 203)
tan (p. 204)

Command Parameters

No parameters are necessary; pi is recognized as a constant.

Examples

```
  ## pi is recognized as a constant
> pi
[1] 3.141593


  ## Use of pi in trigonometry
> cos(45 * pi/180) # Convert degrees to radians
[1] 0.7071068


> acos(0.5) * 180/pi # Convert radians to degrees
[1] 60


  ## 1 radian ~57 degrees
> 180/pi
[1] 57.29578
```

COMMAND NAME

sin
asin
sinh
asinh

These commands deal with the sine. The commands calculate the sine, arc-sine, and hyperbolic equivalents. Angles are in radians (a right angle is π / 2 radians).

Common Usage

```
sin(x)
asin(x)
sinh(x)
asinh(x)
```

Related Commands

cos (p. 202)
tan (p. 204)
pi (p. 203)

Command Parameters

x   A numeric value to evaluate. Can be numeric vectors or complex objects. Angles are in radians.

Examples

```
> sin(45) # In radians
[1] 0.8509035

> sin(45 * pi/180) # Convert degrees to radians
[1] 0.7071068

> asin(0.5) * 180/pi # To get answer in degrees
[1] 30

> asin(sqrt(3)/2) * 180/pi # To get answer in degrees
[1] 60

> sinh(0.4) # Hyperbolic function
[1] 0.4107523
```

COMMAND NAME

```
tan
atan
atan2
tanh
atanh
```

These commands deal with the tangent. The commands calculate the tangent, arc-tangent, and hyperbolic equivalents. The atan2 command calculates the angle between the x-axis and the vector from the origin to (x, y). Angles are in radians (a right angle is π / 2 radians).

Common Usage

```
tan(x)
atan(x)
atan2(y, x)
tanh(z)
atanh(x)
```

Related Commands

cos (p. 202)
sin (p. 203)
pi (p. 203)

Command Parameters

x   A numeric value to evaluate. Can be numeric vectors or complex objects. Angles are in radians.

y, x   For atan2 command y, x, are coordinates.

Examples

```
> tan(45) # In radians
[1] 1.619775

> tan(45 * pi/180) # Convert degrees to radians
[1] 1

> atan(0.6) * 180/pi # Get answer in degrees
[1] 30.96376

> atan(sqrt(3)) * 180/pi # Get answer in degrees
[1] 60

> tanh(0.2) # Hyperbolic function
[1] 0.1973753

  ## Find angle between coordinates and x-axis (in degrees)
> atan2(5, 5) * 180/pi
[1] 45

> atan2(10, 5) * 180/pi
[1] 63.43495

> atan2(5, 10) * 180/pi
[1] 26.56505
```

HYPERBOLIC FUNCTIONS

 SEE "Trigonometry."

MATRIX MATH

A matrix is a rectangular array with rows and columns. Many R commands are designed expressly to deal with matrix math.

COMMAND NAME

```
backsolve
forwardsolve
```

These commands solve a system of linear equations where the coefficient matrix is upper ("right", "R") or lower ("left", "L") triangular.

 SEE also `forwardsolve` in "Matrix Math."

Common Usage

```
backsolve(r, x, k = ncol(r), upper.tri = TRUE, transpose = FALSE)
forwardsolve(l, x, k = ncol(l), upper.tri = FALSE, transpose = FALSE)
```

Related Commands

`solve` (p. 220)
`chol` (p. 207)
`qr` (p. 219)

Command Parameters

`r, l`	A matrix giving the coefficients for the system to be solved. Only the upper or lower triangle is used and other values are ignored.
`x`	A matrix whose columns give the right-hand sides for the equations.
`k`	The number of columns for `r` (or `l`) and rows of `x` to use.
`upper.tri =`	If TRUE, the upper triangle of the coefficient matrix is used; use `upper.tri = FALSE` to use the lower triangle.
`transpose = FALSE`	If set to TRUE, the transposed matrix is used; that is, y is solved in the equation `r' y = x`.

Examples

```
  ## Make a coefficient matrix
> (mx = cbind(1,1:3,c(2,0,1)))
     [,1] [,2] [,3]
[1,]    1    1    2
[2,]    1    2    0
[3,]    1    3    1

  ## The right-hand sides of the equations
> x = c(8, 4, 2)

  ## Solve
> backsolve(mx, x) # The upper triangular solution
[1] 2 2 2

> forwardsolve(mx, x) # The lower triangular solution
[1]   8 -2   0

> backsolve(mx, x, upper.tri = FALSE) # Same as previous
[1]   8 -2   0

> backsolve(mx, x, transpose = TRUE) # Transpose matrix
[1]    8   -2  -14
```

COMMAND NAME

chol

This command computes the Choleski factorization of a real matrix. The matrix must be symmetric, positive-definite. The result returned is the upper triangular factor of the Choleski decomposition, that is, the matrix R such that R'R = x.

Common Usage

```
chol(x, pivot = FALSE,  LINPACK = pivot)
```

Related Commands

svd (p. 221)
qr (p. 219)
det (p. 209)

Command Parameters

x	A matrix that is real, symmetric, and positive-definite.
pivot = FALSE	If TRUE, pivoting is used. This can enable the decomposition of a positive semi-definite matrix to be computed.
LINPACK = FALSE	If set to TRUE, then for non-pivoting, the LINPACK routines are used (thus providing compatibility with older versions).

Examples

```
  ## Make a matrix
> (mx = matrix(c(5,1,1,3), ncol = 2))
     [,1] [,2]
[1,]    5    1
[2,]    1    3

  ## Choleski decomposition
> (cm = chol(mx))
          [,1]      [,2]
[1,] 2.236068 0.4472136
[2,] 0.000000 1.6733201

  ## Original matrix can be reconstructed from Choleski
> crossprod(cm)
     [,1] [,2]
[1,]    5    1
[2,]    1    3

> t(cm) %*% cm
     [,1] [,2]
[1,]    5    1
[2,]    1    3
```

COMMAND NAME

crossprod
tcrossprod

These commands calculate the cross-products of two matrix objects. They are equivalent to t(x) %*% y (for the crossprod command) and x %*% t(y) (for the tcrossprod command).

Common Usage

```
crossprod(x, y = NULL)
tcrossprod(x, y = NULL)
```

Related Commands

outer (p. 218)
%*% (p. 216)
matmult (p. 216)
%o% (p. 218)

Command Parameters

x, y   Matrix objects (can be complex numbers). If y is missing it is assumed to be the same matrix as x.

Examples

```
  ## Make matrix objects
> (x = cbind(1,1:3,c(2,0,1)))
     [,1] [,2] [,3]
[1,]    1    1    2
[2,]    1    2    0
[3,]    1    3    1

> (y = c(1, 3, 2))
[1] 1 3 2

> (y1 = matrix(1:3, nrow = 1))
     [,1] [,2] [,3]
[1,]    1    2    3

  ## Cross-products
> crossprod(x, y)    # Same as t(x) %*% y
     [,1]
[1,]    6
[2,]   13
[3,]    4

> crossprod(x, y1) # Gives error as y1 wrong "shape"
Error in crossprod(x, y1) : non-conformable arguments

> tcrossprod(x, y1) # Same as x %*% t(y1)
     [,1]
[1,]    9
[2,]    5
[3,]   10
```

COMMAND NAME

```
det
determinant
```

The determinant command calculates the modulus of the determinant (optionally as a logarithm) and the sign of the determinant. The det command calculates the determinant of a matrix (it is a wrapper for the determinant command).

Common Usage

```
det(x)
determinant(x, logarithm = TRUE)
```

Related Commands

qr (p. 219)
svd (p. 221)
chol (p. 207)

Command Parameters

x	A numeric matrix.
logarithm = TRUE	If TRUE (the default), the natural logarithm of the modulus of the determinant is calculated.

Examples

```
  ## Make a matrix
> x = cbind(1,1:3,c(2,0,1))
> x
     [,1] [,2] [,3]
[1,]    1    1    2
[2,]    1    2    0
[3,]    1    3    1

  ## The determinant
> det(x)
[1] 3

  ## The longer command produces a list as a result
> determinant(x)
$modulus
[1] 1.098612
attr(,"logarithm")
[1] TRUE

$sign
[1] 1

attr(,"class")
[1] "det"

  ## Make result more readable (shows log)
> unlist(determinant(x))
 modulus     sign
1.098612 1.000000

  ## Unlist result but show non-log determinant
> unlist(determinant(x, logarithm = FALSE))
modulus    sign
      3       1
```

COMMAND NAME

`diag`

Matrix diagonals. This command has several uses; it can extract or replace the diagonal of a matrix. Alternatively, the command can construct a diagonal matrix. See the following command parameters for details.

Common Usage

```
diag(x = 1, nrow, ncol)
diag(x) <- value
```

Related Commands

`lower.tri` (p. 215)
`upper.tri` (p. 222)
`matrix` (p. 10)

Command Parameters

x There are various options for x:

- If x is a matrix, the diagonal is extracted.

- If x is missing and `nrow` is specified, an identity matrix is returned.

- If x is a single value and the only parameter, a square identity matrix is returned (of size given by x).

- If x is a vector (> 1 element) or `nrow` specified, a matrix is returned with the given diagonal and zero off-diagonal entries.

`nrow` Number of rows for the identity matrix (if x is not a matrix).

`ncol` Number of columns for the identity matrix (if x is not a matrix).

`value` A numerical value for the diagonal. This should be either a single number or a vector equal to the length of the current diagonal.

Examples

```
  ## Make a matrix
> x = cbind(1,1:3,c(2,0,1))
> x
     [,1] [,2] [,3]
[1,]    1    1    2
[2,]    1    2    0
[3,]    1    3    1
```

```
   ## Get the current diagonal
> diag(x)
[1] 1 2 1

   ## Reset current diagonal
> diag(x) <- c(2, 1, 2)
> x
     [,1] [,2] [,3]
[1,]    2    1    2
[2,]    1    1    0
[3,]    1    3    2

   ## Make identity matrix
> diag(x = 3) # Simple identity matrix
     [,1] [,2] [,3]
[1,]    1    0    0
[2,]    0    1    0
[3,]    0    0    1

> diag(x = 3, nrow = 3) # Set diagonal and rows
     [,1] [,2] [,3]
[1,]    3    0    0
[2,]    0    3    0
[3,]    0    0    3

> diag(c(6, 9)) # Specify diagonal
     [,1] [,2]
[1,]    6    0
[2,]    0    9

> diag(c(7, 4), nrow = 4) # Extra rows (must be multiple of diagonal)
     [,1] [,2] [,3] [,4]
[1,]    7    0    0    0
[2,]    0    4    0    0
[3,]    0    0    7    0
[4,]    0    0    0    4
```

COMMAND NAME

drop

This command examines an object and if there is a dimension with only a single entry, the dimension is removed.

 SEE droplevels in Theme 1, "Data" for removing unused levels of a factor. See drop1 in "Analysis of Variance and Linear Modeling" for dropping terms of a model.

Common Usage

drop(x)

Related Commands

diag (p. 211)

Command Parameters

x   An array or matrix object.

Examples

```
  ## Simple matrix multiplication
> 1:3 %*% 2:4 # Makes a matrix with single entry
     [,1]
[1,]   20

  ## Drop redundant dimension
> drop(1:3 %*% 2:4) # Single value (vector) result
[1] 20

  ## Make an array
> my.arr = array(1:6, dim = c(3, 1, 2))
> my.arr
, , 1

     [,1]
[1,]    1
[2,]    2
[3,]    3

, , 2

     [,1]
[1,]    4
[2,]    5
[3,]    6

  ## Drop redundant dimension
> drop(my.arr)
     [,1] [,2]
[1,]    1    4
[2,]    2    5
[3,]    3    6
```

COMMAND NAME

eigen

Computes eigenvalues and eigenvectors for matrix objects; that is, carries out spectral decomposition. The result is a list containing $values and $vectors.

Common Usage

```
eigen(x, symmetric, only.values = FALSE, EISPACK = FALSE)
```

Related Commands

svd (p. 221)
qr (p. 219)
chol (p. 207)
det (p. 209)
diag (p. 211)

Command Parameters

x	A matrix.
symmetric	If set to TRUE, the matrix is assumed to be symmetric and only its lower triangle and diagonal are included.
only.values = FALSE	If TRUE, only the eigenvalues are computed and returned, otherwise both eigenvalues and eigenvectors are returned.
EISPACK = FALSE	By default eigen uses the LAPACK routines DSYEVR, DGEEV, ZHEEV, and ZGEEV, whereas eigen(EISPACK = TRUE) provides an interface to the EISPACK routines RS, RG, CH, and CG.

Examples

```
  ## Make a matrix
> x = cbind(1,1:3,c(2,0,1))
> x
     [,1] [,2] [,3]
[1,]   1    1    2
[2,]   1    2    0
[3,]   1    3    1

  ## Default eigenvalues and eigenvectors
> eigen(x)
$values
[1] 3.6779935+0.0000000i 0.1610033+0.8886732i 0.1610033-0.8886732i

$vectors
                 [,1]                  [,2]                  [,3]
[1,] -0.6403310+0i   0.7948576+0.0000000i   0.7948576+0.0000000i
[2,] -0.3816052+0i  -0.3503987-0.1693260i  -0.3503987+0.1693260i
[3,] -0.6665986+0i  -0.1582421+0.4378473i  -0.1582421-0.4378473i
```

```
## Return eigenvalues/vectors for lower triangle and diagonal
> eigen(x, symmetric = TRUE)
$values
[1]   5.0340418   0.5134648 -1.5475066

$vectors
             [,1]         [,2]         [,3]
[1,] -0.3299702   0.9425338 -0.05243658
[2,] -0.7164868  -0.2862266 -0.63617682
[3,] -0.6146269  -0.1723493  0.76975935

  ## Get values only (n.b. unlist makes result a vector)
> unlist(eigen(x, only.values = TRUE, symmetric = TRUE))
   values1     values2     values3
 5.0340418   0.5134648 -1.5475066
```

COMMAND NAME

forwardsolve

This command solves a system of linear equations where the coefficient matrix is upper ("right", "R") or lower ("left", "L") triangular.

 SEE backsolve.

COMMAND NAME

lower.tri

Returns a logical value (TRUE) for the lower triangle of a matrix. The rest of the matrix returns as FALSE. The diagonal can be included.

Common Usage

```
lower.tri(x, diag = FALSE)
```

Related Commands

upper.tri (p. 222)
diag (p. 211)
matrix (p. 10)

Command Parameters

x   A matrix object.

diag   If diag = TRUE, the diagonals are returned as TRUE.

Examples

```
  ## Make a matrix
> x = cbind(1,1:3,c(2,0,1))
> x
     [,1] [,2] [,3]
[1,]    1    1    2
[2,]    1    2    0
[3,]    1    3    1

  ## Get logical lower triangle
> lower.tri(x)
       [,1]  [,2]  [,3]
[1,] FALSE FALSE FALSE
[2,]  TRUE FALSE FALSE
[3,]  TRUE  TRUE FALSE

  ## Set lower triangle and diagonal to a value
> x[lower.tri(x, diag = 1)] = 99
> x
     [,1] [,2] [,3]
[1,]   99    1    2
[2,]   99   99    0
[3,]   99   99   99
```

COMMAND NAME

```
matmult
%*%
```

The %*% symbol is used to perform matrix multiplication.

Common Usage

```
x %*% y
```

Related Commands

diag (p. 211)
matrix (p. 10)
eigen (p. 213)

Command Parameters

x, y   Matrix or vector objects.

Examples

```
  ## Make some matrix objects
> (x = cbind(1,1:3,c(2,0,1)))
     [,1] [,2] [,3]
[1,]    1    1    2
[2,]    1    2    0
[3,]    1    3    1

> (y = c(1, 3, 2))
[1] 1 3 2

> (y1 = matrix(1:3, nrow = 1))
     [,1] [,2] [,3]
[1,]    1    2    3

> (z = matrix(3:1, ncol = 1))
     [,1]
[1,]    3
[2,]    2
[3,]    1

  ## Various matrix multiplications
> x %*% y
     [,1]
[1,]    8
[2,]    7
[3,]   12

> x %*% y1 # Order can be important
Error in x %*% y1 : non-conformable arguments

> y1 %*% x
     [,1] [,2] [,3]
[1,]    6   14    5

> x %*% z
     [,1]
[1,]    7
[2,]    7
[3,]   10

> z %*% x # Order is important
Error in z %*% x : non-conformable arguments

> y %*% y # Matrix multiplication of two vectors
     [,1]
[1,]   14
```

COMMAND NAME

```
outer
%o%
```

The `outer` command calculates the outer product of arrays and matrix objects. The `%o%` symbol is a convenience wrapper for `outer(X, Y, FUN = "*")`.

Common Usage

```
outer(X, Y, FUN = "*")
X %o% Y
```

Related Commands

`matmult` (p. 216)
`%*%` (p. 216)
`diag` (p. 211)
`eigen` (p. 213)

Command Parameters

X   The first argument for FUN, typically a numeric vector or array (including matrix objects).

Y   The second argument for FUN, typically a numeric vector or array (including matrix objects).

FUN = "*"   A function to use on the outer products, e.g., "*" is equivalent to X * Y.

Examples

```
   ## Multiplication
> outer(1:3, 1:3, FUN = "*")
     [,1] [,2] [,3]
[1,]    1    2    3
[2,]    2    4    6
[3,]    3    6    9


> 1:3 %o% 1:3 # Same as previous

   ## Power function
> outer(1:3, 1:3, FUN = "^")
     [,1] [,2] [,3]
[1,]    1    1    1
[2,]    2    4    8
[3,]    3    9   27

   ## Addition
> outer(1:3, 1:3, FUN = "+")
     [,1] [,2] [,3]
[1,]    2    3    4
[2,]    3    4    5
[3,]    4    5    6
```

COMMAND NAME

`qr`

This command computes the QR decomposition of a matrix. It provides an interface to the techniques used in the LINPACK routine DQRDC or the LAPACK routines DGEQP3 and (for complex matrices) ZGEQP3. The result holds a `class` attribute "qr".

Common Usage

```
qr(x, tol = 1e-07 , LAPACK = FALSE)
```

Related Commands

solve (p. 220)
eigen (p. 213)
svd (p. 221)
det (p. 209)

Command Parameters

x	A matrix object.
tol = 1e-07	The tolerance for detecting linear dependencies in the columns of x. Only used if LAPACK = FALSE and x is real.
LAPACK = FALSE	If TRUE use LAPACK; otherwise, use LINPACK (if x is real).

Examples

```
  ## Make a matrix
> (x = cbind(1,1:3,c(2,0,1)))
     [,1] [,2] [,3]
[1,]   1    1    2
[2,]   1    2    0
[3,]   1    3    1


  ## QR decomposition (result is a list with class = "qr")
> qr(x)
$qr
          [,1]        [,2]        [,3]
[1,] -1.7320508 -3.4641016 -1.7320508
[2,]  0.5773503 -1.4142136  0.7071068
[3,]  0.5773503  0.9659258  1.2247449

$rank
[1] 3
```

```
$qraux
[1] 1.577350 1.258819 1.224745

$pivot
[1] 1 2 3

attr(,"class")
[1] "qr"
```

COMMAND NAME

solve

Solves a system of equations. This command solves the equation a %*% x = b for x, where b can
be either a vector or a matrix.

Common Usage

```
solve(a, b, tol, LINPACK = FALSE)
```

Related Commands

backsolve (p. 206)
qr (p. 219)
svd (p. 221)
lm (p. 312)

Command Parameters

a	A square numeric or complex matrix containing the coefficients of the linear system.
b	A numeric or complex vector or matrix giving the right-hand side(s) of the linear system. If missing, b is taken to be an identity matrix and solve will return the inverse of a.
tol	The tolerance for detecting linear dependencies in the columns of a.
LINPACK = FALSE	If LINPACK = FALSE (the default), the LAPACK routine is used.

Examples

```
   ## Make a matrix (coefficients of linear system)
> (x = cbind(1,1:3,c(2,0,1)))
     [,1] [,2] [,3]
[1,]    1    1    2
[2,]    1    2    0
[3,]    1    3    1
```

```
  ## Make vector for rhs of linear system
> (b = 1:3)
[1] 1 2 3


  ## Solve
> solve(x, b)
[1] 0 1 0


> solve(x) # Omit b to return inverse of matrix
          [,1]       [,2]       [,3]
[1,]   0.6666667  1.6666667 -1.3333333
[2,]  -0.3333333 -0.3333333  0.6666667
[3,]   0.3333333 -0.6666667  0.3333333


> solve(x, b = c(3, 2, 4))
[1] 0 1 1
```

COMMAND NAME

svd

The svd command computes the singular-value decomposition of a rectangular matrix. The result is a list containing $d, the singular values of x. If nu > 0 and nv > 0, the result also contains $u and $v, the left singular and right singular vectors of x.

Common Usage

```
svd(x, nu = min(n, p), nv = min(n, p), LINPACK = FALSE)
```

Related Commands

qr (p. 219)
eigen (p. 213)
solve (p. 220)
lm (p. 312)

Command Parameters

x	A matrix (can be numeric, logical, or complex).
nu = min(n, p)	The number of left singular vectors to be computed. This must between 0 and the number of rows in x.
nv = min(n, p)	The number of right singular vectors to be computed. This must be between 0 and the number of columns in x.
LINPACK = FALSE	If LINPACK = FALSE (the default), the LAPACK routine is used.

Examples

```
  ## Make a matrix
> (x = cbind(1,1:3,c(2,0,1)))
     [,1] [,2] [,3]
[1,]    1    1    2
[2,]    1    2    0
[3,]    1    3    1


  ## Determine SVD and left/right vectors (result is a list)
> svd(x)
$d
[1] 4.3622821 1.6738238 0.4108637


$u
           [,1]       [,2]       [,3]
[1,] -0.4560266  0.8514870 -0.2588620
[2,] -0.4734978 -0.4784171 -0.7395383
[3,] -0.7535513 -0.2146786  0.6213481


$v
           [,1]        [,2]       [,3]
[1,] -0.3858246  0.09462844 -0.9177063
[2,] -0.8398531 -0.44770719  0.3069284
[3,] -0.3818195  0.88915900  0.2522104


  ## SVD only (result unlisted as vector)
> unlist(svd(x, nu = 0, nv = 0))
       d1        d2        d3
4.3622821 1.6738238 0.4108637
```

COMMAND NAME

`upper.tri`

Returns a logical value (TRUE) for the upper triangle of a matrix. The rest of the matrix returns as FALSE. The diagonal can be included.

Common Usage

`upper.tri(x, diag = FALSE)`

Related Commands

`lower.tri` (p. 215)
`diag` (p. 211)
`matrix` (p. 10)

Command Parameters

x   A matrix object.

`diag = FALSE`   If `diag = TRUE`, the diagonals are returned as TRUE.

Examples

```
  ## Make a matrix
> x = cbind(1,1:3,c(2,0,1))
> x
     [,1] [,2] [,3]
[1,]    1    1    2
[2,]    1    2    0
[3,]    1    3    1

  ## Get logical upper triangle
> upper.tri(x)
      [,1]  [,2]  [,3]
[1,] FALSE  TRUE  TRUE
[2,] FALSE FALSE  TRUE
[3,] FALSE FALSE FALSE

  ## Set upper triangle and diagonal to a value
> x[upper.tri(x, diag = 1)] = 99
> x
     [,1] [,2] [,3]
[1,]   99   99   99
[2,]    1   99   99
[3,]    1    3   99
```

Summary Statistics

A summary statistic is a mathematical way of summarizing one aspect of a data sample. Allied to these summaries is the distribution of a sample (that is, its shape).

What's In This Topic:

- **Simple summary stats** (p. 223)
- **Tests of distribution** (p. 235)

SIMPLE SUMMARY STATS

R provides various commands that produce simple summary statistics of data samples.

 SEE also Theme 1, "Data: Summarizing Data."

COMMAND NAME

```
cummax
cummin
cumprod
cumsum
```

These commands provide functions for carrying out cumulative operations. The commands return values for cumulative maxima, minima, product, and sum. If used with the `seq_along` command, they can provide cumulative values for other functions.

Common Usage

```
cummax(x)
cummin(x)
cumprod(x)
cumsum(x)
```

Related Commands

max (p. 178)
min (p. 179)
sum (p. 186, 232)
seq_along (p. 27)
seq (p. 27)

Command Parameters

x   An R object, usually a vector.

Examples

```
   ## Make a vector
> vec = c(3:1, 2:0, 4:2)
> vec
[1] 3 2 1 2 1 0 4 3 2

   ## Cumulative operations
> cummax(vec)
[1] 3 3 3 3 3 3 3 4 4 4

> cummin(vec)
[1] 3 2 1 1 1 0 0 0 0

> cumsum(1:10)
 [1]  1  3  6 10 15 21 28 36 45 55

> cumprod(1:7)
[1]    1    2    6   24  120  720 5040
```

COMMAND NAME

`fivenum`

This command produces Tukey's five-number summary for the input data. The values returned are minimum, lower-hinge, median, upper-hinge, and maximum.

Common Usage

```
fivenum(x, na.rm = TRUE)
```

Related Commands

```
quantile (p. 229)
median (p. 228)
IQR (p. 225)
range (p. 230)
```

Command Parameters

x   An R object, usually a vector.

na.rm = TRUE   By default, any NA items are omitted before carrying out the calculations.

Examples

```
  ## Some numbers
> vec = c(2:5, 4:5, 6:8, 9, 12, 17)
> vec
 [1]  2  3  4  5  4  5  6  7  8  9 12 17

  ## Summarize
> fivenum(vec)
[1]  2.0  4.0  5.5  8.5 17.0
```

COMMAND NAME

IQR

Calculates the inter-quartile range.

Common Usage

```
IQR(x, na.rm = FALSE)
```

Related Commands

```
fivenum (p. 224)
quantile (p. 229)
range (p. 230)
mad (p. 226)
```

Command Parameters

x   A vector of values.

na.rm = FALSE   If set to TRUE, NA items are omitted.

Examples

```
  ## Some numbers
> vec = c(2:5, 4:5, 6:8, 9, 12, 17)
> vec
 [1]  2  3  4  5  4  5  6  7  8  9 12 17

  ## Summarize
> IQR(vec)
[1] 4.25
```

COMMAND NAME

`length`

Determines how many elements are in an object. The command can get or set the number of elements.

 SEE Theme 1, "Data: Summarizing Data."

COMMAND NAME

`mad`

This command calculates the median absolute deviation for a numeric vector. It also adjusts (by default) by a factor for asymptotically normal consistency.

Common Usage

```
mad(x, center = median(x), constant = 1.4826, na.rm = FALSE,
    low = FALSE, high = FALSE)
```

Related Commands

`IQR` (p. 225)
`median` (p. 228)
`range` (p. 230)

Command Parameters

`x`	A vector.
`center = median(x)`	The center to use; the default is the `median`.
`constant = 1.4826`	The adjustment factor; set this to 1 for no adjustment.
`na.rm = FALSE`	If `na.rm = TRUE`, NA items are omitted.
`low = FALSE`	If `low = TRUE`, the median is calculated as the lower of the two middle values for an even sample size.
`high = FALSE`	If `high = TRUE`, the median is calculated as the higher of the two middle values for an even sample size.

Examples

```
  ## Some numbers
> vec = c(2:5, 4:5, 6:8, 9, 12, 17)
> vec
 [1]  2  3  4  5  4  5  6  7  8  9 12 17

  ## Summarize
> mad(vec)
[1] 2.9652

  ## This gives the same result
> median(abs(vec - median(vec))) * 1.4826
[1] 2.9652

  ## Alter median calculation for even sample size
> mad(vec, low = TRUE)
[1] 2.2239

> mad(vec, high = TRUE)
[1] 3.7065
```

COMMAND NAME

max
pmax

The max command returns the maximum value in a numerical vector or object. The pmax command returns the parallel maxima by comparing two objects.

 SEE "Mathematical Operations: Math."

COMMAND NAME

mean

Calculates the mean value for the specified data.

Common Usage

mean(x, trim = 0, na.rm = FALSE)

Related Commands

median (p. 228)
summary (p. 132, 233, 522)

Command Parameters

`x`	An R object. Many kinds of objects return a result, including vectors, matrixes, arrays, and data frames.
`trim = 0`	A fraction of observations (0 to 0.5) to be trimmed from each end before the mean is calculated.
`na.rm = FALSE`	If `na.rm = TRUE`, NA items are omitted. The command will produce a result of NA if NA items are present and `na.rm = FALSE`.

Examples

```
  ## Make some objects
> newmat = matrix(1:12, nrow = 3) # A matrix
> newdf = data.frame(col1 = 1:3, col2 = 4:6, col3 = 5:3) # A data frame
> newvec = c(2:5, 4:5, 6:8, 9, 12, 17) # numeric vector

  ## Mean values
> mean(newmat) # Mean for entire matrix
[1] 6.5

> mean(newdf) # Gives column means for data frame
col1 col2 col3
   2    5    4

> mean(newvec)
[1] 6.833333

> mean(newvec, trim = 0.1) # Trimmed mean
[1] 6.3
```

COMMAND NAME

`median`

This command calculates the median value for an object.

Common Usage

`median(x, na.rm = FALSE)`

Related Commands

`quantile` (p. 229)
`mean` (p. 227)

Command Parameters

x   An R object. Generally, the object is a vector, matrix, or array.

na.rm = FALSE   If na.rm = TRUE, NA items are omitted. The command will produce a result of NA if NA items are present and na.rm = FALSE.

Examples

```
  ## Make some objects
> newmat = matrix(1:12, nrow = 3) # A matrix
> newvec = c(2:5, 4:5, 6:8, 9, 12, 17) # numeric vector

  ## Median values
> median(newmat) # Median for entire matrix
[1] 6.5

> median(newvec)
[1] 5.5
```

COMMAND NAME

```
min
pmin
```

The min command returns the minimum value in a vector or object (which can be character). The pmin command returns the parallel minima by comparing two objects.

 SEE "Mathematical Operations: Math."

COMMAND NAME

```
quantile
```

Returns quantiles for a sample corresponding to given probabilities. The default settings produce five quartile values.

Common Usage

```
quantile(x, probs = seq(0, 1, 0.25), na.rm = FALSE, names = TRUE)
```

Related Commands

fivenum (p. 224)
median (p. 228)
ecdf (p. 152)

Command Parameters

x	An R object, usually a vector.
probs =	The probabilities required (0 to 1). The default setting produces quartiles, that is, probabilities of 0, 0.25, 0.5, 0.75, and 1.
na.rm = FALSE	If na.rm = TRUE, NA items are omitted.
names = TRUE	By default the names of the quantiles are shown (as a percentage).

Examples

```
  ## Make a vector
> newvec = c(2:5, 4:5, 6:8, 9, 12, 17) # numeric vector

  ## Quantiles
> quantile(newvec) # The defaults, quartiles
   0%   25%   50%   75%  100%
 2.00  4.00  5.50  8.25 17.00

> quantile(newvec, type = 3) # Different type, used by SAS
  0%  25%  50%  75% 100%
   2    4    5    8   17

> quantile(newvec, type = 6) # Used by MiniTab and SPSS
   0%   25%   50%   75%  100%
 2.00  4.00  5.50  8.75 17.00

> quantile(newvec, probs = c(0.3, 0.7), names = FALSE) # Suppress names
[1] 4.3 7.7
```

COMMAND NAME

range

Gives the range for a given sample; that is, a vector containing the minimum and maximum values.

Common Usage

```
range(..., na.rm = FALSE)
```

Related Commands

IQR (p. 225)
max (p. 178)
min (p. 179)

Command Parameters

...	Numeric or character objects.
na.rm = FALSE	If na.rm = TRUE, NA items are omitted.

Examples

```
  ## Make objects
> newvec = c(2:5, 4:5, 6:8, 9, 12, 17) # numeric vector
> vec = c(11, 15, 99, 45) # numeric vector

  ## Range
> range(newvec) # A vector containing min and max of the object
[1]  2 17

> range(newvec, vec) # The range for the two named objects combined
[1]  2 99
```

COMMAND NAME

sd

Calculates standard deviation for vector, matrix, and data frame objects. If the data are a matrix or data frame, the standard deviation is calculated for each column.

 SEE also sd in "Simple Summary Stats."

Common Usage

sd(x, na.rm = FALSE)

Related Commands

var (p. 235)
mad (p. 226)
IQR (p. 225)

Command Parameters

x	An R object; usually a vector, matrix, or data frame.
na.rm = FALSE	If na.rm = TRUE, NA items are omitted. If NA items are present they will cause the result to be NA unless omitted.

Examples

```
  ## Make objects
> newdf = data.frame(C1 = c(1, 2, 12), C2 = c(1, 2, 25), C3 = c(1, 2, 50))
> newmat = matrix(c(1, 2, 12, 1, 2, 25, 1, 2, 50), ncol = 3)
> newvec = c(2:5, 4:5, 6:8, 9, 12, NA, 17) # Numeric vector

  ## Std Dev.
> sd(newdf)
       C1         C2         C3
 6.082763 13.576941 28.005952

> sd(newvec, na.rm = TRUE)
[1] 4.239068

> sd(newvec) # NA items not omitted by default
[1] NA

> sd(newmat)
[1]   6.082763 13.576941 28.005952
```

COMMAND NAME

sum

This command returns the sum of the values present.

Common Usage

```
sum(..., na.rm = FALSE)
```

Related Commands

summary (p. 132, 233, 522)
colSums (p. 124)

Command Parameters

...	R objects.
na.rm = FALSE	If na.rm = TRUE, NA items are omitted. If NA items are present they will cause the result to be NA unless omitted.

Examples

```
  ## Make objects
> newdf = data.frame(C1 = c(1, 2, 12), C2 = c(1, 2, 25), C3 = c(1, 2, 50))
> newmat = matrix(c(1, 2, 12, 1, 2, 25, 1, 2, 50), ncol = 3)
```

```
> newvec = c(2:5, 4:5, 6:8, 9, 12, NA, 17) # Numeric vector

  ## Sum
> sum(newdf) # Sums entire data frame
[1] 96

> sum(newvec, na.rm = TRUE)
[1] 82

> sum(newmat) # Sums entire matrix
[1] 96

> sum(newmat, newvec, na.rm = TRUE) # Combine items to sum
[1] 178
```

COMMAND NAME

summary

Summarizes an object. This command is very general and the result depends on the class of the object being examined. Some results objects have a special `class` attribute and possibly a dedicated summary routine to display them.

 SEE also Theme 1, "Data: Summarizing Data."

 SEE also aov and lm.

Common Usage

summary(object)

Related Commands

fivenum (p. 224)
str (p. 102)
attributes (p. 76)
class (p. 79)

Command Parameters

object An R object to summarize. R will look at the `class` attribute of the object and then see if there is a command `summary.class`, where `class` matches the object `class` attribute. If there is a matching command it is executed; otherwise, the default `summary` command is performed.

Examples

```
## Make some data
> dat = data.frame(pred = c(1:5, 3:7, 4:8),
 resp = gl(3, 5, labels = c("x", "y", "z")))

> summary(dat$pred) # Summary for numeric vector object
  Min. 1st Qu. Median   Mean 3rd Qu.   Max.
 1.000   3.500  5.000  4.667   6.000  8.000

> summary(dat$resp) # Summary for factor object
x y z
5 5 5

> summary(dat) # Summary for data frame
     pred         resp
 Min.   :1.000   x:5
 1st Qu.:3.500   y:5
 Median :5.000   z:5
 Mean   :4.667
 3rd Qu.:6.000
 Max.   :8.000

  ## Carry out ANOVA
> dat.aov = aov(pred ~ resp, data = dat)
> class(dat.aov) # Holds 2 classes
[1] "aov" "lm"

  ## Default summary uses class: "aov" (there is a summary.aov command)
> summary(dat.aov)

            Df Sum Sq Mean Sq F value  Pr(>F)
resp         2 23.333  11.667  4.6667 0.03168 *
Residuals   12 30.000   2.500
---
Signif. codes:  0 '***' 0.001 '**' 0.01 '*' 0.05 '.' 0.1 ' ' 1
```

COMMAND NAME

sd

Calculates standard deviation for vector, matrix, and data frame objects. If the data are a matrix or data frame, the standard deviation is calculated for each column.

Common Usage

```
sd(x, na.rm = FALSE)
```

Related Commands

var (p. 235)
mad (p. 226)

Command Parameters

x	A numerical object. Usually a vector but if it is a data frame or matrix the result gives the standard deviation of the columns.
na.rm = FALSE	If na.rm = TRUE, NA items are omitted.

Examples

```
  ## Make a vector
> newvec = c(13:18)

  ## Make a data frame
> mydf = data.frame(col1 = 1:6, col2 = 7:12)

  ## Compute standard deviation
> sd(newvec)
[1] 1.870829

> sd(mydf)
    col1      col2
1.870829  1.870829
```

COMMAND NAME

var

This command calculates the variance of numeric vectors.

 SEE var in "Correlations and Associations."

TESTS OF DISTRIBUTION

The distribution of a data sample (that is, its "shape") is important because statistical inference can only be made if the distribution is known.

COMMAND NAME

density

This command computes kernel density estimates. You can use it to visualize the distribution of a data sample as a graph and can also compare to a known distribution by overlaying the plot onto a histogram, for example.

Common Usage

density(x)

Related Commands

hist (p. 368)

x   The data for which the estimate of kernel density is to be computed.

Examples

```
  ## Make data
> set.seed(75)                      # Set random number seed
> x = rnorm(100, mean = 5, sd = 2)  # Normal distribution
> set.seed(75)                      # Set random number seed again
> y = rpois(100, lambda = 5)        # Poisson distribution

  ## Create histogram and density overlay (Figure 2-1)
> hist(x, freq = FALSE, xlim = c(0, 12)) # Histogram

> lines(density(y), lwd = 3) # Overlay density
```

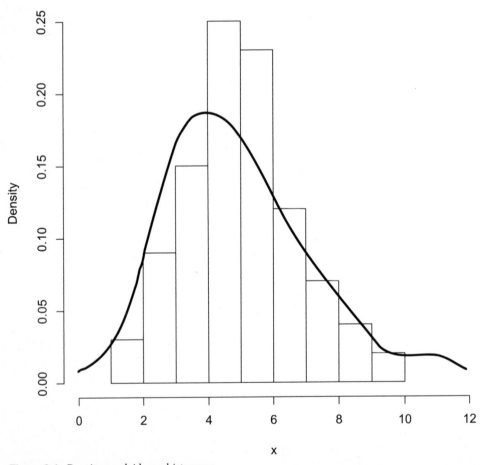

Figure 2-1: Density overlaid on a histogram

```
     ## Make density object
> (dy = density(y))

Call:
        density.default(x = y)

Data: y (100 obs.); Bandwidth 'bw' = 0.7851

        x                 y
  Min.    :-2.355   Min.    :5.768e-05
  1st Qu.: 1.572    1st Qu.:9.115e-03
  Median : 5.500    Median :3.117e-02
  Mean   : 5.500    Mean    :6.359e-02
  3rd Qu.: 9.428    3rd Qu.:1.167e-01
  Max.   :13.355    Max.    :1.866e-01

> names(dy) # View elements of density result
[1] "x"         "y"         "bw"       "n"         "call"      "data.name" "has.na"
```

COMMAND NAME

`hist`

This command makes histograms.

 SEE Theme 3, "Graphics."

COMMAND NAME

`ks.test`

This command carries out one- or two-sample Kolmogorov-Smirnov tests. The result is a list with the `class` attribute `"htest"`. The `ks.test` command can compare two distributions or one sample to a "known" distribution.

Common Usage

```
ks.test(x, y, alternative = "two.sided", exact = NULL)
```

Related Commands

`shapiro.test` (p. 239)
`qqnorm` (p. 385)

Command Parameters

x   A vector of numeric values.

y   A sample to test x against. This can be in several forms:

- A vector of numeric values.

- A cumulative distribution function (e.g., pnorm).

- A character string naming a cumulative distribution function.

alternative   Indicates the alternative hypothesis. The default is `"two.sided"` with `"less"` or `"greater"` as other possible values.

exact = NULL   If TRUE, an exact p-value is computed (not for the one-sided two-sample test).

Examples

```
  ## Some data samples to test
> dat = c(1:3, 4:7, 6:9, 7:11)
> d2 = c(6, 7, 7, 7, 11, 12, 12, 16)

  ## Compare to normal distribution (1-sample test)
> ks.test(dat, "pnorm", mean = 6, sd = 2)

        One-sample Kolmogorov-Smirnov test

data:  dat
D = 0.254, p-value = 0.2534
alternative hypothesis: two-sided

  ## Two-sample test
> ks.test(dat, d2)

        Two-sample Kolmogorov-Smirnov test

data:  dat and d2
D = 0.4375, p-value = 0.2591
alternative hypothesis: two-sided

  ## Compare to normal distribution (as Two-sample test)
> ks.test(dat, pnorm(q = 15, mean = 5, sd = 1), alternative = "greater")

        Two-sample Kolmogorov-Smirnov test

data:  dat and pnorm(q = 15, mean = 5, sd = 1)
D^+ = 0, p-value = 1
alternative hypothesis: the CDF of x lies above that of y
```

COMMAND NAME

`qqline`

This command adds a line to a normal quantile-quantile plot. The line passes through the first and third quantiles.

 SEE Theme 3, "Graphics."

COMMAND NAME

`qqnorm`

This command produces a normal quantile-quantile plot.

 SEE Theme 3, "Graphics."

COMMAND NAME

`qqplot`

This command produces a quantile-quantile plot of two sets of data.

 SEE Theme 3, "Graphics."

COMMAND NAME

`shapiro.test`

This command carries out a Shapiro-Wilk test on a sample. The result shows departure from the normal distribution. The result is a list with a `class` attribute `"htest"`.

Common Usage

`shapiro.test(x)`

Related Commands

`ks.test` (p. 237)
`qqnorm` (p. 385)

Command Parameters

x   A numeric vector of data values.

```
  ## Make data samples to test
> dat = c(1:3, 4:7, 6:9, 7:11)
> d2 = c(6, 7, 7, 7, 8, 9, 12, 16)

  ## Test for normality
> shapiro.test(dat) # Result not significantly different from normal

        Shapiro-Wilk normality test

data:  dat
W = 0.9681, p-value = 0.8065

> shapiro.test(d2) # Result is significantly different from normal

        Shapiro-Wilk normality test

data:  d2
W = 0.8078, p-value = 0.03466
```

Differences Tests

In a general sense *differences tests* examine differences between samples. This is in contrast to those tests that examine links between samples such as correlation or association.

Some commands use the `formula` syntax; this notation allows for the representation of complicated analytical situations.

 SEE also `formula` in "Analysis of Variance and Linear Modeling."

What's In This Topic:

- **Parametric tests** (p. 241)

  - Tests for differences in normally distributed samples

  - Tests for assumptions for normally distributed samples (e.g., homogeneity of variance)

  - Power of parametric tests

- **Non-parametric tests** (p. 252)

  - Tests for differences in non-parametric samples

  - Tests for assumptions for non-parametric samples (for example, differences in scale parameters)

  - Power of non-parametric tests

PARAMETRIC TESTS

Parametric tests generally involve data that is normally distributed. Included in this section are commands that also test for some of the assumptions of these tests.

COMMAND NAME

`bartlett.test`

This command carries out the Bartlett test for homogeneity of variances. In other words, it tests if the variances in several samples are the same. The command can accept a `formula` (see the following common usage examples and command parameters). The result is a list with a `class` attribute `"htest"`.

Common Usage

`bartlett.test(x)`

`bartlett.test(x, g)`

`bartlett.test(formula, data, subset, na.action)`

Related Commands

`var.test` (p. 251)
`fligner.test` (p. 254)
`ansari.test` (p. 252)
`mood.test` (p. 259)
`aov` (p. 285)
`lm` (p. 312)

Command Parameters

`x`	The data to test. This can be in one of several forms:

- A numeric vector of data values (with groups given by `g`).

- A list of data values (each item in the list is a separate sample).

- A fitted linear model object (with a `class` attribute `"lm"`).

`g`	A vector or factor object giving the groups for the corresponding data in `x`. This is ignored if `x` is a list.
`formula`	A formula describing the data values and grouping of the form `values ~ groups`.
`data`	The matrix or data frame that contains the items specified in the `formula`.
`subset`	A subset of observations to be used; of the form `subset = group %in% c("a", "b", ...)`.
`na.action`	What to do if the data contains `NA` items. The default is to use the current settings (usually `"na.omit"`).

Examples

```
  ## Make some data
> x = c(1, 2, 3, 3, 5)  # A vector
> y = c(3, 3, 3, 4, 4)  # A vector
> z = c(1, 4, 7, 9, 12) # A vector

> d1 = data.frame(x = x, y = y, z = z) # A data frame

> d2 = stack(d1) # Stack data to make response, predictor
> names(d2) <- c("resp", "pred") # rename columns

  ## Run Bartlett tests
> bartlett.test(list(x, y, z)) # Give samples as list

        Bartlett test of homogeneity of variances

data:  list(x, y, z)
Bartlett's K-squared = 11.9435, df = 2, p-value = 0.00255

  ## Data x, y, z, specified in different forms
  ## All return same result as previous example
> bartlett.test(d1) # Multiple samples in one data frame
> bartlett.test(d2$resp, g = d2$pred) # Specify groups
> bartlett.test(resp ~ pred, data = d2) # Formula syntax

  ## Use a subset
> bartlett.test(resp ~ pred, data = d2, subset = pred %in% c("x", "y"))

        Bartlett test of homogeneity of variances

data:  resp by pred
Bartlett's K-squared = 3.0642, df = 1, p-value = 0.08004
```

COMMAND NAME

oneway.test

This command tests whether means from two or more samples are different. The result is a list with a class attribute "htest".

Common Usage

```
oneway.test(formula, data, subset, na.action, var.equal = FALSE)
```

Related Commands

t.test (p. 248)
kruskal.test (p. 258)
aov (p. 285)

Command Parameters

formula A formula of the form `values ~ groups` that specifies the samples to test.

data A matrix or data frame that contains the variables specified in the `formula`.

subset A subset of observations to be used; of the form `subset = group %in% c("a", "b", ...)`.

na.action What to do if the data contains `NA` items. The default is to use the current settings (usually `"na.omit"`).

var.equal = FALSE By default, the variance of the samples is not assumed to be equal; in which case a Welch test is carried out. If `TRUE`, a one-way ANOVA is conducted.

Examples

```
  ## Make data
> x = c(1, 2, 3, 3, 5) # A vector
> y = c(3, 3, 3, 4, 4) # A vector
> z = c(1, 4, 7, 9, 12) # A vector

> d1 = data.frame(x = x, y = y, z = z) # Data frame

> d2 = stack(d1) # Stack to form response, predictor
> names(d2) <- c("resp", "pred") # Rename variables

  ## One-Way testing
> oneway.test(resp ~ pred, data = d2) # Welch test

        One-way analysis of means (not assuming equal variances)

data:  resp and pred
F = 1.6226, num df = 2.000, denom df = 6.038, p-value = 0.2729

> oneway.test(resp ~ pred, data = d2, var.equal = TRUE) # ANOVA

        One-way analysis of means

data:  resp and pred
F = 3.0096, num df = 2, denom df = 12, p-value = 0.08723
```

```
  ## Same result as previous
> anova(lm(resp ~ pred, data = d2))
Analysis of Variance Table

Response: resp
          Df Sum Sq Mean Sq F value  Pr(>F)
pred       2 41.733 20.8667  3.0096 0.08723 .
Residuals 12 83.200  6.9333
---
Signif. codes:  0 '***' 0.001 '**' 0.01 '*' 0.05 '.' 0.1 ' ' 1

  ## Use subset
> oneway.test(resp ~ pred, data = d2, subset = pred %in% c("x", "y"))

        One-way analysis of means (not assuming equal variances)

data:  resp and pred
F = 0.72, num df = 1.000, denom df = 5.071, p-value = 0.4344
```

COMMAND NAME

p.adjust

Adjusts p-values for multiple comparisons. This command can be called in two ways:

- As a standalone command
- As a parameter in another command (e.g., pairwise.t.test)

The result is a vector of adjusted p-values if called as a standalone command. If used as a parameter, the p-values are adjusted for the result object.

Common Usage

```
p.adjust(p, method = p.adjust.methods, n = length(p))
```

Related Commands

pairwise.t.test (p. 245)
pairwise.wilcox.test (p. 261)

Command Parameters

p	A vector of p-values.
method = p.adjust.methods	The correction method. The method names are contained in a vector, p.adjust.methods (see the following examples). The default is "holm". Other options are "hochberg", "hommel", "bonferroni", "BH", "BY", "fdr", and "none".

```
n = length(p)
```
The number of comparisons; the default is the number of p-values given in p. Note that you can set n larger than `length(p)`, which means the unobserved p-values are assumed to be greater than all the observed p for `"bonferroni"` and `"holm"` methods and equal to 1 for the other methods. Do not attempt this unless you know what you are doing!

Examples

```
   ## Show p-value adjust methods
> p.adjust.methods
[1] "holm"       "hochberg"  "hommel"     "bonferroni" "BH"         "BY"
[7] "fdr"        "none"

   ## Generate some p-values
> p = seq(from = 0.001, by = 0.007, length.out = 5)
> p
[1] 0.001 0.008 0.015 0.022 0.029

> p.adjust(p, method = "holm")
[1] 0.005 0.032 0.045 0.045 0.045

> p.adjust(p, method = "BY")
[1] 0.01141667 0.04566667 0.05708333 0.06279167 0.06621667

   ## Select all methods except "fdr", which is same as "BH"
> pp.adjust.M = p.adjust.methods[p.adjust.methods != "fdr"]

   ## Apply all corrections to p and give result as a matrix
> p.adj = sapply(p.adjust.M, function(meth) p.adjust(p, meth))
> p.adj
      holm hochberg hommel bonferroni    BH        BY    none
[1,] 0.005    0.005  0.005      0.005 0.0050 0.01141667 0.001
[2,] 0.032    0.029  0.029      0.040 0.0200 0.04566667 0.008
[3,] 0.045    0.029  0.029      0.075 0.0250 0.05708333 0.015
[4,] 0.045    0.029  0.029      0.110 0.0275 0.06279167 0.022
[5,] 0.045    0.029  0.029      0.145 0.0290 0.06621667 0.029
```

COMMAND NAME

```
pairwise.t.test
```

Carries out multiple t-tests with corrections for multiple testing. The result is an object with a class attribute `"pairwise.htest"`.

Common Usage

```
pairwise.t.test (x, g, p.adjust.method = p.adjust.methods,
                pool.sd = !paired, paired = FALSE,
                alternative = "two.sided")
```

Related Commands

pairwise.wilcox.test (p. 261)
t.test (p. 248)
TukeyHSD (p. 298)

Command Parameters

x	A vector of values (the response).
g	A vector or factor specifying the groups.
p.adjust.method	The method used for adjusting for multiple tests. Defaults to "holm". Other options are "hochberg", "hommel", "bonferroni", "BH", "BY", "fdr", and "none".
pool.sd	This can be set to TRUE or FALSE to enable pooling of standard deviations (not appropriate for paired tests).
paired = FALSE	If set to TRUE, a paired t-test is carried out for each comparison.
alternative = "two.sided"	Specifies the alternative hypothesis; the default is "two.sided" with "greater" or "less" being other options.

Examples

```
  ## Make some data
> resp = c(1, 2, 3, 3, 5, 3, 3, 3, 4, 4, 1, 4, 7, 9, 12) # Data
> pred = gl(3, 5, labels = c("x", "y", "z")) # Factor with 3 levels
> d1 = data.frame(resp, pred) # Data frame

  ## Pairwise t-tests
> pairwise.t.test(d1$resp, g = d1$pred) # Default

        Pairwise comparisons using t tests with pooled SD
data:   d1$resp and d1$pred
  x    y
y 0.72 -
z 0.12 0.16
P value adjustment method: holm

  ## Conservative adjustment
> pairwise.t.test(d1$resp, g = d1$pred, p.adjust = "bonferroni")

        Pairwise comparisons using t tests with pooled SD
data:   d1$resp and d1$pred
  x    y
y 1.00 -
z 0.12 0.24
P value adjustment method: bonferroni


> pairwise.t.test(d1$resp, g = d1$pred, paired = TRUE) # Paired t-tests
```

```
        Pairwise comparisons using paired t tests
data:  d1$resp and d1$pred
   x    y
y 0.30 -
z 0.12 0.27
P value adjustment method: holm


> pairwise.t.test(d1$resp, g = d1$pred, pool.sd = FALSE) # No pooled SD

        Pairwise comparisons using t tests with non-pooled SD
data:  d1$resp and d1$pred
   x    y
y 0.43 -
z 0.36 0.36
P value adjustment method: holm
```

COMMAND NAME

`power.t.test`

This command computes the power of a t-test. It can also determine the parameters required to achieve a certain power (one of the first five parameters must be given as NULL to do this). The result is an object holding a `class` attribute `"power.htest"`.

Common Usage

```
power.t.test (n = NULL, delta = NULL, sd = 1, sig.level = 0.05,
              power = NULL, type = "two.sample",
              alternative = "two.sided", strict = FALSE)
```

Related Commands

`t.test` (p. 248)
`pairwise.t.test` (p. 245)
`power.anova.test` (p. 295)

Command Parameters

`n = NULL`	The number of observations (replicates) per group.
`delta = NULL`	The true difference in means.
`sd = 1`	The standard deviation.
`sig.level = 0.05`	The significance level for a Type I error probability.
`power = NULL`	The power of the test, that is, 1 minus (Type II error probability).
`type = "two.sample"`	The type of t-test; the default is `"two.sample"`. Alternatives are `"one.sided"` or `"paired"`.
`alternative = "two.sided"`	The default `"two.sided"` indicates a two-sided test; the alternative is `"one.sided"`.
`strict = FALSE`	If `strict = TRUE` is used, the power will include the probability of rejection in the opposite direction of the true effect, in the two-sided case. Without this the power will be half the significance level if the true difference is zero.

Examples

```
## Determine power
> power.t.test(n = 20, delta = 1)

        Two-sample t test power calculation

              n = 20
          delta = 1
             sd = 1
      sig.level = 0.05
          power = 0.8689528
    alternative = two.sided

 NOTE: n is number in *each* group

  ## Determine number of replicates to achieve given power
> power.t.test(delta = 1, power = 0.9)

        Two-sample t test power calculation

              n = 22.02110
          delta = 1
             sd = 1
      sig.level = 0.05
          power = 0.9
    alternative = two.sided

 NOTE: n is number in *each* group
```

COMMAND NAME

t.test

This command carries out the Student's t-test. Options include one-sample, two-sample, and paired tests. The command can accept input in the form of a `formula`. The result of the command is a list with a `class` attribute "htest".

Common Usage

```
t.test(x, ...)

t.test(x, y = NULL, alternative = "two.sided", mu = 0,
       paired = FALSE, var.equal = FALSE, conf.level = 0.95, ...)

t.test(formula, data, subset, na.action, ...)
```

Related Commands

wilcox.test (p. 265)
pairwise.t.test (p. 245)
power.t.test (p. 247)

Command Parameters

x	A vector of numeric values. A formula can be specified instead of x and y.
y	A vector of numeric values. If y is missing or NULL, a one-sample test is carried out on x.
alternative = "two.sided"	Specifies the alternative hypothesis; the default is "two.sided", with "greater" or "less" as other options.
mu = 0	A value for the mean. This represents the true value of the mean for a one-sample test or the difference in means for a two-sample test.
paired = FALSE	If paired = TRUE, a matched pairs test is conducted. If TRUE, x and y must be the same length and missing values are removed pairwise.
var.equal = FALSE	If var.equal = TRUE, the variances are assumed equal (the "classic" t-test). The default, FALSE, carries out the Welch (Satterthwaite) approximation for degrees of freedom.
conf.level = 0.95	A value for the confidence level that is reported.
formula	For two-sample tests, the data can be specified as a formula of the form response ~ grouping.
data	A data frame or matrix that contains the variables specified in the formula.
subset	A subset of observations to be used; of the form subset = group %in% c("a", "b", ...).
na.action	What to do if the data contains NA items. The default is to use the current settings (usually "na.omit").
...	Other parameters.

Examples

```
## Make data
> x = c(2, 4, 5, 4, 7, 6) # A vector
> y = c(7, 8, 6, 8, 9, 7) # A vector
> z = c(1, 2, 2, 4, 2, 5) # A vector
> dat2 = data.frame(resp = c(x, y, z),
  pred = gl(3, 6, labels = c("x", "y", "z"))) # A data frame
```

```
  ## t-tests
> t.test(x, y, var.equal = TRUE) # Classic t-test


        Two Sample t-test

data:  x and y
t = -3.4, df = 10, p-value = 0.006771
alternative hypothesis: true difference in means is not equal to 0
95 percent confidence interval:
 -4.690116 -0.976551
sample estimates:
mean of x mean of y
 4.666667  7.500000


> t.test(y, z, paired = TRUE) # Paired test


        Paired t-test

data:  y and z
t = 6.4524, df = 5, p-value = 0.001330
alternative hypothesis: true difference in means is not equal to 0
95 percent confidence interval:
 2.907779 6.758888
sample estimates:
mean of the differences
              4.833333


> t.test(resp ~ pred, data = dat2, subset = pred %in% c("x", "z"),
  conf.level = 0.99) # Use subset


        Welch Two Sample t-test

data:  resp by pred
t = 2.1213, df = 9.78, p-value = 0.0605
alternative hypothesis: true difference in means is not equal to 0
99 percent confidence interval:
 -1.003145   5.003145
sample estimates:
mean in group x mean in group z
       4.666667        2.666667


> t.test(y, mu = 8, alternative = "less") # One-sample test


        One Sample t-test

data:  y
t = -1.1677, df = 5, p-value = 0.1478
alternative hypothesis: true mean is less than 8
95 percent confidence interval:
      -Inf 8.362792
```

```
sample estimates:
mean of x
      7.5
```

COMMAND NAME

`var.test`

This command carries out an F-test to compare the variances of two samples (assumed to be normally distributed). The result is a list with a `class` attribute `"htest"`. The command can accept input in the form of a `formula`.

Common Usage

```
var.test(x, y, ratio = 1, alternative = "two.sided", conf.level = 0.95)

var.test(formula, data, subset, na.action, ...)
```

Related Commands

`bartlett.test` (p. 241)
`ansari.test` (p. 252)
`mood.test` (p. 259)

Command Parameters

`x, y`	Numeric vectors of data. The data can also be specified as a `formula`.
`ratio = 1`	The hypothesized ratio of variances of `x` and `y`.
`alternative = "two.sided"`	Specifies the alternative hypothesis; the default is `"two.sided"`, with `"greater"` or `"less"` as other options.
`conf.level = 0.95`	A value for the confidence level that is reported.
`formula`	A formula giving the data in the form `response ~ grouping`.
`data`	A data frame or matrix that contains the variables specified in the `formula`.
`subset`	A subset of observations to be used; of the form `subset = group %in% c("a", "b", ...)`.
`na.action`	What to do if the data contains `NA` items. The default is to use the current settings (usually `"na.omit"`).
`...`	Other parameters.

Examples

```
  ## Make data
> x = c(2, 4, 5, 4, 7, 6) # A vector
> y = c(7, 8, 6, 8, 9, 7) # A vector
> z = c(1, 2, 2, 4, 2, 9) # A vector
> dat2 = data.frame(resp = c(x, y, z),
 pred = gl(3, 6, labels = c("x", "y", "z"))) # A data frame
```

```
  ## Variance tests
> var.test(x, y) # Basic test

        F test to compare two variances

data:  x and y
F = 2.7879, num df = 5, denom df = 5, p-value = 0.2849
alternative hypothesis: true ratio of variances is not equal to 1
95 percent confidence interval:
  0.3901105 19.9232463
sample estimates:
ratio of variances
          2.787879

  ## Use a subset
> var.test(resp ~ pred, data = dat2, subset = pred %in% c("y", "z"))

        F test to compare two variances

data:  resp by pred
F = 0.1269, num df = 5, denom df = 5, p-value = 0.0408
alternative hypothesis: true ratio of variances is not equal to 1
95 percent confidence interval:
  0.01776047 0.90704077
sample estimates:
ratio of variances
          0.1269231
```

NON-PARAMETRIC

Non-parametric tests involve data that is not normally distributed. Included in this section are commands that also test for some of the assumptions of these tests.

COMMAND NAME

`ansari.test`

This command carries out the Ansari-Bradley two-sample test for a difference in scale parameters. The result is a list with a `class` attribute `"htest"`. The command can accept input in the form of a `formula`.

Common Usage

```
ansari.test(x, y, alternative = "two.sided", conf.level = 0.95)

ansari.test(formula, data, subset, na.action, ...)
```

Related Commands

`mood.test` (p. 259)
`fligner.test` (p. 254)
`var.test` (p. 251)
`bartlett.test` (p. 241)

Command Parameters

`x, y`	Numeric vectors of data. The data can also be specified as a `formula`.
`alternative = "two.sided"`	Specifies the alternative hypothesis; the default is `"two.sided"`, with `"greater"` and `"less"` as other options.
`conf.level = 0.95`	A value for the confidence level that is reported.
`formula`	A formula giving the data in the form `response ~ grouping`.
`data`	A data frame or matrix that contains the variables specified in the `formula`.
`subset`	A subset of observations to be used; of the form `subset = group %in% c("a", "b", ...)`.
`na.action`	What to do if the data contains `NA` items. The default is to use the current settings (usually `"na.omit"`).
`...`	Other parameters.

Examples

```
  ## Make data
> x = c(2, 4, 5, 4, 7, 6) # A vector
> y = c(7, 8, 6, 8, 9, 7) # A vector
> z = c(1, 2, 2, 4, 2, 9) # A vector
> dat2 = data.frame(resp = c(x, y, z),
 pred = gl(3, 6, labels = c("x", "y", "z"))) # A data frame

  ## Test scale parameters
> ansari.test(x, y) # Basic test

        Ansari-Bradley test

data:  x and y
AB = 20.5, p-value = 0.8645
alternative hypothesis: true ratio of scales is not equal to 1

  ## Use formula and a subset
> ansari.test(resp ~ pred, data = dat2, subset = pred %in% c("y", "z"))

        Ansari-Bradley test

data:  resp by pred
AB = 25.5, p-value = 0.1247
alternative hypothesis: true ratio of scales is not equal to 1
```

COMMAND NAME

`binom.test`

This command carries out an exact binomial test.

 SEE `binom.test` in "Association and Goodness of Fit."

COMMAND NAME

`fligner.test`

This command carries out a Fligner-Killeen (median) test of homogeneity of variances. In other words, it tests the null hypothesis that the variances in each of the groups (samples) are the same. The result is a list with a `class` attribute `"htest"`. The command can accept input in the form of a `formula`.

Common Usage

`fligner.test(x)`

`fligner.test(x, g)`

`fligner.test(formula, data, subset, na.action)`

Related Commands

`ansari.test` (p. 252)
`mood.test` (p. 259)
`var.test` (p. 251)
`bartlett.test` (p. 241)

Command Parameters

`x`	A numeric vector for the data; can also be a list.
`g`	A vector or factor object giving the groups for the corresponding elements of `x`. This is ignored if `x` is a list.
`formula`	A formula giving the data in the form `response ~ grouping`.
`data`	A data frame or matrix that contains the variables specified in the `formula`.
`subset`	A subset of observations to be used; of the form `subset = group %in% c("a", "b", ...)`.
`na.action`	What to do if the data contains `NA` items. The default is to use the current settings (usually `"na.omit"`).

Examples

```
  ## Make data
> x = c(2, 4, 5, 4, 7, 6) # A vector
> y = c(7, 8, 6, 8, 9, 7) # A vector
> z = c(1, 2, 2, 4, 2, 9) # A vector

> dat1 = c(x, y, z) # Combine vectors

  ## 3-level factor for x, y, z groups
> grp = gl(3, 6, labels = c("x", "y", "z"))

> dat2 = data.frame(resp = dat1, pred = grp) # A data frame

  ## Fligner-Killeen tests
> fligner.test(dat1, grp) # Basic test

        Fligner-Killeen test of homogeneity of variances

data:  dat1 and grp
Fligner-Killeen:med chi-squared = 0.7509, df = 2, p-value = 0.687

  ## Formula input and subset
> fligner.test(resp ~ pred, data = dat2, subset = pred %in% c("y", "z"))

        Fligner-Killeen test of homogeneity of variances

data:  resp by pred
Fligner-Killeen:med chi-squared = 0.0136, df = 1, p-value = 0.9071

> fligner.test(list(x, y, z)) # Use list as input

        Fligner-Killeen test of homogeneity of variances

data:  list(x, y, z)
Fligner-Killeen:med chi-squared = 0.7509, df = 2, p-value = 0.687
```

COMMAND NAME

`friedman.test`

This command carries out a Friedman rank sum test on unreplicated blocked data. The test is sometimes erroneously called a non-parametric two-way ANOVA. The result is a list with a `class` attribute `"htest"`. The command can accept input in several forms:

- As a `matrix` arranged with columns as groups and rows as blocks
- As three separate vectors (data, groups, and blocks)
- As a `formula`

Common Usage

```
friedman.test(y)

friedman.test(y, groups, blocks)

friedman.test(formula, data, subset, na.action)
```

Related Commands

quade.test (p. 263)
kruskal.test (p. 258)
aov (p. 285)

Command Parameters

y	A numeric vector of data values or a matrix. If y is a matrix, the columns are taken as the groups and the rows as the blocks.
groups	A vector giving the groups for the corresponding elements of y. This is ignored if y is a matrix.
blocks	A vector giving the blocks for the corresponding elements of y. This is ignored if y is a matrix.
formula	A formula giving the data in the form response ~ group | block.
data	A data frame or matrix that contains the variables specified in the formula.
subset	A subset of observations to be used; of the form subset = group %in% c("a", "b", ...).
na.action	What to do if the data contains NA items. The default is to use the current settings (usually "na.omit").

Examples

```
   ## Make data (vectors for data, group, block)
> temp = c(22.6, 13.5, 5.8, 22.4, 14.4, 5.9, 22.9, 14.2, 6.0, 23.2, 13.8, 5.8)
> depth = rep(c(1, 5, 12), 4)
> date = gl(4, 3, labels = c("May", "Jun", "Jul", "Aug"))

   ## Construct data frame with columns for data, group and block
> lt = data.frame(temp, depth, date)
> lt
   temp depth date
1  22.6     1  May
2  13.5     5  May
```

```
3    5.8    12  May
4   22.4     1  Jun
5   14.4     5  Jun
6    5.9    12  Jun
7   22.9     1  Jul
8   14.2     5  Jul
9    6.0    12  Jul
10  23.2     1  Aug
11  13.8     5  Aug
12   5.8    12  Aug

  ## Construct matrix; columns are groups and rows are blocks
> lt2 = matrix(temp, nrow = 4, byrow = TRUE,
 dimnames = list(month.abb[5:8], c("1", "5", "12")))
> lt2
       1    5   12
May 22.6 13.5 5.8
Jun 22.4 14.4 5.9
Jul 22.9 14.2 6.0
Aug 23.2 13.8 5.8

  ## Friedman tests
  ## Separate vectors for data, group, block
> friedman.test(temp, depth, date)

        Friedman rank sum test

data:  temp, depth and date
Friedman chi-squared = 8, df = 2, p-value = 0.01832

  ## Data frame with columns for data, group, block
  ## Same result as previous
> friedman.test(temp ~ depth | date, data = lt)

  ## Use entire matrix set out with columns as group, rows as block
  ## Same result as previous
> friedman.test(lt2)

  ## Use a subset
> friedman.test(temp ~ depth | date, data = lt, subset = depth %in% c(1, 12))

        Friedman rank sum test

data:  temp and depth and date
Friedman chi-squared = 4, df = 1, p-value = 0.0455
```

COMMAND NAME

`kruskal.test`

This command carries out the Kruskal-Wallis rank sum test. This is sometimes called a non-parametric 1-way ANOVA. The result is a list with a `class` attribute `"htest"`. The command can accept input in several forms:

- As separate vectors, one for the data and one for the grouping
- As a `list`, with each element representing a sample
- As a data frame with each column being a sample
- As a `formula`

Common Usage

`kruskal.test(x)`

`kruskal.test(x, g)`

`kruskal.test(formula, data, subset, na.action)`

Related Commands

`wilcox.test` (p. 265)
`friedman.test` (p. 255)
`aov` (p. 285)

Command Parameters

x	The numeric data. This can be:

- A vector of data.
- A list where each element is a sample.
- A data frame where each column is a sample.

g	A vector or factor giving the grouping for the corresponding elements of x. This is ignored if x is a data frame or list.
formula	A formula giving the data in the form `response ~ group`.
data	A data frame or matrix that contains the variables specified in the `formula`.
subset	A subset of observations to be used; of the form `subset = group %in% c("a", "b", ...)`.
na.action	What to do if the data contains `NA` items. The default is to use the current settings (usually `"na.omit"`).

Examples

```
  ## Make data
> x = c(2, 4, 5, 4, 7, 6) # A vector
> y = c(7, 8, 6, 8, 9, 7) # A vector
> z = c(1, 2, 2, 4, 2, 9) # A vector

> dat = data.frame(x, y, z) # Data frame
> dat1 = c(x, y, z) # Combine vectors

  ## 3-level factor for x, y, z groups
> grp = gl(3, 6, labels = c("x", "y", "z"))


> dat2 = data.frame(resp = dat1, pred = grp) # A data frame

  ## Kruskal-Wallis tests
  ## Use data frame (each column is sample)
> kruskal.test(dat)

        Kruskal-Wallis rank sum test

data:  dat
Kruskal-Wallis chi-squared = 7.6153, df = 2, p-value = 0.0222

  ## Use separate vectors for data and group
  ## Same result as previous
> kruskal.test(dat1, grp)

  ## Use data frame where columns are data and grouping
  ## Same result as previous
> kruskal.test(resp ~ pred, data = dat2)

  ## Use formula and subset
> kruskal.test(resp ~pred, data = dat2, subset = pred %in% c("x", "z"))

        Kruskal-Wallis rank sum test

data:  resp by pred
Kruskal-Wallis chi-squared = 1.9479, df = 1, p-value = 0.1628
```

COMMAND NAME

`mood.test`

This command carries out the Mood test for differences in scale parameter. The command can accept input in the form of a `formula`. The result is a list with a `class` attribute `"htest"`.

Common Usage

```
mood.test(x, y, alternative = "two.sided", ...)

mood.test(formula, data, subset, na.action, ...)
```

Related Commands

fligner.test (p. 254)
ansari.test (p. 252)
var.test (p. 251)
bartlett.test (p. 241)

Command Parameters

x, y	Numeric vectors of data values. The input can also be given as a formula.
alternative = "two.sided"	Specifies the alternative hypothesis; the default is "two.sided", with "greater" and "less" as other options.
formula	A formula giving the data in the form response ~ grouping.
data	A data frame or matrix that contains the variables specified in the formula.
subset	A subset of observations to be used; of the form subset = group %in% c("a", "b", ...).
na.action	What to do if the data contains NA items. The default is to use the current settings (usually "na.omit").

Examples

```
   ## Make data
> x = c(2, 4, 5, 4, 7, 6) # A vector
> y = c(7, 8, 6, 8, 9, 7) # A vector
> z = c(1, 2, 2, 4, 2, 9) # A vector
> dat2 = data.frame(resp = c(x, y, z),
 pred = gl(3, 6, labels = c("x", "y", "z"))) # A data frame

   ## Test scale parameters
> mood.test(x, y) # Basic test


      Mood two-sample test of scale

data:  x and y
Z = 0.0998, p-value = 0.9205
alternative hypothesis: two.sided
```

```
  ## Use formula and a subset
> mood.test(resp ~ pred, data = dat2, subset = pred %in% c("y", "z"))

        Mood two-sample test of scale

data:  resp by pred
Z = -1.4974, p-value = 0.1343
alternative hypothesis: two.sided
```

COMMAND NAME

`pairwise.wilcox.test`

This command carries out pairwise Wilcoxon rank sum tests with corrections for multiple testing. The result is an object with a `class` attribute `"pairwise.htest"`.

Common Usage

```
pairwise.wilcox.test(x, g, p.adjust.method = p.adjust.methods, paired = FALSE)
```

Related Commands

`wilcox.test` (p. 265)
`p.adjust` (p. 244)

Command Parameters

x	A vector of values (the response).
g	A vector or factor specifying the groups.
p.adjust.method	The method used for adjusting for multiple tests. Defaults to `"holm"`. Other options are `"hochberg"`, `"hommel"`, `"bonferroni"`, `"BH"`, `"BY"`, `"fdr"`, and `"none"`.
paired = FALSE	If set to `TRUE`, a paired test is carried out for each comparison.

Examples

```
  ## Make data
> resp = c(1, 2, 3, 3, 5, 3, 3, 3, 4, 4, 1, 4, 7, 9, 12) # Data
> pred = gl(3, 5, labels = c("x", "y", "z")) # Factor with 3 levels

  ## Pairwise tests
> pairwise.wilcox.test(resp, g = pred) # Default

        Pairwise comparisons using Wilcoxon rank sum test

data:  resp and pred

  x    y
y 0.52 -
z 0.52 0.52

P value adjustment method: holm
```

```
  ## Conservative adjustment
> pairwise.wilcox.test(resp, g = pred, p.adjust = "bonferroni")

        Pairwise comparisons using Wilcoxon rank sum test

data:  resp and pred

  x    y
y 1.00 -
z 0.52 0.60

P value adjustment method: bonferroni

  ## Paired test
> pairwise.wilcox.test(resp, g = pred, paired = TRUE)

        Pairwise comparisons using Wilcoxon signed rank test

data:  resp and pred

  x    y
y 0.38 -
z 0.30 0.38

P value adjustment method: holm
```

COMMAND NAME

`power.prop.test`

Calculates the power of a proportion test or determines the parameters required to achieve a certain power.

 SEE `power.prop.test` in "Association and Goodness of Fit."

COMMAND NAME

`prop.test`

Tests for equal (or given) proportions. This can be used for testing the null hypothesis to ensure that the proportions (probabilities of success) in several groups are the same, or that they equal certain given values.

 SEE `prop.test` in "Association and Goodness of Fit."

COMMAND NAME

`quade.test`

The Quade test for unreplicated blocked data. This command analyzes unreplicated complete block experimental data where there is only one replicate for each combination of block and group. The result is a list with a `class` attribute `"htest"`. The command can accept input in several forms:

- As a `matrix` arranged with columns as groups and rows as blocks
- As three separate vectors (data, groups, and blocks)
- As a `formula`

Common Usage

```
quade.test(y)
```

```
quade.test(y, groups, blocks)
```

```
quade.test(formula, data, subset, na.action)
```

Related Commands

`friedman.test` (p. 255)
`kruskal.test` (p. 258)
`aov` (p. 285)

Command Parameters

y	A numeric vector of data values or a matrix. If y is a matrix, the columns are taken as the groups and the rows as the blocks.
groups	A vector giving the groups for the corresponding elements of y. This is ignored if y is a matrix.
blocks	A vector giving the blocks for the corresponding elements of y. This is ignored if y is a matrix.
formula	A formula giving the data in the form `response ~ group	block`.
data	A data frame or matrix that contains the variables specified in the `formula`.
subset	A subset of observations to be used; of the form `subset = group %in% c("a", "b", ...)`.
na.action	What to do if the data contains NA items. The default is to use the current settings (usually `"na.omit"`).

Examples

```
## Make data (vectors for data, group and block)
> temp = c(22.6, 13.5, 5.8, 22.4, 14.4, 5.9, 22.9, 14.2, 6.0, 23.2, 13.8, 5.8)
> depth = rep(c(1, 5, 12), 4)
> date = gl(4, 3, labels = c("May", "Jun", "Jul", "Aug"))
```

```
> lt = data.frame(temp, depth, date) # Make a data frame
> lt # Data frame columns are data, group, block
   temp depth date
1  22.6     1  May
2  13.5     5  May
3   5.8    12  May
4  22.4     1  Jun
5  14.4     5  Jun
6   5.9    12  Jun
7  22.9     1  Jul
8  14.2     5  Jul
9   6.0    12  Jul
10 23.2     1  Aug
11 13.8     5  Aug
12  5.8    12  Aug

> lt2 = matrix(temp, nrow = 4, byrow = TRUE,
  dimnames = list(month.abb[5:8], c("1", "5", "12"))) # Make a matrix
> lt2 # Matrix columns are groups and rows are blocks
       1    5   12
May 22.6 13.5  5.8
Jun 22.4 14.4  5.9
Jul 22.9 14.2  6.0
Aug 23.2 13.8  5.8


  ## Quade tests
  ## Separate vectors for data, group, block
> quade.test(temp, depth, date)


        Quade test

data:   temp, depth and date
Quade F = 15, num df = 2, denom df = 6, p-value = 0.00463


  ## Data frame with columns for data, group, block
  ## Same result as previous
> quade.test(temp ~ depth | date, data = lt)


  ## Use entire matrix set out with columns as group, rows as block
  ## Same result as previous
> quade.test(lt2)


  ## Use a subset
> quade.test(temp ~ depth | date, data = lt, subset = depth %in% c(1, 12))


        Quade test

data:   temp and depth and date
Quade F = 15, num df = 1, denom df = 3, p-value = 0.03047
```

COMMAND NAME

`wilcox.test`

This command carries out Wilcoxon rank sum and signed rank tests (that is, one and two-sample tests). The two-sample test is also known as the Mann-Whitney U-test. The result is a list with a `class` attribute `"htest"`. The command can accept input in the form of a `formula`.

Common Usage

```
wilcox.test(x, y = NULL, alternative = "two.sided", mu = 0,
            paired = FALSE, exact = NULL, correct = TRUE,
            conf.int = FALSE, conf.level = 0.95)


wilcox.test(formula, data, subset, na.action, ...)
```

Related Commands

`kruskal.test` (p. 258)
`pairwise.wilcox.test` (p. 245)
`t.test` (p. 248)
`p.adjust` (p. 244)

Command Parameters

`x, y`	Numeric vectors specifying the data; if `y` is omitted or is `NULL`, a one-sample test is carried out.
`alternative = "two.sided"`	Specifies the alternative hypothesis; the default is `"two.sided"`, with `"greater"` or `"less"` as other options.
`mu = 0`	A value for the location shift. This represents the true value of the median for a one-sample test or the difference in medians for a two-sample test.
`paired = FALSE`	If `paired = TRUE`, a matched pairs test is conducted. If `TRUE`, `x` and `y` must be the same length and missing values are removed pairwise.
`exact = NULL`	If `exact = TRUE`, an exact p-value is computed.
`correct = TRUE`	By default, a continuity correction is applied in the normal approximation of the p-value.
`conf.int = FALSE`	If `conf.int = TRUE`, confidence intervals are computed.
`conf.level = 0.95`	A value for the confidence level that is reported if `conf.int = TRUE`.
`formula`	For two-sample tests, the data can be specified as a `formula` of the form `response ~ grouping`.
`data`	A data frame or matrix that contains the variables specified in the `formula`.
`subset`	A subset of observations to be used; of the form `subset = group %in% c("a", "b", ...)`.
`na.action`	What to do if the data contains `NA` items. The default is to use the current settings (usually `"na.omit"`).
`...`	Other parameters.

Examples

```
  ## Make data
> x = c(2, 4, 5, 2, 8, 3)
> y = c(7, 8, 6, 8, 9, 7)
> z = c(1, 2, 2, 4, 2, 5)

> dat2 = data.frame(resp = c(x, y, z),
 pred = gl(3, 6, labels = c("x", "y", "z")))

  ## Carry out Wilcox tests
> wilcox.test(x, mu = 5, exact = FALSE) # One-sample test

        Wilcoxon signed rank test with continuity correction

data:  x
V = 4, p-value = 0.4098
alternative hypothesis: true location is not equal to 5

> wilcox.test(x, y, exact = FALSE, correct = FALSE) # Two-sample test

        Wilcoxon rank sum test

data:  x and y
W = 4, p-value = 0.02347
alternative hypothesis: true location shift is not equal to 0

> wilcox.test(y, z, paired = TRUE, exact = FALSE, conf.int = TRUE,
 conf.level = 0.9) # Matched pair test

        Wilcoxon signed rank test with continuity correction

data:  y and z
V = 21, p-value = 0.03501
alternative hypothesis: true location shift is not equal to 0
90 percent confidence interval:
 3.000091 6.499983
sample estimates:
(pseudo)median
      4.999967

  ## Formula input using subset
> wilcox.test(resp ~ pred, data = dat2,
 subset = pred %in% c("x", "z"), exact = FALSE)

        Wilcoxon rank sum test with continuity correction

data:  resp by pred
W = 25, p-value = 0.2787
alternative hypothesis: true location shift is not equal to 0
```

Correlations and Associations

Correlations and *associations* are analytical approaches that look to find links between things. These approaches contrast to differences tests. Correlations tests usually compare numeric variables that are "continuous" whereas association tests generally look at categorical data.

What's In This Topic:

- **Correlation** (p. 267)
    - Correlation matrices
    - Correlation tests
    - Covariance
- **Association and goodness of fit** (p. 275)
    - Chi-squared test
    - Binomial test
    - Fisher's Exact test
    - Kolmogorov-Smirnov test
    - Proportion test

THEME 2: MATH AND STATISTICS

CORRELATION

Correlation is a general term referring to the linking of two numeric continuous variables.

COMMAND NAME

cor

This command carries out correlation on vectors of data or columns of data frames or matrix objects. You can use three methods:

- Pearson Product Moment
- Spearman's Rho Rank correlation
- Kendall's Tau Rank correlation

The result is either a numeric vector or a matrix, depending on the data being correlated.

Common Usage

```
cor(x, y = NULL, use = "everything", method = "pearson")
```

Related Commands

cor.test (p. 269)
cov (p. 271)
var (p. 235)
cov2cor (p. 272)

Command Parameters

x	Numeric data; this can be a vector, matrix, or data frame.
y = NULL	A vector, matrix, or data frame with compatible dimensions to x. If x is a matrix or data frame, y can be missing (or NULL).
use = "everything"	This optional character string defines how to deal with missing values. The default is "everything", but other options are "all.obs", "complete.obs", "na.or.complete", and "pairwise.complete.obs".
method = "pearson"	There are three methods of calculating correlation; the default is "pearson". Other options are "spearman" and "kendall".

Examples

```
  ## Make data
> w = c(2, 5, 6, 3, 8, 1)
> x = c(2, 4, 5, 2, 8, 3)
> y = c(7, 8, 6, 8, 9, 7)
> z = c(1, 2, 2, 4, 2, 5)

> d1 = data.frame(w, x, y, z)
> d2 = data.frame(w, z)

  ## Correlations
> cor(w, y, method = "kendall") # Two vectors
[1] 0.3580574

> cor(d1) # Entire data frame using default "pearson"
           w          x         y          z
w  1.0000000  0.8971800 0.3973597 -0.4865197
x  0.8971800  1.0000000 0.4181210 -0.2912759
y  0.3973597  0.4181210 1.0000000  0.0000000
z -0.4865197 -0.2912759 0.0000000  1.0000000

> cor(d1$x, d1, method = "spearman") # 1 variable against the remainder
          w x         y          z
[1,] 0.8116794 1 0.2089785 -0.09240617

> cor(d1$w, d1[,3:4]) # One variable against some of the others
             y          z
[1,] 0.3973597 -0.4865197

> cor(d1, d2, method = "pearson") # One data frame against another
           w          z
w  1.0000000 -0.4865197
x  0.8971800 -0.2912759
y  0.3973597  0.0000000
z -0.4865197  1.0000000
```

COMMAND NAME

`cor.test`

This command carries out correlation significance tests using one of several methods:

- Pearson Product Moment
- Spearman's Rho Rank correlation
- Kendall's Tau Rank correlation

The result is a list with a `class` attribute `"htest"`. The command accepts input in the form of a `formula`.

Common Usage

```
cor.test(x, ...)

cor.test(x, y, alternative = "two.sided", method = "pearson", exact = NULL,
         conf.level = 0.95, continuity = FALSE, ...)

cor.test(formula, data, subset, na.action, ...)
```

Related Commands

cor (p. 267)
cov (p. 271)
var (p. 273)
cov2cor (p. 272)

Command Parameters

`x, y`	Numeric vectors of data values; these must be of the same length.
`alternative = "two.sided"`	Specifies the alternative hypothesis; the default is `"two.sided"`, with `"greater"` or `"less"` as other options.
`method = "pearson"`	There are three methods of calculating correlation; the default is `"pearson"`. Other options are `"spearman"` and `"kendall"`.
`exact = NULL`	If `exact = TRUE`, for Spearman and Kendall methods an exact p-value is calculated.
`conf.level = 0.95`	The confidence level used for the Pearson method.
`continuity = FALSE`	If `continuity = TRUE`, a continuity correction is used for Spearman and Kendall methods.
`formula`	The data can be specified as a `formula` of the form ~ x + y.
`data`	A data frame or matrix that contains the variables specified in the `formula`.

subset	A subset of observations to be used; of the form subset = group %in% c("a", "b", ...).
na.action	What to do if the data contains NA items. The default is to use the current settings (usually "na.omit").
...	Other parameters.

Examples

```
  ## Make data
> w = c(2, 5, 6, 3, 8, 1)
> x = c(2, 4, 5, 2, 8, 3)
> y = c(7, 8, 6, 8, 9, 7)
> z = c(1, 2, 2, 4, 2, 5)
> d1 = data.frame(w, x, y, z)

  ## Correlation Tests
  ## Use two vectors
> cor.test(w, y, method = "kendall", exact = FALSE)

        Kendall's rank correlation tau

data:  w and y
z = 0.9744, p-value = 0.3299
alternative hypothesis: true tau is not equal to 0
sample estimates:
      tau
0.3580574

  ## Use formula input and default method = "pearson"
> cor.test(~ w + z, data = d1)

        Pearson's product-moment correlation

data:  w and z
t = -1.1137, df = 4, p-value = 0.3278
alternative hypothesis: true correlation is not equal to 0
95 percent confidence interval:
 -0.9306304  0.5371173
sample estimates:
       cor
-0.4865197
```

```
## Formula input
> cor.test(~ x + z, data = d1, method = "spearman",
 exact = FALSE, continuity = TRUE)

        Spearman's rank correlation rho

data:  x and z
S = 38.2342, p-value = 0.907
alternative hypothesis: true rho is not equal to 0
sample estimates:
        rho
-0.09240617
```

COMMAND NAME

cov

This command calculates covariance on vectors of data or columns of data frames or matrix objects. The result is either a vector or a matrix, depending on the input data. A covariance matrix can be converted to a correlation matrix using the cov2cor command.

Common Usage

```
cov(x, y = NULL, use = "everything", method = "pearson")
```

Related Commands

var (p. 273)
cor (p. 267)
cor.test (p. 269)
cov2cor (p. 272)

Command Parameters

x	Numeric data; this can be a vector, matrix, or data frame.
y = NULL	A vector, matrix, or data frame with compatible dimensions to x. If x is a matrix or data frame, y can be missing (or NULL).
use = "everything"	This optional character string defines how to deal with missing values. The default is "everything" but other options are "all.obs", "complete.obs", "na.or.complete", and "pairwise.complete.obs".
method = "pearson"	You have three methods of calculating covariance; the default is "pearson". Other options are "spearman" and "kendall".

Examples

```
  ## Make data
> w = c(2, 5, 6, 3, 8, 1)
> x = c(2, 4, 5, 2, 8, 3)
> y = c(7, 8, 6, 8, 9, 7)
> z = c(1, 2, 2, 4, 2, 5)

> d1 = data.frame(w, x, y, z)
> d2 = data.frame(w, z)

  ## Covariance
> cov(w, y, method = "kendall") # Two vectors
[1] 10

> cov(d1) # Entire data frame
          w    x   y          z
w  6.966667  5.4 1.1 -1.933333
x  5.400000  5.2 1.0 -1.000000
y  1.100000  1.0 1.1  0.000000
z -1.933333 -1.0 0.0  2.266667

> cov(d1$x, d1, method = "spearman") # 1 variable against the remainder
      w   x   y    z
[1,] 2.8 3.4 0.7 -0.3

> cov(d1$w, d1[,3:4]) # One variable against some of the others
       y         z
[1,] 1.1 -1.933333

> cov(d1, d2, method = "pearson") # One frame against another
          w         z
w  6.966667 -1.933333
x  5.400000 -1.000000
y  1.100000  0.000000
z -1.933333  2.266667
```

COMMAND NAME

cov2cor

This command produces a correlation matrix from a covariance matrix.

Common Usage

cov2cor(V)

Related Commands

cov (p. 271)
cor (p. 267)
var (p. 273)

Command Parameters

v   A symmetric numeric matrix, usually a covariance matrix.

Examples

```
  ## Make data
> w = c(2, 5, 6, 3, 8, 1)
> x = c(2, 4, 5, 2, 8, 3)
> y = c(7, 8, 6, 8, 9, 7)
> z = c(1, 2, 2, 4, 2, 5)

> d1 = data.frame(w, x, y, z)

  ## Make covariance matrix
> (cv1 = cov(d1))
        w      x    y         z
w  6.966667   5.4 1.1 -1.933333
x  5.400000   5.2 1.0 -1.000000
y  1.100000   1.0 1.1  0.000000
z -1.933333  -1.0 0.0  2.266667

  ## Produce correlation matrix from covariance
  ## Same result as cor(d1)
> cov2cor(cv1)
           w           x         y          z
w  1.0000000  0.8971800 0.3973597 -0.4865197
x  0.8971800  1.0000000 0.4181210 -0.2912759
y  0.3973597  0.4181210 1.0000000  0.0000000
z -0.4865197 -0.2912759 0.0000000  1.0000000
```

COMMAND NAME

var

This command calculates the variance of numeric vectors. If more than one vector is given or the input is a matrix or data frame, the command determines covariance.

Common Usage

```
var(x, y = NULL, na.rm = FALSE, use)
```

Related Commands

sd (p. 231)
cov (p. 271)
cor (p. 267)
cov2cor (p. 272)

Command Parameters

x	Numeric data; this can be a vector, matrix, or data frame.
y = NULL	A vector, matrix, or data frame with compatible dimensions to x. If x is a matrix or data frame, y can be missing (or NULL).
na.rm = FALSE	If na.rm = TRUE, NA items are omitted.
use = "everything"	This optional character string defines how to deal with missing values. The default is "everything" but other options are "all.obs", "complete.obs", "na.or.complete", and "pairwise.complete.obs".

Examples

```
  ## Make data
> w = c(2, 5, 6, 3, 8, 1)
> x = c(2, 4, 5, 2, 8, 3)
> y = c(7, 8, 6, 8, 9, 7)
> z = c(1, 2, 2, 4, 2, 5)

> d1 = data.frame(w, x, y, z)
> d2 = data.frame(w, z)

  ## Variance
> var(w) # Variance of a single vector
[1] 6.966667

> var(w, z) # Covariance for two vectors
[1] -1.933333

> var(d1) # Covariance of entire data frame
          w    x   y         z
w  6.966667  5.4 1.1 -1.933333
x  5.400000  5.2 1.0 -1.000000
y  1.100000  1.0 1.1  0.000000
z -1.933333 -1.0 0.0  2.266667

> var(d1$w, d1) # Covariance of one variable to rest of data frame
           w   x   y         z
[1,] 6.966667 5.4 1.1 -1.933333

> var(d1, d2) # Covariance of two data frames
          w         z
w  6.966667 -1.933333
x  5.400000 -1.000000
y  1.100000  0.000000
z -1.933333  2.266667
```

ASSOCIATION AND GOODNESS OF FIT

Association tests differ from correlations in that data are categorical (sometimes called "count" or "frequency" data).

COMMAND NAME

`binom.test`

This command carries out an exact binomial test. In other words, it tests the probability of success in a Bernoulli experiment. The result is a list with a `class` attribute `"htest"`.

Common Usage

```
binom.test(x, n, p = 0.5, alternative = "two.sided", conf.level = 0.95)
```

Related Commands

`prop.test` (p. 281)
`fisher.test` (p. 278)

Command Parameters

`x`	A numeric value for the number of successes. Can also be a vector of two values giving the successes and failures, respectively.
`n`	The number of trials. This is ignored if x is a vector of length 2.
`p = 0.5`	The hypothesized probability of success; the default is 0.5.
`alternative = "two.sided"`	A character string specifying the alternative hypothesis. The default is `"two.sided"`, with `"greater"` or `"less"` as other options.
`conf.level = 0.95`	The confidence level for the confidence interval reported in the result.

Examples

```
## Make data
## Mendelian genetics: cross between two genotypes produces
## 1/4 progeny "dwarf", 3/4 progeny "giant"
## Experimental trials produce results:
> dwarf = 243
> giant = 682
```

```
## Binomial test
> binom.test(giant, dwarf + giant, p = 3/4) # Assume "giant" is success

        Exact binomial test

data: giant and dwarf + giant
number of successes = 682, number of trials = 925, p-value = 0.3825
alternative hypothesis: true probability of success is not equal to 0.75
95 percent confidence interval:
 0.7076683 0.7654066
sample estimates:
probability of success
              0.7372973


> binom.test(c(dwarf, giant), p = 1/4) # Assume "dwarf" is success

        Exact binomial test

data:  c(dwarf, giant)
number of successes = 243, number of trials = 925, p-value = 0.3825
alternative hypothesis: true probability of success is not equal to 0.25
95 percent confidence interval:
 0.2345934 0.2923317
sample estimates:
probability of success
              0.2627027
```

COMMAND NAME

`chisq.test`

This command carries out chi-squared tests of association or goodness of fit. The result is a list with a `class` attribute "htest". The command accepts input in various ways and this determines whether an association or goodness of fit test is carried out:

- If you provide a two-dimensional contingency table (as a matrix or data frame), an association test is conducted.

- If you provide two factors, a contingency table is constructed from those and an association test is conducted.

- If you provide a one-dimensional input, a goodness of fit test is conducted. If you also provide the probabilities, these are used in the test; if not, the test assumes equal probability.

Common Usage

```
chisq.test(x, y = NULL, correct = TRUE, p = rep(1/length(x), length(x)),
          rescale.p = FALSE, simulate.p.value = FALSE, B = 2000)
```

Related Commands

ks.test (p. 237)
fisher.test (p. 278)
binom.test (p. 275)

Command Parameters

x	A numeric vector or matrix. Can also be a factor. If x and y are both factors, a contingency table is constructed and a test of association conducted. If x is a matrix with more than one row or column, and y is not given, a test of association is conducted.
y = NULL	A numeric vector or matrix. Can also be a factor. If y is not given and x is a vector or a matrix with a single row (or column), a goodness of fit test is carried out.
correct = TRUE	By default, the Yates' correction is applied to 2×2 contingency tables. Use correct = FALSE to not apply the correction.
p	A vector of probabilities the same length as x. If p is given, a goodness of fit test is conducted. If p is not given, the goodness of fit test assumes equal probabilities.
rescale.p = FALSE	If rescale.p = TRUE, the values in p are rescaled so that they sum to 1.
simulate.p.value = FALSE	If this is TRUE, a Monte Carlo simulation is used to compute p-values.
B = 2000	The number of replicates to use in the simulation of the p-value.

Examples

```
  ## Make data
> Gdn = c(47, 19, 50) # Count data
> Hdg = c(10, 3, 0) # Count data
> Prk = c(40, 5, 10) # Count data

> ct = data.frame(Gdn, Hdg, Prk) # Make a data frame
> rownames(ct) = c("Bbrd", "Cfnc", "GrtT") # Assign row names

> (ct.cs = chisq.test(ct)) # The chi-sq test of association

        Pearson's Chi-squared test

data:  ct
X-squared = 22.5888, df = 4, p-value = 0.0001530

Warning message:
In chisq.test(ct) : Chi-squared approximation may be incorrect
```

```
> names(ct.cs) # Show items in result
[1] "statistic" "parameter" "p.value" "method" "data.name" "observed" "expected"
[8] "residuals"

> ct.cs$obs # Observed values
     Gdn Hdg Prk
Bbrd  47  10  40
Cfnc  19   3   5
GrtT  50   0  10

> ct.cs$exp # Expected values
          Gdn       Hdg        Prk
Bbrd 61.15217 6.853261 28.994565
Cfnc 17.02174 1.907609  8.070652
GrtT 37.82609 4.239130 17.934783

> ct.cs$res # Pearson residuals
           Gdn        Hdg        Prk
Bbrd -1.8097443  1.2020211  2.043849
Cfnc  0.4794923  0.7909219 -1.080877
GrtT  1.9794042 -2.0589149 -1.873644

  ## Use Mont-Carlo simulation
> chisq.test(ct, simulate.p.value = TRUE)

 Pearson's Chi-squared test with simulated p-value
 (based on 2000 replicates)

data:  ct
X-squared = 22.5888, df = NA, p-value = 0.0004998

  ## A Goodness of Fit test
> chisq.test(Gdn, p = Prk, rescale.p = TRUE)

        Chi-squared test for given probabilities

data:  Gdn
X-squared = 62.9515, df = 2, p-value = 2.139e-14
```

COMMAND NAME

`fisher.test`

This command carries out Fisher's exact test of association. The result is a list with a class attribute "htest".

Common Usage

```
fisher.test(x, y = NULL, hybrid = FALSE, or = 1,
            alternative = "two.sided", conf.int = TRUE,
            conf.level = 0.95, simulate.p.value = FALSE, B = 2000)
```

Related Commands

chisq.test (p. 276)
binom.test (p. 275)

Command Parameters

x	A two-dimensional contingency table or a factor object.
y = NULL	A factor object. If x is a contingency table, y is ignored. If x is also a factor, a contingency table is constructed from x and y. Vectors are coerced into factors.
hybrid = FALSE	For tables larger than 2×2 if hybrid = TRUE, a hybrid approximation of the probabilities is computed instead of an exact probability.
or = 1	For tables larger than 2×2, the hypothesized odds ratio.
alternative = "two.sided"	For 2×2 tables this specifies the alternative hypothesis; other options are "greater" and "less".
conf.int = TRUE	By default, the confidence intervals are computed.
conf.level = 0.95	The confidence level used.
simulate.p.value = FALSE	If this is TRUE, a Monte Carlo simulation is used to compute p-values for tables larger than 2×2.
B = 2000	The number of replicates to use in the simulation of the p-value.

Examples

```
  ## Make data
  ## Do two plant species tend to grow together?
  ## Make matrix contingency table (1st cell shows co-occurrence)
> nd = matrix(c(9, 3, 4, 5), nrow = 2,
  dimnames = list(Dock = c("d+", "d-"), Nettle = c("n+", "n-")))

> nd
    Nettle
Dock n+ n-
  d+  9  4
  d-  3  5

> fisher.test(nd) # Carry out test

        Fisher's Exact Test for Count Data

data:  nd
p-value = 0.2031
alternative hypothesis: true odds ratio is not equal to 1
95 percent confidence interval:
  0.4284363 35.6068875
```

```
sample estimates:
odds ratio
  3.502144


  ## Data as factors
  ## Presence/absence data
> nettle = c(1,1,1,1,1,1,1,1,1,1,1,1,0,0,0,0,0,0,0,0,0)
> dock = c(1,1,1,1,1,1,1,1,1,0,0,0,1,1,1,1,0,0,0,0,0)

> fisher.test(nettle, dock) # Same result as previous
```

COMMAND NAME

power.prop.test

Calculates the power of a proportion test or determines the parameters required to achieve a certain power. The result is an object with the class attribute "power.htest".

Common Usage

```
power.prop.test(n = NULL, p1 = NULL, p2 = NULL, sig.level = 0.05,
                power = NULL, alternative = "two.sided", strict = FALSE)
```

Related Commands

prop.test (p. 281)
binom.test (p. 275)

Command Parameters

n = NULL	The number of observations (per group).
p1 = NULL	The probability in one group.
p2 = NULL	The probability in other group.
sig.level = 0.05	The significance level (Type I error probability). This must be specified as NULL if you wish to compute it for other given parameters.
power = NULL	The power of the test, that is, 1 minus (Type II error probability).
alternative = "two.sided"	By default, a two-sided test is computed; use alternative = "one.sided" for a one-sided test.
strict = FALSE	If strict = TRUE, the strict interpretation is used in the two-sided case.

Examples

```
  ## Power of Proportion Test
> power.prop.test(n = 100, p1 = 0.5, p2 = 0.7) # Find power of test

     Two-sample comparison of proportions power calculation

              n = 100
             p1 = 0.5
             p2 = 0.7
      sig.level = 0.05
          power = 0.8281094
    alternative = two.sided


NOTE: n is number in *each* group

> power.prop.test(p1 = 0.5, p2 = 0.7, power = 0.9) # Find n given others

     Two-sample comparison of proportions power calculation

              n = 123.9986
             p1 = 0.5
             p2 = 0.7
      sig.level = 0.05
          power = 0.9
    alternative = two.sided


NOTE: n is number in *each* group

  ## Significance must be specified as NULL to find it given others
> power.prop.test(n = 100, p1 = 0.5, p2 = 0.7, power = 0.9, sig.level = NULL)

     Two-sample comparison of proportions power calculation

              n = 100
             p1 = 0.5
             p2 = 0.7
      sig.level = 0.1026686
          power = 0.9
    alternative = two.sided


NOTE: n is number in *each* group
```

COMMAND NAME

`prop.test`

Tests for equal (or given) proportions. This can be used for testing the null hypothesis that the proportions (probabilities of success) in several groups are the same, or that they equal certain given values. The result is a list with a `class` attribute "htest".

Common Usage

```
prop.test(x, n, p = NULL, alternative = "two.sided",
          conf.level = 0.95, correct = TRUE)
```

Related Commands

binom.test (p. 275)
power.prop.test (p. 280)

Command Parameters

x	A vector giving the counts of successes. Can also give successes and failures as a table (or matrix) with two columns.
n	A vector giving the number of trials; ignored if x is a matrix or table.
p = NULL	A vector giving the probabilities of success. By default this is NULL, whereby the probability is assumed to be equal (or 0.5 if there is only one group).
alternative = "two.sided"	The alternative hypothesis: the default is "two.sided" but "greater" and "less" are other options.
conf.level = 0.95	The confidence level of the computed confidence interval. Only used when testing that a single proportion equals a given value, or that two proportions are equal.
correct = TRUE	By default, Yates' correction is applied where possible.

Examples

```
  ## Proportion Test
  ## Test equality of proportions
> smokers  = c( 83, 90, 129, 70 )
> patients = c( 86, 93, 136, 82 )

> prop.test(smokers, n = patients)

 4-sample test for equality of proportions without continuity correction

data:  smokers out of patients
X-squared = 12.6004, df = 3, p-value = 0.005585
alternative hypothesis: two.sided
sample estimates:
   prop 1    prop 2    prop 3    prop 4
0.9651163 0.9677419 0.9485294 0.8536585
```

```
  ## Flip a coin
> prop.test(45, n = 100) # One set of trials

        1-sample proportions test with continuity correction

data:  45 out of 100, null probability 0.5
X-squared = 0.81, df = 1, p-value = 0.3681
alternative hypothesis: true p is not equal to 0.5
95 percent confidence interval:
 0.3514281 0.5524574
sample estimates:
   p
0.45


  ## Multiple trials
> prop.test(c(33, 43, 53), n = rep(100, 3), p = rep(0.5, 3)) # 3 sets

        3-sample test for given proportions without continuity correction

data:  c(33, 43, 53) out of rep(100, 3), null probabilities rep(0.5, 3)
X-squared = 13.88, df = 3, p-value = 0.003073
alternative hypothesis: two.sided
null values:
prop 1 prop 2 prop 3
   0.5    0.5    0.5
sample estimates:
prop 1 prop 2 prop 3
  0.33   0.43   0.53


  ## Give data as success/failure
> sf = cbind(result = c(33, 43, 53), fail = c(67, 57, 47))
> sf # Success/fail matrix
     result fail
[1,]     33   67
[2,]     43   57
[3,]     53   47


> prop.test(sf, p = rep(0.5, 3)) # Same result as previous
```

Analysis of Variance and Linear Modeling

Analysis of variance (ANOVA) and linear modeling are important and widely used methods of analysis. The commands rely on input being in the form of a `formula`. A `formula` allows a complex analytical situation to be described in a logical manner.

 SEE also `formula` for details.

What's In This Topic:

- **Analysis of variance (ANOVA)** (p. 284)
  - Model formulae
  - Model terms
  - Multivariate analysis of variance
  - Post-hoc testing (Tukey's HSD)
  - Replications
- **Linear modeling** (p. 300)
  - Best-fit lines
  - Coefficients
  - Confidence intervals
  - Generalized linear modeling
  - Model building
  - Model distribution families
  - Residuals

ANOVA

Analysis of variance and linear modeling are very similar. ANOVA tends to be used when you have discrete levels of variables and linear modeling is used for when the variables are continuous. The commands rely on input being in the form of a `formula`. A `formula` allows a complex analytical situation to be described in a logical manner.

 SEE `formula` for details.

COMMAND NAME

anova

This command computes analysis of variance (or deviance) tables for one or more fitted-model objects. You can use this to compare multiple models or to produce the "classic" ANOVA table from a linear model result. Multiple models are compared in the order they are specified (they must be based on the same data set).

 SEE anova under "Linear Modeling."

COMMAND NAME

`aov`

Carries out analysis of variance. The input uses a `formula`, which specifies the variables and how they are to be modeled. The `aov` command is essentially a call to the `lm` command, but it differs in that an `Error` term can be specified. Multiple response variables can be given. The default contrasts used in R are not orthogonal and it is often advisable to have them so.

 SEE `formula` and `manova` for details. See `contrasts` for details of contrast options.

Common Usage

```
aov(formula, data = NULL, projections = FALSE, qr = TRUE,
    contrasts = NULL, ...)
```

Related Commands

`lm` (p. 312)
`manova` (p. 292)
`anova` (p. 284)
`TukeyHSD` (p. 298)

Command Parameters

`formula`	A formula that specifies the variables and how they are to be modeled. See `formula`. Multiple response variables can be given; see `manova` for details.
`data`	Specifies a data frame where the variables to be modeled are to be found.
`projections = FALSE`	If `TRUE`, the projections are returned as part of the result object.
`qr = TRUE`	By default, the QR decomposition is returned as part of the result object.
`contrasts = NULL`	A list of contrasts to be used for some of the factors in the formula. These are not used for any `Error` term, and supplying contrasts for factors only in the `Error` term will give a warning.
`...`	Other commands can be used; e.g., `subset` and `na.action`.

Examples

```
## Make data
> height = c(9, 11, 6, 14, 17, 19, 28, 31, 32, 7, 6, 5, 14, 17, 15, 44, 38, 37)
> plant = gl(2, 9, labels = c("vulgaris", "sativa"))
> water = gl(3, 3, 18, labels = c("mid", "hi", "lo"))
```

```
> aov1 = aov(height ~ plant * water) # two-way anova with interaction
> summary(aov1) # Summary "classic" anova table
             Df  Sum Sq Mean Sq  F value    Pr(>F)
plant         1   14.22   14.22   2.4615  0.142644
water         2 2403.11 1201.56 207.9615 4.863e-10 ***
plant:water   2  129.78   64.89  11.2308  0.001783 **
Residuals    12   69.33    5.78
---
Signif. codes:  0 '***' 0.001 '**' 0.01 '*' 0.05 '.' 0.1 ' ' 1

> names(aov1) # The elements in the result object
 [1] "coefficients" "residuals"    "effects"      "rank"         "fitted.values"
 [6] "assign"       "qr"           "df.residual"  "contrasts"    "xlevels"
[11] "call"         "terms"        "model"

> aov2 = aov(height ~ plant) # one-way anova
> summary(aov2)
             Df  Sum Sq Mean Sq F value Pr(>F)
plant         1   14.22  14.222  0.0874 0.7713
Residuals    16 2602.22 162.639

  ## Use explicit Error term (not a sensible model!)
> aov3 = aov(height ~ plant + Error(water)) # Explicit Error term
> summary(aov3)

Error: water
          Df Sum Sq Mean Sq F value Pr(>F)
Residuals  2 2403.1  1201.6

Error: Within
          Df  Sum Sq Mean Sq F value Pr(>F)
plant      1  14.222  14.222       1 0.3343
Residuals 14 199.111  14.222
```

COMMAND NAME

contrasts

C

contr.xxxx

These commands get and set contrast options for factor objects that are used in linear modeling (including ANOVA). Replace xxxx with the type of contrast you wish to set (see the following common usage and examples).

Common Usage

```
contrasts(x, contrasts = TRUE, sparse = FALSE)
contrasts(x, how.many) <- value

C(object, contr, how.many, ...)

contr.helmert(n, contrasts = TRUE, sparse = FALSE)
contr.poly(n, scores = 1:n, contrasts = TRUE, sparse = FALSE)
contr.sum(n, contrasts = TRUE, sparse = FALSE)
contr.treatment(n, base = 1, contrasts = TRUE, sparse = FALSE)
contr.SAS(n, contrasts = TRUE, sparse = FALSE)
```

Related Commands

aov (p. 285)
lm (p. 312)
glm (p. 310)

Command Parameters

x	A factor or logical variable.
contrasts = TRUE	If contrasts = FALSE, an identity matrix is returned. If contrasts = TRUE, the contrasts are returned from the current contrasts option. The parameter is ignored if x is a matrix with a contrasts attribute.
sparse = FALSE	If TRUE, a sparse matrix is returned.
how.many	The number of contrasts to create; defaults to one less than the number of levels in x.
object	A factor (can be ordered).
contr	Which contrasts to use. This can be given as a matrix with one row for each level of the factor or a suitable function like contr.xxxx or a character string giving the name of the function.
...	Additional parameters to pass to contr.xxxx.
n	A vector of levels for a factor or the number of levels required.
scores = 1:n	The set of values over which orthogonal polynomials are to be computed.
base	An integer specifying which group is considered the baseline group. Ignored if contrasts is FALSE.

Examples

```
  ## Make data
> res = c(9, 6, 14, 19, 28, 32, 7, 5, 14, 15, 44, 37)
> pr1 = gl(2, 6, labels = c("A", "B"))
> pr2 = gl(3, 2, 12, labels = c("m", "h", "l"))
> dat = data.frame(res, pr1, pr2)
```

```
> contrasts(pr1) # Get current contrasts from options if not set already
  B
A 0
B 1
> contrasts(pr1) = "contr.helmert" # Set contrasts explicitly
> contrasts(pr1) # See the new settings
  [,1]
A   -1
B    1


> contrasts(pr1) = "contr.treatment"
> attributes(pr1) # See the $contrasts setting with the others
$levels
[1] "A" "B"

$class
[1] "factor"

$contrasts
[1] "contr.treatment"

> attr(pr1, which = "contrasts") # View contrast attr explicitly
[1] "contr.treatment"

> contrasts(pr2, contrasts = FALSE) # Identity matrix
  m h l
m 1 0 0
h 0 1 0
l 0 0 1

> options("contrasts") # See general setting
$contrasts
        unordered           ordered
"contr.treatment"       "contr.poly"

  ## New setting
> op = options(contrasts = c("contr.helmert", "contr.poly"))
  ## Various commands that require these contrast settings e.g. aov()
> options(op) # Set back to original

> contr.SAS(pr1) # Make contrast matrix using SAS style contrasts
  A A A A A A B B B B
A 1 0 0 0 0 0 0 0 0 0
A 0 1 0 0 0 0 0 0 0 0
A 0 0 1 0 0 0 0 0 0 0
A 0 0 0 1 0 0 0 0 0 0
A 0 0 0 0 1 0 0 0 0 0
A 0 0 0 0 0 1 0 0 0 0
B 0 0 0 0 0 0 1 0 0 0
B 0 0 0 0 0 0 0 1 0 0
```

```
B 0 0 0 0 0 0 0 0 1 0 0
B 0 0 0 0 0 0 0 0 0 1 0
B 0 0 0 0 0 0 0 0 0 0 1
B 0 0 0 0 0 0 0 0 0 0 0

> C(pr1, contr = contr.treatment) # Set contrasts
 [1] A A A A A A B B B B B B
attr(,"contrasts")
   2
A 0
B 1
Levels: A B

> contr.helmert(3) # Contrast matrix for 3 levels
  [,1] [,2]
1   -1   -1
2    1   -1
3    0    2
```

COMMAND NAME

effects

This command returns the (orthogonal) effects from a fitted-model object. The result is a named vector with a class attribute "coef".

Common Usage

effects(object)

Related Commands

coef (p. 304)
coefficients (p. 304)

Command Parameters

object   An R object; usually one resulting from a model fitting command; e.g., lm.

Examples

```
  ## Make data
> count = c(9, 25, 15, 2, 14, 25, 24, 47)
> speed = c(2, 3, 5, 9, 14, 24, 29, 34)

> fw.lm = lm(count ~ speed) # A simple linear model
> summary(fw.lm)
```

```
Call:
lm(formula = count ~ speed)

Residuals:
    Min      1Q  Median      3Q     Max
-13.377  -5.801  -1.542   5.051  14.371

Coefficients:
            Estimate Std. Error t value Pr(>|t|)
(Intercept)   8.2546     5.8531   1.410   0.2081
speed         0.7914     0.3081   2.569   0.0424 *
---
Signif. codes:  0 '***' 0.001 '**' 0.01 '*' 0.05 '.' 0.1 ' ' 1

Residual standard error: 10.16 on 6 degrees of freedom
Multiple R-squared: 0.5238,     Adjusted R-squared: 0.4444
F-statistic: 6.599 on 1 and 6 DF,  p-value: 0.0424

> effects(fw.lm) # Orthogonal effects
(Intercept)        speed
-56.9220959  26.1028966    0.6904209 -14.0717679  -4.2745040
                           2.3200240  -0.8827121

 19.9145519
attr(,"assign")
[1] 0 1
attr(,"class")
[1] "coef"
```

COMMAND NAME

`formula`

The `formula` syntax is used by many commands to describe a model situation. The general form is often `response ~ predictor` but some commands also use `response ~ groups | blocks`. See the following command parameters for details. The `formula` command extracts the formula used to create a result (see the following examples).

Common Usage

```
formula(object)
```

```
y ~ x
```

Related Commands

aov (p. 285)
lm (p. 312)

Command Parameters

In the following, A, B, and C represent factors, whereas x and y represent numerical variables.

y ~ A	One-way analysis of variance.
y ~ A + x	Single classification analysis of covariance model of y, with classes determined by A and covariate x.
y ~ A * B y ~ A + B + A:B	Two-factor non-additive analysis of variance of y on factors A and B, that is, with interactions.
y ~ B %in% A y ~ A/B	Nested analysis of variance with B nested in A.
y ~ A + B %in% A y ~ A + A:B	Nested analysis of variance with factor A plus B nested in A.
y ~ A * B * C y ~ A + B + C + A:B + A:C + B:C + A:B:C	Three-factor experiment with complete interactions between factors A, B, and C.
y ~ (A + B + C)^2 y ~ (A + B + C) * (A + B + C) y ~ A * B * C – A:B:C y ~ A + B + C + A:B + A:C + B:C	Three-factor experiment with model containing main effects and two-factor interactions only.
y ~ A * B + Error(C)	An experiment with two treatment factors, A and B, and error strata determined by factor C. For example, a split plot experiment, with whole plots (and hence also sub-plots), determined by factor C. The Error term can be used only with the aov command.
y ~ A + I(A + B) y ~ A + I(A^2)	The I() insulates the contents from the formula meaning and allows mathematical operations. In the first example, you have an additive two-way analysis of variance with A and the sum of A and B. In the second example, you have a polynomial analysis of variance with A and the square of A.

Examples

```
  ## Make data
> count = c(9, 25, 15, 2, 14, 25, 24, 47)
> speed = c(2, 3, 5, 9, 14, 24, 29, 34)

> fw.lm = lm(count ~ speed) # A linear model

> formula(fw.lm) # Extract the formula
count ~ speed
```

COMMAND NAME

`interaction.plot`

Provides a graphical illustration of possible factor interactions. The command plots the mean (or other summary) of the response variable for two-way combinations of factors.

 **SEE** Theme 3, "Graphics."

COMMAND NAME

manova

This command carries out multivariate analysis of variance. An Error term cannot be included. Essentially the manova command is a wrapper for aov, but with special extra parameters and a summary method. The result of a manova is an object with a class attribute "manova". The result of summary.manova is an object with a class attribute "summary.manova".

 SEE also aov.

Common Usage

```
manova(formula, data, ...)

summary.manova(object, test = "Pillai", intercept = FALSE, tol = 1e-7, ...)
```

Related Commands

aov (p. 285)
lm (p. 312)

Command Parameters

formula	A formula giving the model to use. The general form is response ~ predictor. The response part must be a matrix or data frame with columns representing each response variable.
data	A data frame that contains the (predictor) variables.
object	An R object with class "manova" or an aov object with multiple response variables.
test = "Pillai"	The test statistic to use; defaults to "Pillai". Other options are "Wilks", "Hotelling-Lawley", and "Roy". The name can be abbreviated.
intercept = FALSE	If TRUE, the intercept is included in the summary.
tol = 1e-7	A tolerance to use if residuals are rank deficient (see qr).
...	Other commands; e.g., subset.

Examples

```
   ## Make data
> height = c(9, 11, 6, 14, 17, 19, 28, 31, 32, 7, 6, 5, 14, 17, 15, 44, 38, 37)
> plant = gl(2, 9, labels = c("vulgaris", "sativa"))
> water = gl(3, 3, 18, labels = c("mid", "hi", "lo"))
> set.seed(9) # Random number seed
> seeds = as.integer(height * runif(18, 0.5, 1.5)) # A new variable

   ## MANOVA. Make response matrix "on the fly"
> pw.man = manova(cbind(seeds, height) ~ water) # Basic manova

> pw.man # Basic result
Call:
   manova(cbind(seeds, height) ~ water)

Terms:
                  water Residuals
resp 1           3159.0     725.5
resp 2        2403.1111  213.3333
Deg. of Freedom       2        15

Residual standard error: 6.954615 3.771236
Estimated effects may be unbalanced

> summary(pw.man) # Summary default Pillai-Bartlett statistic
          Df  Pillai approx F num Df den Df    Pr(>F)
water      2 0.92458    6.448      4     30 0.0007207 ***
Residuals 15
---
Signif. codes:  0 '***' 0.001 '**' 0.01 '*' 0.05 '.' 0.1 ' ' 1

> summary(pw.man, test = "Wilks") # Summary with different statistic
          Df    Wilks approx F num Df den Df    Pr(>F)
water      2 0.080835   17.620      4     28 2.485e-07 ***
Residuals 15
---
Signif. codes:  0 '***' 0.001 '**' 0.01 '*' 0.05 '.' 0.1 ' ' 1

> anova(pw.man) # ANOVA table
Analysis of Variance Table

            Df  Pillai approx F num Df den Df    Pr(>F)
(Intercept)  1 0.96977  224.556      2     14 2.307e-11 ***
water        2 0.92458    6.448      4     30 0.0007207 ***
Residuals   15
---
Signif. codes:  0 '***' 0.001 '**' 0.01 '*' 0.05 '.' 0.1 ' ' 1
```

```
> pw.aov = aov(cbind(seeds, height) ~ water)  # Use aov command

> summary(pw.aov)
 Response seeds :
          Df Sum Sq Mean Sq F value    Pr(>F)
water      2 3159.0 1579.50  32.657 3.426e-06 ***
Residuals 15  725.5   48.37
---
Signif. codes:  0 '***' 0.001 '**' 0.01 '*' 0.05 '.' 0.1 ' ' 1

 Response height :
          Df  Sum Sq Mean Sq F value    Pr(>F)
water      2 2403.11 1201.56  84.484 6.841e-09 ***
Residuals 15  213.33   14.22
---
Signif. codes:  0 '***' 0.001 '**' 0.01 '*' 0.05 '.' 0.1 ' ' 1
```

COMMAND NAME

`model.tables`

This command computes some tables of results from aov model fits.

Common Usage

`model.tables(x, type = "effects", se = FALSE, cterms)`

Related Commands

aov (p. 285)
lm (p. 312)
anova (p. 284)
replications (p. 297)

Command Parameters

x	A fitted-model result.
type = "effects"	The type of table to produce; the default is "effects" with "means" as an alternative.
se = FALSE	If se = TRUE, standard errors are computed (only for balanced designs).
cterms	A character vector giving the tables to produce; the default is all tables.

Examples

```
  ## Make data
> height = c(9, 11, 6, 14, 17, 19, 28, 31, 32, 7, 6, 5, 14, 17, 15, 44, 38, 37)
> plant = gl(2, 9, labels = c("vulgaris", "sativa"))
> water = gl(3, 3, 18, labels = c("mid", "hi", "lo"))

> aov1 = aov(height ~ plant * water) # Two-way with interaction (balanced)

  ## Show mean tables and std error for interaction term only
> model.tables(aov1, se = TRUE, type = "means", cterms = "plant:water")
Tables of means
Grand mean

19.44444


 plant:water
         water
plant     mid    hi    lo
  vulgaris  8.67 16.67 30.33
  sativa    6.00 15.33 39.67


Standard errors for differences of means
        plant:water
              1.963
replic.           3

  ## Show effects tables and std error for "water" only
> model.tables(aov1, se = TRUE, type = "effects", cterms = "water")
Tables of effects

 water
water
    mid      hi      lo
-12.111  -3.444  15.556


Standard errors of effects
        water
        0.9813
replic.      6
```

COMMAND NAME

power.anova.test

Calculates the power of a one-way ANOVA (balanced) or determines the parameters required to achieve a certain power. You can also determine the value of any one parameter by setting all the others to NULL.

Common Usage

```
power.anova.test(groups = NULL, n = NULL, between.var = NULL,
                within.var = NULL, sig.level = 0.05, power = NULL)
```

Related Commands

anova (p. 284)
lm (p. 312)

Command Parameters

groups = NULL	The number of groups.
n = NULL	The number of observations (per group).
between.var = NULL	The between-group variance.
within.var = NULL	The within-group variance (the variance of the error term).
sig.level = 0.05	The significance level (Type I error probability). If you wish to determine this when other parameters are given you set this to NULL.
power = NULL	The power of the test, that is, 1 minus (Type II error probability).

Examples

```
## Determine power given all the other parameters
> power.anova.test(groups = 4, n = 6, between.var = 2, within.var = 3)

     Balanced one-way analysis of variance power calculation

          groups = 4
               n = 6
     between.var = 2
      within.var = 3
       sig.level = 0.05
           power = 0.7545861

 NOTE: n is number in each group

 ## Determine significance for given power and other parameters
> power.anova.test(groups = 4, n = 6, between.var = 2, within.var = 3,
 power = 0.9, sig.level = NULL)

     Balanced one-way analysis of variance power calculation

          groups = 4
               n = 6
     between.var = 2
      within.var = 3
       sig.level = 0.1438379
           power = 0.9

 NOTE: n is number in each group
```

COMMAND NAME

`replications`

Determines the number of replicates for each term in a model. The variables must be in a data frame for this to work properly. If the model is balanced, the result is a vector; otherwise, it is a list object. This can be used as the basis for a test of balance (see the following examples).

Common Usage

```
replications(formula, data = NULL, na.action)
```

Related Commands

`model.tables` (p. 294)

Command Parameters

`formula`   A formula; usually this will be of the form `response ~ predictor`.

`data = NULL`   The data frame where the variables contained in the `formula` are to be found. If the `formula` is a data frame and `data = NULL`, all the factors in the specified data frame are used.

`na.action`   A function for handling missing values; defaults to whatever is set in `options("na.action")`; usually this is `"na.omit"`, which omits NA items.

Examples

```
  ## Make a data frame (response and two factors)
> my.df = data.frame(resp = 1:12, pr1 = gl(3,4), pr2 = gl(2,1,12))

> replications(my.df) # Entire data frame
pr1 pr2
  4   6
Warning message:
In replications(my.df) : non-factors ignored: resp

> replications(resp ~ pr1 * pr2, data = my.df) # Show replicates
   pr1     pr2 pr1:pr2
     4       6       2


  ## Test of balance (produces TRUE as it is balanced)
> !is.list(replications(resp ~ pr1 * pr2, data = my.df))
[1] TRUE

> my.df[4, 2] = 2 # Make the data slightly unbalanced

> replications(resp ~ pr1 * pr2, data = my.df) # Show replicates
$pr1
pr1
1 2 3
3 5 4
```

```
$pr2
[1] 6

$`pr1:pr2`
   pr2
pr1 1 2
   1 2 1
   2 2 3
   3 2 2


  ## Test of balance (produces FALSE as it is unbalanced)
> !is.list(replications(resp ~ pr1 * pr2, data = my.df))
[1] FALSE
```

COMMAND NAME

TukeyHSD

Carries out Tukey's Honest Significant Difference post-hoc tests. This command creates a set of confidence intervals on the differences between means of the levels of factors. These confidence intervals are based on the Studentized range statistic. The result of the command is a list containing the statistics for each factor requested.

 SEE also qtukey in Theme 1, "Data: Distribution of Data."

Common Usage

```
TukeyHSD(x, which, ordered = FALSE, conf.level = 0.95)
```

Related Commands

aov (p. 285)
qtukey (p. 158)
model.tables (p. 294)

Command Parameters

x	A fitted-model object, usually from aov.
which	A character vector giving the terms of the model for which confidence intervals are required. The default is all terms.
ordered = FALSE	If ordered = TRUE, the levels of the factors are ordered in increasing mean. The result is that all differences in means are reported as positive values.
conf.level = 0.95	The confidence level to use; defaults to 0.95.

Examples

```
## Make data
> height = c(9, 11, 6, 14, 17, 19, 28, 31, 32, 7, 6, 5, 14, 17, 15, 44, 38, 37)
> plant = gl(2, 9, labels = c("A", "B"))
> water = gl(3, 3, 18, labels = c("m", "h", "l"))

> aov1 = aov(height ~ plant * water) # An ANOVA

> TukeyHSD(aov1, ordered = TRUE) # Post-hoc test
  Tukey multiple comparisons of means
    95% family-wise confidence level
    factor levels have been ordered

Fit: aov(formula = height ~ plant * water)

$plant
        diff        lwr      upr     p adj
B-A 1.777778 -0.6910687 4.246624 0.142644


$water
         diff       lwr      upr     p adj
h-m  8.666667  4.964266 12.36907 0.0001175
l-m 27.666667 23.964266 31.36907 0.0000000
l-h 19.000000 15.297599 22.70240 0.0000000


$`plant:water`
              diff         lwr      upr     p adj
A:m-B:m  2.666667 -3.92559686  9.258930 0.7490956
B:h-B:m  9.333333  2.74106981 15.925597 0.0048138
A:h-B:m 10.666667  4.07440314 17.258930 0.0016201
A:l-B:m 24.333333 17.74106981 30.925597 0.0000004
B:l-B:m 33.666667 27.07440314 40.258930 0.0000000
B:h-A:m  6.666667  0.07440314 13.258930 0.0469217
A:h-A:m  8.000000  1.40773647 14.592264 0.0149115
A:l-A:m 21.666667 15.07440314 28.258930 0.0000014
B:l-A:m 31.000000 24.40773647 37.592264 0.0000000
A:h-B:h  1.333333 -5.25893019  7.925597 0.9810084
A:l-B:h 15.000000  8.40773647 21.592264 0.0000684
B:l-B:h 24.333333 17.74106981 30.925597 0.0000004
A:l-A:h 13.666667  7.07440314 20.258930 0.0001702
B:l-A:h 23.000000 16.40773647 29.592264 0.0000007
B:l-A:l  9.333333  2.74106981 15.925597 0.0048138


## Plot the Tukey result (Figure 2-2)
> plot(TukeyHSD(aov1, ordered = TRUE), las = 1, cex.axis = 0.8)
```

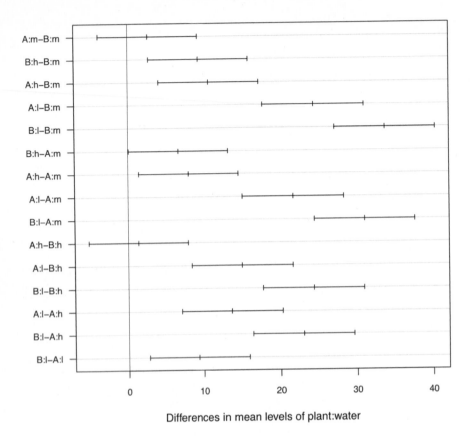

Figure 2-2: Plot of TukeyHSD result.

LINEAR MODELING

Linear modeling is carried out with various commands in R. Various "helper" commands also undertake a variety of useful associated functions.

COMMAND NAME

`abline`

Adds straight lines to a plot. This command can be used to add lines of best fit to fitted models. The command can accept input in various ways:

- Intercept and slope given explicitly

- Intercept and slope taken from fitted-model object

The command can also add vertical or horizontal lines to an existing plot.

SEE also Theme 3, "Graphics."

Common Usage

```
abline( a = NULL, b = NULL, reg = NULL, coef = NULL, untf = FALSE, ...)
```

Related Commands

plot (p. 382)
lm (p. 312)
fitted (p. 309)

Command Parameters

a = NULL	The intercept.
b = NULL	The slope.
reg = NULL	An R object with a coef method.
coef = NULL	A vector of length 2, giving the intercept and slope.
untf = FALSE	If untf = TRUE, and one or both axes are log-transformed, a curve is drawn corresponding to a line in original coordinates; otherwise, a line is drawn in the transformed coordinate system.
...	Other graphical parameters including col, lty, and lwd.

Examples

```
  ## Make data
> count = c(9, 25, 15, 2, 14, 25, 24, 47)
> speed = c(2, 3, 5, 9, 14, 24, 29, 34)

  ## Linear model
> lm1 = lm(count ~ speed)

  ## Plot variables (not shown)
> plot(count ~ speed)

  ## Lines of best fit
> abline(reg = lm1) # From model result
> abline(coef = coef(lm1)) # Coefficients
> abline(a = 8.25, b = 0.79) # Intercept and Slope
```

COMMAND NAME

add1

Adds all possible single terms to a model. This command is used to build a model by adding the "best" variable to an existing model. The result shows the AIC value for each possible term. Optionally, you can show a significance statistic.

Common Usage
```
add1(object, scope, test = "none")
```

Related Commands
drop1 (p. 306)
step (p. 315)
lm (p. 312)

Command Parameters

object	An R object, usually a fitted-model.
scope	A formula giving the terms to be considered for adding to the existing model.
test = "none"	A character string giving the name of a test statistic to compute for each variable as if it had been added to the original model. The default is "none"; other options are "Chisq" and "F". The F-test is only appropriate for lm and aov models. The Chi-squared test can be an exact test for lm models, or a likelihood ratio test, or test of the reduction in scaled deviance depending on the model type.

Examples
```
> data(swiss) # Link to data (in package:datasets)
> names(swiss) # Show variables
[1] "Fertility"      "Agriculture"    "Examination"    "Education"
[5] "Catholic"       "Infant.Mortality"

  ## Build a linear model
  ## Start with "blank" model containing intercept only
> lm1 = lm(Fertility ~ 1, data = swiss)
> lm1

Call:
lm(formula = Fertility ~ 1, data = swiss)

Coefficients:
(Intercept)
      70.14

  ## Evaluate each term to be added to existing model singly
> add1(lm1, scope = swiss, test = "F")
Single term additions

Model:
Fertility ~ 1
            Df Sum of Sq    RSS    AIC F value    Pr(F)
<none>                   7178.0 238.34
Agriculture  1     894.8 6283.1 234.09  6.4089 0.014917 *
Examination  1    2994.4 4183.6 214.97 32.2087 9.450e-07 ***
```

```
Education        1    3162.7 4015.2 213.04 35.4456 3.659e-07 ***
Catholic         1    1543.3 5634.7 228.97 12.3251  0.001029 **
Infant.Mortality 1    1245.5 5932.4 231.39  9.4477  0.003585 **
---
Signif. codes:  0 '***' 0.001 '**' 0.01 '*' 0.05 '.' 0.1 ' ' 1
```

COMMAND NAME

anova

This command computes analysis of variance (or deviance) tables for one or more fitted-model objects. You can use this to compare multiple models or to produce the "classic" ANOVA table from a linear model result. Multiple models are compared in the order they are specified (they must be based on the same data set).

Common Usage

```
anova(object, ...)
```

Related Commands

aov (p. 285)
lm (p. 312)
coefficients (p. 304)
effects (p. 289)
fitted (p. 309)
residuals (p. 314)

Command Parameters

object   An object containing the results obtained by a model fitting such as lm or glm.

...   Additional fitted-model objects.

Examples

```
  ## Make data
> height = c(9, 11, 6, 14, 17, 19, 28, 31, 32, 7, 6, 5, 14, 17, 15, 44, 38, 37)
> plant = gl(2, 9, labels = c("vulgaris", "sativa"))
> water = gl(3, 3, 18, labels = c("mid", "hi", "lo"))

  ## Make linear models
> lm1 = lm(height ~ plant + water) # Additive
> lm2 = lm(height ~ plant * water) # Interaction

  ## Make ANOVA tables
> anova(lm1) # Classic ANOVA table
```

```
Analysis of Variance Table

Response: height
          Df  Sum Sq Mean Sq F value    Pr(>F)
plant      1   14.22   14.22   1.000    0.3343
water      2 2403.11 1201.56  84.484 1.536e-08 ***
Residuals 14  199.11   14.22
---
Signif. codes:  0 '***' 0.001 '**' 0.01 '*' 0.05 '.' 0.1 ' ' 1


> anova(lm1, lm2) # Compare models
Analysis of Variance Table

Model 1: height ~ plant + water
Model 2: height ~ plant * water
  Res.Df     RSS Df Sum of Sq      F   Pr(>F)
1     14 199.111
2     12  69.333  2    129.78 11.231 0.001783 **
---
Signif. codes:  0 '***' 0.001 '**' 0.01 '*' 0.05 '.' 0.1 ' ' 1
```

COMMAND NAME

```
coef
coefficients
```

This command extracts model coefficients from fitted-model objects. The `coefficients` command is an alias for the generic command `coef`.

Common Usage

```
coef(object)
coefficients(object)
```

Related Commands

fitted (p. 309)
residuals (p. 314)
lm (p. 312)

Command Parameters

object   An R object that contains coefficients; the result of `lm` or `glm`, for example.

Examples

```
  ## Make data
> count = c(9, 25, 15, 2, 14, 25, 24, 47)
> speed = c(2, 3, 5, 9, 14, 24, 29, 34)
```

```
   ## A linear model
> lm1 = lm(count ~ speed)

   ## The coefficients
> coef(lm1)
(Intercept)        speed
  8.2545956    0.7913603

   ## Produce the same result
> coefficients(lm1)
> lm1$coefficients

> ## Data for ANOVA
> height = c(9, 11, 6, 14, 17, 19, 28, 31, 32, 7, 6, 5, 14, 17, 15, 44, 38, 37)
> plant = gl(2, 9, labels = c("A", "B"))
> water = gl(3, 3, 18, labels = c("m", "h", "l"))

   ## Make an aov object
> aov1 = aov(height ~ plant * water)

   ## The coefficients
> coef(aov1)
  (Intercept)       plantB        waterh        waterl  plantB:waterh  plantB:waterl
     8.666667    -2.666667      8.000000     21.666667       1.333333      12.000000
```

COMMAND NAME

confint

This command computes confidence intervals for one or more parameters in a fitted-model (for example, resulting from lm or glm).

Common Usage

confint(object, parm, level = 0.95)

Related Commands

fitted (p. 309)
abline (p. 300)
lm (p. 312)

Command Parameters

object   A fitted-model object; from lm, for example.

parm   A vector of numbers or characters stating which parameters are to be given
               confidence intervals. If not given, all parameters are used.

level = 0.95   The confidence level required.

```
  ## Make data
> count = c(9, 25, 15, 2, 14, 25, 24, 47)
> speed = c(2, 3, 5, 9, 14, 24, 29, 34)
> algae = c(75, 66, 54, 45, 48, 23, 9, 11)

  ## A linear model
> lm1 = lm(count ~ speed + algae)

  # CI for all terms
> confint(lm1, level = 0.99)
                 0.5 %       99.5 %
(Intercept) -210.594559 128.830182
speed         -2.614892    6.881866
algae         -1.698137    3.100186

  ## CI for only one term
> confint(lm1, parm = "algae")
         2.5 %    97.5 %
algae -0.828495 2.230544
```

COMMAND NAME

drop1

This command takes a fitted-model object and removes terms one by one. The result allows you to decide if terms can be dropped from the model as part of a backwards deletion process.

 SEE drop for reducing dimensions of arrays. See droplevels for dropping unused levels of a factor, in Theme 1, "Data."

Common Usage

drop1(object, scope, test = "none")

Related Commands

add1 (p. 301)
step (p. 315)
lm (p. 312)

Command Parameters

object   A fitted-model object.

scope   A formula giving the terms to be considered for dropping from the existing model.

test = "none"   A character string giving the name of a test statistic to compute for each variable as if it had been added to the original model. The default is "none"; other options are "Chisq" and "F". The F-test is only appropriate for lm and aov models. The Chi-squared test can be an exact test for lm models, or a likelihood ratio test, or test of the reduction in scaled deviance depending on the model type.

Examples

```
> data(swiss) # Link to data (in package:datasets)
> names(swiss) # Show the variables
[1] "Fertility"      "Agriculture"   "Examination"   "Education"
[5] "Catholic"       "Infant.Mortality"

  ## A linear model, note use of . to denote "everything else"
> lm1 = lm(Fertility ~ ., data = swiss) # A model with all terms

> drop1(lm1, scope = lm1, test = "Chisq")
Single term deletions

Model:
Fertility ~ Agriculture + Examination + Education + Catholic +
    Infant.Mortality
                 Df Sum of Sq    RSS     AIC    Pr(Chi)
<none>                        2105.0  190.69
Agriculture       1    307.72 2412.8  195.10  0.011332 *
Examination       1     53.03 2158.1  189.86  0.279550
Education         1   1162.56 3267.6  209.36  5.465e-06 ***
Catholic          1    447.71 2552.8  197.75  0.002608 **
Infant.Mortality  1    408.75 2513.8  197.03  0.003877 **
---
Signif. codes:  0 '***' 0.001 '**' 0.01 '*' 0.05 '.' 0.1 ' ' 1
```

COMMAND NAME

family

This command provides a mechanism to query or specify distribution model parameters for fitted models. The command is used in two main ways:

- To query the distribution model parameters of an object.

- To specify a distribution type in a model such as a generalized linear model via the glm command.

Common Usage

```
family(object)

binomial(link = "logit")
gaussian(link = "identity")
Gamma(link = "inverse")
inverse.gaussian(link = "1/mu^2")
poisson(link = "log")
quasi(link = "identity", variance = "constant")
quasibinomial(link = "logit")
quasipoisson(link = "log")
```

Related Commands

glm (p. 310)

Command Parameters

object An R object for which you wish to know the distribution model.

link The model link function; usually specified as a character string.

Examples

```
  ## Data for glm binomial model
> lat = c(48.1, 45.2, 44.0, 43.7, 43.5, 37.8, 36.6, 34.3)
> a90 = c(47, 177, 1087, 187, 397, 40, 39, 30)
> a100 = c(139, 241, 1183, 175, 671, 14, 17, 0)

  ## Use family to set the distribution type
> glm1 = glm(cbind(a100, a90) ~ lat, family = binomial)

> family(glm1) # Get the distribution family from result

Family: binomial
Link function: logit

  ## A linear model
> lm1 = lm(1:10 ~ c(5:10, 1:4))

> family(lm1) # Get the distribution family

Family: gaussian
Link function: identity
```

COMMAND NAME

```
fitted
fitted.values
```

This command extracts model fitted values from objects that are created by modeling commands, for example `lm`, and `glm`. The `fitted.values` command is an alias for the `fitted` command.

Common Usage

```
fitted(object)
fitted.values(object)
```

Related Commands

coef (p. 304)
residuals (p. 314)
lm (p. 312)
glm (p. 310)

Command Parameters

object   An R object that contains fitted values, usually from a command that produces a fitted-model; for example, aov, lm, glm.

Examples

```
## A binomial generalized linear model (logistic regression)
## The data
> lat = c(48.1, 45.2, 44.0, 43.7, 43.5, 37.8, 36.6, 34.3)
> a90 = c(47, 177, 1087, 187, 397, 40, 39, 30)
> a100 = c(139, 241, 1183, 175, 671, 14, 17, 0)

## The generalized linear model
> glm1 = glm(cbind(a100, a90) ~ lat, family = binomial)

## A linear model
## The data
> count = c(9, 25, 15, 2, 14, 25, 24, 47)
> speed = c(2, 3, 5, 9, 14, 24, 29, 34)
> algae = c(75, 66, 54, 45, 48, 23, 9, 11)

## The linear model
> lm1 = lm(count ~ speed + algae)

## Fitted values
> fitted(glm1)
        1         2         3         4         5         6         7         8
0.7202510 0.6053128 0.5531198 0.5398384 0.5309514 0.2902269 0.2481226 0.1795320
> fitted(lm1)
         1         2         3         4         5         6         7         8
15.961615 11.785882  7.640563  9.865292 22.635800 26.445059 27.298153 39.367636
```

```
## Access fitted values via model result directly
> glm1$fitted # Same as before
> lm1$fitted  # Same as before
```

COMMAND NAME

glm

This command carries out generalized linear modeling. The modeling can use a variety of
distribution functions. The result is a list object with a class attribute "glm".

 SEE also family.

Common Usage

```
glm(formula, family = gaussian, data, subset, na.action)
```

Related Commands

anova (p. 284)
aov (p. 285)
lm (p. 312)

Command Parameters

formula	A formula giving a symbolic description of the model to be fitted. Usually this is in the form response ~ predictor.
family = gaussian	A description of the error distribution and link function to be used in the model. This can be specified as a family function or a character string.
data	The data frame containing the variables specified in the formula.
subset	An optional subset of observations to be used, usually in the form subset = predictor %in% c("a", "b", ...).
na.action	A function for handling missing values; defaults to whatever is set in options("na.action"). Usually this is "na.omit", which omits NA items.

Examples

```
  ## A Poisson model
> counts <- c(18,17,15,20,10,20,25,13,12)
> outcome <- gl(3,1,9)
> treatment <- gl(3,3)
```

```
> glm1 = glm(counts ~ outcome + treatment, family = poisson)
> anova(glm1, test = "Chisq")
Analysis of Deviance Table

Model: poisson, link: log

Response: counts

Terms added sequentially (first to last)


          Df Deviance Resid. Df Resid. Dev P(>|Chi|)
NULL                         8      10.5814
outcome    2    5.4523       6       5.1291   0.06547 .
treatment  2    0.0000       4       5.1291   1.00000
---
Signif. codes:  0 '***' 0.001 '**' 0.01 '*' 0.05 '.' 0.1 ' ' 1

   ## A binomial generalized linear model (logistic regression)
   ## The data
> lat = c(48.1, 45.2, 44.0, 43.7, 43.5, 37.8, 36.6, 34.3)
> a90 = c(47, 177, 1087, 187, 397, 40, 39, 30)
> a100 = c(139, 241, 1183, 175, 671, 14, 17, 0)

> glm1 = glm(cbind(a100, a90) ~ lat, family = binomial)
> anova(glm1, test = "Chisq")
Analysis of Deviance Table

Model: binomial, link: logit

Response: cbind(a100, a90)

Terms added sequentially (first to last)


      Df Deviance Resid. Df Resid. Dev P(>|Chi|)
NULL                      7     153.633
lat    1   83.301         6      70.333 < 2.2e-16 ***
---
Signif. codes:  0 '***' 0.001 '**' 0.01 '*' 0.05 '.' 0.1 ' ' 1

   ## A gaussian linear model
   ## The data
> count = c(9, 25, 15, 2, 14, 25, 24, 47)
> speed = c(2, 3, 5, 9, 14, 24, 29, 34)
> algae = c(75, 66, 54, 45, 48, 23, 9, 11)
```

```
  ## Same result as lm
> glm1 = glm(count ~ speed + algae, family = gaussian)
> anova(glm1, test = "F")
Analysis of Deviance Table

Model: gaussian, link: identity

Response: count

Terms added sequentially (first to last)


      Df Deviance Resid. Df Resid. Dev      F  Pr(>F)
NULL                     7    1300.88
speed  1   681.36        6     619.51 7.0258 0.04539 *
algae  1   134.62        5     484.90 1.3881 0.29174
---
Signif. codes:  0 '***' 0.001 '**' 0.01 '*' 0.05 '.' 0.1 ' ' 1
```

COMMAND NAME

lm

This command is used to fit linear models. The model is described in a formula which enables complex models to be symbolized. The lm command is something of a workhorse, and allows regression, analysis of variance, and covariance to be carried out. For some models the aov command is more appropriate; Error terms, for example, are not used in lm. The result of using lm is a list object that has a class attribute "lm".

 SEE also formula in "ANOVA."

Common Usage

lm(formula, data, subset, na.action)

Related Commands

glm (p. 310)
aov (p. 285)
anova (p. 284)

Command Parameters

formula	A formula giving a symbolic description of the model to be fitted. Usually this is in the form `response ~ predictor`.
data	The data frame containing the variables specified in the `formula`.
subset	An optional subset of observations to be used, usually in the form `subset = predictor %in% c("a", "b", ...)`.
na.action	A function for handling missing values; defaults to whatever is set in `options("na.action")`. Usually this is `"na.omit"`, which omits NA items.

Examples

```
  ## Some data
> count = c(9, 25, 15, 2, 14, 25, 24, 47)  # Response
> speed = c(2, 3, 5, 9, 14, 24, 29, 34)    # Predictor
> algae = c(75, 66, 54, 45, 48, 23, 9, 11) # Predictor

  ## The model
> lm1 = lm(count ~ speed + algae)

> summary(lm1)

Call:
lm(formula = count ~ speed + algae)

Residuals:
    1      2      3      4      5      6      7      8
-6.962 13.214  7.359 -7.865 -8.636 -1.445 -3.298  7.632

Coefficients:
            Estimate Std. Error t value Pr(>|t|)
(Intercept)  -40.882     42.090  -0.971    0.376
speed          2.134      1.178   1.812    0.130
algae          0.701      0.595   1.178    0.292

Residual standard error: 9.848 on 5 degrees of freedom
Multiple R-squared: 0.6273,     Adjusted R-squared: 0.4782
F-statistic: 4.207 on 2 and 5 DF, p-value: 0.08483

> anova(lm1)
Analysis of Variance Table

Response: count
          Df Sum Sq Mean Sq F value  Pr(>F)
speed      1 681.36  681.36  7.0258 0.04539 *
algae      1 134.62  134.62  1.3881 0.29174
Residuals  5 484.90   96.98
---
Signif. codes:  0 '***' 0.001 '**' 0.01 '*' 0.05 '.' 0.1 ' ' 1
```

COMMAND NAME

```
resid
residuals
```

This command extracts residuals from fitted-model objects that have been returned by modeling functions. The `residuals` command is the generic command and `resid` is an alias for it.

Common Usage

```
resid(object)
residuals(object)
```

Related Commands

```
coef (p. 304)
fitted (p. 309)
```

Command Parameters

object   An R object containing residuals; for example, the result from aov, `lm`, or `glm` commands.

Examples

```
   ## Logistic (binomial) regression
> lat = c(48.1, 45.2, 44.0, 43.7, 43.5, 37.8, 36.6, 34.3)
> a90 = c(47, 177, 1087, 187, 397, 40, 39, 30)
> a100 = c(139, 241, 1183, 175, 671, 14, 17, 0)

   ## The glm
> glm1 = glm(cbind(a100, a90) ~ lat, family = binomial)
> resid(glm1)
          1          2          3          4          5          6          7
 0.8307678 -1.1982004 -3.0582160 -2.1493279  6.4204595 -0.5070130  0.9392368
          8
-3.4456961

> glm1$residuals # Same as resid()

   ## Linear regression
> count = c(9, 25, 15, 2, 14, 25, 24, 47)
> speed = c(2, 3, 5, 9, 14, 24, 29, 34)
> algae = c(75, 66, 54, 45, 48, 23, 9, 11)

   ## The lm
> lm1 = lm(count ~ speed + algae)
> resid(lm1)
          1          2          3          4          5          6          7          8
-6.961615 13.214118  7.359437 -7.865292 -8.635800 -1.445059 -3.298153  7.632364

> lm1$residuals # Same as resid()
```

COMMAND NAME

step

This command conducts stepwise model building using forwards or backwards algorithms. AIC is used in the decision-making process.

Common Usage

```
step(object, scope, direction = "both", trace = 1, steps = 1000, k = 2)
```

Related Commands

add1 (p. 301)
drop1 (p. 306)
lm (p. 312)

Command Parameters

object	An object representing the initial model; this could be a model result or a formula.
scope	This defines the range of models to be considered. Usually this is defined using a list that gives the lower and upper models as formulae (see the following examples).
direction = "both"	Sets the direction for the model building operation. The default is "both", with "forward" and "backward" as other options.
trace = 1	If trace = 0, no intermediate steps are reported. Setting a value > 1 can give additional information.
steps = 1000	The number of steps to use; the default is 1000.
k = 2	Sets the multiple of the number of degrees of freedom used for the penalty. Use k = 2 (the default) for AIC. Setting k = log(n) equates to BIC (aka SBC).
...	Additional parameters; for example, test (see anova).

Examples

```
  ## Make data
> count = c(9, 25, 15, 2, 14, 25, 24, 47)        # Response
> speed = c(2, 3, 5, 9, 14, 24, 29, 34)          # Predictor
> algae = c(75, 66, 54, 45, 48, 23, 9, 11)       # Predictor
> oxyge = c(35, 68, 40, 42, 44, 80, 72, 95)      # Predictor
> lmdat = data.frame(count, speed, algae, oxyge) # Make data frame

 ## Start with intercept and run forwards
  ## Only single term (oxyge) is added
> step(lm(count~1, data = lmdat), scope = list(lower = ~1, upper = lmdat),
 direction = "forward", trace = 1, test = "F")
Start:  AIC=42.73
count ~ 1
```

```
          Df Sum of Sq    RSS    AIC F value    Pr(F)
+ oxyge  1    1082.40  218.48 30.458 29.7254 0.001584 **
+ speed  1     681.36  619.51 38.796  6.5990 0.042401 *
+ algae  1     497.67  803.20 40.873  3.7177 0.102108
<none>                1300.88 42.731
---
Signif. codes:  0 '***' 0.001 '**' 0.01 '*' 0.05 '.' 0.1 ' ' 1

Step:  AIC=30.46
count ~ oxyge

         Df Sum of Sq    RSS    AIC F value  Pr(F)
<none>                218.48 30.458
+ algae  1   14.5897 203.89 31.905  0.3578 0.5758
+ speed  1    0.8597 217.62 32.426  0.0198 0.8937


Call:
lm(formula = count ~ oxyge, data = lmdat)

Coefficients:
(Intercept)        oxyge
   -13.2702       0.5613


> data(swiss)  # Data are in package:datasets
> names(swiss) # View variables (Fertility = response)
[1] "Fertility"      "Agriculture"    "Examination"      "Education"
[5] "Catholic"       "Infant.Mortality"

  ## Start with everything and run backwards
  ## One term is dropped (Examination) from model
> step(lm(Fertility~., data = swiss), scope = list(lower = ~1, upper = swiss),
 direction = "backward", trace = 1, test = "F")
Start:  AIC=190.69
Fertility ~ Agriculture + Examination + Education + Catholic +
    Infant.Mortality

                  Df Sum of Sq    RSS    AIC F value    Pr(F)
- Examination      1     53.03 2158.1 189.86  1.0328  0.315462
<none>                         2105.0 190.69
- Agriculture      1    307.72 2412.8 195.10  5.9934  0.018727 *
- Infant.Mortality 1    408.75 2513.8 197.03  7.9612  0.007336 **
- Catholic         1    447.71 2552.8 197.75  8.7200  0.005190 **
- Education        1   1162.56 3267.6 209.36 22.6432 2.431e-05 ***
---
Signif. codes:  0 '***' 0.001 '**' 0.01 '*' 0.05 '.' 0.1 ' ' 1

Step:  AIC=189.86
Fertility ~ Agriculture + Education + Catholic + Infant.Mortality
```

```
                Df Sum of Sq    RSS    AIC F value     Pr(F)
<none>                        2158.1 189.86
- Agriculture       1    264.18 2422.2 193.29  5.1413   0.02857 *
- Infant.Mortality  1    409.81 2567.9 196.03  7.9757   0.00722 **
- Catholic          1    956.57 3114.6 205.10 18.6165 9.503e-05 ***
- Education         1   2249.97 4408.0 221.43 43.7886 5.140e-08 ***
---
Signif. codes:  0 '***' 0.001 '**' 0.01 '*' 0.05 '.' 0.1 ' ' 1

Call:
lm(formula = Fertility ~ Agriculture + Education + Catholic +
    Infant.Mortality, data = swiss)

Coefficients:
    (Intercept)     Agriculture     Education      Catholic
        62.1013        -0.1546        -0.9803        0.1247
Infant.Mortality
         1.0784
```

Miscellaneous Methods

The analytical methods outlined in this section do not fit easily into the previous categories. The first group of commands deals with clustering. The second group covers ordination, which has foundations in matrix math. The third group covers analytical methods connected with time series. The fourth group covers non-linear modeling.

What's In This Topic:

- **Clustering** (p. 318)

  - Dissimilarity indices

  - Hierarchical clustering

  - K-means

  - Tree cutting

- **Ordination** (p. 324)

  - Multidimensional scaling (principal coordinates analysis)

  - Principal components analysis

- **Time series** (p. 331)

- **Non-linear modeling and optimization** (p. 333)

  - Locally weighted polynomial regression (scatter plot smoothing)

  - Non-linear modeling

  - Optimization

CLUSTERING

R has a range of commands connected with analytical routines concerned with clustering. These methods include the construction of distance matrices and hierarchical dendrograms as well as k-means analysis.

COMMAND NAME

`cutree`

This command cuts a tree into groups of data. Generally the tree will have been created by the `hclust` command. You can specify the number of groups to produce or the cut height(s) to use to cut the tree.

Common Usage

```
cutree(tree, k = NULL, h = NULL)
```

Related Commands

`hclust` (p. 321)
`dist` (p. 319)

Command Parameters

`tree`   A hierarchical clustering tree object, usually produced by `hclust`.

`k = NULL`   The number of groups desired.

`h = NULL`   The heights where the tree should be cut.

Examples

 USE cd data in `Essential.RData` file for these examples.

```
> load("Essential.RData") # Get datafile
> rownames(cd)            # Rows are used as samples
 [1] "ML1" "ML2" "MU1" "MU2" "PL2" "PU2" "SL1" "SL2" "SU1" "SU2"

  ## Create Hierarchical cluster object
> cd.eu = dist(cd, method = "euclidian")     # Distance matrix
> cd.hc = hclust(cd.eu, method = "complete") # Hierarchical cluster

  ## Assign 5 groups and show membership
> cutree(cd.hc, k = 5)
ML1 ML2 MU1 MU2 PL2 PU2 SL1 SL2 SU1 SU2
  1   2   2   1   3   4   4   5   5   5
```

```
   ## Show multiple groups.. grp 1 is trivial
> cutree(cd.hc, k = 1:5)
    1 2 3 4 5
ML1 1 1 1 1 1
ML2 1 1 2 2 2
MU1 1 1 2 2 2
MU2 1 1 1 1 1
PL2 1 2 3 3 3
PU2 1 1 2 2 4
SL1 1 1 2 2 4
SL2 1 2 3 4 5
SU1 1 2 3 4 5
SU2 1 2 3 4 5

> cd.hc$height # View cut heights
[1] 11.46996 15.22104 15.63458 16.20247 16.90444 21.83941 22.11063 26.38863
[9] 26.81567

   ## Select height and show membership
> cutree(cd.hc, h = 20)
ML1 ML2 MU1 MU2 PL2 PU2 SL1 SL2 SU1 SU2
  1   2   2   1   3   4   4   5   5   5
```

COMMAND NAME

dist

This command computes distance matrices (that is, dissimilarity). Various algorithms can be used (see the following command parameters). The result is an object with a class attribute "dist". There is a dedicated print routine for "dist" objects.

Common Usage

```
dist(x, method = "euclidian", diag = FALSE, upper = FALSE, p = 2)
```

Related Commands

hclust (p. 321)
cutree (p. 318)

Command Parameters

x	Numerical data in a data frame or matrix.
method = "euclidian"	The method used to generate the distances; the default is "euclidian". Other options are "maximum", "manhattan", "canberra", "binary", and "minkowski".

diag = FALSE	If diag = TRUE, the diagonal of the matrix is given. This actually sets an attribute of the result so it is possible to create a "dist" object with diag = FALSE but use print with diag = TRUE (see the following examples).
upper = FALSE	If upper = TRUE, the upper quadrant is given (in addition to the lower). This sets an attribute of the result so it is possible to create a "dist" object with one setting and print the opposite.
p = 2	The power of the Minkowski distance.

Examples

 USE cd data in Essential.RData file for these examples.

```
> load("Essential.RData") # Get datafile
> rownames(cd)              # Rows are used as samples
 [1] "ML1" "ML2" "MU1" "MU2" "PL2" "PU2" "SL1" "SL2" "SU1" "SU2"

  ## Use Euclidian algorithm
> cd.eu = dist(cd, method = "euclidian")
> print(cd.eu, digits = 4) # Show the result
      ML1   ML2   MU1   MU2   PL2   PU2   SL1   SL2   SU1
ML2 21.82
MU1 20.42 16.90
MU2 15.63 22.35 24.73
PL2 26.34 21.78 23.21 25.90
PU2 21.84 18.64 21.61 26.39 23.17
SL1 25.12 19.89 21.84 25.20 19.01 15.22
SL2 21.14 21.25 22.47 21.86 18.46 19.52 17.62
SU1 26.35 24.85 26.13 26.82 20.83 23.59 19.58 16.20
SU2 24.45 25.79 26.39 25.49 22.11 23.45 21.38 11.47 13.12

  ## Use Binary algorithm
> cd.bn = dist(cd, method = "binary", upper = TRUE, diag = TRUE)
> print(cd.bn, digits = 2, diag = FALSE)
     ML1  ML2  MU1  MU2  PL2  PU2  SL1  SL2  SU1  SU2
ML1       0.59 0.50 0.55 0.92 0.76 0.93 0.92 0.95 0.95
ML2 0.59       0.46 0.42 0.84 0.77 0.86 0.89 0.87 0.95
MU1 0.50 0.46       0.48 0.87 0.72 0.88 0.88 0.86 0.91
MU2 0.55 0.42 0.48       0.88 0.81 0.89 0.91 0.92 0.97
PL2 0.92 0.84 0.87 0.88       0.80 0.79 0.81 0.82 0.89
PU2 0.76 0.77 0.72 0.81 0.80       0.83 0.87 0.88 0.88
SL1 0.93 0.86 0.88 0.89 0.79 0.83       0.75 0.66 0.80
SL2 0.92 0.89 0.88 0.91 0.81 0.87 0.75       0.69 0.75
SU1 0.95 0.87 0.86 0.92 0.82 0.88 0.66 0.69       0.61
SU2 0.95 0.95 0.91 0.97 0.89 0.88 0.80 0.75 0.61
```

COMMAND NAME

hclust

This command carries out hierarchical clustering. The command takes a matrix of distances (dissimilarity) and creates an object with a class attribute "hclust". There is a special version of the plot command for "hclust" objects; see the following examples.

 SEE also plot in Theme 3.

Common Usage

hclust(d, method = "complete")

Related Commands

cutree (p. 318)
dist (p. 319)
kmeans (p. 322)

Command Parameters

d A dissimilarity matrix; usually this is produced by the dist command.

method = "complete" The method of agglomeration to be used; the default is "complete", with other options being "ward", "single", "average", "mcquitty", "median", and "centroid".

Examples

 USE cd data in Essential.RData file for these examples.

```
> load("Essential.RData") # Get datafile
> rownames(cd)            # Rows are used as samples
 [1] "ML1" "ML2" "MU1" "MU2" "PL2" "PU2" "SL1" "SL2" "SU1" "SU2"

  ## Create Hierarchical cluster object
> cd.eu = dist(cd, method = "euclidian")    # Distance matrix

> cd.hc = hclust(cd.eu, method = "complete") # Hierarchical cluster
> cd.hc         # The result

Call:
hclust(d = cd.eu, method = "complete")

Cluster method   : complete
Distance         : euclidean
Number of objects: 10
```

```
> names(cd.hc) # Show result components
[1] "merge"        "height"      "order"       "labels"      "method"      "call"
[7] "dist.method"

  ## Use plot to create dendrogram (Figure 2-3)
> plot(cd.hc)
```

Cluster Dendrogram

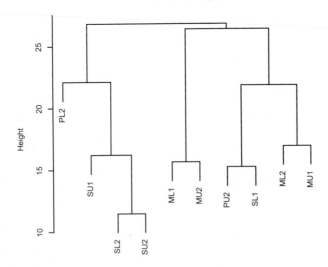

cd.eu
hclust (*, "complete")

Figure 2-3: Dendrogram of hierarchical cluster analysis

COMMAND NAME

kmeans

This command carries out k-means clustering on a data matrix.

Common Usage

kmeans(x, centers, iter.max = 10, nstart = 1, algorithm = "Hartigan-Wong")

Related Commands

hclust (p. 321)

Command Parameters

x	An R object containing numeric data; usually this is a matrix or data frame.
centers	Either the number of clusters required or a set of initially distinct cluster centers. If this is a single number, a random set of distinct rows in x is chosen as the initial centers.

iter.max = 10	The maximum number of iterations allowed.
nstart = 1	Used for the random selection of centers to start. Setting a value > 1 can be helpful when differentiating between clusters.
algorithm = "Hartigan-Wong"	Sets the algorithm to use for the analysis; the default is "Hartigan-Wong", but other options are "Lloyd", "Forgy", and "MacQueen".

Examples

```
  ## Some data for k-means analysis
> data(iris)  # Morphological data for 3 putative species
> names(iris) # See variables
[1] "Sepal.Length" "Sepal.Width"  "Petal.Length" "Petal.Width"  "Species"

  ## K-means with 3 clusters (there are 3 putative species)
  ## Use columns 1:4 as data (column 5 is species labels/names)
> iris.k = kmeans(iris[,1:4], centers = 3)
> iris.k # Show result
K-means clustering with 3 clusters of sizes 38, 62, 50

Cluster means:
  Sepal.Length Sepal.Width Petal.Length Petal.Width
1     6.850000    3.073684     5.742105    2.071053
2     5.901613    2.748387     4.393548    1.433871
3     5.006000    3.428000     1.462000    0.246000

Clustering vector:
  [1] 2 2 2 2 2 2 2 2 2 2 2 2 2 2 2 2 2 2 2 2 2 2 2 2 2 2 2 2 2 2 2 2 2 2 2 2
 [37] 2 2 2 2 2 2 2 2 2 2 2 2 2 2 1 1 3 1 1 1 1 1 1 1 1 1 1 1 1 1 1 1 1 1 1 1
 [73] 1 1 1 1 1 3 1 1 1 1 1 1 1 1 1 1 1 1 1 1 1 1 1 1 1 1 1 3 1 3 3 3 3 1 3
[109] 3 3 3 3 3 1 1 3 3 3 3 1 3 1 3 1 3 3 1 1 3 3 3 3 3 3 1 3 3 3 3 1 3 3 3 1 3
[145] 3 3 1 3 3 1

Within cluster sum of squares by cluster:
[1] 23.87947 39.82097 15.15100
 (between_SS / total_SS =  88.4 %)

Available components:

[1] "cluster"     "centers"     "totss"      "withinss"    "tot.withinss"
[6] "betweenss"   "size"

  ## Visualize using two of the morphological variables (Figure 2-4)
> plot(iris[, c(1,4)], pch = iris.k$cluster) # Clusters with different points

  ## Add centers
> points(iris.k$centers[, c(1,4)], pch = 8, cex = 2)  # Asterisk
> points(iris.k$centers[, c(1,4)], pch = 20, cex = 2) # Solid circle
```

```
## Show group membership
> table(iris$Species, iris.k$cluster)

            1  2  3
  setosa    0  0 50
  versicolor 2 48  0
  virginica 36 14  0
```

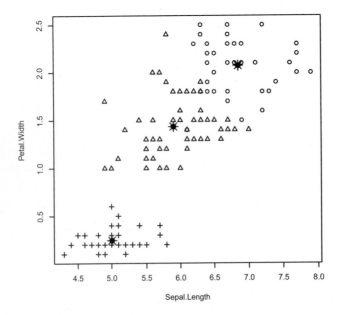

Figure 2-4: K-means cluster analysis for Iris morphological data

ORDINATION

There are two main kinds of ordination built into the base distribution of R. Principal components analysis (PCA) is a method of dealing with multivariate data. Two commands carry out PCA: prcomp and princomp. The commands use slightly different mathematical approaches. Classical multidimensional scaling (also called principal coordinates analysis) is conducted via the cmdscale command.

COMMAND NAME

cmdscale

This command carries out classical multidimensional scaling, which is also known as principal coordinates analysis. The command takes a set of dissimilarities (see dist), and returns a set of points as x, y, coordinates. The distance between the points is broadly equal to the dissimilarities. The result is a matrix object with columns [1] and [2] that are analogous to the x and y coordinates, respectively. Additional dimensions can be specified in the command, so extra columns may result.

Common Usage

```
cmdscale(d, k = 2, eig = FALSE, add = FALSE, x.ret = FALSE)
```

Related Commands

dist (p. 319)
prcomp (p. 326)
princomp (p. 329)

Command Parameters

d	A dissimilarity matrix; usually created with the dist command.
k = 2	The dimensions of the result to return. Usually k = 2 is sufficient but additional columns of coordinates can be returned by increasing the value of k.
eig = FALSE	If TRUE, the eigenvalues are computed and returned as part of the result.
add = FALSE	If TRUE, an additive constant c* is computed. This is added to all non-diagonal dissimilarities such that all n-1 eigenvalues are non-negative.
x.ret = FALSE	If TRUE, the doubly centered symmetric distance matrix is returned.

Examples

 USE moss data in Essential.RData file for these examples.

```
> load(file = "Essential.RData") # Load file

  ## View row names (the data samples)
> rownames(moss)
[1] "BN2" "LT1" "LT2" "PE3" "PO2" "PT1" "PT3" "QA1" "QR1"

  ## Create dissimilarity matrix using Euclidian algorithm
> moss.eu = dist(moss, method = "euclidian")

  ## Simplest default multidimensional scaling
> moss.pco = cmdscale(moss.eu)

  ## Result is simple matrix. Columns can be used as basis for plot
> moss.pco
            [,1]        [,2]
BN2  -0.4446475  34.8789419
LT1 -18.1046921   2.8738551
LT2 -22.5535658  -0.1146282
PE3  39.2108396  -2.0936131
PO2 -29.1878891 -13.1531653
PT1  31.1197817   3.1753791
PT3  45.2687047 -13.5379996
QA1 -24.0843294  -7.6439190
QR1 -21.2242021  -4.3848508
```

```
## If additional parameters are specified the result is a list
## Distance coordiantes $points
## Eigenvalues $eig
## Goodness of Fit of eigenvalues $GOF

> moss.pco = cmdscale(moss.eu, k = 2, eig = TRUE)
> moss.pco
$points
            [,1]        [,2]
BN2  -0.4446475  34.8789419
LT1 -18.1046921   2.8738551
LT2 -22.5535658  -0.1146282
PE3  39.2108396  -2.0936131
PO2 -29.1878891 -13.1531653
PT1  31.1197817   3.1753791
PT3  45.2687047 -13.5379996
QA1 -24.0843294  -7.6439190
QR1 -21.2242021  -4.3848508


$eig
[1] 7.274282e+03 1.673219e+03 4.010192e+02 3.237306e+02 1.945114e+02
[6] 5.300512e+01 3.839127e+01 1.849303e+01 9.928362e-13

$x
NULL

$ac
[1] 0

$GOF
[1] 0.896844 0.896844
```

COMMAND NAME

prcomp

This command carries out principal components analysis on a data matrix. The result is an object with a class attribute "prcomp". The PCA is carried out using svd, which is a slightly different approach to the princomp command. There is a special plotting command for the result, biplot. The command can accept input using a formula.

Common Usage

```
prcomp(formula, data = NULL, subset, na.action,
       retx = TRUE, center = TRUE, scale = FALSE, tol = NULL)
```

Related Commands

princomp (p. 329)
biplot (p. 353)
svd (p. 221)
eigen (p. 213)
cmdscale (p. 324)

Command Parameters

formula	A formula with no response variable, e.g., of the form ~ predictor. The variables should be numeric. Alternatively the formula can be a numeric matrix or data frame.
data = NULL	An optional data frame that contains the variables in the formula.
subset	An optional vector giving the rows to use from the data matrix.
na.action	A function that details what to do with NA items. The default is usually na.omit, which omits missing data.
retx = TRUE	By default the rotated variables are returned in the result object.
center = TRUE	If TRUE, the variables are shifted to be zero centered. You can also give a vector of length equal to the number of variables (columns in the data matrix).
scale = FALSE	If scale = TRUE, the variables are scaled to have unit variance before the analysis (this is generally advisable). You can also give a vector of length equal to the number of variables (columns in the data matrix).
tol = NULL	A value indicating the magnitude below which components should be omitted; this equates to the product of tol and the standard deviation of first component.

Examples

```
  ## Use datasets:USArrests
> data(USArrests)  # Get datafile
> names(USArrests) # View variable names
[1] "Murder"   "Assault"  "UrbanPop" "Rape"

  ## Scaled PCA using entire data.frame
> pca1 = prcomp(USArrests, scale = TRUE)

  ## Both following commands produce same PCA as previous
> pca2 = prcomp(~., data = USArrests, scale = TRUE)
> pca3 = prcomp(~ Murder + Assault + Rape + UrbanPop,
 data = USArrests, scale = TRUE)

> pca1 # View result
Standard deviations:
[1] 1.5748783 0.9948694 0.5971291 0.4164494
```

```
Rotation:
                  PC1         PC2         PC3         PC4
Murder    -0.5358995  0.4181809 -0.3412327  0.64922780
Assault   -0.5831836  0.1879856 -0.2681484 -0.74340748
UrbanPop  -0.2781909 -0.8728062 -0.3780158  0.13387773
Rape      -0.5434321 -0.1673186  0.8177779  0.08902432

> names(pca1) # View elements in result object
[1] "sdev"     "rotation" "center"   "scale"    "x"

> summary(pca1) # Summary
Importance of components:
                        PC1    PC2     PC3     PC4
Standard deviation    1.575 0.9949 0.59713 0.41645
Proportion of Variance 0.620 0.2474 0.08914 0.04336
Cumulative Proportion  0.620 0.8675 0.95664 1.00000

  ## Plots for results...
  ## Scree-plot of variances (Figure 2-5)
> plot(pca1, type = "lines", main = "PCA for USArrests")
```

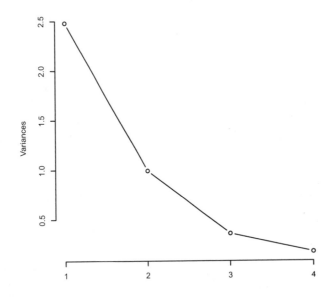

Figure 2-5: Scree-plot of variances from principal components analysis

```
  ## Bi-plot of result (Figure 2-6)
> biplot(pca1, col = 1, cex = c(0.8, 1.2), expand = 0.9)
```

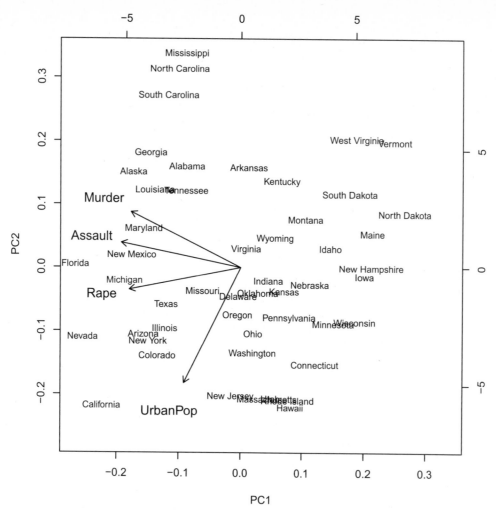

Figure 2-6: Bi-plot of principal components analysis

COMMAND NAME

princomp

This command carries out principal components analysis on a data matrix. The result is an object with a class attribute "princomp". The PCA is carried out using eigen, which is a slightly different approach to the prcomp command (the prcomp approach is generally preferable). The biplot plotting command is used for the result. The command can accept input using a formula.

Common Usage

```
princomp(formula, data = NULL, subset, na.action, cor = FALSE,
        scores = TRUE, covmat = NULL
```

Related Commands

prcomp (p. 326)
biplot (p. 353)
eigen (p. 213)
cor (p. 267)
cmdscale (p. 324)

Command Parameters

formula	A formula with no response variable, e.g., of the form ~ predictor. The variables should be numeric. Alternatively, the formula can be a numeric matrix or data frame.
data = NULL	An optional data frame that contains the variables in the formula.
subset	An optional vector giving the rows to use from the data matrix.
na.action	A function that details what to do with NA items. The default is usually na.omit, which omits missing data.
cor = FALSE	If cor = TRUE, the correlation matrix is used (only if no constant variables exist); the default is to use the covariance matrix. Using cor = TRUE is equivalent to scale = TRUE in the prcomp command.
scores = TRUE	If TRUE (the default), the score on each principal component is calculated.
covmat = NULL	A covariance matrix. If supplied, this is used instead of calculating it from the data given.

Examples

```
  ## Use datasets:USArrests
> data(USArrests)  # Get datafile
> names(USArrests) # View variable names
[1] "Murder"   "Assault"  "UrbanPop" "Rape"

> pca1 = princomp(USArrests, cor = TRUE)

  ## Both following commands produce same PCA as previous
> pca2 = princomp(~., data = USArrests, cor = TRUE)
> pca3 = princomp(~ Murder + Assault + Rape + UrbanPop,
 data = USArrests, cor = TRUE)

> pca1 # View result
Call:
princomp(x = USArrests, cor = TRUE)

Standard deviations:
   Comp.1    Comp.2    Comp.3    Comp.4
1.5748783 0.9948694 0.5971291 0.4164494
```

```
 4  variables and  50 observations.

> names(pca1) # View elements in result object
[1] "sdev"    "loadings" "center"    "scale"    "n.obs"    "scores"    "call"

> summary(pca1) # Summary
Importance of components:
                          Comp.1    Comp.2    Comp.3    Comp.4
Standard deviation     1.5748783 0.9948694 0.5971291 0.41644938
Proportion of Variance 0.6200604 0.2474413 0.0891408 0.04335752
Cumulative Proportion  0.6200604 0.8675017 0.9566425 1.00000000

  ## Plots for results...
  ## Scree-plot of variances (refer to Figure 2-5)
> plot(pca1, type = "lines", main = "PCA for USArrests")

  ## Bi-plot of data (refer to Figure 2-6)
> biplot(pca1, col = 1, cex = c(0.8, 1.2), expand = 0.9)
```

TIME SERIES

This section shows commands related to time-series data.

COMMAND NAME

`Box.test`

This command carries out Box-Pierce or Ljung-Box tests for examining independence in time series. These tests are also called "portmanteau" tests. The result is a list with a `class` attribute `"htest"`.

Common Usage

```
Box.test(x, lag = 1, type = "Box-Pierce", fitdf = 0)
```

Related Commands

`ts` (p. 13)
`PP.test` (p. 332)

Command Parameters

`x`	A numeric vector or a univariate time-series object.
`lag = 1`	The lag to use for the autocorrelation coefficients.
`type = "Box-Pierce"`	The test to carry out; defaults to `"Box-Pierce"` with `"Ljung-Box"` as an alternative. You can use an abbreviation.
`fitdf = 0`	The number of degrees of freedom to be subtracted if x is a series of residuals.

```
> data(lynx) # Canadian annual lynx trapped

> Box.test(lynx, lag = 1, type = "Box-Pierce")

        Box-Pierce test

data:  lynx
X-squared = 57.6, df = 1, p-value = 3.209e-14

> Box.test(lynx, lag = 1, type = "Ljung-Box")

        Box-Ljung test

data:  lynx
X-squared = 59.1292, df = 1, p-value = 1.477e-14
```

COMMAND NAME

PP.test

This command carries out the Phillips-Perron test for the null hypothesis that x has a unit root against a stationary alternative. The result is a list with a class attribute "htest".

Common Usage

PP.test(x, lshort = TRUE)

Related Commands

ts (p. 13)
Box.test (p. 331)

Command Parameters

x	A numeric vector or a univariate time series.
lshort = TRUE	If TRUE (the default), the short version of the truncation lag parameter is used.

Examples

```
> data(lynx) # Canadian annual lynx trapped

> PP.test(lynx)

        Phillips-Perron Unit Root Test

data:  lynx
Dickey-Fuller = -4.5852, Truncation lag parameter = 4, p-value = 0.01
```

```
> set.seed(55)    # Set random number seed
> x = rnorm(1000) # Make 1000 random values from normal distribution

> PP.test(x)

        Phillips-Perron Unit Root Test

data:  x
Dickey-Fuller = -31.4208, Truncation lag parameter = 7, p-value = 0.01

> y = cumsum(x) # This should have unit root
> PP.test(y)

        Phillips-Perron Unit Root Test

data:  y
Dickey-Fuller = -0.8208, Truncation lag parameter = 7, p-value = 0.9598
```

NON-LINEAR MODELING AND OPTIMIZATION

In non-linear modeling the observed data are modeled by a function that does not necessarily conform to a strict linear pattern. The technique of non-linear modeling uses successive approximations to fit the model.

In a similar vein, locally weighted polynomial regression is a method often used to visualize relationships by fitting a kind of best-fit line. Rather than being straight, the line is "influenced" by the points it passes by. It is often called scatter plot smoothing.

COMMAND NAME

loess

This command carries out local polynomial regression fitting. A common use for this is to produce a locally fitted model that can be added to a scatter plot as a trend line to help visualize the relationship. The trend line is not a straight line but weaves through the scatter of points; thus loess is often referred to as a *scatter plot smoother*.

Common Usage

```
loess(formula, data, weights, subset, na.action,
      model = FALSE, span = 0.75, degree = 2, family = "gaussian")
```

Related Commands

lowess (p. 335)
lines (p. 398)
fitted (p. 309)

Command Parameters

`formula`	A formula that describes the regression. You specify the response and up to four numeric predictors. The formula is usually of the form `response ~ p1 * p2 * p3 * p4`, but additive predictors are allowed.
`data`	A data frame specifying where the variables in the `formula` are to be found.
`weights`	Optional weights for each case; usually specified as a vector.
`subset`	A subset of observations, usually of the form `subset = group %in% c("a", "b", ...)`.
`na.action`	A function indicating what to do if `NA` items are present. The default is `na.omit`, which omits the `NA` items.
`model = FALSE`	If `TRUE`, the model frame is returned as part of the result (essentially the original data).
`span = 0.75`	A numerical value that controls the degree of smoothing. Smaller values result in less smoothing.
`degree = 2`	The degree of the polynomials to use; this is normally 1 or 2.
`family = "gaussian"`	The kind of fitting carried out. The default, `"gaussian"`, uses least-squares. The alternative, `"symmetric"`, uses a re-descending M estimator with Tukey's biweight function.

Examples

```
  ## Use cars data from R datasets
> data(cars) # Make sure data are ready

  ## Make a local ploynomial regression
> cars.loess = loess(dist ~ speed, data = cars)

  ## View the result (a summary)
> cars.loess
Call:
loess(formula = dist ~ speed, data = cars)

Number of Observations: 50
Equivalent Number of Parameters: 4.78
Residual Standard Error: 15.29

  ## Look at names of items in result
> names(cars.loess)
 [1] "n"         "fitted"    "residuals" "enp"      "s"        "one.delta"
 [7] "two.delta" "trace.hat" "divisor"   "pars"     "kd"       "call" [13] "terms"
"xnames"    "x"         "y"         "weights"

  ## Make a basic scatter plot of the original data (Figure 2-7)
> plot(cars)
```

```
  ## Add loess line
> lines(cars.loess$x, cars.loess$fitted, lwd = 3)

  ## Give a title
> title(main = "loess smoother")
```

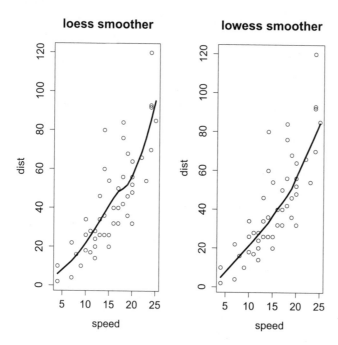

Figure 2-7: Two forms of scatter plot smoother compared

COMMAND NAME

`lowess`

This command carries out scatter plot smoothing. The algorithm uses a locally weighted polynomial regression. A common use for this is to produce a locally fitted model that can be added to a scatter plot as a trend line to help visualize the relationship.

Common Usage

```
lowess(x, y = NULL, f = 2/3, iter = 3,
       delta = 0.01 * diff(range(xy$x[o])))
```

Related Commands

loess (p. 333)
lines (p. 398)
fitted (p. 309)

Command Parameters

x, y = NULL   Vectors that give the coordinates of the points in the scatter plot. Alternatively, if x is an object with a plotting structure (that is, it contains x and y components) then y can be missing.

f = 2/3   Controls the smoothness by giving the proportion of points in the plot that influence the smoothing at each value. Larger values result in smoother curves.

iter = 3   The number of iterations performed; this helps robustness of the result. Larger values take more computing power and run slower.

delta   Allows the computation to speed up at the expense of some smoothness. The default value is 1/100 of the range of x. Instead of computing the local polynomial fit for each point, some points are skipped and interpolation is used. Larger values result in more interpolation.

Examples

```
  ## Use cars data from R datasets (built into R)
> data(cars) # Make sure data are ready

  ## Make a local ploynomial regression
> cars.lowess = lowess(cars$speed, cars$dist)
> cars.lowess # Result contains x and y elements
$x
 [1]  4  4  7  7  8  9 10 10 10 11 11 12 12 12 12 13 13 13 13 14 14 14 14 15
[25] 15 15 16 16 17 17 17 18 18 18 18 19 19 19 20 20 20 20 20 22 23 24 24 24
[49] 24 25

$y
 [1]  4.965459  4.965459 13.124495 13.124495 15.858633 18.579691 21.280313
 [8] 21.280313 21.280313 24.129277 24.129277 27.119549 27.119549 27.119549
[15] 27.119549 30.027276 30.027276 30.027276 30.027276 32.962506 32.962506
[22] 32.962506 32.962506 36.757728 36.757728 36.757728 40.435075 40.435075
[29] 43.463492 43.463492 43.463492 46.885479 46.885479 46.885479 46.885479
[36] 50.793152 50.793152 50.793152 56.491224 56.491224 56.491224 56.491224
[43] 56.491224 67.585824 73.079695 78.643164 78.643164 78.643164 78.643164
[50] 84.328698

  ## Make a basic scatter plot of the original data (refer to Figure 2-7)
> plot(cars)

  ## Add lowess line
> lines(cars.lowess, lwd = 3)

  ## Add graph title
> title(main = "lowess smoother")
```

COMMAND NAME

nlm

This command carries out a minimization of a function using a Newton-type algorithm.

Common Usage

nlm(f, p, ..., hessian = FALSE, print.level = 0)

Related Commands

nls (p. 338)
optim (p. 340)
uniroot (p. 344)
polyroot (p. 342)

Command Parameters

f	The function to be minimized.
p	The starting parameter values for the minimization.
...	Additional arguments to f.
hessian = FALSE	If hessian = TRUE, the hessian of f at the minimum is returned.
print.level = 0	Controls the information shown through the minimization process: if 0, no information is shown; if 1, only initial and final details are shown; if 2, all tracing information through the iteration process is shown.

Examples

```
  ## Make a simple function to minimize
> f = function(x, a) sum((x-a)^2)

> nlm(f, p = c(6, 9), a = c(2, 4), hessian = TRUE)
$minimum
[1] 5.482287e-26

$estimate
[1] 2 4

$gradient
[1]  3.659295e-13 -2.917666e-13

$hessian
             [,1]         [,2]
[1,] 2.000000e+00 8.271806e-17
[2,] 8.271806e-17 2.000000e+00
```

```
$code
[1] 1

$iterations
[1] 2
```

COMMAND NAME

nls

This command carries out non-linear regression; it determines the non-linear (weighted) least-squares estimates of the parameters of a given model. The result is a list with a `class` attribute "nls".

Common Usage

```
nls(formula, data, start, algorithm, trace, subset, weights, na.action)
```

Related Commands

SSlogis (p. 343)
nlm (p. 337)

Command Parameters

formula	A formula for the non-linear model, which should include variables and parameters.
data	A data frame that contains the variables in the `formula`.
start	Starting estimates, given as a list.
algorithm	A character string that gives the algorithm to be used. The default is a Gauss-Newton algorithm; options are "default", "plinear", and "port".
trace = FALSE	If `trace` = TRUE, the iteration process is displayed.
subset	An optional subset of the data set.
weights	An optional vector of fixed weights. If present, the objective function is weighted least squares.
na.action	A function indicating what to do if NA items are present. The default is na.omit, which omits the NA items.

Examples

```
  ## Make data (substrate concentration and rate of reaction)
> conc = c(1, 1.5, 2, 2.7, 5, 7.7, 10)
> vel = c(9, 12.5, 16.7, 20, 28.6, 37, 38.5)
> mm = data.frame(conc, vel)

  ## Fit a Michaelis Menten model
> mm.nlm = nls(vel ~ Vm * conc / (K + conc), data = mm,
  start = list(K = 1, Vm = 1))
```

```
> coef(mm.nlm) # The coefficients
        K        Vm
 5.602863 61.518487


  ## Plot model (see Figure 2-8)
> plot(vel ~ conc, data = mm, type = "b") # Original data
> lines(spline(mm$conc, fitted(mm.nlm)), lwd = 3) # Add fitted curve
```

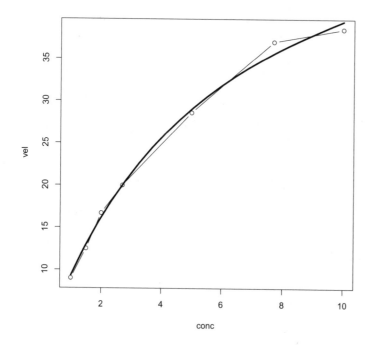

Figure 2-8: Plot of a Michaelis-Menten model using non-linear modeling (nls)

```
  ## using a selfStart model
  ## More data
> data(DNase) # Get data from datasets
> DNase1 <- subset(DNase, Run == 1) # Use only part of data


  ## The model
> fm1DNase1 <- nls(density ~ SSlogis(log(conc), Asym, xmid, scal), DNase1)
> summary(fm1DNase1)


Formula: density ~ SSlogis(log(conc), Asym, xmid, scal)


Parameters:
     Estimate Std. Error t value Pr(>|t|)
Asym  2.34518    0.07815   30.01 2.17e-13 ***
xmid  1.48309    0.08135   18.23 1.22e-10 ***
scal  1.04146    0.03227   32.27 8.51e-14 ***
```

```
---
Signif. codes:  0 '***' 0.001 '**' 0.01 '*' 0.05 '.' 0.1 ' ' 1

Residual standard error: 0.01919 on 13 degrees of freedom

Number of iterations to convergence: 0
Achieved convergence tolerance: 3.281e-06

> coef(fm1DNase1) # Get coefficients only
    Asym     xmid     scal
2.345180 1.483090 1.041455
```

COMMAND NAME

optim

This command carries out general-purpose optimization based on Nelder–Mead, quasi-Newton, and conjugate-gradient algorithms. It includes an option for box-constrained optimization and simulated annealing.

Common Usage

```
optim(par, fn, gr = NULL, ..., method = "Nelder-Mead",
      lower = -Inf, upper = Inf, control = list(), hessian = FALSE)
```

Related Commands

nlm (p. 337)
optimize (p. 341)

Command Parameters

par	Initial values for the parameters to be optimized.
fn	A function to be minimized (or maximized); the first argument must be a vector of parameters over which the minimization is to take place.
gr = NULL	A function to return the gradient.
...	Additional arguments to pass to fn and gr.
method = "Nelder-Mead"	The method for the optimization. The default is "Nelder-Mead". Other options are "BFGS", "CG", "L-BFGS-B", and "SANN".
lower = -Inf	Lower bound on the variables for the "L-BFGS-B" method.
upper = Inf	Upper bound on the variables for the "L-BFGS-B" method.
control = list()	A list of control parameters.
hessian = FALSE	If TRUE, a differentiated Hessian matrix is returned.

Examples

```
  # Make a simple function to optimize
> f = function(x, a) sum((x-a)^2)

> optim(c(6, 9), f, a = c(2, 4), hessian = TRUE)
$par
[1] 1.999964 4.000290

$value
[1] 8.549353e-08

$counts
function gradient
      63       NA

$convergence
[1] 0

$message
NULL

$hessian
              [,1]           [,2]
[1,]   2.000000e+00 -8.131516e-17
[2,]  -8.131516e-17  2.000000e+00
```

COMMAND NAME

```
optimise
optimize
```

These commands carry out one-dimensional optimization. The `optimise` command is simply an alias for `optimize`. The command searches a given interval, from the lower end to the upper, for a minimum or maximum of a given function with respect to its first argument.

Common Usage

```
optimize(f, interval, ...,
         lower = min(interval), upper = max(interval),
         maximum = FALSE, tol = .Machine$double.eps^0.25)
```

Related Commands

optim (p. 340)
uniroot (p. 344)

Command Parameters

f	The function to be optimized. The function is either minimized or maximized over its first argument depending on the value of maximum.
interval	A vector that gives the endpoints of the interval to be searched for the minimum.
...	Additional arguments to be passed to the function, f.
lower = min(interval)	The lower end point of the interval to be searched.
upper = max(interval)	The upper end point of the interval to be searched.
maximum = FALSE	If maximum = TRUE, the function is maximized rather than minimized.
tol	A value for the accuracy.

Examples

```
  ## Make a simple function to optimize
> f = function(x, a) sum((x-a)^2)

> optimize(f, interval = c(6, 9), a = c(2, 4))
$minimum
[1] 6.000076

$objective
[1] 20.00091

> optimize(f, interval = c(6, 9), a = c(2, 4), maximum = TRUE)
$maximum
[1] 8.999924

$objective
[1] 73.99818
```

COMMAND NAME

polyroot

This command finds zeros of real or complex polynomials using the Jenkins-Traub algorithm.

Common Usage

polyroot(z)

Related Commands

uniroot (p. 344)
optimize (p. 341)

Command Parameters

z   A vector of polynomial coefficients in increasing order.

Examples

```
> polyroot(c(4, 2))
[1] -2+0i

> polyroot(c(4, 2, 3))
[1] -0.333333+1.105542i -0.333333-1.105542i

> polyroot(c(4, 2, 3, 2))
[1]  0.068000+1.103572i -1.635999+0.000000i  0.068000-1.103572i
```

COMMAND NAME

SSlogis

This command creates self-starting non-linear models. The command evaluates the logistic function and its gradient, which creates starting estimates for the parameters.

Common Usage

SSlogis(input, Asym, xmid, scal)

Related Commands

nls (p. 338)

Command Parameters

input   A numeric vector of values used to evaluate the model.

Asym   A numeric value representing the asymptote.

xmid   A numeric value representing the x value at the inflection point of the curve.

scal   A value for the scale parameter.

Examples

```
> data(DNase) # Data from datasets
> DNase1 <- subset(DNase, Run == 1) # Use only part of the data

  ## A self-starting non-linear model
> fm1DNase1 <- nls(density ~ SSlogis(log(conc), Asym, xmid, scal), DNase1)
> coef(fm1DNase1)
    Asym     xmid     scal
2.345180 1.483090 1.041455
```

```
  ## Estimate starting values
> SSlogis(log(DNase1$conc), Asym = 2.5, xmid = 1.5, scal = 1) # Response only
 [1] 0.02694401 0.02694401 0.10440049 0.10440049 0.20043094 0.20043094
 [7] 0.37110918 0.37110918 0.64628190 0.64628190 1.02705657 1.02705657
[13] 1.45596838 1.45596838 1.84021742 1.84021742


> Asym = 2.5; xmid = 1.5; scal = 1 # Set values

  ## Use set values
> SSlogis(log(DNase1$conc), Asym, xmid, scal) # Response and gradient
 [1] 0.02694401 0.02694401 0.10440049 0.10440049 0.20043094 0.20043094
 [7] 0.37110918 0.37110918 0.64628190 0.64628190 1.02705657 1.02705657
[13] 1.45596838 1.45596838 1.84021742 1.84021742
attr(,"gradient")
            Asym        xmid        scal
 [1,] 0.01077760 -0.02665362  0.1204597
 [2,] 0.01077760 -0.02665362  0.1204597
 [3,] 0.04176020 -0.10004070  0.3134430
 [4,] 0.04176020 -0.10004070  0.3134430
 [5,] 0.08017238 -0.18436192  0.4498444
 [6,] 0.08017238 -0.18436192  0.4498444
 [7,] 0.14844367 -0.31602037  0.5520434
 [8,] 0.14844367 -0.31602037  0.5520434
 [9,] 0.25851276 -0.47920978  0.5049495
[10,] 0.25851276 -0.47920978  0.5049495
[11,] 0.41082263 -0.60511849  0.2181850
[12,] 0.41082263 -0.60511849  0.2181850
[13,] 0.58238735 -0.60803081 -0.2022198
[14,] 0.58238735 -0.60803081 -0.2022198
[15,] 0.73608697 -0.48565736 -0.4981527
[16,] 0.73608697 -0.48565736 -0.4981527
```

COMMAND NAME

uniroot

This command carries out one-dimensional root (zero) finding. It searches the given interval from the lower to the upper to find a root (zero) of the given function, with respect to its first argument.

Common Usage

```
uniroot(f, interval, ..., lower = min(interval), upper = max(interval),
        tol = .Machine$double.eps^0.25, maxiter = 1000)
```

Related Commands

polyroot (p. 342)
optimize (p. 341)

Command Parameters

`f`	The function for which the root is required.
`interval`	A vector that gives the endpoints of the interval to be searched for the root.
`...`	Additional arguments to be passed to the function, `f`.
`lower = min(interval)`	The lower end point of the `interval` to be searched.
`upper = max(interval)`	The upper end point of the `interval` to be searched.
`tol`	A value for the accuracy.
`maxiter = 1000`	The maximum number of iterations.

Examples

```
## Make a function
> f = function (x, a) x - a

## Find root
> uniroot(f, interval = c(0, 1), a= 0.2)
$root
[1] 0.2

$f.root
[1] 0

$iter
[1] 1

$estim.prec
[1] 0.8
```

THEME 3: GRAPHICS

This theme is concerned with all things connected to graphics. This includes the production of various types of graphs, adding text, lines, and points to graphs, and altering a range of additional graphical parameters. This theme also covers saving graphs to other programs and to disk in various graphical formats.

Topics In This Theme

COMMANDS IN THIS THEME:

Making Graphs

You can create various sorts of graphs with a few basic commands covered in this topic. You can transfer your graphs to other programs or save them to disk in a variety of graphical formats (for example, pdf, jpeg, tiff, and so on).

What's In This Topic:

- **Types of graphs** (p. 349)
- **Saving graphs** (p. 389)
    - Creating blank graph windows
    - Managing open graph windows
    - Types of graphics files

Types of Graphs

The R program can produce several types of graphs. The commands that produce these graphs are covered in this section. You can customize and embellish your graphs in many ways. Note that many of the parameters used by the various graphics commands are shared by several commands.

 SEE also "Adding to Graphs."

 SEE also "Graphical Parameters."

COMMAND NAME

`barplot`

This command creates bar charts. The bars can be drawn as vertical or horizontal.

Common Usage

```
barplot(height, width = 1, space = NULL,
        names.arg = NULL, legend.text = NULL, beside = FALSE,
        horiz = FALSE, density = NULL, angle = 45,
        col = NULL, border = par("fg")
        main = NULL, sub = NULL, xlab = NULL, ylab = NULL,
        xlim = NULL, ylim = NULL,
        cex.axis = par("cex.axis"), cex.names = par("cex.axis"),
        plot = TRUE, add = FALSE, args.legend = NULL, ...)
```

Related Commands

`hist` (p. 368)
`dotchart` (p. 366)
`plot` (p. 382)
`rect` (p. 420)

Command Parameters

`height`	The data giving the heights of the bars. This can be a vector of numeric values or a matrix.
`width = 1`	The widths of the bars. This can be specified as a vector of values or as a single number. If a single number is specified, there will be no effect unless `xlim` is also given.

`space = NULL`	The amount of space (as a fraction of the average bar width) left before each bar. You can specify a single number or one number per bar. If `height` is a matrix and `beside = TRUE`, space can be specified by two numbers, where the first is the space between bars in the same group, and the second is the space between the groups. If not given explicitly, it defaults to `c(0,1)` if `height` is a matrix and `beside = TRUE`, and to 0.2 otherwise.
`names.arg = NULL`	The names to be displayed beneath the bars (or groups of bars). If omitted, the names are taken from data specified in `height`. If the data are a matrix, the names are taken from the column names. If the data are a vector, the names are taken from the `names` attribute.
`legend.text = NULL`	A vector of text to use for a legend. If `legend.text = TRUE`, the names are constructed from the row names of the data.
`beside = FALSE`	By default, stacked bars are produced if the data are a matrix with multiple rows. Each column forms a stack. If `beside = TRUE`, the bars are shown in groups.
`horiz = FALSE`	If `horiz = TRUE`, the bars are drawn horizontally. In this case the bottom axis is still regarded as the x-axis and the vertical axis as the y-axis.
`col = NULL`	Colors to use for the bars. The default is a range of gray shades.
`border`	The border color for the bars.
`density = NULL`	The density of shading lines in lines per inch. The default is `NULL`, which suppresses lines.
`angle = 45`	The angle of shading lines in degrees. This is measured as a counter-clockwise rotation.
`main = NULL`	A character string giving the main title for the plot.
`sub = NULL`	A character string giving the subtitle for the plot.
`xlab = NULL`	A character string giving the title for the x-axis.
`ylab = NULL`	A character string giving the title for the y-axis.
`cex.axis = 1`	A numeric value that sets the expansion factor for the numeric axis labels.
`cex.names = 1`	A numeric value that sets the expansion factor for the bar names.
`plot = TRUE`	If `plot = FALSE`, nothing is plotted.
`add = FALSE`	If `add = TRUE`, the bars are added to an existing plot.
`args.legend = NULL`	A list of arguments to be passed to the legend (see the `legend` command).

Examples

```
  ## Make values for basic barplot
> rain = c(34, 32, 23, 15, 10, 8, 6, 9, 12, 21, 24, 29) # Vector
> month = month.abb[1:12] # Make labels

  ## Now draw the plot (Figure 3-1)
  ## Increase y-axis limits and add titles
> barplot(rain, ylim = c(0, 35), names = month,
  main = "Rainfall", xlab = "Month", ylab = "Rainfall in mm")
```

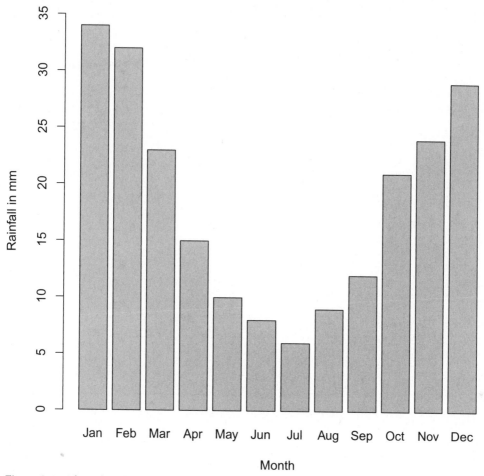

Figure 3-1: A basic bar chart

```
  ## More data, this time as a matrix
> data(VADeaths) # Data are in R datasets

  ## Draw stacked bar chart with horizontal bars (Figure 3-2)
  ## Note that xlab annotates bottom axis
  ## There is no legend automatically
> barplot(VADeaths, xlab = "Deaths per 1000", horiz = TRUE)

  ## Add main title afterwards
> title(main = "Death Rates in Virginia (1940)")
```

Death Rates in Virginia (1940)

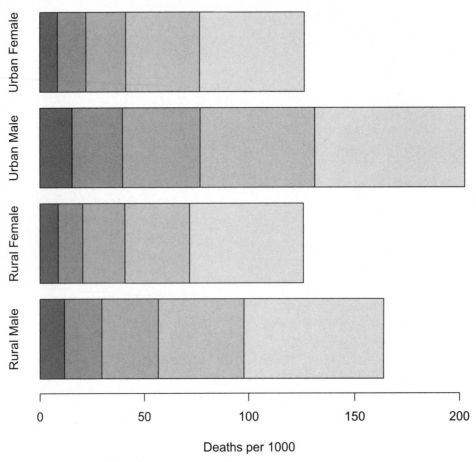

Figure 3-2: A stacked bar chart

```
  ## Same data as previous - a Matrix
> data(VADeaths) # Data are in R datasets

  ## Draw bar chart with adjacent bars (Figure 3-3)
  ## Add a legend. Note parameters passed to legend command
> barplot(VADeaths, beside = TRUE, legend = TRUE,
 args.legend = list(bty = "n", title = "Age category"))

  ## Add titles afterwards
> title(ylab = "Deaths per 1000", xlab = "Category")
```

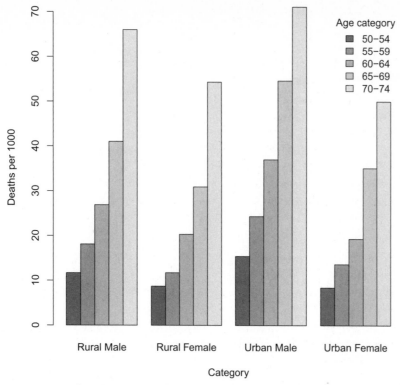

Figure 3-3: A bar chart with adjacent (grouped) bars and a legend

COMMAND NAME

`biplot`

This command produces biplots. Essentially, a *biplot* is two series of x, y coordinates. The data are plotted using separate axis scales and you have the option to add arrows to the second series. The main use for biplots is showing the result of multivariate analysis. The command will accept input in two different ways: as the result of a multivariate analysis or as two separate two-column matrix objects.

Common Usage

```
biplot(x, y, var.axes = TRUE, col, cex = rep(par("cex"), 2),
       xlabs = NULL, ylabs = NULL, expand = 1,
       xlim  = NULL, ylim  = NULL, arrow.len = 0.1,
       main = NULL, sub = NULL, xlab = NULL, ylab = NULL, ...)

biplot(x, choices = 1:2, scale = 1, pc.biplot = FALSE, ...)
```

Related Commands

prcomp (p. 326)
princomp (p. 329)
matplot (p. 374)

Command Parameters

x	The data that forms the first set of points. This can be a two-column matrix or the result of a multivariate analysis. If the object is the latter, x is taken from the results of the rows (samples).
y	The data that forms the second set of points. If x is given as the result of a multivariate analysis, y can be missing. In this case, the data will be taken from the results of the columns (variables).
var.axes = TRUE	By default, the second set of points has arrows pointing to them from the origin.
col	The colors for the points and arrows.
cex	The character expansion factor for the points. Two values can be given for the first and second set, respectively.
xlabs = NULL	A vector of character strings to use as the labels for the individual points for the first data set. The default uses the row names if set, or numbers if names are not set.
ylabs = NULL	A vector of character strings to use as the labels for the individual points for the second data set. The default uses the row names if set, or numbers if names are not set.
expand = 1	An expansion factor to apply to the axes for the second set of points relative to the first.
xlim = NULL	A vector of two values giving the limits of the x-axis for the first data set.
ylim = NULL	A vector of two values giving the limits of the y-axis for the first data set.
arrow.len = 0.1	The length of the arrow heads if var.axes = TRUE. Use arrow.len = 0 to suppress arrow heads.
main = NULL sub = NULL xlab = NULL ylab = NULL ...	Additional graphical parameters can be given. These include main and subtitles for the plot as well as titles for x- and y-axes.
choices = 1:2	If the data are from a multivariate analysis and have a class attribute "prcomp" or "princomp", you can specify which axes to plot (two values are required). The default is to use 1:2, which relates to the first two axes.
scale = 1	A scale factor (between 0 and 1). This affects the way the scales of the variables (columns) and observations (rows) are drawn relative to one another.
pc.plot = FALSE	If pc.plot = TRUE, the observations are scaled up by sqrt(n) and the variables scaled down by sqrt(n).

Examples

 USE moss data in `Essential.RData` file for these examples.

```
## Use Principal Components to make multivariate result
> moss.pca = prcomp(moss, scale = TRUE)

## View the result as a bi-plot (Figure 3-4)
## Note use of two colors and two cex (2nd set smaller)
> biplot(moss.pca, scale = 0, col = c("black", 'gray50'),
  cex = c(1, 0.7))
```

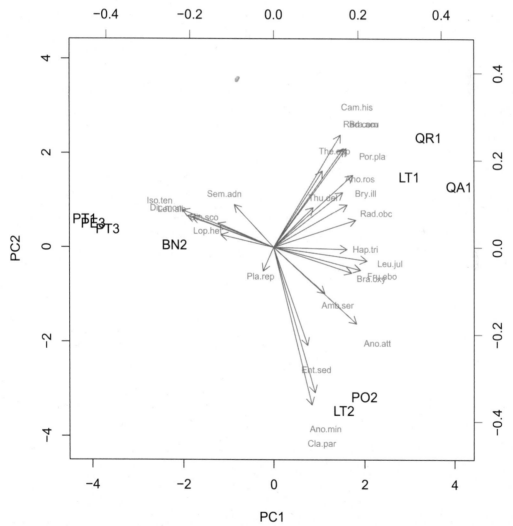

Figure 3-4: A biplot from a principal components analysis

```
## Use data from two matrix objects
## Make data
> mat1 = matrix(c(7, -5, 5, 6, 0, 1, 2, -1, 7, 4), ncol = 2)
> rownames(mat1) = LETTERS[1:5] # Make row names (become plot labels)
> colnames(mat1) = c("Column 1", "Column 2") # Become axis titles

> mat2 = matrix(c(10, -6, -8, 3, 15, -8, 8, -5), ncol = 2)
> rownames(mat2) = letters[1:4] # Make rownames (become plot labels)

## Draw the biplot (Figure 3-5)
## make the arrows slightly smaller and all points larger
> biplot(mat1, mat2, expand = 0.5, col = c("black", "gray30"),
  cex = 1.5)
```

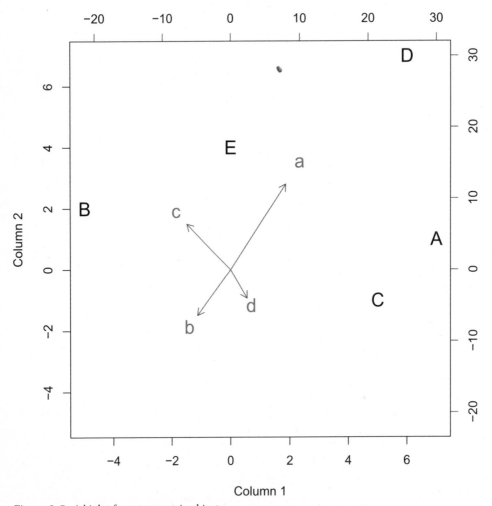

Figure 3-5: A biplot from two matrix objects

COMMAND NAME

`boxplot`

This command produces box-whisker plots. The command accepts data in several forms:

- As one or more vectors of values
- As an object containing multiple numeric variables (for example, data frame, matrix, or list)
- As a `formula`

The command takes your input data and calculates the values required to create the plot. These values are then passed to the `bxp` command for the actual plotting.

Common Usage

```
boxplot(formula, data = NULL, ..., subset, na.action = NULL)

boxplot(x, ..., range = 1.5, width = NULL, varwidth = FALSE,
        notch = FALSE, outline = TRUE, names, plot = TRUE,
        border = par("fg"), col = NULL,
        pars = list(boxwex = 0.8, staplewex = 0.5),
        horizontal = FALSE, add = FALSE, at = NULL)
```

Related Commands

bxp (p. 360)

Command Parameters

`formula`	A formula of the form $y \sim grp$, where y is the response variable and `grp` is one or more predictor (grouping) variables.
`data = NULL`	A data frame (or list) from which the variables in the `formula` are to be found.
`subset`	A subset of the observations to be used in the plot.
`na.action = NULL`	What to do if the data contains NA items. The default is to ignore them.
`x`	If the input data are not specified as a formula, x specifies the data to be used. This can be one or more vectors (separate names using commas) or a data frame, matrix, or list.
`range = 1.5`	Specifies how far the whiskers extend; this is range multiplied by the inter-quartile range. To make the whiskers extent to the max-min, use `range = 0`. See the `outline` parameter.
`width = NULL`	A vector of values giving the relative widths of the boxes.
`varwidth = FALSE`	If `varwidth = TRUE`, the boxes have widths proportional to the square root of the number of observations.
`notch = FALSE`	If `notch = TRUE`, a notch is drawn as an indicator of significant difference (an approximate 95% confidence indicator).

outline = TRUE	If outline = FALSE, outliers are not shown. By default, points that lie beyond the range of the whiskers are shown as outliers.
names	Group labels for the boxes. The labels are taken from the names attribute if available.
plot = TRUE	If plot = FALSE, the plot is not drawn and the boxplot statistics are given instead. These are in the form of a list. These statistics could be passed to the bxp command.
border	A vector of colors for the borders of the boxes.
col	The colors for the fill of the boxes. If a single value is given it is used for all boxes, otherwise the values are used sequentially and recycled as necessary.
pars = list()	A list of additional parameters to pass to the bxp command. The defaults specify boxwex and staplewex.
boxwex = 0.8	A scale factor to apply to all boxes.
staplewex = 0.5	The width of the staple line (the ends of the whiskers) compared to box width.
horizontal = FALSE	If TRUE, the boxes and whiskers are drawn horizontally. In this case the bottom axis is still regarded as the x-axis and the vertical axis as the y-axis.
add = FALSE	If add = TRUE, the boxplot is drawn into the existing plot window.
at = NULL	A vector of values specifying the locations where the boxes are to be drawn. The locations are relative to the number of boxes across the x-axis.
...	Additional graphical parameters.

Examples

```
  ## Make data
> dat1 = c(4, 5, 6, 4, 3, 5, 7, 8)
> dat2 = c(8, 6, 5, 5, 4, 6, 3, 9)

  ## Draw box-plot (Figure 3-6)
  ## Names must be given explicitly when using separate vectors
  ## Boxes made thinner using boxwex
> boxplot(dat1, dat2, names = c("Data 1", "Data 2"),
  col = "gray80", boxwex = 0.7,
  xlab = "Treatment", ylab = "Count")
```

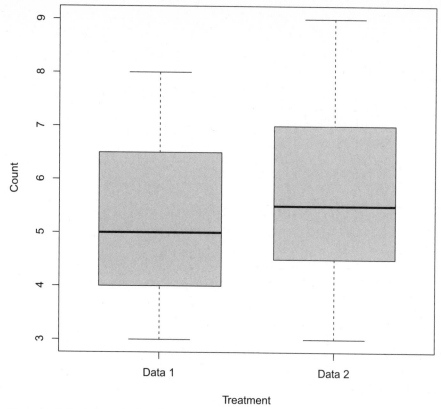

Figure 3-6: Basic box-whisker plot

```
  ## Use data from datasets
> data(PlantGrowth) # Make sure data is ready
> names(PlantGrowth) # See what the columns are called
[1] "weight" "group"

  ## Make boxplot, (Figure 3-7)
  ## Use horizontal boxes, las = 1 rotates axis labels
  ## Use formula to specify data
  ## Boxes automatically labeled as data in data frame
  ## Note outlier (use range = 0 to extend whiskers)
> boxplot(weight ~ group, data = PlantGrowth, horizontal = TRUE,
  las = 1)

  ## Add titles, make them slightly larger than default
  ## Note xlab still refers to bottom axis
  ## note also expression used for subscript
> title(xlab = expression("Growth"["in grams"]),
  ylab = 'Treatment', cex.lab = 1.3)
```

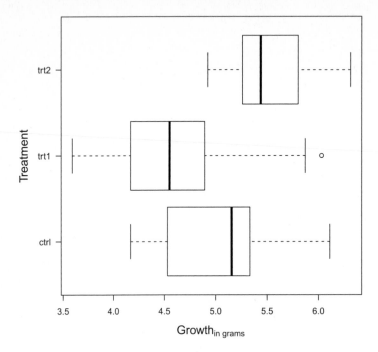

Figure 3-7: A horizontal boxplot

COMMAND NAME

bxp

This command draws box-whisker plots. The data are usually taken from summary statistics produced by the boxplot command, but you could generate the values in another way.

Common Usage

```
bxp(z, notch = FALSE, width = NULL, varwidth = FALSE,
    outline = TRUE, notch.frac = 0.5,
    border = par("fg"), pars = NULL, frame.plot = axes,
    horizontal = FALSE, add = FALSE, at = NULL, show.names = NULL,
    ...)
```

Related Commands

boxplot (p. 357)

Command Parameters

z	A list that contains the elements used to create the plot. Usually this will be created by the boxplot command.
notch = FALSE	If notch = TRUE, a notch is drawn as an indicator of significant difference (an approximate 95% confidence indicator).
width = NULL	A vector of values giving the relative widths of the boxes.
varwidth = FALSE	If varwidth = TRUE, the boxes have widths proportional to the square root of the number of observations.
outline = TRUE	If outline = FALSE, outliers are not shown. By default, points that lie beyond the range of the whiskers are shown as outliers.
notch.frac = 0.5	A value between 0 and 1 that determines what fraction of the box width the notch should use.
border	A vector of colors for the borders of the boxes. The color set is also used as the default for other colors: boxcol, medcol, whiskcol, staplecol, and outcol.
pars = NULL	Additional graphical parameters can be specified as a list. See the ... parameter.
frame.plot = axes	Specifies if a frame should be drawn around the plot. The default is effectively TRUE, unless axes = FALSE is specified. The frame can be suppressed using frame.plot = FALSE.
horizontal = FALSE	If TRUE, the boxes and whiskers are drawn horizontally. In this case the bottom axis is still regarded as the x-axis and the vertical axis as the y-axis.
add = FALSE	If add = TRUE, the boxplot is drawn into the existing plot window.
at = NULL	A vector of values specifying the locations where the boxes are to be drawn. The locations are relative to the number of boxes across the x-axis.
show.names = NULL	Set to TRUE or FALSE to override the defaults on whether an x-axis label is printed for each group.
...	Additional graphical parameters can be specified. (See "Graphical Parameters.") Any parameters set override those set via the pars parameter.

Additional graphical parameters for the bxp command can be applied to various components of the plot. The parameters are generally based on the equivalents in the par command:

boxwex	A scale factor applied to all boxes. The default = 0.8.
staplewex, outwex	A width expansion factor for the staple (end of whisker) and outlier line proportional to box width. The default = 0.5.
boxlty, boxlwd, boxcol, boxfill	Sets the box outline type, width, color, and fill color.

medlty, medlwd, medpch, medcex, medcol, medbg	Sets parameters for the median indicator: line type, width, character, expansion factor, color, and background. The default medpch = NA suppresses the character. To suppress the line, use medlty = "blank".
whisklty, whisklwd, whiskcol	Sets parameters for the whiskers: line type (the default is "dashed"), width, and color.
staplelty, staplelwd, staplecol	Sets parameters for the staple (the end of the whiskers): line type, width, and color.
outlty, outlwd, outpch, outcex, outcol, outbg	Sets parameters for the outliers: line type, width, character, expansion factor, color, and background. The default outlty = "blank" suppresses the lines. To suppress the points, use outpch = NA.

Examples

```
  ## Use data from datasets
> data(PlantGrowth) # Make sure data is ready

  ## Use boxplot to create statistics for plot but do not plot it
> bp = boxplot(weight ~ group, data = PlantGrowth, plot = FALSE)
> bp # See the results
$stats
      [,1] [,2]  [,3]
[1,] 4.170 3.59 4.920
[2,] 4.530 4.17 5.260
[3,] 5.155 4.55 5.435
[4,] 5.330 4.89 5.800
[5,] 6.110 5.87 6.310

$n
[1] 10 10 10

$conf
         [,1]     [,2]     [,3]
[1,] 4.755288 4.190259 5.165194
[2,] 5.554712 4.909741 5.704806

$out
[1] 6.03

$group
[1] 2

$names
[1] "ctrl" "trt1" "trt2"
```

```
## Use bxp to draw boxplot (Figure 3-8).
## Various parameters altered: horizontal plot, outlier symbol
## median line removed and replaced by symbol
## axis labels all horizontal, add notch (gives error for these data)
> bxp(bp, notch = TRUE, horiz = TRUE, outpch = 16,
  medlty = "blank", medpch = 16, las = 1)

Warning message:
In bxp(bp, notch = TRUE, horiz = TRUE, outpch = 16, medlty = "blank",  :
  some notches went outside hinges ('box'): maybe set notch=FALSE
```

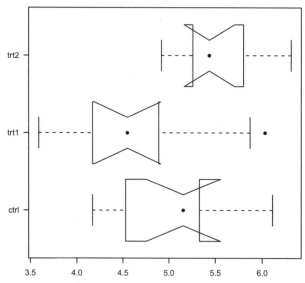

Figure 3-8: A boxplot drawn and customized using the bxp command

COMMAND NAME

`coplot`

This command produces conditioning plots. The command requires that the input be in the form of a `formula`. The panels of the plot can be customized using the `panel` parameter, which is in the form of a `function`.

Common Usage

```
coplot(formula, data, given.values, panel = points, rows, columns,
       show.given = TRUE, col = par("fg"), pch = par("pch"),
       bar.bg = c(num = gray(0.8), fac = gray(0.95)),
       xlab = c(x.name, paste("Given :", a.name)),
       ylab = c(y.name, paste("Given :", b.name)),
       subscripts = FALSE,
       axlabels = function(f) abbreviate(levels(f)),
       number = 6, overlap = 0.5, xlim, ylim, ...)
```

Related Commands

pairs (p. 377)

Command Parameters

formula	A formula of the general form y ~ x | a * b, where y and x are the variables to plot, and a and b are the conditioning variables. If there is only one conditioning variable, the formula will be y ~ x | a.
data	The name of the data frame containing the variables in the formula.
given.values	These values determine how the plot is arranged by specifying the order in which the conditioning plots are shown and applied. If there is one conditioning variable, there will be one set of values corresponding to the levels of the conditioning variable.
panel = points	A function that determines how the plot is produced. The default is points. Any custom function must include x and y parameters (see also the subscripts parameter).
rows	The number of rows for the main plot.
columns	The number of columns for the main plot.
show.given = TRUE	If FALSE, the levels of the conditioning variables are not shown. If two conditioning variables exist, two values must be given.
col	The colors for the points.
pch	The plotting symbols for the points.
bar.bg	A vector with two named components: "num" and "fac". These give the color of the shingle bars (see the following examples) for numeric and factor variables, respectively.
xlab	A character vector containing the names for the x-axis and the first conditioning variable. If a single value is given it is used for the x-axis, and the default is used for the conditioning variable.
ylab	A character vector containing the names for the y-axis and the second conditioning variable. If a single value is given it is used for the y-axis, and the default is used for the conditioning variable.
subscripts	If subscripts = TRUE, the custom function in panel can include a subscripts parameter.
axlabels	A function to create axis (tick) labels when x or y are factors.
number	An integer value to control the number of conditioning intervals if the conditioning variable is not a factor. If you have two conditioning variables you can specify two values.
overlap	A numeric value < 1, which determines the fraction of overlap of the conditioning variables. If you have two conditioning variables you can specify two values. If overlap < 0, there will be gaps between the data slices.

xlim	The extent of the x-axis; you must give the starting and ending values.
ylim	The extent of the y-axis; you must give the starting and ending values.
...	Additional graphical parameters can be used within the panel function.

Examples

 USE pw data in Essential.RData file for this example.

```
> Index = seq(length=nrow(pw)) # index of rows

  ## Draw plot (Figure 3-9)
  ## height is response data, Index plots individual values
  ## plant * water are conditioning variables
> coplot(height ~ Index | plant * water, data = pw,
  col = 'gray60', pch = 16, cex = 2, bar.bg = c(fac = "gray80"))
```

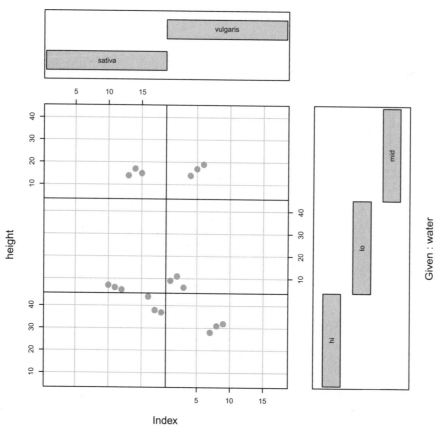

Figure 3-9: A coplot, a response variable, and two conditioning variables

THEME 3: GRAPHICS

COMMAND NAME

curve

This command draws a curve corresponding to a mathematical function. The command can create a new plot or add the curve to an existing plot window.

 SEE curve in "Adding Data" and curve in "Adding Lines."

COMMAND NAME

density

This command computes kernel density estimates. You can use it to visualize the distribution of a data sample as a graph, for example, plot(density(x)). You can also compare to a known distribution by overlaying the plot onto a histogram using the lines command.

 SEE hist.

COMMAND NAME

dotchart

This command produces Cleveland dot plots. These can be used as an alternative to bar charts and pie charts. You can also add a summary statistic to the plot.

Common Usage

```
dotchart(x, labels = NULL, groups = NULL, gdata = NULL,
         cex = par("cex"), pch = 21, gpch = 21, bg = par("bg"),
         color = par("fg"), gcolor = par("fg"), lcolor = "gray",
         xlim = range(x[is.finite(x)]),
         main = NULL, xlab = NULL, ylab = NULL, ...)
```

Related Commands

barplot (p. 349)
pie (p. 380)

Command Parameters

x	The data to plot, usually a vector or a matrix. If x is a matrix, the rows are taken as the data and the columns are taken as the groups.
labels = NULL	A vector of labels for the points. For a vector the names are used, for a matrix the rownames are used.
groups = NULL	A factor indicating the grouping of the data.
gdata = NULL	A data value for each group, such as the mean.
cex	A character expansion factor, values > 1 make text larger, values < 1 make it smaller.
pch = 21	The plotting symbol to use for the data points.
gpch = 21	The plotting symbol to use for the grouping summary.
bg	The background color for the plotting symbols.
color	The colors to use for data points and labels.
gcolor	The color to use for group labels and values.
lcolor = "gray"	The colors to use for the horizontal lines.
xlim	The x-axis scale, e.g., the limits of the horizontal axis. You must specify both start and end values.
main = NULL	An overall title for the plot.
xlab = NULL	A title for the x-axis.
ylab = NULL	A title for the y-axis.
...	Additional graphical parameters.

Examples

```
  ## Use data from datasets (VADeaths is a matrix)
> data(VADeaths) # make sure data ready

  ## Create dotchart (Figure 3-10), use colMeans to get summary mean
  ## Alter symbol for summary stat, add some titles
> dotchart(VADeaths, gdata = colMeans(VADeaths), gpch = "+",
  xlab = "Deaths per 1000", main = "Virginia (1940)")

  ## Add y-axis title and marginal text (top axis, on the right end)
> title(ylab = "Categories")
> mtext(text = "Grouping summary = mean", side = 3, adj = 1, font = 3)
```

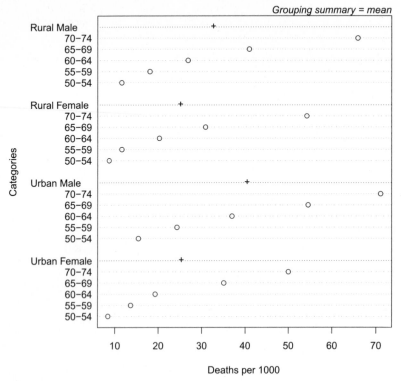

Figure 3-10: Cleveland dot chart with group summary statistic

COMMAND NAME

`hist`

This command creates histograms. The command computes the required values before plotting the histogram. These values can be saved as a named object, which holds a `class` attribute `"histogram"`.

Common Usage

```
hist(x, breaks = "Sturges",
    freq = NULL, right = TRUE,
    density = NULL, angle = 45, col = NULL, border = NULL,
    main = paste("Histogram of" , xname),
    xlim = range(breaks), ylim = NULL,
    xlab = xname, ylab,
    axes = TRUE, plot = TRUE, labels = FALSE, ...)
```

Related Commands

density (p. 366)
stem (p. 388)
barplot (p. 349)
table (p. 142)
rect (p. 420)

Command Parameters

x	A vector of values.
breaks = "Sturges"	Specifies the breakpoints between the histogram bars. Can be one of:

- An integer specifying the number of breaks required

- A vector of values, each one being a breakpoint

- A custom function to calculate breakpoints

- A character string giving an algorithm to use. The default is "Sturges"; other options are "Scott" and "FD", which is an abbreviation for "Freedman-Diaconis".

freq = NULL	If freq = TRUE, the histogram axis represents frequency. If FALSE, density is used (so the total area sums to 1). If the breakpoints are equidistant, the value defaults to TRUE.
right = TRUE	By default, the histogram cells are right-closed (left open) intervals.
density = NULL	The density of shading lines in lines per inch. The default is NULL, which suppresses lines.
angle = 45	The angle of shading lines in degrees. This is measured as a counter-clockwise rotation.
col = NULL	The color for the bars. The default, NULL, gives unfilled bars.
border = NULL	The border color for the bars. The default uses the standard foreground color.
main	A main title for the plot. To omit the title, use main = NULL.
xlim	The limits of the x-axis. You must specify both starting and ending values.
ylim	The limits of the y-axis. You must specify both starting and ending values.
xlab	A character vector giving a title for the x-axis.
ylab	A character vector giving a title for the y-axis.
axes = TRUE	If FALSE, the axes are not drawn.
plot = TRUE	If plot = FALSE, the values to create the histogram are computed but the plot is not drawn.
labels = FALSE	A vector of labels to place above the bars. For this to be successful you will need to know how many bars will be produced.
...	Additional graphical parameters can be used.

```
  ## Make some data
> set.seed(99) # Set random number generator
> dat = rnorm(50, mean = 10, sd = 1.5) # Values from normal distribution


  ## Draw histogram (Figure 3-11)
  ## Extend x-axis limits, add density fill lines
> hist(dat, xlim = c(4, 14), density = 15, angle = 60)
```

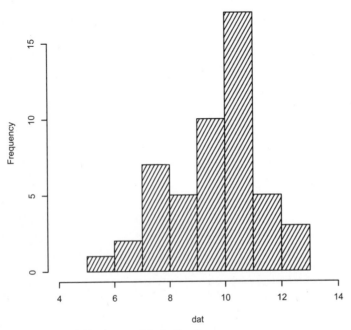

Figure 3-11: A histogram with shading lines

```
  ## View data used to draw histogram
> hist(dat, plot = FALSE)
$breaks
[1]   5  6  7  8  9 10 11 12 13

$counts
[1]   1  2  7  5 10 17  5  3

$intensities
[1] 0.02 0.04 0.14 0.10 0.20 0.34 0.10 0.06

$density
[1] 0.02 0.04 0.14 0.10 0.20 0.34 0.10 0.06
```

```
$mids
[1]  5.5  6.5  7.5  8.5  9.5 10.5 11.5 12.5

$xname
[1] "dat"

$equidist
[1] TRUE

attr(,"class")
[1] "histogram"

  ## Add density overlay and use unequal bars (Figure 3-12)
> hist(dat, breaks = c(5, 7, 9, 10, 11, 13), xlim = c(3, 13),
  main = NULL, col = "gray90", axes = FALSE)

  ## Add axes
> axis(2) # The default y-axis
  ## Draw x-axis
> axis(1, pos = 0) # Use pos to move axis up to bottom of bars

  ## Add density line as overlay
> lines(density(dat), lwd = 2) # lwd makes line wider
```

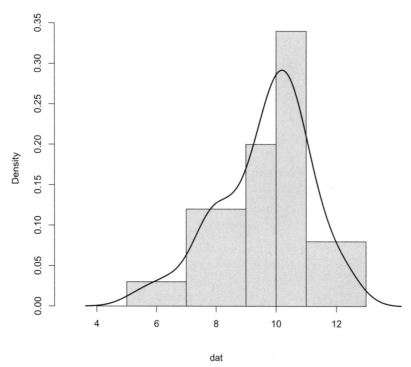

Figure 3-12: Histogram with unequal breakpoints and a density plot overlay

COMMAND NAME

`interaction.plot`

This command plots the mean or other summary statistic of a response variable for two-way combinations of factors. It can be seen as a quick graphical way to visualize potential factor interactions.

 SEE also aov in Theme 2, "Math and Statistics."

Common Usage

```
interaction.plot(x.factor, trace.factor, response, fun = mean,
            type = "l", legend = TRUE,
            trace.label = deparse(substitute(trace.factor)),
            fixed = FALSE,
            xlab = deparse(substitute(x.factor)),
            ylab = ylabel,
            ylim = range(cells, na.rm=TRUE),
            lty = nc:1, col = 1, pch = c(1:9, 0, letters),
            leg.bg = par("bg"), leg.bty = "n", ...)
```

Related Commands

`matplot` (p. 374)
`aov` (p. 285)

Command Parameters

`x.factor`	A factor whose levels will form the x-axis.
`trace.factor`	A factor whose levels will form the trace, e.g., the groupings of the plot.
`response`	A numeric variable giving the response variable to plot on the y-axis.
`fun = mean`	The summary function to apply to the response variable; the mean is the default.
`type = "l"`	The type of plot. The default is to use lines; other options are `"p"` for points and `"b"` for both lines and points.
`legend = TRUE`	If `legend = TRUE`, a legend is added.
`trace.label`	A title for the legend.
`fixed = FALSE`	By default, the trace factor is shown in the legend in the order of the level. If `fixed = TRUE`, the levels are shown in order of the summary function (at the right-hand end).
`xlab`	A title for the x-axis.
`ylab`	A title for the y-axis.
`ylim`	The limits of the y-axis. You must specify both starting and ending values.
`lty = nc:1`	The line types for the trace variable. The defaults use a range of numeric values.
`col = 1`	The colors for the plot. The default is black for everything.

pch	The plotting symbols to use if `type` = `"p"` or `"b"`. The defaults use numbers 1–9 followed by lowercase letters if needed.
leg.bg	A color to use for the legend. This only works if `leg.bty` = `"o"`.
leg.bty = "n"	By default, a box is not drawn around the legend. To draw one, use `leg.bty` = `"o"`.
...	Other graphical parameters can be specified.

Examples

 USE pw data in `Essential.RData` file for this example.

```
> names(pw) # A reminder of the variables
[1] "height" "plant"  "water"

  ## Draw the interaction plot (Figure 3-13)
> interaction.plot(pw$plant, pw$water, pw$height, fun = mean,
  xlab = "Plant Species", ylab = "Mean height",
  trace.label = "Water\nTreatment",
  type = "b", pch = c(16, 18, 21),
  lwd = 2, leg.bty = "o", las = 1)
```

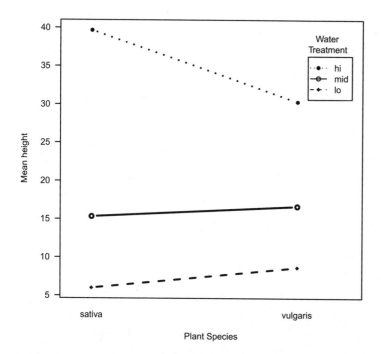

Figure 3-13: An interaction plot

COMMAND NAME

```
matplot
matpoints
matlines
```

The `matplot` command produces multiple series graphs. The command works by plotting the columns of one matrix against the columns of another matrix. The `matpoints` and `matlines` commands add points and lines to existing plots.

 SEE also `matlines` in "Adding to Graphs," `matlines` and `matpoints` in "Adding Lines," and `matpoints` in "Adding Data."

Common Usage

```
matplot(x, y, type = "p", lty = 1:5, lwd = 1, pch = NULL,
        col = 1:6, cex = NULL, bg = NA,
        xlab = NULL, ylab = NULL, xlim = NULL, ylim = NULL,
        ..., add = FALSE

matpoints(x, y, type = "p", lty = 1:5, lwd = 1, pch = NULL,
        col = 1:6, ...)

matlines (x, y, type = "l", lty = 1:5, lwd = 1, pch = NULL,
        col = 1:6, ...)
```

Related Commands

```
plot (p. 382)
points (p. 402)
lines (p. 398)
```

Command Parameters

`x, y` Matrix or vectors of numeric data to plot. The number of rows should match. If only one matrix or vector is given, it is taken as y with x being a simple index based on the number of rows in the given data.

`type = "p"` The type of plot to create. The default is "p", producing points. Other options are "l" and "b", producing lines and both lines and points, respectively. Different types can be specified for each column of y.

`lty = 1:5`	The line type to use for each column of y; defaults to values 1 to 5 and is recycled as necessary.
`lwd = 1`	The line widths for each column of y.
`pch = NULL`	The plotting symbols to use for each column of y. The default uses numbers 1–9 and lowercase letters.
`col = 1:6`	The colors to use for each column of y. Colors are recycled as necessary.
`cex = NULL`	The character expansion factor for each column of y.
`bg = NA`	The background colors to use for plotting symbols (if appropriate) for each column of y.
`xlab = NULL`	A title for the x-axis.
`ylab = NULL`	A title for the y-axis.
`xlim = NULL`	The limits of the x-axis. You must specify both starting and ending values.
`ylim = NULL`	The limits of the y-axis. You must specify both starting and ending values.
`...`	Additional graphical parameters.
`add = FALSE`	If `add = TRUE`, the plot is added to the current plot window; otherwise, a new plot is created.

 SEE also par.

Examples

```
  ## Make some data (matrix for response and matrix for predictor)
> resp = matrix(c(2, 4, 7, 12, 10, 15, 19, 14, 15, 11, 6, 4), ncol = 2)
> pred = matrix(c(2, 3, 5, 8, 12, 15), ncol = 1)

  ## Create matrix plot as lines+points (Figure 3-14)
  ## Use custom symbols, line width, colors and styles
> matplot(pred, resp, type = 'b', pch = c(21,23), lwd = c(1, 2),
 col = 1:2, lty = 1:2)

  ## Add a legend, make sure parameters match original plot
  ## Check pch, lty and so on match
> legend("topright", legend = c("Spp1", "Spp2"), bty = "n", pch = c(21, 23),
 col = 1:2, lty = 1:2, title = "Species")
```

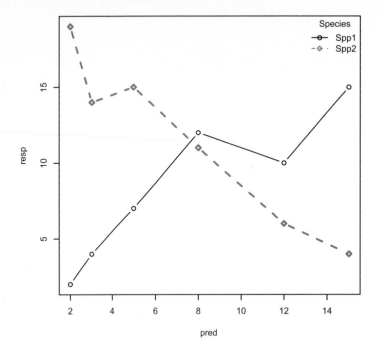

Figure 3-14: A matrix plot with legend

```
   ## Create some data (vectors)
 > Sp3 = c(15, 9, 5, 2, 3, 8)
 > Sp4 = c(3, 5, 8, 12, 13, 9)

   ## Make a blank plot (Figure 3-15)
 > plot(0:15, 0:15, type = "n")

   ## matpoints can add to any plot and can also draw lines!
   ## Note that data can be a vector
   ## Specify plotting character, color and so on to help match in legend
 > matpoints(pred, Sp3, type = "b", col = "blue", lwd = 3, lty = 3,
   pch = 25)

   # matlines can draw points!
 > matlines(pred, Sp4, type = "b", col = "black", pch = 24)

   ## Add a legend
 > legend("bottomleft", legend = c("Sp3", "Sp4"),
   col = c("blue", "black"), lty = c(3, 1), pch = 25:24)
```

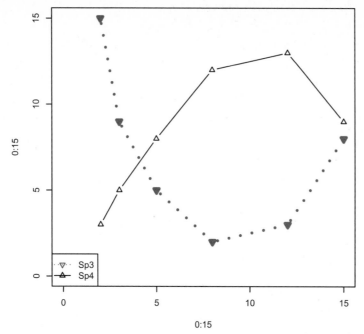

Figure 3-15: The matpoints and matlines commands used to add data to an existing plot

COMMAND NAME

`pairs`

This command produces multiple scatter plots within one plot window; that is, it produces a matrix of scatter plots. The command can accept input in two forms:

- As a matrix or data frame with numeric columns

- As a `formula`

Common Usage

```
pairs(formula, data = NULL, ..., subset,
    na.action = stats::na.pass)

pairs(x, labels, panel = points, ...,
    lower.panel = panel, upper.panel = panel,
    diag.panel = NULL, text.panel = textPanel,
    label.pos = 0.5 + has.diag/3,
    cex.labels = NULL, font.labels = 1,
    row1attop = TRUE, gap = 1)
```

Related Commands

`plot` (p. 382)
`coplot` (p. 363)

Command Parameters

`formula`	A formula with no response variable, only predictors, of the form `~ x + y + z`.
`data = NULL`	A data frame or list containing the variables given in the `formula`.
`subset`	A subset of observations to use.
`na.action`	A function defining what to do if `NA` items are in the data. The default is to pass missing values on to the panel functions, but `na.action = na.omit` will cause cases with missing values in any of the variables to be omitted entirely.
`x`	A data frame or matrix whose columns form the variables to be plotted.
`labels`	The names for the variables.
`panel = points`	A `function(x, y, ...)`, used to plot the contents of the panels.
`...`	Additional graphical parameters.
`lower.panel = panel`	A `function(x, y, ...)`, used for plotting in the lower triangle of panels.
`upper.panel = panel`	A `function(x, y, ...)`, used for plotting in the upper triangle of panels.
`diag.panel = NULL`	A `function(x, ...)`, used to apply to the diagonal.
`text.panel = textPanel`	A `function(x, y, labels, cex, font, ...)`, which is applied to the diagonals.
`label.pos`	The y position of the labels in the text panel.
`cex.labels = NULL`	An expansion factor for the labels in the text panel.
`font.labels = 1`	The font style to use for the text panel.
`row1attop = TRUE`	If `TRUE`, the layout is matrix-like, with row 1 at the top. If `FALSE`, it is graph-like with row 1 at the bottom.
`gap = 1`	Sets the distance between sub-plots in margin lines.

Examples

 USE `mf` data in `Essential.RData` file for these examples.

```
> names(mf) # as a reminder of variable names
[1] "Length" "Speed"  "Algae"  "NO3"    "BOD"    "site"

  ## Make pairs plot using some of the variables (Figure 3-16)
> pairs(~ Length + Speed + Algae, data = mf)
```

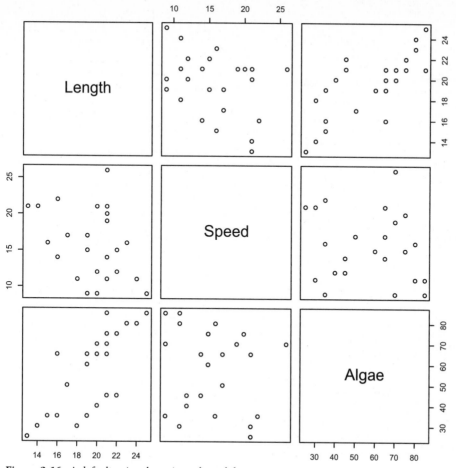

Figure 3-16: A default pairs plot using selected data

```
  ## Make a special function to display best-fit line
> panel.lm = function(x, y, ...) {  # Set-up function and define inputs
    par("new" = TRUE)                 # do not wipe a new plot
    plot(x, y)                        # plot the x, y values
    abline(lm(y ~ x), col = "blue") # add a best-fit line in blue
    par("new" = FALSE) } # reset the new parameter and end the function

  ## Make pairs plot (Figure 3-17) and use new function
  ## to place scatter + best-fit in lower panels
> pairs(~Length + Speed + Algae + NO3, data=mf, lower.panel = panel.lm)
```

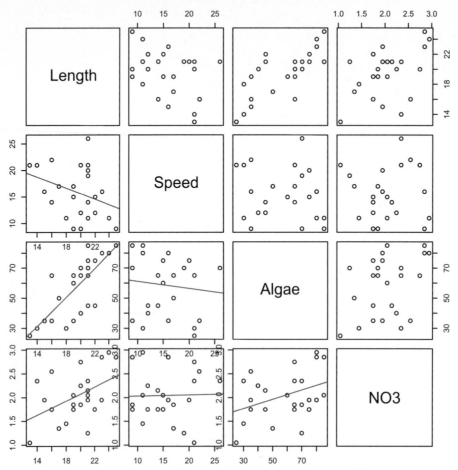

Figure 3-17: A pairs plot with a customized function for the lower panels

COMMAND NAME

pie

This command produces pie charts.

Common Usage

```
pie(x, labels = names(x), edges = 200, radius = 0.8,
    clockwise = FALSE, init.angle = if(clockwise) 90 else 0,
    density = NULL, angle = 45, col = NULL, border = NULL,
    lty = NULL, main = NULL, ...)
```

Related Commands

dotchart (p. 366)
barplot (p. 349)

Command Parameters

x	A vector of numeric values, these will form the pie slices and must be non-negative.
labels = names(x)	Labels for the pie slices. The default is to use the names attribute of x.
edges = 200	A value that controls how smooth the circular outline of the pie is. The greater the value, the more segments of polygon are used, so the smoother the circle.
radius = 0.8	The proportion of the plot area that the pie fills. Smaller size may be necessary to accommodate labels.
clockwise = FALSE	By default, the slices of pie are drawn counter-clockwise.
init.angle	A value specifying the starting angle in degrees. The default is 0 (3 o'clock) unless clockwise = TRUE, in which case it is 90 (12 o'clock).
density = NULL	The density of shading lines in lines per inch. The default is NULL, which suppresses lines.
angle = 45	The angle of shading lines in degrees. This is measured as a counter-clockwise rotation.
col = NULL	Colors used for filling the slices. The default is a set of six pastel colors.
border = NULL	The border color for the slices.
lty = NULL	The line type for the slices.
main = NULL	An overall title for the plot.
...	Additional graphical parameters can be supplied, but the only ones with an effect relate to labels and main title.

Examples

```
  ## Make data
> rain = c(34, 32, 23, 15, 10, 8, 6, 9, 12, 21, 24, 29) # A vector
> names(rain) = month.abb[1:12] # Make labels
> rain # View the data
Jan Feb Mar Apr May Jun Jul Aug Sep Oct Nov Dec
 34  32  23  15  10   8   6   9  12  21  24  29

  ## Make a pie chart using all default settings (Figure 3-18)
  ## Labels are shown for slices as names were set
> pie(rain)
```

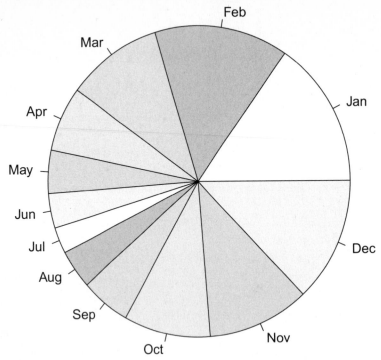

Figure 3-18: A pie chart

COMMAND NAME

`plot`

This command is a generic function for plotting R objects. The basic form of the command produces scatter plots. However, many objects have a dedicated plotting routine and variants of the plot command will produce plots according to the `class` attribute of the object. You have three ways to specify the input to plot:

- As separate x and y coordinates

- As a `formula`

- As an object that has a plotting structure (that is, it has a dedicated plot command of its own)

Many graphical parameters can be specified and most are shared with other commands that produce a plot window. The `par` command gives access to all the graphical parameters.

 SEE also `plot` in "Adding Lines."

Common Usage

`plot(x, y, ...)`

Related Commands

par (p. 437)
points (p. 402)
lines (p. 398)

Command Parameters

x, y	The coordinates to plot. These can be separate x and y vectors or a formula. You can also specify an object, which holds a print structure.
frame.plot	If frame.plot = TRUE, the default, a box is drawn around the plot region.
type	The type of plot to produce. The general default is type = "p", which produces points. The main options are "p" for points, "l" for lines, "b" for both, and "n" for nothing.
main sub xlab ylab	Titles. Titles can be specified using a character string (or expression). You can produce titles for the overall plot and a subtitle, as well as for x- and y-axes.
log	Allows plotting of axes on a log scale. Use a character string as follows: "x" for the x-axis to be logarithmic, "y" for the y-axis, and "xy" or "yx" for both.
...	Additional graphical parameters.

Many graphical parameters can be used with the plot command. Additionally, the par command allows you to alter the current settings. Most of the parameters accessible via par can be used directly from the plotting command but some can only be set using the par command.

 SEE also par.

Examples

 USE mf data in Essential.RData file for this example.

```
> names(mf) # As a reminder of the variables
[1] "Length" "Speed"  "Algae"  "NO3"    "BOD"    "site"

  ## A scatter plot in x, y style (Figure 3-19)
  ## Expression used in x-axis label to get superscript
  ## plotting symbol 21 can be colored in ("gray85") and larger
> plot(mf$Speed, mf$Length,
 xlab = expression(Speed~ms^-1), ylab = "Length in mm",
pch = 21, bg = "gray85", cex = 2)

  ## Add a main title and alter the font to italic
> title(main = "Mayflies", font.main = 3)
```

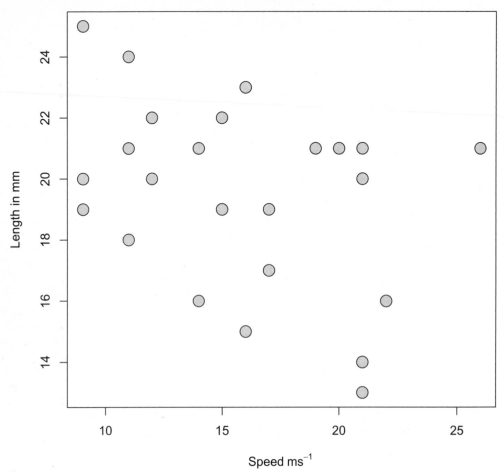

Figure 3-19: A scatter plot

```
  ## Use cars data from R datasets
> data(cars) # make sure data are ready
> names(cars) # A reminder of the variables
[1] "speed" "dist"

  ## Make plot (Figure 3-20), use formula to specify data
  ## Use lines (type = "l") and widen them (lwd = 1.5)
  ## Add titles and ensure axis annotations are horizontal (las = 1)
> plot(dist ~ speed, data = cars, type = "l", lwd = 1.5,
 xlab = "Speed, mph", ylab = "Distance, ft.",
 main = "Stopping Distances (1920s)", las = 1)
```

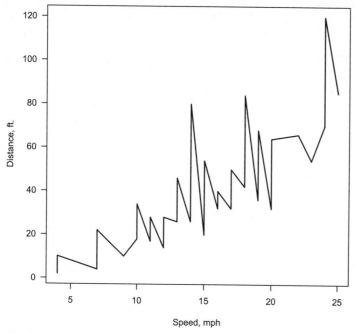

Stopping Distances (1920s)

Figure 3-20: A plot using lines rather than points

COMMAND NAME

qqnorm

This command draws quantile-quantile plots. The command takes a numeric sample and plots it against theoretical quantiles based on a normal distribution. In this way, you can visualize the normality of the data distribution.

 SEE also Theme 2: "Math and Statistics: Tests of Distribution."

Common Usage

```
qqnorm(y, ylim, main = "Normal Q-Q Plot",
     xlab = "Theoretical Quantiles", ylab = "Sample Quantiles",
     plot.it = TRUE, datax = FALSE, ...)
```

Related Commands

qqplot (p. 387)
qqline (p. 411)
plot (p. 382)

Command Parameters

y	The data sample to plot, usually a vector.
ylim	The limits of the y-axis; you must specify both starting and ending values.
main	The main title for the plot. The title can be omitted using main = NULL.
xlab ylab	Titles for x- and y-axes; the defaults place sensible titles. If you specify NULL, the title is not omitted; "x" and "y" are used for the x- and y-axis, respectively. To suppress an axis, use "", a pair of empty quotes.
plot.it = TRUE	If plot.it = FALSE, the data for the plot is computed but nothing is actually plotted.
datax = FALSE	By default, the sample quantiles are plotted on the y-axis. If datax = TRUE, the theoretical quantiles are plotted on the y-axis and the sample quantiles are plotted on the x-axis.
...	Additional graphical parameters can be used.

 SEE also par.

Examples

 USE pw data in Essential.RData file for this example.

```
## Draw the QQ plot (Figure 3-21). Set plotting symbol, color & size.
> qqnorm(pw$height, cex = 2, pch = 21, bg = "gray85")

## Add a QQ line to help estimate normality
> qqline(pw$height, lwd = 2, lty = 3)
```

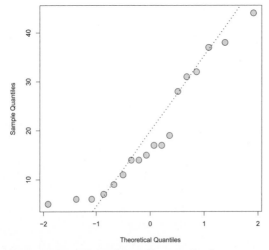

Figure 3-21: A normal quantile-quantile plot

COMMAND NAME

qqplot

This command produces a quantile-quantile plot of two variables.

 SEE also Theme 2: "Math and Statistics: Tests of Distribution."

Common Usage

```
qqplot(x, y, plot.it = TRUE, xlab = deparse(substitute(x)),
       ylab = deparse(substitute(y)), ...)
```

Related Commands

qqnorm (p. 385)
plot (p. 382)
abline (p. 404)

Command Parameters

x, y   Numeric samples to plot. They do not need to be the same length because it is
                the quantiles that are plotted, not the original data.

plot.it = TRUE If plot.it = FALSE, the data for the plot is computed but nothing is actually
                plotted.

xlab   Titles for x- and y-axes; the defaults place sensible titles. If you specify NULL,
ylab   the title is not omitted; "sx" and "sy" are used for the x- and y-axis, respec-
                tively. To suppress an axis, use "", a pair of empty quotes.

Examples

```
  ## Make some data
> set.seed(55) # Reset the random number generator

  ## Make random numbers from two distributions
> nd = rnorm(n = 50, mean = 5, sd = 1) # Normal (Gaussian) data
> ud = runif(n = 40, min = 3, max = 7) # Uniform distribution

  ## Make QQ plot to compare samples (Figure 3-22)
> qqplot(nd, ud, cex = 1.5, xlab = "Gaussian", ylab = "Uniform")

  ## If samples matched, the line would "fit"
> abline(0, 1, lwd = 1.5, lty = 4)
```

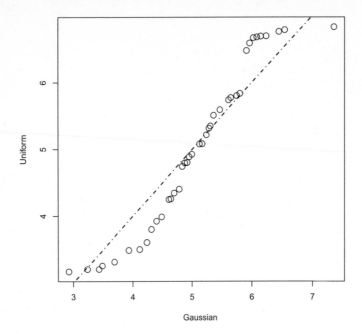

Figure 3-22: A QQ plot comparing Gaussian and Uniform distribution

COMMAND NAME

stem

This command creates stem-and-leaf plots. The command does not open a graphical window but produces a text-based representation of the data distribution in the console window.

Common Usage

```
stem(x, scale = 1, width = 80)
```

Related Commands

hist (p. 368)
density (p. 366)

Command Parameters

x   A numeric vector.

scale = 1   Sets the length of the plot; essentially creates more bins. You can specify values < 1.

width = 80 Sets the width of the plot in the console window. Any truncated values are represented by +n, where n shows the number of missing values.

Examples

```
  ## Make some data
> set.seed(55) # Set random number generator

  ## Make 50 values from a normal distribution
> nd = rnorm(n = 50, mean = 5, sd = 1)

  ## Stem-leaf plot using defaults
> stem(nd)

  The decimal point is at the |

  2 | 9
  3 | 24
  3 | 5579
  4 | 12334
  4 | 55667788999
  5 | 0012233334
  5 | 5667889
  6 | 0011224
  6 | 56
  7 | 4

  ## Make scale smaller
> stem(nd, scale = 0.5)

  The decimal point is at the |

  2 | 9
  3 | 245579
  4 | 1233455667788999
  5 | 00122333345667889
  6 | 001122456
  7 | 4
```

Saving Graphs

You can save your graphs to other programs in two ways: using copy and paste or by saving your graph to disk as a graphics file. You can save graphs in various formats; for example, JPEG, PNG, TIFF, BMP, and PDF.

Sometimes you want to create a graphics window ready to accept a plot. Creating a window leaves an old graph intact and readies a new graphics window for subsequent plots. You can also have several graphics windows open at the same time. R provides commands that allow you to manage the various graphics windows.

COMMAND NAME

bmp
jpeg
png
tiff
dev.new

These commands open a link to a file on disk and send graphical commands to it. The file remains open and any graphical commands are sent to the file until the command dev.off is used to close the file.

 SEE also jpeg, png, tiff, and dev.new in "Saving Graphs."

Common Usage

```
bmp(filename = "Rplot%03d.bmp",
    width = 480, height = 480, units = "px",
    pointsize = 12, bg = "white", res = NA)

jpeg(filename = "Rplot%03d.jpeg",
     width = 480, height = 480, units = "px",
     pointsize = 12, quality = 75, bg = "white", res = NA)

png(filename = "Rplot%03d.png",
    width = 480, height = 480, units = "px",
    pointsize = 12, bg = "white",  res = NA)

tiff(filename = "Rplot%03d.tiff",
     width = 480, height = 480, units = "px", pointsize = 12,
     compression = "none", bg = "white", res = NA)

dev.new(...)
```

Related Commands

dev.off (p. 392)
quartz (p. 395)
dev.new (p. 390, 395)
pdf (p. 394)

Command Parameters

filename	A filename to write the subsequent graphics file. This must be in quotes. The file will be written to the current working directory unless the path is written explicitly.
width = 480	The width of the graphic. The default is 480 (pixels).
height = 480	The height of the graphic. The default is 480 (pixels).
units = "px"	The units for height and width. The default is "px" (pixels). Other options are "in" (inches), "cm" (centimeters), and "mm" (millimeters).

pointsize = 12	The default point-size of plotted text characters. It works out at 1/72 inch at res dpi.
quality = 75	For jpeg this sets the quality of the image as a percentage. Essentially this controls the file size. Smaller values will be smaller files, but greater compression leads to poorer quality.
compression = "none"	For tiff this sets the type of compression to use. The default is "none". Other options are "rle", "lzw", "jpeg", and "zip".
bg	Sets the background color. The default setting is "white".
res = NA	The resolution for the final image in dpi. If you do not specify a value, the image will use 72 dpi but not have a dpi value recorded in the meta data.
...	Any appropriate commands for the device.

Examples

```
  ## Use cars data from R datasets
> names(cars) # A reminder of the variables
[1] "speed" "dist"

  ## Draw the plot to screen (not shown)
> plot(dist ~ speed, data = cars, main = "Scatter plot", cex=2, las = 1)
> abline(lm(dist ~ speed, data = cars), lty = 2, lwd = 2)
> text(5, 100, "Correlation = 0.8", pos = 4)

  ## Send to disk as PNG using res = 300
  ## Open the device driver
> png(file = "dpi300.png", height = 2100, width = 2100,
  res = 300, bg = "white")

  ## Use graphical commands
> plot(dist ~ speed, data = cars, main = "Scatter plot", cex=2, las = 1)
> abline(lm(dist ~ speed, data = cars), lty = 2, lwd = 2)
> text(5, 100, "Correlation = 0.8", pos = 4)

  ## Close the device and finish writing the file
> dev.off()

## Compare the screen plot to the disk file
```

COMMAND NAME

```
dev.copy
dev.print
```

These commands copy the current graphics device to a new device. The most useful purpose is to copy a graphic from the screen to a disk file (which you can also do via the GUI in Windows). The dev.copy command makes the new device the current one and leaves it open so further graphical commands can be issued (use dev.off to close the file). The dev.print command closes the device immediately.

Common Usage

```
dev.copy(device, ..., which = dev.next())

dev.print(device, ...)
```

Related Commands

dev.off (p. 392)
dev.cur (p. 392)
bmp (p. 390)
pdf (p. 394)
png (p. 390)
jpeg (p. 390)
tiff (p. 390)

Command Parameters

device	A device to send the current plot to. This will usually be bmp, png, pdf, jpeg, or tiff.
...	Parameters to pass to the device; e.g., filename, height, width, and res.
which = dev.next()	If a device is already open, it can be specified using which. You cannot specify both device and which parameters.

Examples

```
  ## Use cars data from R datasets
> data(cars) # make sure data is ready

  ## Plot to screen (not shown)
> plot(dist ~ speed, data = cars, main = "Scatter plot",
  cex = 2, las = 1)

  ## Send graphic to a jpeg file and close device immediately
> dev.print(jpeg, height = 2100, width = 2100, res = 300,
  file = "A_test.jpg")
```

COMMAND NAME

```
dev.cur
dev.list
dev.next
dev.off
dev.prev
dev.set
```

These commands manage the graphics device(s). You can see what the current device is, list all active devices, turn off any or all devices (and so complete the writing of a graphics file to disk), and switch between graphics devices (on screen or disk). The commands and their tasks are as follows:

- dev.cur shows which is the current device.

- dev.list lists all open devices.

- dev.next makes the next device current.

- dev.off closes a device.

- dev.prev makes the previous device current.

- dev.set sets a specific device as current.

- graphics.off closes all devices.

Common Usage

```
dev.cur()
dev.list()
dev.next(which = dev.cur())
dev.off(which = dev.cur())
dev.prev(which = dev.cur())
dev.set(which = dev.next())
graphics.off()
```

Related Commands

```
dev.copy (p. 391)
dev.print (p. 391)
png (p. 390)
pdf (p. 394)
bmp (p. 390)
tiff (p. 390)
jpeg (p. 390)
```

Command Parameters

which   The graphics device to use. Usually a simple integer value. The number 1 is always the "null device" and cannot be used.

Examples

```
> graphics.off() # Turn off all graphics devices
> dev.cur() # What is current? Nothing!
null device
         1

  ## Open a new blank window
> windows(height = 7, width = 7, title = "My Graphics Window")
> dev.cur() # Device 2 is current (1 is always null)
windows
     2

  ## Open another window
> quartz(height = 7, width = 7, title = "My other Graphics Window")
> dev.list() # Show the list
windows windows
     2       3
```

```
> dev.cur() # Window 3 is current
windows
      3
> dev.prev() # set to previous window
windows
      2
```

COMMAND NAME

jpeg

Opens a link to a file on disk and sends graphical commands to a JPEG file.

 SEE bmp and pdf.

COMMAND NAME

pdf

Opens a link to a file on disk and sends graphical commands to a PDF file.

Common Usage

```
pdf(file = ifelse(onefile, "Rplots.pdf", "Rplot%03d.pdf"),
    width, height, onefile, family, title,
    paper, bg, fg, pointsize, pagecentre, colormodel)
```

Related Commands

dev.off (p. 392)
dev.new (p. 390, 395)
png (p. 390)
bmp (p. 390)
tiff (p. 390)
jpeg (p. 390)

Command Parameters

file	A filename to write the subsequent graphics file. This must be in quotes. The file will be written to the current working directory unless the path is written explicitly. The default filename depends on the onefile setting.
width	The width of the plot in inches. The usual default is 7, but this can be altered.
height	The height of the plot in inches. The usual default is 7, but this can be altered.
onefile	If onefile = TRUE, multiple figures will be sent to a single PDF file.
family	The font family to use. The default is "Helvetica" (or "sans"). Other options are "AvantGarde", "Bookman", "Courier" (or "mono"), "Helvetica-Narrow", "NewCenturySchoolbook", "Palatino", and "Times" (or "serif"). These are standard Adobe PostScript fonts.

title	A title comment embedded in the file. The default is "R Graphics Output".
paper = "special"	The target paper size. Basic options are "a4", "letter", "legal" (or "us"), and "executive". Also, "a4r" and "USr" can be used for landscape (rotated) orientation. The default, "special", takes the paper size from the height and width.
bg = "transparent"	The background color to use. The default is "transparent".
fg = "black"	The foreground color to use. The default is "black".
pointsize = 12	The default point size to use. This is only approximate and defaults to 12.
pagecentre = TRUE	If paper is not "special", by default the graphic is centered on the page.
colormodel	A character string that specifies the color model to be used; the default is "rgb". Other options are "gray" and "cmyk".

Examples

```
  ## Create a link to a file and start the PDF device driver
  ## Set the device to create greyscale
> pdf(file = "My_graphic.pdf", height = 7, width = 7,
  colormodel = "gray")

  ## Create a plot
plot(dist ~ speed, data = cars, main = "Scatter plot", cex = 2, las = 1)

  ## Close the device, which writes/finishes the file
dev.off()
```

COMMAND NAME

png

Opens a link to a file on disk and sends graphical commands to a PNG file.

 SEE bmp and pdf.

COMMAND NAME

quartz
windows
X11
dev.new

These commands open a blank graphics window. Usually this will be on-screen but the quartz command can open a link to a file (which must be closed using dev.off). The different commands operate on different operating systems:

- For Macintosh, use quartz and X11

- For Windows, use windows and X11

- For Linux, use X11 (x11 is an alias)

The `dev.new` command opens a graphics device appropriate for the operating system.

 SEE also x11 in "Saving Graphs."

Common Usage

```
quartz(title, width, height, pointsize, family,
       type, file = NULL, bg, canvas, dpi)

windows(width, height, pointsize, xpinch, ypinch, bg, canvas,
        gamma, title, family)

X11(width, height, pointsize, gamma, bg, canvas, title, type)

dev.new(...)
```

Related Commands

`dev.cur` (p. 392)
`dev.list` (p. 392)

Command Parameters

`title`	A character string that will appear in the title bar of the graphics window.
`width`	The width of the graphics window in inches. The default is 7.
`height`	The height of the graphics window in inches. The default is 7.
`pointsize`	The point size to use. The default is 12.
`dpi`	The resolution of the output. For on-screen graphics windows, this defaults to the resolution of the screen. For off-screen graphics, the default is 72.
`xpinch` `ypinch`	The resolution of the output in the horizontal and vertical directions.
`bg`	The initial background color to use; defaults to `"transparent"`.
`canvas`	The canvas color to use for on-screen windows. The default is `"white"`.
`type = "native"`	The type of display to use. The default, `"native"`, uses the screen. Other options are dependent on the OS and include `"png"`, `"jpeg"`, `"tiff"`, `"gif"`, `"psd"`, and `"pdf"`.
`file = NULL`	A target for the graphics device. Used when `type` is set to an off-screen device. Any filename must be in quotes and will go to the current working directory unless the path is specified explicitly.

family	The family name of the font series to be used. The default depends on the operating system.
. . .	Parameters to pass to selected device. If left blank, the default screen device is used.

Examples

```
  ## Start a new blank screen 5 inches in size (Windows OS)
> windows(height = 5, width = 5, title = "My graphics")

  ## Start a new window 4 inches is size (on any OS)
> dev.new(height = 4, width = 4, title = "My small graphic")

> graphics.off() # close all graphics
```

COMMAND NAME

`tiff`

Opens a link to a file on disk and sends graphical commands to a TIFF file.

 SEE bmp and pdf.

COMMAND NAME

`windows`

Opens a blank graphics window. The different commands operate on different operating systems.

 SEE also windows in "Saving Graphs."

 SEE quartz in "Saving Graphs."

COMMAND NAME

`X11`
`x11`

Opens a blank graphics window. The x11 command is an alias for X11.

 SEE quartz.

Adding to Graphs

You can add various elements to graphs. You can add data, represented by points or lines. You can also add various sorts of lines to plots, such as lines of best-fit or curves representing mathematical functions. You can also add text to graphs, either in the main plot area or in the margins and along the axes. You can also add legends.

What's In This Topic:

ADDING DATA

Once you have created a graph of some sort you can add data to it in various ways. You can add data as `points` or as `lines`. You can also use the `lines` command to make lines of best-fit.

COMMAND NAME

`curve`

This command plots a mathematical function, either as a new plot or to an existing one.

 SEE "Adding Lines."

COMMAND NAME

`lines`

 SEE also `lines` in "Adding Lines."

This command adds connected line segments to an existing plot. The data can be specified in two main ways:

- As x and y coordinates

- As an object that contains a valid plotting structure (that is, x and y coordinates)

You can think of the `lines` and `points` commands as equivalent; you can alter the parameters of either to produce the same result.

Common Usage

```
lines(x, y = NULL, type = "l", ...)
```

Related Commands

`points` (p. 402)
`abline` (p. 404)
`plot` (p. 382)
`spline` (p. 414)
`curve` (p. 408)
`par` (p. 437)

Command Parameters

`x, y` Vectors of numeric values that describe the coordinates to plot. If x is an object with a valid plotting structure, y can be missing. This object could be a list with named x and y elements, a two-column matrix or data frame, or a time series object.

`type = "l"` The type of line to produce. The default, `"l"`, produces segments of line. Other options include:

- `"p"`—Points

- `"b"`—Both points and lines

- `"o"`—Points and lines overplotted

- `"c"`—Unconnected line segments

- `"n"`—Nothing

`...` Other graphical parameters can be used. Especially noteworthy are:

- `lwd`—Line width

- `lty`—Line type

- `col`—Line color

 SEE the `par` command for a comprehensive list.

Examples

```
## Use cars data from R datasets
> data(cars) # make sure data are ready

## Draw scatter plot (Figure 3-23)
> plot(dist ~ speed, data = cars, main = "Scatter plot", cex=2, las = 1)

## Make a linear model of relationship
> cars.lm = lm(dist ~ speed, data = cars)

## Use fitted model values to add a line (x = speed, y = fitted)
> lines(cars$speed, fitted(cars.lm), lwd = 2)
```

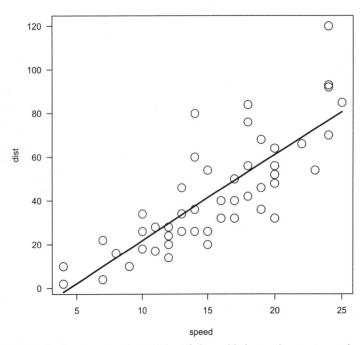

Figure 3-23: A scatter plot with best-fit line added using lines command

COMMAND NAME

locator

The locator command reads the position of the cursor when you click the mouse. The results are returned as x, y coordinates. A common use for the locator command is to allow the user to place a legend or text in a graphic window by clicking with the mouse.

Common Usage

```
locator(n = 512)
```

Related Commands

```
legend (p. 432)
text (p. 428)
```

Command Parameters

n = 512   The number of points to locate. The coordinates of mouse clicks will be recorded until the default number of clicks is reached (512) or the ESC key is pressed.

Examples

```
> plot(0:10,0:10) # Make a simple plot

  ## Set one mouse-click and get the coordinates
> locator(1)
$x
[1] 3.357639

$y
[1] 8.821705

  ## Set two clicks and return coordinates
> locator(2)
$x
[1] 2.020833 6.829861

$y
[1] 7.736434 4.538760
```

COMMAND NAME

```
matlines
matpoints
```

These commands add data as lines or points to an existing plot (usually one created using `matplot`).

 SEE matplot in "Types of Graphs."

THEME 3: GRAPHICS

COMMAND NAME

`points`

This command adds points to an existing plot. The data can be specified in two main ways:

- As x and y coordinates
- As an object that contains a valid plotting structure (that is, x and y coordinates)

You can think of the `points` and `lines` commands as equivalent; you can alter the parameters of either to produce the same result.

Common Usage

```
points(x, y = NULL, type = "p", ...)
```

Related Commands

`lines` (p. 398)
`par` (p. 437)
`plot` (p. 382)

Command Parameters

x, y   Vectors of numeric values that describe the coordinates to plot. If x is an object with a valid plotting structure, y can be missing. This object could be a list with named x and y elements, a two-column matrix or data frame, or a time series object.

type = "p"   The type of line to produce. The default, "p", produces points. Other options include:

- "1"—Lines
- "b"—Both points and lines
- "o"—Points and lines overplotted
- "c"—Unconnected line segments
- "n"—Nothing

...   Other graphical parameters can be used. Especially noteworthy are:

- pch—Plotting symbol
- cex—Character expansion for plotting symbols
- col—Color for plotting symbols (and line)
- bg—Background color for open style plotting symbols (pch = 21:25)

Examples

```
  ## make a simple plot (Figure 3-24)
> plot(1:10, 1:10, cex = 2)

  ## Add points to the plot
> points(10:1, 1:10, pch = 23, bg = "gray80", cex = 2)

  ## Some data (as vectors)
> x = c(1, 4, 6, 3, 4, 7)
> y = c(3, 6, 4, 5, 9, 6)

  ## Add the vectors as points
> points(x, y, pch = 21, bg = "black", cex = 2)
```

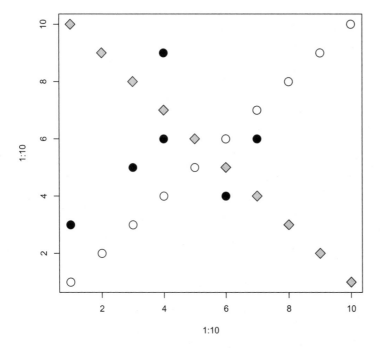

Figure 3-24: Scatter plot with extra data added using the points command

ADDING LINES

You can add various sorts of lines to existing plots. These include lines of best-fit (straight or curved), sections of straight line, arrows, and curves representing mathematical functions.

COMMAND NAME

`abline`

This command can add one or more straight lines to a plot. Lines can be drawn horizontally, vertically, or with a specified slope and intercept. The command can accept input in two main ways:

- Values given explicitly

- Values taken from an object, which contains `coefficients`

Common Usage

```
abline(a = NULL, b = NULL, h = NULL, v = NULL, reg = NULL,
       coef = NULL, untf = FALSE, ...)
```

Related Commands

`lines` (p. 398)
`fitted` (p. 309)
`loess` (p. 333)
`lowess` (p. 335)
`spline` (p. 414)

Command Parameters

`a = NULL`	The intercept for the line as a numeric value.
`b = NULL`	The slope of the line as a numeric value.
`h = NULL`	The y value for a horizontal line.
`v = NULL`	The x value for a vertical line.
`reg = NULL`	An object that contains coefficients, such as the result of `lm`.
`coef = NULL`	A vector containing two values, the intercept and slope.
`untf = FALSE`	If `untf = TRUE`, and at least one axis was drawn log-transformed, the line is drawn corresponding to the original coordinates. If `untf = FALSE`, the line is drawn using the transformed coordinate system. Horizontal and vertical lines always use the original coordinate system.
`...`	Additional graphics commands can be used. Of particular use are:

- `col`—The line color

- `lwd`—The line width

- `lty`—The line type

SEE the par command for a comprehensive list.

Examples

```
  ## Use cars data from R datasets
> data(cars) # make sure data is ready

  ## Make the basic scatter plot (Figure 3-25)
> plot(dist ~ speed, data = cars, cex = 2)

  ## Add horizontal lines using a sequence
> abline(h = seq(from = 20, to = 100, by = 20), lty = 3, col = "gray50")

  ## Add a vertical line at the mean speed
> abline(v = mean(cars$speed), lty = "dotted", col = "gray50")

  ## Do a regression
> cars.lm = lm(dist ~ speed, data = cars)

  ## Add line of best-fit using regression result
> abline(cars.lm, lwd = 2.5)

  ## View coefficients of regression (intercept, slope)
> coef(cars.lm)
(Intercept)        speed
 -17.579095     3.932409

  ## Add line approximating to intercept, slope
  ## by giving vector of two values
> abline(c(-20, 4), lwd = 2, lty = 2)

  ## add a line by specifying intercept and slope separately
> abline(0, 1)
```

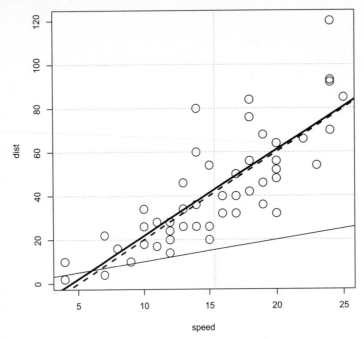

Figure 3-25: Using the abline command to add to a plot

COMMAND NAME

`arrows`

This command adds arrows to a plot by connecting pairs of coordinates.

Common Usage

```
arrows(x0, y0, x1 = x0, y1 = y0,
       length = 0.25, angle = 30, code = 2,
       col = par("fg"), lty = par("lty"), lwd = par("lwd"),
       ...)
```

Related Commands

`segments` (p. 413)

Command Parameters

`x0, y0`	The coordinates for the starting point.
`x1, y1`	The coordinates for the ending point.
`length = 0.25`	The length of the arrow head, in inches.

`angle = 30`	The angle of the arrow head to the shaft.
`code = 2`	The style of arrow to draw. If `code = 1`, an arrow head is drawn at the starting end. If `code = 2` (the default), an arrow head is drawn at the end. If `code = 3`, arrow heads are drawn at both ends. If `code = 0`, no heads are drawn.
`col`	The color for the arrow.
`lty`	The line type: 1= solid, 2 = dashed, 3 = dotted.
`lwd`	The line width.
`...`	Additional graphical commands can be given.

 SEE also par in "Using the par Command."

Examples

```
## Draw an empty plot (Figure 3-26)
> plot(1:10, 1:10, type = "n")

## Draw arrows to "join the dots", using defaults
> arrows(1:9, 1:9, 2:10, 2:10)

## Set some coordinates
> xc = 2:8
> yc = rep(5, 7)

## Use coordinates to add points
> points(xc, yc)

## Use arrows to add "error style" bars vertically
> arrows(xc, yc + 0.5, xc, yc - 0.5, code = 3, lwd = 3, angle = 90)

## Use arrows to add "error style" bars horizontally
> arrows(xc - 0.3, yc, xc + 0.3, yc, code = 3, length = 0.1,
  lty = 2, angle = 90)

## More arrows and annotation
> arrows(2,8, 4, 8, code = 3)
> arrows(2,7, 4, 7, code = 2)
> arrows(2,6, 4, 6, code = 1)
> arrows(2,9, 4, 9, code = 0)
> text(4, 9, "Code 0", pos = 4)
> text(4, 6, "Code 1", pos = 4)
> text(4, 7, "Code 2", pos = 4)
> text(4, 8, "Code 3", pos = 4)
```

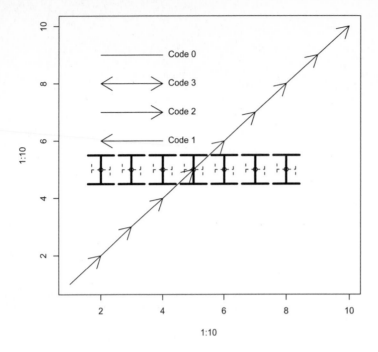

Figure 3-26: Various arrows added to a plot

COMMAND NAME

```
curve
plot
```

These commands draw curves representing mathematical functions. The `plot` command is very general and will plot those functions already built in to R. The `curve` command permits you to specify any function, which is then plotted.

Common Usage

```
curve(expr, from = NULL, to = NULL, n = 101, add = FALSE,
      type = "l", ylab = NULL, log = NULL, xlim = NULL, ...)

plot(x, y = 0, to = 1, from = y, xlim = NULL, ...)
```

Related Commands

```
lines (p. 398)
spline (p. 414)
plot (p. 382)
```

Command Parameters

`expr`	An expression of a function of x or the name of a function to plot.
`x`	A numeric R function.
`from`	The starting/lower value for x.
`to`	The ending/upper value for x.
`n = 101`	The number of x values to evaluate.
`add = FALSE`	If `add = TRUE`, the curve plotted is added to an existing plot window.
`type = "l"`	The type of plot. The default, `"l"`, plots lines. Other options include `"p"` for points and `"b"` for both lines and points.
`ylab = NULL`	A label for the y-axis.
`y`	An alias for `from`. This maintains compatibility with the `plot` command.
`log = NULL`	A character string stating which (if any) axes should be on a log scale. The options are `"x"`, `"y"`, and `"xy"`.
`xlim = NULL`	The limits of the x-axis; two values must be given, the starting and ending values.
`...`	Additional graphical parameters can be used. The most useful ones are likely to be:

- `col`—Color of lines/points
- `lty`—Line type
- `lwd`—Line width
- `pch`—Plotting character

 SEE the `par` command for a comprehensive list.

Examples

```
## Plot a trig function (Figure 3-27)
## curve command would give same result
## Set x-axis to go from -2*pi to +2*pi and lengthen y-axis for legend
> plot(sin, from = -pi*2, to =  pi*2,
  lty = 2, lwd = 1.5, ylim = c(-1, 1.5), ylab = "y-value")

## Plot the cosine, use curve command and set add = TRUE to overlay
> curve(cos, from = -pi*2, to = pi*2, lty = 3, add = TRUE)

## Add a legend, be careful to styles from the plot
> legend("topright", legend = c("Sine", "Cosine"),
  lty = c(2, 3), lwd = c(1.5, 1), bty = "n")

## Give a main title
> title(main = "Sine and Cosine functions")
```

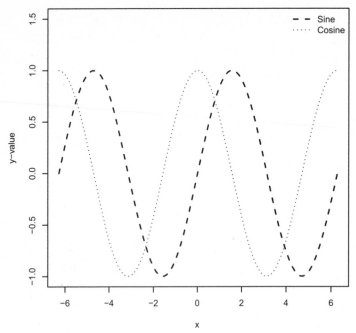

Sine and Cosine functions

Figure 3-27: Plotting mathematical functions

COMMAND NAME

`lines`

This command adds connected line segments to an existing plot.

 SEE "Adding Data."

COMMAND NAME

`loess`

This command carries out local polynomial regression fitting. A common use for this is to produce a locally fitted model that can be added to a scatter plot as a trend line to help visualize the relationship.

 SEE Theme 2, "Math and Statistics."

COMMAND NAME

`lowess`

This command carries out scatter plot smoothing. The algorithm uses a locally weighted polynomial regression. A common use for this is to produce a locally fitted model that can be added to a scatter plot as a trend line to help visualize the relationship. The trend line is not a straight line, but weaves through the scatter of points; thus, `lowess` is often referred to as a scatter plot smoother.

 SEE Theme 2, "Math and Statistics."

COMMAND NAME

`matlines`
`matpoints`

These commands add data as lines or points to an existing plot (usually one created using `matplot`).

 SEE `matplot` in "Types of Graphs."

COMMAND NAME

`qqline`

This command adds a line to a normal QQ plot, which passes through the first and third quartiles.

 SEE also Theme 2, "Tests of Distribution."

Common Usage

`qqline(y, datax = FALSE, ...)`

Related Commands

`qqnorm` (p. 385)
`qqplot` (p. 387)

Command Parameters

`y`	The numerical sample from which the QQ plot was derived.
`datax = FALSE`	By default, the sample quantiles are plotted on the y-axis. If `datax = TRUE`, the theoretical quantiles are plotted on the y-axis and the sample quantiles are plotted on the x-axis.
`...`	Additional graphical parameters may be used. The most useful ones are likely to be:

- `col`—The color of the line.

- `lty`—The line type.

- `lwd`—The line width.

SEE the par command for a more comprehensive list.

Examples

```
  ## make some data
> set.seed(22) # Set random number generator

  ## Random values from Gamma distribution
> dat = rgamma(50, shape = 3)

  ## Make a Normal QQ plot (Figure 3-28)
> qqnorm(dat, cex = 1.5)

  ## Add a line - not a good fit!
> qqline(dat, lty = "dotdash", lwd = 2)
```

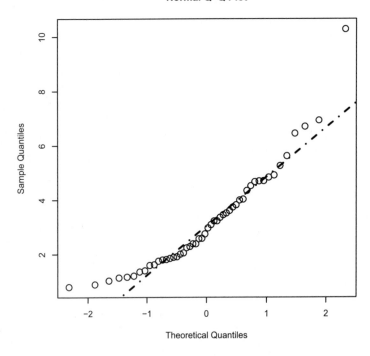

Figure 3-28: Adding a QQ-line to a normal QQ plot

COMMAND NAME

segments

This command adds line segments to a plot by connecting pairs of coordinates.

Common Usage

```
segments(x0, y0, x1 = x0, y1 = y0,
        col = par("fg"), lty = par("lty"), lwd = par("lwd"),
        ...)
```

Related Commands

arrows (p. 406)
lines (p. 398)
curve (p. 408)

Command Parameters

x0, y0   The coordinates for the starting point.

x1, y1   The coordinates for the ending point.

col   The color for the lines.

lty   The line type: 1= solid, 2 = dashed, 3 = dotted.

lwd   The line width.

...   Additional graphical commands can be given:

 SEE also par.

Examples

```
  ## Use VADeaths data from R datasets
> data(VADeaths) # make sure data is ready

  ## Calculate means for columns
> VADmean = colMeans(VADeaths)

  ## Calculate std. deviation
> VADsd = apply(VADeaths, MARGIN = 2, FUN = sd)

  ## Calculate std. error
> VADerr = VADsd / sqrt(5) # There are 5 rows

  ## Before plotting, set clipping to allow spill-over into margin
  ## as top-hat will reach top of plot area
> opt = par("xpd" = TRUE)
```

```
## Bar chart of means (Figure 3-29)
## Note setting of name for plot object
> bp = barplot(VADmean, ylim = c(0, 50), ylab = "Mean Deaths per 1000")


## Use segments to draw error bars (top to bottom)
> segments(bp, VADmean + VADerr, bp, VADmean - VADerr, lwd = 2)


## Add top hats (left to right)
> segments(bp - 0.1, VADmean + VADerr, bp + 0.1, VADmean + VADerr, lwd=2)


> par(opt) # Reset clipping back to previous setting
```

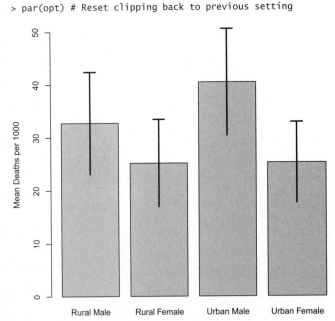

Figure 3-29: Using the segments command to add error bars

COMMAND NAME

`spline`

This command uses spline interpolation on a series of coordinate data. If you use this within a `lines` command, you can produce a smoothed curve.

Common Usage

```
spline(x, y = NULL, n = 3*length(x), method = "fmm",
    xmin = min(x), xmax = max(x), xout, ties = mean)
```

Related Commands

lines (p. 398)
loess (p. 333)
lowess (p. 335)

Command Parameters

x, y = NULL	Vectors giving the coordinates of the points to be interpolated. Alternatively, x can be an object with a plotting structure, such as a list with x and y elements (in which case y can be missing).
n	If xout is unspecified, the interpolation takes place at n equally spaced points between xmin and xmax.
method = "fmm"	The method of interpolation. The default is "fmm"; other options are "natural", "periodic", and "monoH.FC".
xmin = min(x)	If xout is unspecified the interpolation takes place at n equally spaced points
xmax = max(x)	between xmin and xmax.
xout	A set of values explicitly stating where the interpolation should take place.
ties = mean	Determines how tied values are dealt with. The default is mean. Other functions can be used as long as they require a single value as an argument and return a single value. Alternatively, you can give the string "ordered".

Examples

 USE bbel data in Essential.RData file for this example.

```
> names(bbel) # Check variable names
[1] "abund" "light"

  ## Plot scatter graph of relationship (Figure 3-30)
> plot(abund ~ light, data = bbel, pch = 16)

  ## Looks polynomial - add a title
> title(main = "Polynomial regression")

  ## Carry out polynomial regression
> bbel.lm = lm(abund ~ light + I(light^2), data = bbel)

  ## Add "best-fit" line (y-data from model fit)
> lines(bbel$light, fitted(bbel.lm), lty = 2)

  ## Regular lines look "clunky" so use spline to smooth curve
> lines(spline(bbel$light, fitted(bbel.lm)), lwd = 2)
```

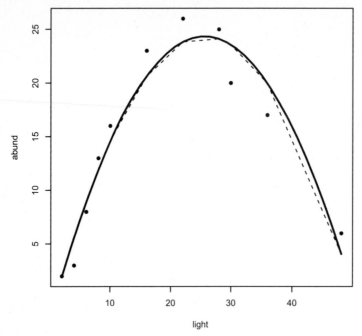

Figure 3-30: Curved line (using spline) of best-fit for a polynomial regression

ADDING SHAPES

Various shapes can be added to plots. The commands that deal with these are `rect`, which adds rectangles, and `polygon`, which adds polygons. In addition, there is the `box` command, which adds a bounding box to a plot.

COMMAND NAME

box

This command adds a box around the current plot in the given color and line style.

 SEE also box in "Altering Axis Parameters."

Common Usage

```
box(which = "plot", lty = "solid", ...)
```

Related Commands

rect (p. 420)
polygon (p. 418)
axis (p. 446)

Command Parameters

which = "plot"   Where the box is to be drawn. The default is "plot", which draws around the plot region (e.g., the extent of the axes and any bars/points). Other options are "inner", "outer", and "figure". Exactly where the box will appear depends on the margin settings.

lty = "solid"   The line type. The default is "solid".

...   Additional graphical commands can be given. The most useful of these are:

- col—The line color

- lwd—The line width

- bty—The box type. The default is "0", producing a complete box. Other options are "L", "C", "U", "7", and "]". The resulting box resembles the character (which can be lowercase). Use bty = "n" (lowercase) for no box.

 SEE the par command for a comprehensive list of other options.

Examples

```
  ## Make some data
> dat = c(23, 15, 6, 9) # A vector
> names(dat) = c("Q1", "Q2", "Q3", "Q4") # Assign names

  ## Draw a pie chart (Figure 3-31)
> pie(dat, clockwise = TRUE, init.angle = 270, radius = 0.9)

  ## Add various boxes
> box(lty = 3, lwd = 1.5, bty = "7") # top and right of plot area
> box(lty = 2, lwd = 2.5, bty = "L") # bottom and left of plot area
> box(lwd = 3, which = "outer")      # around the outer margin
```

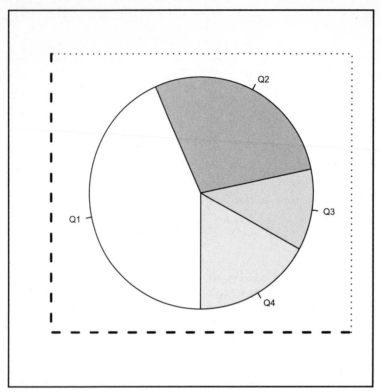

Figure 3-31: A pie chart with various plot boxes added using the box command

COMMAND NAME

`polygon`

Draws shapes into the current plot window by connecting a series of coordinates.

Common Usage

```
polygon(x, y = NULL, density = NULL, angle = 45,
      border = NULL, col = NA, lty = par("lty"),
      ..., fillOddEven = FALSE)
```

Related Commands

segments (p. 413)
rect (p. 420)

Command Parameters

x, y	Vectors containing the x and y coordinates to plot. If x contains a plotting structure (e.g., a list with x and y elements, or a two-column matrix or data frame), y can be missing. In any event the polygon is assumed to be closed and the last pair of coordinates are joined to the first.
density = NULL	The density of shading lines in lines per inch. The default is NULL, which suppresses lines.
angle = 45	The angle of shading lines in degrees. This is measured as a counter-clockwise rotation.
border = NULL	The color to draw the border. The default uses the current par("fg") setting. Use border = NA to omit borders.
col = NA	The fill color for the polygon(s). If density is not NULL, the specified color is used for the density lines.
lty	The line type to use.
...	Additional graphical parameters can be given, e.g., lwd.
fillOddEven = FALSE	Controls the way that self-intersecting polygons are colored/filled.

 SEE the par command for details.

Examples

```
## Make a plot without data to set a coordinate system (Figure 3-32)
> plot(0:10, 0:10, type = "n")

## Make data for shape coordinates and draw
## Use vector data
> tri1x = 0:2
> tri1y = c(0, 2, 0)

## Draw this shape
> polygon(tri1x, tri1y, lty = 2) # Dotted border

## Make more data, matrix
> tri2mat = matrix(c(4, 2, 6, 0, 4, 4), ncol = 2)

## Draw this shape with fill color and wide line
> polygon(tri2mat, col = "lightblue", lwd = 2)

## More data as a list
> xc = c(6, 8, 6, 10, 4, 5, 6, 9, 8, 10) # vector for x
> yc = c(0, 4, 6, 9, 10, 8, 9, 6, 4, 0) # vector for y
> poly1 = list(x = xc, y = yc) # put data into a list
```

```
## Draw the shape using the list data
> polygon(poly1, col = "pink", border = NA) # Turn off border
> polygon(poly1$y, poly1$x, col = "gray90") # Switch co-ordinates
```

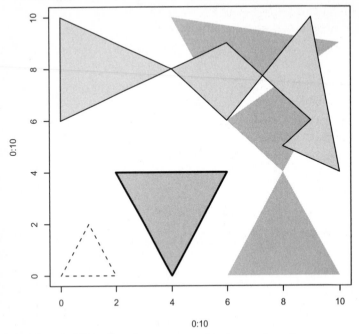

Figure 3-32: Using the polygon command to draw various shapes

COMMAND NAME

rect

This command draws one or more rectangles into an existing plot window. Other plotting commands such as hist and barplot use the command.

Common Usage

```
rect(xleft, ybottom, xright, ytop, density = NULL, angle = 45,

    col = NA, border = NULL, lty = par("lty"), lwd = par("lwd"),

    ...)
```

Related Commands

box (p. 416)
polygon (p. 418)
segments (p. 413)
hist (p. 368)
barplot (p. 349)

Command Parameters

xleft ybottom xright ytop	The coordinates for the rectangle(s). A vector of left x positions. A vector of bottom y positions. A vector of right x positions. A vector of top y positions. You are essentially describing the coordinates for the bottom-left point and the top-right point of each rectangle you want to draw.
density = NULL	The density of shading lines in lines per inch. The default is NULL, which suppresses lines.
angle = 45	The angle of shading lines in degrees. This is measured as a counter-clockwise rotation.
col = NA	The color to fill the rectangles with. The default NA, (also NULL) equates to no fill.
border = NULL	The color to draw the border. The default uses the current par("fg") setting. Use border = NA to omit borders. Use border = TRUE to set the color of the border to the same as the shading lines (if density is used).
lty	The line type.
lwd	The line width.
...	Additional graphical parameters can be used.

Examples

```
## Make some data
> dat = c(2, 3, 4, 4, 4, 5, 5, 5, 5, 5, 6, 6, 6, 6, 7)
> table(dat) # Look at the frequencies
dat
2 3 4 5 6 7
1 1 3 5 4 1


  ## Make your own histogram!
  ## Use hist to determine breakpoints on x-axis
> hist(dat, plot = FALSE)$breaks # computes breakpoints
[1] 2 3 4 5 6 7
> breaks = hist(dat, plot = FALSE)$breaks # make a variable for result

> hist(dat, plot = FALSE)$counts # computes frequencies
[1] 2 3 5 4 1
> counts = hist(dat, plot = FALSE)$counts # make a variable for result

  ## Make a blank plot as a coordinate system (basis for Figure 3-33)
  ## Leave out everything!
> plot(2:7, 0:5, type = "n", axes = FALSE, xlab = NA, ylab = NA)

  ## Add basic axes (adding to Figure 3-33)
> axis(2)          # the y-axis
> axis(1, pos = 0) # the x-axis, shift this up a bit
```

```
  ## Create a histogram using rectangles, one for each bar
> for (i in 1:length(counts)) {
  rect(breaks[i], 0, breaks[i+1], counts[i], col = "gray90") }

  ## Add titles (finishing Figure 3-33)
> title(xlab = "Breakpoints", ylab = "Counts")
```

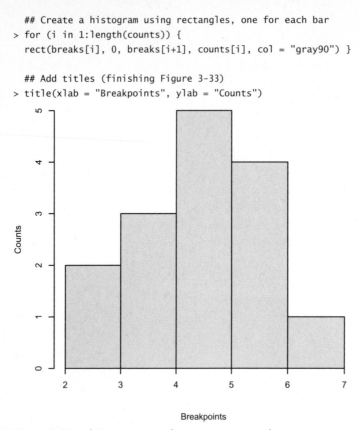

Figure 3-33: A histogram created using rect command

ADDING TEXT

You can add text to graphs in several ways. You can create titles for plots and axes and you can place text in the plot area or in the margins. R also provides a means to create complicated expressions, for example, containing superscript, subscript, and mathematical symbols.

COMMAND NAME

```
expression
is.expression
as.expression
```

The `expression` command allows you to create text strings containing superscript and subscript elements. It also allows the use of math and other symbols. This allows you to create text labels for use as titles and text in graphics windows. An expression object holds a `class` attribute "expression"; the `is.expression` and `as.expression` commands allow you to test for and set this attribute.

 SEE also Theme 1, "Data Types."

Common Usage

```
expression(...)
is.expression(x)
as.expression(x)
```

Related Commands

`text` (p. 428)
`mtext` (p. 425)
`title` (p. 430)
`locator` (p. 400)

Command Parameters

...   R objects, text, or symbols to create the `expression`.

x   An R object to test or coerce to an `expression`.

The following are some of the expressions you can create; use `help(plotmath)` in R for a comprehensive list. You can also type `demo(plotmath)` for more details.

TEXT ELEMENTS

~   A space.

*   A connector.

^   Superscript. Text following the caret is superscripted.

[]   Subscript. Text within the brackets is subscripted.

\n   Newline character.

FONT FACE

`plain()`	The text in parentheses is plain text.
`italic()`	The text in parentheses is *italic* text.
`bold()`	The text in parentheses is **bold** text.
`bolditalic()`	The text in parentheses is ***bold and italic*** text.
`underline()`	The text in parentheses is <u>underlined</u>.

MATH EXPRESSIONS

`x + y`	Produces $x + y$.
`x - y`	Produces $x - y$.
`x == y`	Produces $x = y$.
`x != y`	Produces $x \ y$.
`x %~~% y`	Produces $x \approx y$.

x %+-% y	Produces x ± y.
x %/% y	Produces x ÷ y.
bar(x)	Produces $\bar{x}$ with an overbar.
frac(x, y)	Produces a fraction with x over y.
x %up% y	Produces an up arrow, x ↑ y.
x %down%y	Produces a down arrow, x ↓ y.
x %->% y	Produces a right arrow, x → y.
x %<-% y	Produces a left arrow, x ← y.
sum(x, a, b)	Produces a sum (capital sigma) symbol, Σ, with optional sub and superscripts.
sqrt(x) sqrt(x, y)	Produces a square root symbol, √x, with optional root, y√x.
infinity	An infinity symbol, ∞.
alpha – omega	Greek letters in lowercase.
Alpha – Omega	Greek letters in uppercase.
180*degree	Produces a degree symbol, 180˚.
x ~ y	A space, x y.

Examples

```
  ## Make a blank plot to set a coordinate system (base for Figure 3-34)
> plot(1:10, 1:10, type = 'n')

  ## Set character expansion to a new level
> opt = par(cex = 1.5)

  ## Make some math expressions and draw them on the plot
> text(1, 1, expression(hat(x)))
> text(2, 1, expression(bar(x)))
> text(2, 2, expression(alpha==x))
> text(3, 3, expression(beta==y))
> text(4, 4, expression(frac(x, y)))
> text(5, 5, expression(sum(x)))
> text(6, 6, expression(sum(x^2)))
> text(7, 7, expression(bar(x) == sum(frac(x[i], n), i==1, n)))
> text(8, 8, expression(sqrt(x)))
> text(9, 9, expression(sqrt(x, 3)))

  ## Reset the character expansion to original
> par(opt)

  ## Make some text expressions and draw on the plot
> text(3, 7, expression(Speed ~ ms^-1), cex = 2)
> text(7, 2, expression(Count[per ~ mm]), cex = 2)
> text(4, 9, expression(Mixed^super*" and"[sub]*" script"), cex = 2)
```

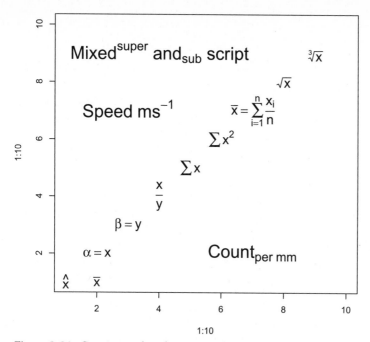

Figure 3-34: Creating math and text using the expression command

COMMAND NAME

`legend`

This command adds a legend to an existing plot window.

 SEE also `legend` in "Adding Legends."

COMMAND NAME

`mtext`

This command adds text to the marginal area of a plot, that is, outside the coordinate system.

Common Usage

```
mtext(text, side = 3, line = 0, outer = FALSE, at = NA,
      adj = NA, padj = NA, cex = NA, col = NA, font = NA, ...)
```

Related Commands

`title` (p. 430)
`expression` (p. 422)
`text` (p. 428)

Command Parameters

`text`	The text to write. This can be a character string or an `expression`.
`side = 3`	The side of the plot to use. The sides are 1 = bottom, 2 = left, 3 = top, 4 = right. The default is the top.
`line = 0`	The line of the margin to use. The default is 0, which is adjacent to the outside of the plot area. Positive values move outward and negative values inward.
`outer = FALSE`	If `outer = TRUE`, the outer margin is used if available.
`at = NA`	How far along the side to place the text in relation to the axis scale. Text is centered on this point.
`adj = NA`	How far along the side to place the text as a proportion. The default is effectively 0.5, which places the text halfway along. If text is oriented parallel to the axis, `adj = 0` will result in left or bottom placement. Text is centered.
`padj = NA`	Adjusts the text perpendicular to the reading direction. This permits "tweaking" of the placement. Positive values place text lower; negative values higher.
`cex = NA`	The character expansion. Values > 1 make text larger; values < 1 make text smaller.
`col = NA`	The color for the text. The default, `NA`, means use the current setting `par("col")`.
`font = NA`	The font to use. The default, `NA`, means use the current setting `par("font")`. Use `font = 1` for regular text; 2 = **bold**, 3 = *italic*, 4 = ***bold+italic***.
`...`	Additional graphics parameters can be used. Of particular interest is `las`, which controls the text direction:

- `las = 0`—Text parallel to axis (default).

- `las = 1`—Text horizontal.

- `las = 2`—Text perpendicular to axis.

- `las = 3`—Text vertical.

 SEE the `par` command for a more comprehensive list.

Examples

```
  ## Make a basic plot
> plot(1:10, 1:10)

  ## Add marginal text, see Figure 3-35 for results
> mtext('mtext(side = 1, line = -1, adj = 1)',
  side = 1, line = -1, adj = 1)

> mtext('mtext(side = 1, line = -1, adj = 0)',
  side = 1, line = -1, adj = 0)
```

```
> mtext('mtext(side = 2, line = -1, font = 3)',
  side = 2, line = -1, font = 3)

> mtext('mtext(side = 3, font = 2)', side = 3, font = 2)

> mtext('mtext(side = 3, line = 1, font = 2)',
  line = 1, side = 3, font = 2)

> mtext('mtext(side = 3, line = 2, font = 2, cex = 1.2)',
  cex = 1.2, line = 2, side = 3, font = 2)

> mtext('mtext(side = 3, line = -2, font = 4, cex = 0.8)',
  cex = 0.8, font = 4, line = -2)

> mtext('mtext(side = 4, line = 0)', side = 4, line = 0)
```

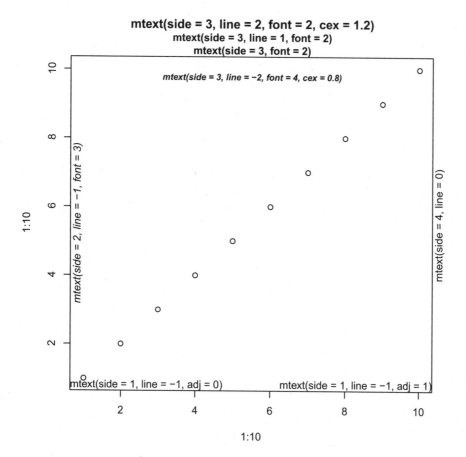

Figure 3-35: Marginal text placed using the mtext command

COMMAND NAME

text

This command adds text to a plot. It is a very general command and you can alter the text in many ways. Text can also be described as an expression.

 SEE also par.

Common Usage

```
text(x, y = NULL, labels = seq_along(x), adj = NULL,
    pos = NULL, offset = 0.5,
    cex = 1, col = NULL, font = NULL, ...)
```

Related Commands

mtext (p. 425)
title (p. 430)
expression (p. 422)
locator (p. 400)

Command Parameters

x, y	The coordinates for positioning of the text. The coordinates can be separate x and y vectors, or y can be missing if x has a plotting structure (a list with x and y elements or a two-column matrix or data frame). You can also use locator(1) to place text with a click of the mouse.
labels	The text labels to place on the plot at the specified coordinates. Can be a character string or an expression. The default attempts to create a numeric index and plots values accordingly; this is not always successful, so it is best to specify labels explicitly!
adj = NULL	An adjustment to the placement coordinates (text is centered on the coordinates). You can specify one or two values (x, y). The default is effectively adj = c(0.5, 0.5), which makes no adjustment. A value of 1 adjusts left (or down). A value of 0 adjusts right (or up). Values > 1 or < 0 are also permitted.

pos = NULL	The positioning of the text relative to the coordinates. This overrides any adj parameter. The default, NULL, results in text centered on the point. Other options are:

- pos = 1—Below point

- pos = 2—Left of point

- pos = 3—Above point

- pos = 4—Right of point

offset = 0.5	When pos is specified, the offset parameter offsets the position of the text by a fraction of the character width. A value of 1 offsets away from the original coordinate, a value of 0 offsets toward the original coordinate. Values > 1 or < 0 are also permitted.
cex = 1	A character expansion factor. Larger values increase size; smaller values decrease size.
col = NULL	The color to use for the labels.
font = NULL	The font to use. The default, NA, means use the current setting par("font"). Use font = 1 for regular text; 2 = **bold**, 3 = *italic*, 4 = ***bold+italic***.
...	Additional graphical parameters may be used. Of particular interest is srt, which sets the rotation of text in degrees. The rotation is counter-clockwise.

 SEE the par command for a more comprehensive list.

Examples

```
  ## Make a basic plot with points
> plot(1:10, 1:10, pch = 3, cex = 1.5)

  ## Add text using various methods of alignment (see Figure 3-36)
> text(4, 4, 'Centered on point')

> text(3, 3, 'Under point (pos = 1)', pos = 1)

> text(5, 5, 'Left of point (pos = 2)', pos = 2)

> text(6, 6, 'Above point (pos = 3)', pos = 3)

> text(7, 7, 'Right of point (pos = 4)', pos = 4)

> text(8, 8, "Upside down! (pos = 4, offset = -0.5)",
  srt = 180, pos = 4, offset = -0.5)

> text(1,1, "Sideways (adj = c(-0.05, 0.5), pos = 4)",
  srt = 90, adj = c(-0.05,0.5))
```

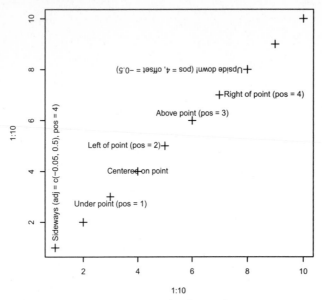

Figure 3-36: Text positioning in the plot window

COMMAND NAME

`title`

This command places titles on plots. It can add labels to the axes as well as an overall title and subtitle. The titles must be characters, but you can specify an `expression`, allowing subscripts, symbols, and so on. Most of the commands that produce graphs will accept the same parameters, but it is sometimes useful to specify titles separately.

Common Usage

```
title(main = NULL, sub = NULL, xlab = NULL, ylab = NULL,
      line = NA, outer = FALSE, ...)
```

Related Commands

`text` (p. 428)
`mtext` (p. 425)
`expression` (p. 422)

Command Parameters

`main = NULL`	The main title at the top of the plot window.
`sub = NULL`	A subtitle.
`xlab = NULL`	A title for the x-axis.
`ylab = NULL`	A title for the y-axis.
`line = NULL`	Allows for offsetting of titles (in marginal lines). A value of 0 places the title just outside the axis. Larger values move the title outward, and smaller values move the title inward.
`outer = FALSE`	If `outer = TRUE`, the title is added to the outer margin.
`...`	Additional graphical parameters can be used. To differentiate between titles, add `.main`, `.sub`, or `.lab` to the parameter required. For example:

- `font.main`, `font.sub`, `font.lab` for font

- `col.main`, `col.sub`, `col.lab` for color

- `cex.main`, `cex.sub`, `cex.lab` for character expansion

 SEE the `par` command for additional parameters.

Examples

```
  ## Set wider margins for plots (save original settings in opt)
> opt = par("mar" = c(7, 5, 5, 3))

  ## Make a simple plot (Figure 3-37). Alter most of the settings!
  ## Include x-axis and y-axis titles here
> plot(1, col.axis = "darkgreen", cex.axis = 1.5, font.axis = 3,
 col.lab = "brown", cex.lab = 2, font.lab = 3,
 xlab = "X-axis", ylab = "Y-axis")

  ## Add main and sub-titles. Alter most of the settings!
> title(main = "Main title", font.main = 4, col.main = "blue",
 cex.main = 2, sub = "Sub-title", font.sub = 1,
 col.sub = "red", cex.sub = "0.75")

  ## Reset margin settings to previous
> par(opt)
```

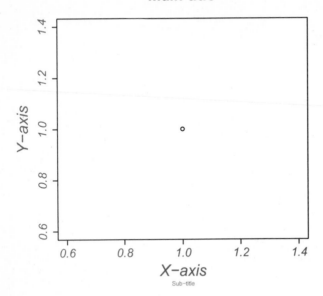

Figure 3-37: Customizing titles

ADDING LEGENDS

Some plot types have a `legend` parameter (for example, `barplot`), which allows the placement of a legend. The `legend` command enables a legend to be created and placed on any plot. The placement of the legend can be achieved in three ways: by coordinate, by keyword, or interactively. See the following command parameters for details.

COMMAND NAME

`legend`

Creates and adds a legend to an existing plot. You have many options and the parameter list is long!

Common Usage

```
legend(x, y = NULL, legend, fill = NULL, col = par("col"),
      border="black", lty, lwd, pch,
      angle = 45, density = NULL, bty = "o", bg = par("bg"),
      box.lwd = par("lwd"), box.lty = par("lty"), box.col = par("fg"),
      pt.bg = NA, cex = 1, pt.cex = cex, pt.lwd = lwd,
      xjust = 0, yjust = 1, x.intersp = 1, y.intersp = 1,
      adj = c(0, 0.5), text.width = NULL, text.col = par("col"),
      merge = do.lines && has.pch,
      ncol = 1, horiz = FALSE, title = NULL,
      inset = 0, title.col = text.col, title.adj = 0.5, seg.len = 2)
```

Related Commands

text (p. 428)
expression (p. 422)
plot (p. 382)
barplot (p. 349)
locator (p. 400)

Command Parameters

x, y = NULL	The coordinates where the legend should be placed. You can specify x and y coordinates explicitly or using a text string. The options are "bottomright", "bottom", "bottomleft", "left", "topleft", "top", "topright", "right", and "center". Abbreviations can be used. You can also place the legend interactively using locator(1) instead of x. The top-left corner of the legend will be placed where you click with the mouse.
legend	The text of the legend. Usually this will be a character or expression vector.
fill = NULL	The fill colors for boxes to appear beside the legend text. If density is given, fill gives the colors for the shading lines. The default, NULL, omits boxes.
col = par("col")	The colors to use for the lines and/or points that appear in the legend. The default uses the current setting in par("col").
border = "black"	The color for the boxes of the legend. Only used if fill is not NULL.
lty	The line types used in the legend. Usually these will match those used in the plot.
lwd	The line widths used in the legend. Usually these will match those used in the plot.
pch	The plotting symbols used in the legend. Usually these will match those used in the plot.
density = NULL	The density of shading lines in lines per inch. The default is NULL, which suppresses lines.
angle = 45	The angle of shading lines in degrees. This is measured as a counter-clockwise rotation.
bty = "o"	The type of box to place around the legend. The default, "o", produces a box. Use bty = "n" to omit the box.
bg = par("bg")	The background color to use for the legend box; only used if bty = "o". The default uses the current setting from par("bg").
box.lty box.lwd box.col	Settings specific to the box around the legend (assuming bty = "o"); they set line type, line width, and color.
pt.bg	The background color for the points that appear in the legend (for open type symbols, pch = 21:25). This will usually match those from the original plot.

`cex`	The character expansion factor. This operates relative to the current setting in `par("cex")`. Specifying a value also sets the expansion for `pt.cex` and `title.cex` (which can also be set independently).
`pt.cex` `pt.lwd`	Settings for the points that appear in the legend. Sets their expansion factor and line width.
`xjust = 0` `yjust = 1`	Adjust the justification of the legend relative to the placement coordinates: 0 = left (or bottom), 0.5 = centered, 1 = right (or top).
`x.intersp = 1` `y.intersp = 1`	Sets the character interspaces for the horizontal or vertical line distances. Larger values allow you to "spread out" the legend over a greater area.
`adj = c(0, 0.5)`	Adjusts the text in the legend box. You can specify one or two values corresponding to the x- and y-axis directions. Increasing the defaults results in text being adjusted to the left (or down). Decreasing the defaults results in text being adjusted right (or up).
`text.width = NULL`	Sets the text width (and so the extent of the legend box), which is usually computed automatically. The value is not in characters; you can determine the value for your text using `strwidth(text)`, where `text` is your character string or `expression`.
`text.col =` `par("col")`	The color of the text in the legend. The default uses the current setting from `par("col")`; usually this is `"black"`.
`merge = TRUE`	If `merge = FALSE`, the points appear at the end of the lines in the legend, rather than in the middle.
`ncol = 1`	The number of columns for the legend. The default is 1.
`horiz = FALSE`	If `TRUE`, the legend is set out horizontally instead of vertically. This has the same effect as increasing the number of columns, but note that you cannot have `horiz = TRUE` and `ncol > 1`.
`title = NULL`	A title for the legend, usually as a character string or `expression`.
`inset = 0`	If the legend is placed using a keyword (rather than x, y coordinates), `inset` specifies the distance to the margin(s). The value is a fraction of the plot region.
`title.col`	The color to use for the title.
`title.adj = 0.5`	Sets the horizontal adjustment for the title (as a proportion of the legend width). The default, 0.5, centers the title. Smaller values shift the title to the right. Larger values shift the title to the left.
`seg.len = 2`	The length of the lines drawn in the legend. Larger values mean longer lines (the units are character widths).

Examples

```
  ## Make an empty plot to create a coordinate system
> plot(0:10, 0:10, type = "n")

  ## Add some points/lines (see Figure 3-38 for final result)
> points(3:5, 4:6, type = "b", lwd=2, lty = 1, pch = 21, col = "black")
> points(2:4, 2:4, type = "b", lwd=2, lty = 2, pch = 24, col = "blue")
> points(5:7, 5:7, type = "b", lwd=2, lty = 3, pch = 25, col = "red")

  ## Make a list of names as labels for each set of lines/points
> mydata = c("Line1", "Line2", "Line3")

  ## Add a legend, take care to match up line/point parameters
> legend("topright", legend = mydata, lty = c(1, 2, 3), lwd = 2,
 col = c("black", "red", "blue"), pch = c(21, 24, 25))

  ## It is often easier to make named objects for colors
  ## and plot characters
> plcols = c("black", "red", "blue")
> plchr = c(21, 24, 25)

  ## Add more legends: note the various options
> legend("bottomleft", legend = mydata, lty = 1:3, col = plcols,
 pch = plchr, bty = "n", title = "Sample\nLegend Title")

> legend("top", legend = mydata, lty = 1:3, col = plcols,
 pch = plchr, horiz = TRUE, inset = 0.01)

> legend(8.5, 1.5, legend = mydata, lty = 1:3, col = plcols,
 pch = plchr, bg = "gray90")

> legend("right", legend = mydata, lty = 1:3, col = plcols,
 pch = plchr, ncol = 2, inset = 0.01, title = "Two-column Layout")

  ## This time go for simple colored boxes
> legend(0, 8, legend = mydata, fill = plcols)
```

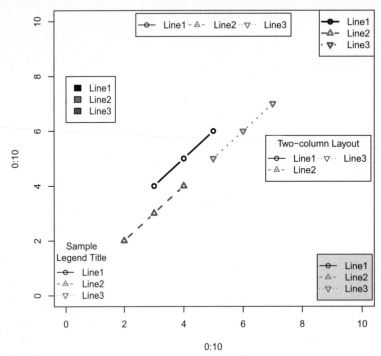

Figure 3-38: A variety of legends

```
## Add a legend using the mouse to set the location
## This adds to the previous example
## Top left of legend appears where you click with the mouse
> legend(locator(1), legend = mydata, lty = 1:3, col = plcols)
```

Graphical Parameters

R provides a mechanism to view current graphical settings and alter them via the par command. The parameters are common to most of the commands that produce graphics. Most settings can be altered (temporarily) by the plotting commands, but a few can only be set via the par command. In addition to the par command, a few other commands have relevance to graphical parameters; for example, the commands that deal with partitioning the plot window and the palette command for creating colors.

What's In This Topic:

- **Using the par command** (p. 437)
- **Altering color** (p. 439)
  - Setting color palettes
  - Color parameters
- **Altering axis parameters** (p. 446)

- **Altering text parameters** (p. 453)
  - Text parameters
  - Plotting characters/symbols
- **Altering line (and box) parameters** (p. 456)
- **Altering plot margins** (p. 459)
- **Altering the graph window** (p. 462)
  - Splitting the window into parts
  - Controlling split windows

USING THE PAR COMMAND

The par command is the management tool for most of the graphical parameters used in R.

COMMAND NAME

par

This command queries or sets the graphical parameters. Some of the parameters are read-only and cannot be set by the user. Many of the remaining parameters can be altered by the separate commands that draw plots, at least for the duration of the plotting. Some parameters can only be set via the par command.

To make it easy to return to previous settings, you can save the current parameters to a named object (a list) as the new settings are applied. See the following examples.

 SEE additional entries for the par command listed under the following headings:

- "Altering Color" (p. 439)
- "Altering Axis Parameters" (p. 446)
- "Altering Text Parameters" (p. 453)
- "Altering Line (and Box) Parameters" (p. 456)
- "Altering Plot Margins" (p. 459)
- "Altering the Graph Window" (p. 462)

Common Usage

```
par(..., no.readonly = FALSE)
```

Related Commands

```
colors (p. 439)
palette (p. 441)
split.screen (p. 469)
layout (p. 462)
```

THEME 3: GRAPHICS

Command Parameters

    ...   A `list` of parameters to be queried or set. Generally, the form is `tag = value`, where `tag` is a character string corresponding to the required parameter. If no `tag` is given, the values of all are reported.

`no.readonly = FALSE`   If `TRUE`, only the parameters that can be set by the user are shown.

Examples

```
  ## List all parameters that you can change (result not shown here)
> par(no.readonly = TRUE)

  ## List some parameters
  ## Character expansion, color, background, plot margin size
> par(list("cex", "col", "bg", "mar"))

$cex
[1] 1

$col
[1] "black"

$bg
[1] "white"

$mar
[1] 5.1 4.1 4.1 2.1

  ## Alter the margin sizes
  ## Note that you make an object; the current setting is saved there
> opt = par("mar" = c(7, 4, 4, 2))

  ## Check the new setting
> par("mar")
[1] 7 4 4 2

  ## See how previous setting was saved
> opt
$mar
[1] 5.1 4.1 4.1 2.1

  ## Restore setting and check it
> par(opt)
> par("mar")
[1] 5.1 4.1 4.1 2.1
```

ALTERING COLOR

Color can be managed in several ways. Various commands deal with color palettes and creation of colors (for example, the RGB specification). Other color parameters are set via the par command.

COMMAND NAME

colors
colours

These commands display the built-in color names. The color names can be used wherever a color is required. Colors are often referred to by a simple integer value. This refers to the position of the color in the current palette.

 SEE the par command to set various default colors.

Common Usage

colors()
colours()

Related Commands

palette (p. 441)
col2rgb (p. 440)

Command Parameters

()   No parameters are required.

Examples

```
## Get colors and save result as an object
> cl = colors()

## How many colors are available?
> length(cl)
[1] 657

## Display the first 20 color names
## Color numbers do not correspond to their position in this list
## but to their position in the current palette
> cl[1:20]
 [1] "white"          "aliceblue"      "antiquewhite"   "antiquewhite1"
 [5] "antiquewhite2"  "antiquewhite3"  "antiquewhite4"  "aquamarine"
 [9] "aquamarine1"    "aquamarine2"    "aquamarine3"    "aquamarine4"
[13] "azure"          "azure1"         "azure2"         "azure3"
[17] "azure4"         "beige"          "bisque"         "bisque1"
```

COMMAND NAME

col2rgb
hcl
hsv
rgb
rgb2hsv

These commands deal with the creation of colors and the translation of specification:

- col2rgb converts a named color to its RGB specification.

- hcl creates a color from hue, chroma, and luminance.

- hsv creates a color from hue, saturation, and value.

- rbg creates a color from red, green, and blue settings.

- rgb2hsv converts RGB values into HSV equivalents.

Common Usage

```
col2rgb(col, alpha = FALSE)

hcl(h = 0, c = 35, l = 85, alpha, fixup = TRUE)

hsv(h = 1, s = 1, v = 1, gamma = 1, alpha)

rgb(red, green, blue, alpha, names = NULL, maxColorValue = 1)

rgb2hsv(r, g = NULL, b = NULL, gamma = 1, maxColorValue = 255)
```

Related Commands

palette (p. 441)
colors (p. 439)

Command Parameters

col
A named color. This can be a character string giving the name or a hexa-decimal string "#rrggbb". You can also give a single integer value, which will return the appropriate value from the current palette.

alpha
The transparency value. Values are:

- col2rgb, set to TRUE or FALSE to display (or not) the result

- hcl, set between 0 and 1 (1 is opaque)

- rgb, set between 0 and maxColorValue

h
A value for "hue." Values are:

- hcl, set between 0 and 360 (0 = red, 120 = green)

- hsv, set between 0 and 1

c	A value for "chroma." The upper limit for this depends on h, "hue" and l, "luminance."
l	A value for "luminance," generally between 0 and 100, but for any combination of h and c only a subset is possible.
fixup = TRUE	If this is TRUE, the resulting color is adjusted so that it is a real color. If fixup = FALSE, an "unreal" color will result in NA.
s, v	Numeric levels for "saturation" and "value." These should be between 0 and 1.
gamma	A gamma correction component.
r, g, b	Integer values for red, green, and blue components of the color. The range of values should be 0 to maxColorValue.
names = NULL	A character vector giving names for the resulting color(s).
maxColorValue	Sets the maximum value for r, g, and b. Values 1 or 255 are most useful.

Examples

```
   ## View current palette colors
> palette()
[1] "black"   "red"      "green3" "blue"     "cyan"     "magenta" "yellow"  "gray"


   ## View current palette colors as RGB
> col2rgb(1:8)
      [,1] [,2] [,3] [,4] [,5] [,6] [,7] [,8]
red      0  255    0    0    0  255  255  190
green    0    0  205    0  255    0  255  190
blue     0    0    0  255  255  255    0  190
```

COMMAND NAME

```
palette
rainbow
heat.colors
terrain.colors
topo.colors
cm.colors
gray
grey
```

These commands create and manage color "sets." The palette command manages the "set" of colors (the palette); you can see the current palette or create a customized range of colors as a palette. The other commands create custom "sets" of colors that can be assigned to the palette (the commands gray and grey are the same). In plotting commands the parameter col = palette() will use the current color "set." Specifying a color simply by an integer value takes the color from its position in the current palette. Using palette("default") returns to base settings and restores the default "set."

Common Usage

```
palette(value)
rainbow(n, s = 1, v = 1, start = 0, end = max(1,n - 1)/n, gamma = 1, alpha = 1)
heat.colors(n, alpha = 1)
terrain.colors(n, alpha = 1)
topo.colors(n, alpha = 1)
cm.colors(n, alpha = 1)
gray(level)
grey(level)
```

Related Commands

colors (p. 439)
col2rgb (p. 440)
hsv (p. 440)

Command Parameters

value   The palette to set; you have several options:

   - Leave empty, view current palette.

   - "default", restores original default palette.

   - Names of colors as character strings, sets new palette to these colors.

   - Color commands, e.g., rainbow(n), to set new palette.

n   The number of colors to be in the palette.

s, v   The "saturation" and "value" to be used in the HSV color descriptions.

start = 0   The starting value for "hue" in the rainbow (between 0 and 1).

end   The ending value for "hue" in the rainbow (between 0 and 1).

gamma   The gamma correction.

alpha   The transparency, between 0 and 1 (1 is opaque).

level   A vector of gray levels, between 0 and 1 (0 is black, 1 is white).

Examples

```
  ## Set plot window into 6 (2 rows, 3 columns)
> opt = par(mfrow = c(2, 3))

  ## Produce color wheels as pie charts (final result in Figure 3-39)
> pie(rep(1,12), col = rainbow(12), radius = 0.95,
 main = "Rainbow Colors")
> box(which = "figure") # a box around the sub-window
```

```
> pie(rep(1,12), col = heat.colors(12), radius = 0.95,
 main = "Heat colors")
> box(which = "figure")

> pie(rep(1,12), col = terrain.colors(12), radius = 0.95,
 main = "Terrain Colors")
> box(which = "figure")

> pie(rep(1,12), col = topo.colors(12), radius = 0.95,
 main = "Topo Colors")
> box(which = "figure")

> pie(rep(1,12), col = cm.colors(12), radius = 0.95, main = "CM Colors")
> box(which = "figure")

> pie(rep(1,12), col = gray(seq(0, 1, len = 12)), radius = 0.95,
 main = "Gray Colors")
> box(which = "figure")

 ## Reset the plot window to previous setting
> par(opt)
```

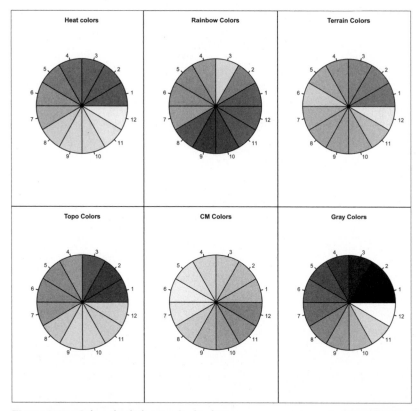

Figure 3-39: Color wheels for standard palettes

```
  ## Set new palette (6 rainbow colors)
> palette(rainbow(6))
> palette()
[1] "red"     "yellow" "green"  "cyan"     "blue"     "magenta"

  ## Set palette to 6 topo colors
> palette(topo.colors(6))
> palette()
[1] "#4C00FF" "#00E5FF" "#00FF4D" "#E6FF00" "yellow"  "#FFE0B3"

  ## View palette colors as RGB
> col2rgb(1:length(palette()))
      [,1] [,2] [,3] [,4] [,5] [,6]
red     76    0    0  230  255  255
green    0  229  255  255  255  224
blue   255  255   77    0    0  179

  ## Reset palette to default
> palette("default")
> palette()
[1] "black"   "red"     "green3" "blue"    "cyan"     "magenta" "yellow" "gray"
```

COMMAND NAME

par

This command queries or sets the various graphical parameters.

 SEE also "Using the par Command."

Common Usage

```
par(tag = value)

par(list(tag1 = value, tag2 = value, ...))
```

Related Commands

palette (p. 441)
col2rgb (p. 440)
colors (p. 439)

Command Parameters

bg   Sets the background color for the plot. If set via par("bg"), "new" is also set to FALSE (see "Altering the Graph Window"). Note that some graphical commands have a bg parameter, which is different than the par setting.

col The overall default plotting color, usually "black". Several variants control colors on plot elements:

- col.axis—Axis annotation

- col.lab—Axis labels (titles)

- col.main—Plot title

- col.sub—Plot subtitle

fg The foreground color for plots. Controls axis color, for example. When set via par("fg"), the "col" parameter is also set to the same color. If you want different values, set "fg" first, then "col" (which you will have to do with a separate par command).

Examples

```
  ## Check current setting of some parameters
> par(list("bg", "col", "fg"))
$bg
[1] "white"

$col
[1] "black"

$fg
[1] "black"

  ## You can make a list of parameters and set them anytime
  ## Use the list for custom settings or as a "default" for restore
> parcols = list(col = "black", fg = "black", bg = "white",
 col.main = "black", col.sub = "black",
 col.lab = "black", col.axis = "black")

## If you assign a name to the par command you can restore later
> opt = par(list(bg = "gray95", fg = "blue", col.main = "red",
 col.sub = "brown"))

  ## The list you made contains the settings that were current
  ## when you made it
> opt
$bg
[1] "white"

$fg
[1] "black"

$col.main
[1] "black"
```

```
$col.sub
[1] "black"

  ## Use your list to restore previous settings
> par(opt)

  ## Or you can use the earlier list
> par(parcols)
```

ALTERING AXIS PARAMETERS

Most axis parameters can be set directly as part of a plotting command, but some can only be altered via the par command. Several separate commands also exist relating to axes.

COMMAND NAME

axis

This command adds an axis to a current plot. It allows you to specify a completely customized axis.

Common Usage

```
axis(side, at = NULL, labels = TRUE, tick = TRUE, line = NA,
    pos = NA, outer = FALSE, font = NA, lty = "solid",
    lwd = 1, lwd.ticks = lwd, col = NULL, col.ticks = NULL,
    hadj = NA, padj = NA, ...)
```

Related Commands

par (p. 437)
pretty (p. 452)
axTicks (p. 448)
plot (p. 382)

Command Parameters

side	An integer value giving the side for the axis: 1 = bottom, 2 = left, 3= top, 4 = right.
at = NULL	The points along the axis where the tick marks are to be placed. If NULL, the default, the tick marks are calculated automatically. Otherwise, you must specify values explicitly.
labels = TRUE	The labels to use for the tick marks. If TRUE, numerical labels are used. You can specify labels as a character string or an expression.
tick = TRUE	If FALSE, the axis line and tick marks are not drawn in.
line = NA	The margin line where the axis will be drawn. Effectively, the default = 0. Positive values move the axis outward, negative values inward.
pos = NA	The coordinate where the axis line is to be drawn. This will be a y-value for sides 1 and 3 and an x-value for sides 2 and 4.

outer = FALSE	If TRUE, the axis is drawn in the outer margin of the plot.
font = NA	The font for the text. The default is effectively par("font").
lty = "solid"	The line type to use. The default is "solid". See "Altering Line (and Box) Parameters."
lwd = 1 lwd.ticks = lwd	The line width for the axis and tick marks. The tick marks default to the same as the lwd setting.
col = NULL col.ticks = NULL	The colors for the axis line and tick marks. If col = NULL, the setting in par("fg") is used. If col.ticks = NULL, the setting is whatever col is set to.
hadj = NA	An adjustment value for all labels parallel to the reading direction. The default is effectively 0.5. Smaller values place labels to the right, larger values to the left.
padj = NA	An adjustment value for all labels perpendicular to the reading direction. The default is effectively 0. Positive values place labels lower, negative values higher.
...	Additional graphical parameters can be used. For example: cex.axis, col.axis and font.axis

 SEE the par command for more details.

Examples

```
  ## Make some data
> rain = c(34, 32, 23, 15, 10, 8, 6, 9, 12, 21, 24, 29) # Vector
> names(rain) = month.abb[1:12] # Make labels
> rain # View the data
Jan Feb Mar Apr May Jun Jul Aug Sep Oct Nov Dec
 34  32  23  15  10   8   6   9  12  21  24  29


  ## Because x-data are categorical a regular plot will show index
  ##  rather than categories we want, so
  ##  draw plot without axes (forms basis for Figure 3-40)
  ## Note that axis labels omitted using NA
> plot(rain, type = "b", lty = "dashed", lwd = 2.5, axes = FALSE,
 main = "Rainfall", xlab = NA, ylab = NA)


  ## Axis 2 (y-axis) is numeric so default is fine but
  ## use las to rotate annotation
> axis(side = 2, las = 1)


  ## New x-axis, at = axis ticks, specify number required
  ## Also give labels
> axis(side = 1, at = 1:length(rain), labels = names(rain))


  ## Add axis labels (final result is Figure 3-40)
> title(xlab = "Month", ylab = "Rainfall in mm")
```

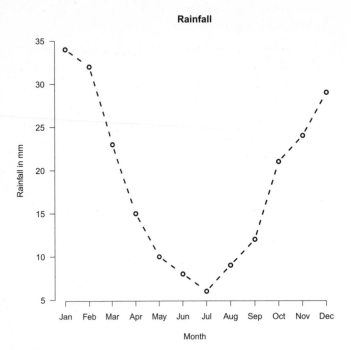

Figure 3-40: Specifying a custom axis

COMMAND NAME

axTicks

This command computes sensible (pretty) locations for tick marks. The locations are the same as calculated using the axis or pretty commands, but axTicks is able to deal with log coordinates.

Common Usage

```
axTicks(side, axp = NULL, usr = NULL, log = NULL)
```

Related Commands

pretty (p. 452)
par (p. 437)
axis (p. 446)

Command Parameters

side	An integer value giving the side for the axis: 1 = bottom, 2 = left, 3= top, 4 = right.
axp = NULL	A numeric vector with three values. You supply the start, end, and number of ticks required. The default values are taken from par("xaxp") or par("yaxp") according to the value of side.

usr = NULL　　A numeric vector with four values. You supply the limits of the coordinate system for x and y directions. The default takes values as in par("usr").

log = NULL　　A logical value indicating is log coordinates are active. The defaults take values from par("xlog") or par("ylog").

 SEE also "Altering the Graph Window."

 SEE also par.

Examples

```
  ## Set x-axis to a log scale
> par(xlog = TRUE)

  ## Determine tick marks locations using 3 algorithms
> axTicks(side = 1, axp = c(1,1000, 2))
[1]    1    5   10   50  100  500 1000

> axTicks(side = 1, axp = c(1,1000, 1))
[1]    1   10  100 1000

> axTicks(side = 1, axp = c(1,1000, 3))
 [1]    1    2    5   10   20   50  100  200  500 1000

  ## Set x-axis back to regular scale
> par(xlog = FALSE)

  ## Make a plot with one axis log, the other not (not shown)
> plot(1:1000, 1:1000, log = "x")

  ## Look at tick mark locations
> axTicks(1)
[1]    1    5   10   50  100  500 1000
> axTicks(2)
[1]    0  200  400  600  800 1000
```

COMMAND NAME

box

This command adds a bounding box around the plot.

 SEE "Adding Shapes."

COMMAND NAME

`par`

This command queries or sets the various graphical parameters.

 SEE also "Using the par Command."

Common Usage

```
par(tag = value)

par(list(tag1 = value, tag2 = value, ...))
```

Related Commands

`axis` (p. 446)
`pretty` (p. 452)
`axTicks` (p. 448)
`box` (p. 416)

Command Parameters

`adj`	Adjusts how text strings are justified. See the `text`, `mtext`, and `title` commands. Generally, 0.5 means centered, 0 means left justified, and 1 means right justified.
`bty`	The type of box to draw around the plot region. The default is `"0"`, producing a complete box. Other options are `"L"`, `"C"`, `"U"`, `"7"`, and `"]"`. The resulting box resembles the character (which can be lowercase). Use `bty = "n"` (lowercase) for no box.
`cex.axis` `cex.lab`	The character expansion to use for axis annotation and axis labels, respectively. The values are relative to the current setting in `par("cex")`. See "Altering Text Parameters."
`col.axis` `col.lab`	The color to use for axis annotation and axis labels, respectively.
`font.axis` `font.lab`	The font to use for axis annotation and axis labels, respectively. Generally, 1 = plain, 2 = **bold**, 3 = *italic*, 4 = ***bold+italic***.
`lab`	This controls approximately how many tick marks and annotations will be used for the axes. You specify three values (`x, y, len`), which correspond to the two axes and the length of the labels (`len` is unused and provides compatibility with the S language). The default is `c(5, 5, 7)`.
`las`	Controls how axis labels are oriented relative to the axes. Specify a numeric value as follows:

- 0—Always parallel to the axis (default)

- 1—Always horizontal

- 2—Always perpendicular to the axis

- 3—Always vertical

`tck = NA`	Controls the length of the tick marks as a fraction of the smallest axis. The default is to use `tcl = -0.5`. Values `>= 0.5` are interpreted as a fraction of the axis. Use `tck = 1` to draw gridlines. Positive values place tick inside the axis, negative values outside.
`tcl = -0.5`	Controls the length of the tick marks as a fraction of the height of a line of text. Using `tcl = NA` sets the value to −0.01 (the default for the S language).
`xaxp` `yaxp`	Controls the number of tick marks and their intervals. For a regular scale (not log), you supply three values: `c(x, y, n)`. These correspond to the extremes of the axis and the required number of tick marks. If the axis is a log scale, the three values have a different meaning. Values for x and y correspond to the powers of 10 and n is a code 1, 2, or 3. It is hard to visualize the result and experimentation is encouraged! Generally, you get more tick marks as the code increases. You can also use negative values, which ignore the log values and give tick marks in the 0–10 range.
`xaxs` `yaxs`	Controls the style of interval calculation for tick marks: ■ `"r"`—Regular (the default) intervals; axis is extended by 4% then subdivided. ■ `"i"`—Internal intervals; axis is subdivided without extension. Use this to get x- and y-axes to "meet" at the origin.
`xaxt` `yaxt`	Sets the axis type. Values of `"s"`, `"l"`, or `"t"` will produce a regular axis, and a value of `"n"` will omit the axis. All other values will give an error.
`xlog` `ylog`	A logical value determining if a log scale is to be used for the axis in question; the default is FALSE. These parameters can only be set using `par`.

Examples

```
  ## Set up plot window for 2 rows and 1 column
  ## par Figure 3-41
> par(mfrow = c(2, 1))

  ## Alter some axis parameters: las = annotation orientation,
  ## adj = justification, xaxs/yaxs = do not extend axis
  ## tcl = tick marks inside
> parax = par(las = 1, adj = 1, xaxs = "i", yaxs = "i", tcl = 0.5)

  ## Draw the plot (Figure 3-41, top)
> plot(0:10, 0:10, main = "Title")

  ## Reset values to previous
> par(parax)

  ## Draw plot again (Figure 3-41, bottom)
> plot(0:10, 0:10, main = "Title")

  ## Reset plot window to single plot
> par(mfrow = c(1, 1))
```

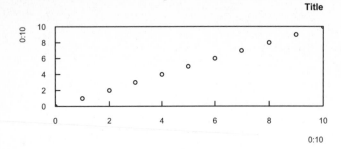

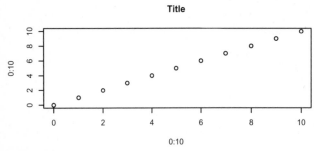

Figure 3-41: Customization of axis parameters

COMMAND NAME

`pretty`

This command calculates breakpoints for an axis. Essentially, the command creates equally spaced intervals spanning the range you specify.

Common Usage

`pretty(x, n = 5, min.n = n %/% 3)`

Related Commands

axTicks (p. 448)
axis (p. 446)
par (p. 437)

Command Parameters

x	A numeric vector or object that can be coerced into one.
n = 5	The desired number of intervals. Generally, the result will be n or n+1 intervals.
min.n	The minimum number of intervals to calculate.

Examples

```
   ## Calculate default axis intervals
> pretty(1:1000)
[1]    0  200  400  600  800 1000

   ## This gives same result
> pretty(100:1000)
[1]    0  200  400  600  800 1000

   ## If you specify min value it must be > n (default n = 5)
> pretty(1:1000, n = 10, min = 9)
 [1]    0  100  200  300  400  500  600  700  800  900 1000
```

ALTERING TEXT PARAMETERS

The par command provides a mechanism to alter many default text parameters. Many of these parameters can also be used from within the various plotting commands.

COMMAND NAME

par

This command queries or sets the various graphical parameters.

 SEE also "Using the par Command."

Common Usage

```
par(tag = value)

par(list(tag1 = value, tag2 = value, ...))
```

Related Commands

text (p. 428)
mtext (p. 425)
title (p. 430)
expression (p. 422)

Command Parameters

adj	Adjusts how text strings are justified. See the text, mtext, and title commands. Generally, 0.5 means centered, 0 means left justified, and 1 means right justified. Note that the adj parameter in the text command will allow adjustment in x and y directions.
cex cex.axis cex.lab cex.main cex.sub	The parameter cex sets the magnification factor for text. Note that some commands have cex as a parameter with different interpretation. The other parameters affect the expansion of text for axis, labels, and titles and operate relative to the setting of cex.

col col.main col.sub col.axis col.lab	The col parameter sets the colors of the plot and text. The other parameters set colors for main and subtitles and axis annotations and labels.
crt	Controls the rotation of characters in degrees. This is generally not a helpful parameter and srt is more useful for rotating strings.
family	The name of the font family to use for drawing text. The default is "", which uses the defaults for the device. Other options include "serif", "sans", and "mono".
font font.main font.sub font.axis font.lab	An integer value determines the style of text: 1 = plain (the default), 2 = **bold**, 3 = *italic*, 4 = ***bold+italic***. The parameters set the font for plotting text, titles, axis annotation, and axis labels.
las	Controls how axis labels are oriented relative to the axes. Specify a numeric value as follows: ■ 0—Always parallel to the axis (default) ■ 1—Always horizontal ■ 2—Always perpendicular to the axis ■ 3—Always vertical
lheight	Specifies the line height multiplier. The default is 1. Larger values create more space between lines of text. This parameter can only be set using par.
pch	The plotting symbols to use. Generally, an integer value between 0 and 25. Values 32–127 give ASCII characters; negative values (< -31) use Unicode characters (if available). Alternatively, a character can be given as a string. Useful symbols include: ■ 19—Solid circle ■ 20—Bullet ■ 21—Filled circle ■ 22—Filled square ■ 23—Filled diamond ■ 24—Filled triangle, point up ■ 25—Filled triangle, point down Characters 21 to 25 have a border, which can be colored separately; col affects the border and bg fills the character. In addition, pch = 46 (or pch = ".") is represented as a special character, a rectangle 0.01 inch in size (if cex = 1). Other symbols are scaled according to the font size.

ps	Sets the point size of text (but not symbols). This parameter can only be set using par.
srt	Sets the string rotation in degrees. The setting only operates for the text command. Text is rotated in a counter-clockwise direction.

Examples

```
## A blank plot to set up a coordinate system
## Final result will be Figure 3-42
> plot(0:10, 0:10, type = "n")

## Some regular text as a baseline
> text(2,10, "Regular text", pos = 4)

## Set text larger and use serif family
> par(list(cex = 2, family = "serif"))

## Add some text
> text(2,8, "Serif Family", pos = 4)

## Alter rotation and set sans serif family
> par(list(srt = 180, family = "sans"))

## Add some text note pos is opposite to previous
> text(2,6, "Sans Family", pos = 2)

## Alter rotation and set monospace family
> par(list(srt = 90, family = "mono"))

 ## Add some text
> text(8,6, "Monospace Family")

## Reset parameters
> par(list(cex = 1, srt = 0, family = ""))

## Create multi-line text
> text(2,4, "Multi-line\ntext with\ndefault spacing", pos = 4)

## Alter line height
> par(lheight = 2)

## More multi-line text
> text(4, 2, "Multi-line\ntext with\ncustom spacing", pos = 4)

## Reset line height
> par(lheight = 1)
```

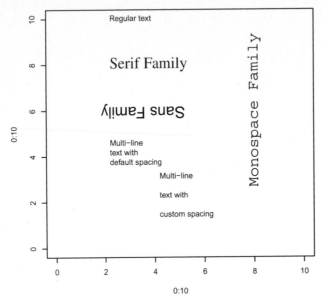

Figure 3-42: Altering text parameters

ALTERING LINE (AND BOX) PARAMETERS

Most graphical commands use lines of one sort or another. Various parameters can be set via the par command. Many of these can also be used directly by the plotting commands that utilize the settings.

COMMAND NAME

par

This command queries or sets the various graphical parameters.

 SEE also "Using the par Command."

Common Usage

```
par(tag = value)

par(list(tag1 = value, tag2 = value, ...))
```

Related Commands

lines (p. 398)
abline (p. 404)
curve (p. 408)
segments (p. 413)
arrows (p. 406)
box (p. 416)
polygon (p. 418)
rect (p. 420)

Command Parameters

bty The type of box to draw around the plot region. The default is "O", producing a complete box. Other options are "L", "C", "U", "7", and "]". The resulting box resembles the character (which can be lowercase). Use bty = "n" (lowercase) for no box.

col Sets colors for the plot. This generally includes any lines drawn.

lend The style of the ends of lines. You can specify an integer or a character string as follows:

- 0 or "round"—Rounded line caps (the default)

- 1 or "butt"—Butt line caps

- 2 or "square"—Square line caps

ljoin This controls how lines are joined. Specify an integer value or a character string as follows:

- 0 or "round"—Rounded joins (the default)

- 1 or "miter"—Mitered line joins

- 2 or "bevel"—Beveled line joins

lmitre Sets the line mitre limit and so controls when mitered line joins are converted to beveled joins. The default is 10; you must set a value > 1.

lty The line type. This can be an integer or a character string as follows:

- 0 or "blank"

- 1 or "solid"

- 2 or "dashed"

- 3 or "dotted"

- 4 or "dotdash"

- 5 or "longdash"

- 6 or "twodash"

Alternatively, you can specify your own pattern using a string of hexadecimal characters. The string defines the length of "on" and "off" segments and must be 2, 4, 6, or 8 characters in length.

lwd The line width; the default is 1. This is similar to an expansion factor and larger values result in thicker lines.

Examples

```
  ## Set plot window to 2 rows and 2 columns
> par(mfrow = c(2, 2))

  ## Set box type and line type/width
> par(list(bty = "L", lty = 2, lwd = 1.5))

  ## Use bbel data from download as basis for plot
  ## (Figure 3-43, top left)
> plot(abund ~ light, data = bbel, type = "b")

  ## Alter parameters again
> par(list(bty = "7", lty = "dashed", lwd = 2))

  ## Redraw plot using new settings (Figure 3-43, top right)
> plot(abund ~ light, data = bbel, type = "b")

  ## Alter parameters again
> par(list(bty = "n", lty = 4, lwd = 2.5))

  ## Redraw (Figure 3-43, bottom left)
> plot(abund ~ light, data = bbel, type = "b")

  ## Alter settings again (these are the usual defaults)
> par(list(bty = "O", lty = 1, lwd = 1))

  ## Plot again (Figure 3-43, bottom right)
> plot(abund ~ light, data = bbel, type = "b")

  ## reset plot window
> par(mfrow = c(1, 1))
```

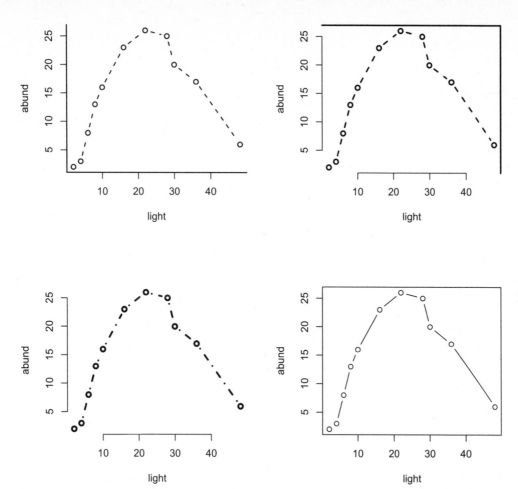

Figure 3-43: Altering line and box parameters

ALTERING PLOT MARGINS

You have various ways to control the margins of your plots. These parameters can only be set via the par command.

 SEE also "Altering the Graph Window."

COMMAND NAME

par

This command queries or sets the various graphical parameters.

Common Usage

```
par(tag = value)

par(list(tag1 = value, tag2 = value, ...))
```

Related Commands

`title` (p. 430)
`mtext` (p. 425)
`axis` (p. 446)

Command Parameters

mai	Sets the margins of the plot in inches. You must specify four values in the form c(bottom, left, top, right), giving the values for the corresponding margins. The defaults are device specific but are often approximately c(1.02, 0.82, 0.82, 0.42). This can only be set using par.
mar	Sets the margins of the plot in lines of text. You must specify four values in the form c(bottom, left, top, right), giving the values for the corresponding margins. The default values are c(5, 4, 4, 2) + 0.1. This can only be set using par.
mex	This sets an expansion factor for describing coordinates in the margin regions. Using values > 1 essentially increases all margins. This can only be set using par.
oma	Sets the outer margins of the plot in lines of text. You must specify four values in the form c(bottom, left, top, right), giving the values for the corresponding margins. The default values are all zero (no outer margin). This can only be set using par.
omd	Sets the region inside the outer margins as a fraction of the plot region (i.e., 0 to 1). You must specify four values, c(x1, x2, y1, y2), defining the region. The default is c(0, 1, 0, 1), which is essentially no outer margin! This can only be set using par.
omi	Sets the outer margins of the plot in inches. You must specify four values in the form c(bottom, left, top, right), giving the values for the corresponding margins. This can only be set using par.

Examples

```
  ## Set margins (in #lines) for outer and regular margins
> par(oma = c(3, 2, 3, 2))
> par(mar = c(7, 6, 6, 4))
```

```
## Draw a plot, with axes but no bounding box (basis for Figure 3-44)
> plot(0:10, 0:10, xlab = "X-axis", ylab = "Y-axis", frame.plot = FALSE)

## Add main and sub-titles
> title(main = "Main Title", sub = "Sub Title")

## Add bounding boxes to various zones
> box(which = "outer")
> box(which = "figure")
> box(which = "plot")

## Add text to show margin areas
> mtext("Regular margin", side = 3, outer = FALSE)
> mtext("Outer Margin", side = 1:4, outer = TRUE)

## Reset margins to default settings
> par(oma = c(0, 0, 0, 0))
> par(mar = c(5, 4, 4, 2) + 0.1)
```

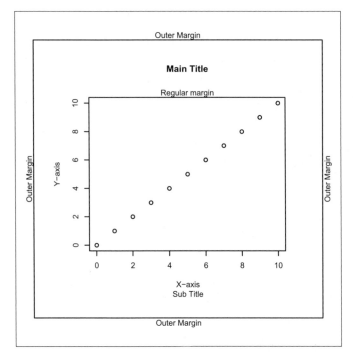

Figure 3-44: Setting and altering margins.

ALTERING THE GRAPH WINDOW

Various commands and graphical parameters alter the graph window in some way. The commands generally either set the dimensions of the plot region or split the plot window in some manner (allowing several graphs to be in one window).

 SEE the `quartz`, `windows`, and `X11` commands to open a new blank plot in "Saving Graphs."

COMMAND NAME

```
layout
layout.show
lcm
```

These commands help split the plot window into sections. The `layout` command does the split; the `layout.show` command allows you to visualize the split. The `lcm` command is a helper function that creates values in centimeters to help sizing of plot windows. Note that the `layout` method of splitting the window is incompatible with the methods, `split.screen` and `par("mfrow")`.

Common Usage

```
layout(mat, widths = rep(1, ncol(mat)),
       heights = rep(1, nrow(mat)), respect = FALSE)

layout.show(n = 1)

lcm(x)
```

Related Commands

```
screen (p. 469)
par("mfrow") (p. 437)
par("mfcol") (p. 437)
dev.cur (p. 392)
```

Command Parameters

`mat`	A matrix that sets out the splits of the screen such that the matrix acts like a map, showing the screen numbers that will be filled for each plotting event (in numerical order). A zero represents an area that will not be plotted.
`widths`	A vector of widths for the plot sections. The values will mirror the columns in `mat`. Values can be specified as relative or as absolute values. To specify absolute value, use the `lcm` command to specify the dimension in centimeters.
`heights`	A vector of heights for the plot sections. The values will mirror the rows in `mat`. Values can be specified as relative or as absolute values. To specify absolute value, use the `lcm` command to specify the dimension in centimeters.

respect = FALSE   This parameter can be given in one of two ways:

- As TRUE or FALSE. If respect = TRUE, a unit column-width will equal a unit column-height for all sections.

- As a matrix of same dimensions as mat. Each value must be 0 (meaning FALSE) or 1 (meaning TRUE).

n = 1   The number of figures to plot/show.

x   A dimension to be interpreted as centimeters.

Examples

```
  ## Use cars data from R datasets
> data(cars) # make sure data is ready
  ## View the variable names
> names(cars)
[1] "speed" "dist"


  ## Work out break points for axes
> xbreak = pretty(cars$speed)
> ybreak = pretty(cars$dist)


  ## Make histogram data (i.e. not plotted)
> xhist = hist(cars$speed, breaks = xbreak, plot = FALSE)
> yhist = hist(cars$dist, breaks = ybreak, plot = FALSE)


  ## Set layout to make 4 areas: one for scatter, one blank,
  ## two for histograms
  ## Make the matrix "map" first
> lout = matrix(c(2, 0, 1, 3), nrow = 2, ncol = 2, byrow = TRUE)
> lout
     [,1] [,2]
[1,]    2    0
[2,]    1    3


  ## Now split the screen using the "map"
  ## The widths and heights are (rows, columns) and are relative
  ## Here we have two rows and two columns (see lout matrix) so
  ## Specify two widths and two heights
> figs = layout(lout, widths = c(3, 1), heights = c(1, 3),
 respect = TRUE)


  ## Show the layout on screen
> layout.show(figs)


  ## Set margins then draw scatter plot final result will be Figure 3-45
> opt.mar = par(mar = c(3, 3, 1, 1))
> plot(dist ~ speed, data = cars)
```

```
  ## Set margins and draw histogram for x-data
> par(mar = c(0, 3, 1, 1)) # Match left margin to first plot
> barplot(xhist$counts, space = 0, axes = FALSE)

  ## Set margins and draw histogram for y-data
> par(mar = c(3, 0, 1, 1)) # Match bottom margin to first plot
> barplot(yhist$counts, space = 0, horiz = TRUE, axes = FALSE)

  ## Reset margins
> par(opt.mar)

  ## Reset to single plot window
> layout(1)
```

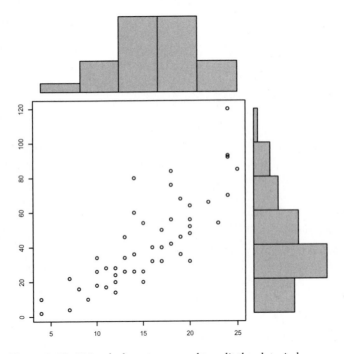

Figure 3-45: Using the layout command to split the plot window

COMMAND NAME

par

This command queries or sets the various graphical parameters.

 SEE also "Using the par Command."

Common Usage

```
par(tag = value)

par(list(tag1 = value, tag2 = value, ...))
```

Related Commands

layout (p. 462)
screen (p. 469)
dev.cur (p. 392)

Command Parameters

ann	If ann = FALSE, annotations are turned off and axis titles and overall titles are not drawn.
ask	If ask = TRUE, the user is asked for input before the figure is drawn. This can only be set using par.
bty	The type of box to draw around the plot region. The default is "O", producing a complete box. Other options are "L", "C", "U", "7", and "]". The resulting box resembles the character (which can be lowercase). Use bty = "n" (lowercase) for no box.
fig	The coordinates of the figure region within the overall plot area as proportions (that is, 0 to 1). You specify four values of the form c(x1, x2, y1, y2). This can only be set using par. The default is c(0, 1, 0, 1), that is, the whole region. This will create a new plot window when set unless new = TRUE is also set.
fin	Sets the figure region in inches as (width, height). This can only be set using par, and will create a new plot window when set.
mfrow	Splits the plot window into sections (rows and columns); you specify c(nr, nc). The subsequent plot window is filled row by row. This can only be set using par. You can skip a section by using plot.new(), and draw directly into a section using par("mfg").
mfcol	Splits the plot window into sections (rows and columns); you specify c(nr, nc). The subsequent plot window is filled column by column. This can only be set using par. You can skip a section by using plot.new(), and draw directly into a section using par("mfg").
mfg	This allows you to draw directly into a section of plot window that has been split using mfrow or mfcol. This can only be set using par. To set a section to plot in next, you specify c(row, column). You can also see which section is current (the last section to have a plot in it). The result shows four values; the first two represent the row, column of the plot section last used. The last two values show the number of rows, columns that are set.
mgp	The margin line (in mex units) for the axis title, axis labels, and axis line. You specify three values; the defaults are c(3, 1, 0). The first value affects the title and the others the axes.
new	This determines if the current plot is wiped when a new plotting instruction is issued. If par("new" = TRUE), the command assumes that the window is clean (new), thus adding to an existing plot. If par("new" = FALSE), the default, the next plotting command wipes the window. This can only be set using par.

pin   This determines the current plot dimensions (width, height) in inches. This can only be set using par.

plt   This determines the plot region as a fraction of the current figure region. You specify four values, c(x1, x2, y1, y2), which represent the coordinates. This can only be set using par.

pty   The type of plot region used. "s" sets a square region and "m" sets a maximal region. This can only be set using par.

usr   The extreme user coordinates of the plotting region. You specify four values: c(x1, x2, y1, y2). If a log scale is in use, the limits will be 10^usr. This can only be set using par.

xpd   Determines the clipping region. If FALSE, plotting is clipped to the plot region. If TRUE, plotting is clipped to the figure region (allowing you to overspill into the margins). If NA, plotting is clipped to the device region.

Examples

```
  ## Splitting the plot window
  ## Make 2 rows, 2 columns, fill plots by column
> par(mfcol = c(2, 2))

  ## Turn off plot box
> par(bty = "n")

  ## First plot starts graphics window (Figure 3-46)
  ## Simple scatter plot, joined points (Figure 3-46, top left)
> plot(log(1:10), 1:10, cex = 1.5, type = "b")

  ## Which plot is current? Result shows row, column of last plot
  ## and row, columns of the split
> par("mfg")
[1] 1 1 2 2

  ## Set random number generator
> set.seed(11)

  ## A histogram of some random numbers (Figure 3-46, bottom left)
> hist(rnorm(n = 50, mean = 5, sd = 1), col = "gray90",
 main = "Normal distribution)

  ## Plot cosine function (Figure 3-46, top right)
> curve(cos, from = -2*pi, to = 2*pi, lwd = 2)

  ## Set some gray colors
> piecol = gray(c(0.55, 0.75, 0.9))
  ## Make some labels
> pielab = c("Cos", "Sin", "Tan")
```

```
## A pie chart (Figure 3-46, bottom right)
> pie(c(cos(45), sin(45), tan(45)), labels = pielab, col = piecol)

## Add text to margin, uses current plot
## still bottom right
> mtext("Trig functions", side = 1, line = 1, font = 2)

## Any command that draws a new plot will wipe window and
## start again top left

## Reset graphic to single window and restore boxes
> par(list(mfcol = c(1, 1), bty = "O"))
```

Figure 3-46: Splitting the plot window and altering window parameters

COMMAND NAME

plot.new

This command causes the current plot to be finished (if there is one) and advances to a new graphics frame. This is useful for skipping plot windows if the frame has been divided into sections.

Common Usage

plot.new()

Related Commands

par("mfrow") (p. 437)
par("mfcol") (p. 437)
layout (p. 462)

Command Parameters

()   No parameters are required.

Examples

```
  ## Split plot window into 2 rows, 2 columns, fill by row
> par(mfrow = c(2, 2))

  ## Turn boxes around plots off
> par(bty = "n")

  ## Set the random number generator
> set.seed(9)

  ## A histogram of some random numbers from Poisson distribution
  ## (Figure 3-47, top left)
hist(rpois(50, lambda = 4), col = "gray95",
 main = "Poisson Distribution")

  ## Skip a plot, and again
> plot.new() # Would have been top right
> plot.new() # Would have been bottom left

  ## A histogram of some random numbers from normal distribution
  ## (Figure 3-47, bottom right)
hist(rnorm(50, mean = 4, sd = 1), col = "gray90",
 main = "Normal Distribution")

  ## Set the next plot to go into row 2, column 1
> par('mfg' = c(2, 1))

  ## A histogram of some random numbers from Student's t distribution
  ## (Figure 3-47, bottom left)
hist(rt(50, df = Inf), col = "gray90",
 main = "Student's-t Distribution")

  ## Reset plot window to single and turn box on
> par(list(bty = "O", mfrow = c(1, 1)))
```

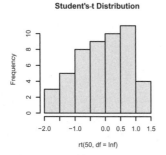

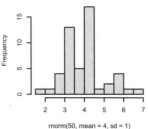

Figure 3-47: Skipping a section of a split window

COMMAND NAME

```
screen
split.screen
erase.screen
close.screen
```

These commands provide a mechanism to split the plotting screen and manage those splits:

- `screen`—Selects the screen to use.

- `split.screen`—Splits the screen (you can also split a previously split section).

- `erase.screen`—Clears a screen by filling with background color.

- `close.screen`—Closes a split.

These commands are incompatible with other means of splitting plot windows, such as `layout` or `par("mfrow")`.

Common Usage

```
split.screen(figs, screen, erase = TRUE)

screen(n = , new = TRUE)

erase.screen(n = )

close.screen(n, all.screens = FALSE)
```

Related Commands

layout (p. 441)
par("mfrow") (p. 437)
par("mfcol") (p. 437)

Command Parameters

figs	Describes how the plot region should be split. You can supply two values giving the number of rows and columns. You can also give a matrix with four columns. Each row represents a section of screen with values for the left, right, bottom, and top (in that order). The values are in NDC units, which are a proportion of the overall plot window, thus 0 to 1.
screen	A number giving the screen to split. The default is the current screen or the whole plot region if no previous splits exist.
erase = TRUE	If erase = FALSE, the selected screen is not cleared before the screen is split.
n	A screen number; close.screen will accept a vector of values. If n is omitted from screen, the current screen number is returned. If n is omitted from close.screen, a vector of values showing the screen numbers is returned.
new = TRUE	If new = FALSE, the screen is not cleared before setting as the current screen. If new = TRUE, the screen is cleared by filling with background color. If this is "transparent", nothing apparently happens! Use par("bg" = "white") to overcome this.
all.screens = FALSE	If TRUE, all screens are closed.

Examples

```
  ## Use cars data from R datasets
> data(cars) # Make sure data is ready

  ## Check if screen is split
> close.screen()
[1] FALSE

  ## Split screen into 2 rows, 1 column
> split.screen(figs = c(2, 1))
[1] 1 2

  ## Prepare screen 1 (at the top)
> screen(1)

  ## A scatter plot (Figure 3-48, top)
> plot(dist ~ speed, data = cars, frame.plot = FALSE)
```

```
  ## Split bottom half (screen 2) into 1 row and 2 columns
> split.screen(figs = c(1, 2), screen = 2)
[1] 3 4

  ## Prepare screen 3 (bottom left)
> screen(3)

  ## A histogram (Figure 3-48, bottom left)
> hist(cars$dist, col = "gray90", main = "Distance")

  ## Prepare screen 4 (bottom right)
> screen(4)

  ## A histogram (Figure 3-48, bottom right)
> hist(cars$speed, col = "gray90", main = "Speed")

  ## Return to screen 1 (top) but do not erase drawing
> screen(1, new = FALSE)

  ## Add title. Generally it is safer to complete one figure
  ## before moving to another
> title(main = "Stopping Distance and Speed")
  ## A reminder of the splits (but not how!)
> close.screen()
[1] 1 2 3 4

  ## Close all splits, this does not wipe the plot
> close.screen(all.screens = TRUE)
```

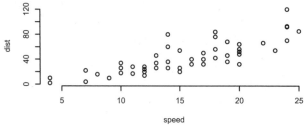

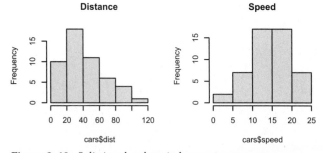

Figure 3-48: Splitting the plot window

```
   ## Make a scatter plot and marginal histograms
   ## Set NDC coordinates for screens as Left, Right, Bottom, Top
   ## NDC are proportional to main window (0 to 1)
> scr1 = c(0, 0.75, 0, 0.75) # NDC coords for screen 1
> scr2 = c(0, 0.75, 0.75, 1) # screen 2
> scr3 = c(0.75, 1, 0, 0.75)
> scr4 = c(0.75, 1, 0.75, 1)

   ## Combine window coordinates in one matrix
> spl = rbind(scr1, scr2, scr3, scr4) # Make a matrix
> colnames(spl) = c("L", "R", "B", "T") # Add column names
> spl # See matrix "map"
        L    R    B    T
scr1 0.00 0.75 0.00 0.75
scr2 0.00 0.75 0.75 1.00
scr3 0.75 1.00 0.00 0.75
scr4 0.75 1.00 0.75 1.00

   ## Use cars data from R datasets
> data(cars) # Make sure data are ready

   ## View the variable names
> names(cars)
[1] "speed" "dist"

   ## Work out break points for axis
> xbreak = pretty(cars$speed)
> ybreak = pretty(cars$dist)

   ## Make histogram data
> xhist = hist(cars$speed, breaks = xbreak, plot = FALSE)
> yhist = hist(cars$dist, breaks = ybreak, plot = FALSE)

   ## Split the screen according to "map"
> split.screen(spl)
[1] 1 2 3 4

   ## Select (and erase) screen 1
> screen(1)

   ## Set margins
> par(mar = c(4, 4, 1, 1))

   ## Draw a scatter plot (Figure 3-49, bottom left)
> plot(dist ~ speed, data = cars, frame.plot = FALSE)

   ## Select and erase screen 2
> screen(2)

   ## Set margins, make sure left margin matches screen 1
> par(mar = c(0, 4, 1, 1))
```

```
  ## Draw the histogram data (Figure 3-49, top left)
> barplot(xhist$counts, space = 0, axes = FALSE)

  ## Select and erase screen 3
> screen(3)

  ## Set margins, make sure bottom margin matches screen 1
> par(mar = c(4, 0, 1 ,1))

  ## Draw histogram data (horizontally, Figure 3-49, bottom right)
> barplot(yhist$counts, space = 0, horiz = TRUE, axes = FALSE)

  ## Select screen 4
> screen(4)

  ## Set all margins to 0
> par(mar = c(0,0,0,0))

  ## A blank plot (Figure 3-49, top right)
> plot(1, type = "n", axes = FALSE)

 ## Add a text message
> text(1,1, "Scatter plot\nand histograms\nfor x/y data")

 ## Remove all splits (window remains until next plot)
> close.screen(all.screens = TRUE)
```

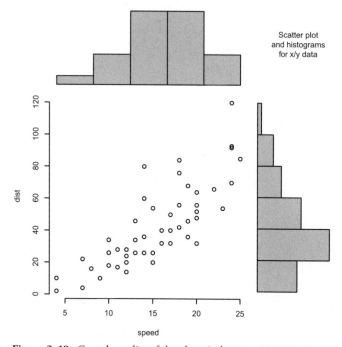

Figure 3-49: Complex splits of the plot window

THEME 4: UTILITIES

This theme covers the commands that are generally useful when accessing the programming aspect of the R language. This theme also covers some commands that do not easily fit into the other three themes of "Data," "Math and Statistics," and "Graphics." Some of these topics include accessing the help system and getting/using additional packages of R commands.

Because R is a programming language, you have great flexibility in how you use it. You can customize R in two main ways:

■ Custom functions

■ Scripts (used as source code)

These two methods differ from one another in the following manner: You can think of functions as short scripts you can type from the keyboard and scripts as longer items that you would use a text editor to create. Once you start to create and use your own custom functions and scripts, you will need to use certain commands that help you undertake the tasks you set R to do and to manage the output (so you can see the results).

Topics in this Theme

COMMANDS IN THIS THEME:

? (p. 482)	# (p. 507)	abbreviate (p. 507)	all (p. 502)
any (p. 503)	apropos (p. 480)	args (p. 491)	body (p. 492)
cat (p. 509)	deparse (p. 510)	detach (p. 486)	dump (p. 498)
else (p. 505)	find (p. 480)	for (p. 504)	formals (p. 494)
function (p. 495)	help (p. 482)	help.start (p. 482)	history (p. 483)
if (p. 505)	install.packages (p. 477)	installed.packages (p. 486)	invisible (p. 512)
letters (p. 527)	LETTERS (p. 527)	library (p. 487)	load (p. 499)
loadhistory (p. 483)	lsf.str (p. 496)	missing (p. 525)	month.abb (p. 527)
month.name (p. 527)	nchar (p. 513)	new.packages (p. 478)	nzchar (p. 513)
old.packages (p. 478)	paste (p. 514)	pi (p. 527)	print (p. 515)
print.xxxx (p. 515)	q (p. 484)	quit (p. 484)	quote (p. 518)
readline (p. 519)	require (p. 487)	return (p. 520)	save (p. 500)
save.image (p. 485)	savehistory (p. 483)	search (p. 489)	searchpaths (p. 489)
source (p. 501)	stop (p. 526)	substitute (p. 521)	summary (p. 522)
summary.xxxx (p. 522)	timestamp (p. 483)	tolower (p. 524)	toupper (p. 524)
update.packages (p. 478)			

Install

The R website at www.r-project.org is a vast repository of all things R-related. This includes the program itself (for all operating systems) as well as additional packages of R commands. The basic installation of R is very powerful, but it can be extended even further by the addition of extra packages of commands (at the time of this writing there were nearly 4000 packages). These packages have been written to carry out a bewildering variety of things. You can browse the R website to see what is available; the Task Views section of the website is very useful because it covers most of the available packages in a topic-based manner. An Internet search will also prove useful if you have a specific topic in mind.

WHAT'S IN THIS TOPIC:

- **Installing R** (p. 477)
- **Installing packages** (p. 477)
  - Installing new additional packages
  - Updating packages

INSTALLING R

The source for all R program installers is the website www.r-project.org, where you can find the appropriate version for your computer. You will need to select a mirror site; choose one local to you to minimize download time. Generally, the link you follow takes you to a page where you can select the version you require. The main program files are called the *R binaries*, whereas additional packages are simply referred to as *packages*.

The installation process will vary according to your operating system; for Windows or Mac it is usually just a matter of running the installation file that you download. For Linux the process may be slightly more complicated, but the website gives instructions.

INSTALLING PACKAGES

Many packages of additional R commands are available for you to use to extend the capabilities of R. The first step is to identify the package you need. The R website at www.r-project.org is a good place to browse the options and the Task Views section gives you a topic-based way of finding what you may need. Once you know the name of the package you require, you can use the appropriate command in R to get and install it.

It is possible to use menu commands if you have Windows or Mac versions of R (using the Packages menu), but it is easier to type the command!

COMMAND NAME

`install.packages`

This command installs a package from the R website onto your computer. You need to be connected to the Internet to download a file, or you can optionally point to a file on your computer if it is already downloaded.

 SEE the `library` command once a package is installed to load and access the commands contained within it.

Common Usage

```
install.packages(pkgs, repos = getOption("repos"), dependencies = NA)
```

Related Commands

`library` (p. 487)
`search` (p. 489)
`update.packages` (p. 478)
`old.packages` (p. 478)
`new.packages` (p. 478)

Command Parameters

`pkgs`	The packages to install. You must give a character vector of the names. If `repos` = `NULL`, you can "point" to a file on your computer by specifying the path (in quotes).
`repos`	A character vector pointing to the repository for the installation files: this can be a URL. The default asks you for a location to select (your mirror site). If you set `repos` = `NULL`, you can install a file from an archive on your computer.
`dependencies = NA`	Some packages require that others be installed before they will work correctly. The default, `NA`, installs these other packages. You can also specify `TRUE` or `FALSE`.

Examples

```
  ## Install a single package from the Internet
> install.packages("gdata")

  ## Multiple packages can be installed
> install.packages(c("ade4", "vegan"))
```

COMMAND NAME

```
new.packages
old.packages
update.packages
```

These commands help you to manage the installation of packages:

- `new.packages` checks for packages that are not already installed and offers to install them.

- `old.packages` checks for packages that are already installed but which have newer versions.

- `update.packages` checks for package updates and offers to install them.

Common Usage

```
new.packages(repos = getOption("repos"), ask = FALSE)

old.packages(repos = getOption("repos"))

update.packages(repos = getOption("repos"), ask = TRUE)
```

Related Commands

library (p. 487)
search (p. 489)
install.packages (p. 477)

Command Parameters

repos   A character vector pointing to the repository for the installation files; this can be a URL. The default asks you for a location to select (your local mirror site). If you set repos = NULL, you can install a file from an archive on your computer.

ask   If ask = TRUE, the user is asked to confirm the installation of each available package. You can also specify "graphics", which brings up an interactive list that enables you to select the packages you want.

Examples

```
## Interactive update using Windows OS (Figure 4-1)
> update.packages(ask = "graphics")
```

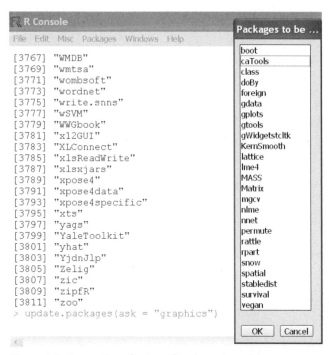

Figure 4-1: Interactive selection of packages to update

Using R

Some commands help your day-to-day operation of R. This topic is concerned with those useful commands and covers several broad themes: the help system and previously typed commands, saving your work (and getting it back), and the management of additional packages.

WHAT'S IN THIS TOPIC:

- **Using the program** (p. 480)
    - The help system
    - Previous command history
    - Saving work
    - Quitting R
- **Additional packages** (p. 486)
    - Opening Packages
    - Closing Packages

USING THE PROGRAM

COMMAND NAME

```
apropos
find
```

These commands find objects by partial matching of their names. The main use for `apropos` is to find commands for which you cannot recall the exact name. The `find` command shows where the object is located in the `search` environment.

Common Usage

```
apropos(what, where = FALSE, ignore.case = TRUE, mode = "any")

find(what, mode = "any", numeric = FALSE, simple.words = TRUE)
```

Related Commands

```
help (p. 482)
help.start (p. 482)
search (p. 489)
ls (p. 67)
mode (p. 89)
```

Command Parameters

what	A character string giving the name to match. For apropos you can also use a regular expression.
where = FALSE numeric = FALSE	If TRUE, the position on the search path is also indicated.
ignore.case = TRUE	By default, the matching is not case sensitive.
mode = "any"	The default is to match objects of any type. If you want to search only for a certain type of object, you must give the mode as a character string.
simple.words = TRUE	Matches only complete words. For partial matching, use simple.words = FALSE.

Examples

```
  ## Show the search path
> search()
 [1] ".GlobalEnv"        "tools:RGUI"        "package:stats"
 [4] "package:graphics"  "package:grDevices" "package:utils"
 [7] "package:datasets"  "package:methods"   "Autoloads"
[10] "package:base"

  ## Partial match for "mean"
> apropos("mean")
 [1] "colMeans"       "kmeans"         "mean"             "mean.Date"
 [5] "mean.POSIXct"   "mean.POSIXlt"   "mean.data.frame"  "mean.default"
 [9] "mean.difftime"  "mean.fw"        "rowMeans"         "weighted.mean"

  ## The find command returns the search path
> find("mean", simple.words = FALSE, numeric = TRUE)
package:stats  package:base
            3            10

  ## Use a regular expression
> apropos("^fw")
 [1] "fw"       "fw.cm"   "fw.cov"  "fw.list" "fw.lm"   "fw.mat"  "fw1"
 [8] "fw2"      "fw3"     "fwe"     "fwi"     "fws"

  ## For find, regular expression works only if simple.words = FALSE
> find("^fw", simple.words = FALSE)
[1] ".GlobalEnv"
```

COMMAND NAME

```
help
?
help.start
```

These commands provide access to the help system. The `?` is a helper function for the `help` command and provides a quick way to access help on a particular topic. The `help.start` command opens a web browser and loads the help index so that you can navigate through the help system. You do not need to be connected to the Internet.

Common Usage

```
help(topic, package = NULL,
     try.all.packages = getOption("help.try.all.packages"),
     help_type = getOption("help_type"))

?topic

help.start()
```

Related Commands

apropos (p. 480)

Command Parameters

`topic`	The topic for which help is required. This should be a character string for the help command, but you can omit the quotation marks by using `?topic`.
`package = NULL`	The name of the package as a character string. This allows access to the help entry even if the package is not on the `search` path (e.g., has not been opened using the `library` command).
`try.all.packages`	The general default is that only packages on the `search` path are searched for a matching help topic. If `TRUE`, all packages are searched.
`help_type`	The default help display method will vary according to your OS. You can attempt to override the default by supplying a character string. The options include "text", "html", and "pdf".

Examples

```
  ## Open the help entry on the mean command using the default
> help("mean")

  ## Also brings up help entry for mean command
> ?mean
```

```
  ## This command is not in the current search path
> ?fitdistr
No documentation for 'fitdistr' in specified packages and libraries:
you could try '??fitdistr'

  ## This searches all packages and
 ## gives an indication of where the command can be found
> ??fitdistr

  ## Look for the command in all packages
> help("fitdistr", try.all.packages = TRUE)

  ## Once you know the package you can get the help entry even if
  ## the package is not currently loaded on the search path
> help("fitdistr", package = "MASS")
```

COMMAND NAME

```
history
savehistory
loadhistory
timestamp
```

These commands provide a way to access and manage the history of previously typed commands. You can also use the up and down arrows to navigate through the list of previously typed commands.

- ■ history shows the last few commands typed.

- ■ savehistory saves the current history of commands to a disk file as plain text.

- ■ loadhistory loads a set of commands into the history.

- ■ timestamp saves a timestamp to the current history.

Common Usage

```
loadhistory(file = ".Rhistory")
savehistory(file = ".Rhistory")

history(max.show = 25, reverse = FALSE, pattern, ignore.case = FALSE)

timestamp()
```

Related Commands

getwd (p. 65)
setwd (p. 70)
file.choose (p. 40)

 SEE the ls command in Theme 1, "Data" for examples of regular expressions.

Command Parameters

`file`	A filename, which must be in quotes. The current working directory is used unless given explicitly. On an OS other than Linux you can use `file.choose()` instead of a filename to read. The file saved/read is plain text, so you can edit or create a history file using a plain text editor.
`max.show = 25`	By default, only the first 25 entries in the history file are shown.
`reverse = FALSE`	If you want the latest entry at the top of the list, use `reverse = TRUE`.
`pattern`	A pattern in the form of a regular expression to match in the history list.
`ignore.case = FALSE`	By default, any `pattern` is case sensitive.

Examples

```
  ## What is the current working directory?
> getwd()
[1] "/Users/markgardener"

  ## Save the current history to a file in the working directory
> savehistory(file = "My_Working_History.RHistory")

  ## Show last 125 entries in history file
> history(max.show = 125)

  ## Use pattern matching
> history(pattern = "barplot")
> history(pattern = "^plot")
> history(pattern = "barplot", reverse = TRUE)
```

COMMAND NAME

```
quit
q
```

These commands exit R. The q command is an alias for `quit`. The command usually offers to save the current workspace. However, this setting may have been altered so you can choose to override the current default. Optionally, you can create a custom `function` called `.Last`, which is executed on quitting.

Common Usage

```
quit(save = "default", runLast = TRUE)
   q(save = "default", runLast = TRUE)

.Last <- function(x) { ...... }
```

Related Commands

save.image (p. 485)
function (p. 495)

Command Parameters

save = "default"	A character string giving one of the options "no", "yes", "ask", or "default". This determines if the workspace is saved to disk. The default is usually "ask".
runLast = TRUE	You can create a custom function called .Last, which is executed on quitting by default. To not run the function, use runLast = FALSE.
{ ......}	Any valid R command or set of commands. The custom function .Last is executed when you quit R.

Examples

```
## Quits R in the normal way and
## asks for save of workspace if that is the default
> q()

## Make sure you save current workspace
> q(save = "yes")

## Set up a function
## Simply displays a message to screen
> .Last = function(x) {cat("Goodbye..")}

## Quit R but don't run .Last function
> q(runLast = FALSE)
```

COMMAND NAME

save.image

This command saves the current workspace to disk.

 SEE also Theme 1, "Data."

Common Usage

save.image()

Related Commands

save (p. 500)

ADDITIONAL PACKAGES

Many packages of additional R commands are available for you to use to extend the capabilities of R.

 SEE also "Installing Packages."

COMMAND NAME

detach

This command detaches a package from the search path. This makes the commands within that package unavailable.

 SEE also Theme 1, "Listing Data."

Common Usage

detach(package:pkgname)

Related Commands

search (p. 500)
library (p. 487)

Command Parameters

package:pkgname   The name of the package. You must give this as a character string; see the following examples.

Examples

```
  ## View the search path to see the MASS package is loaded
> search()
 [1] ".GlobalEnv"       "package:MASS"      "tools:RGUI"
 [4] "package:stats"    "package:graphics"  "package:grDevices"
 [7] "package:utils"    "package:datasets"  "package:methods"
[10] "Autoloads"        "package:base"

  ## Detach the MASS package
> detach("package:MASS")
```

COMMAND NAME

installed.packages

This command shows a list of all the packages currently installed. The result can be very extensive if you have a lot of packages installed on your system. You can also use library(pkg), if the package is not installed, the command will fail.

Common Usage

```
installed.packages()
```

Related Commands

```
library (p. 487)
install.packages (p. 477)
new.packages (p. 478)
update.packages (p. 478)
```

Command Parameters

() If no parameters are given, the command searches all the library locations to list packages.

Examples

```
## Get the list of installed packages and save result (it is a matrix)
> ip = installed.packages()

## See the headings of the result
> colnames(ip)
 [1] "Package"   "LibPath"   "Version"   "Priority" "Depends"  "Imports"
 [7] "LinkingTo" "Suggests"  "Enhances"  "OS_type"  "License"  "Built"

## View the first 5 rows for the "Package" column (the name)
> ip[1:5, "Package"]
      abind     accuracy        ade4    ade4TkGUI       adegenet
    "abind"   "accuracy"      "ade4"  "ade4TkGUI"    "adegenet"

## The fifth column shows the dependencies, that is
## the other packages that must be loaded for them to work
> ip[1:5, c(1,5)]
          Package      Depends
abind     "abind"      "R (>= 1.5.0)"
accuracy  "accuracy"   NA
ade4      "ade4"       NA
ade4TkGUI "ade4TkGUI"  "ade4 (>= 1.4-3), tcltk"
adegenet  "adegenet"   "methods, MASS"
```

COMMAND NAME

```
library
require
```

These commands load additional packages of commands. The require command is intended to be called by other commands because it returns a warning, rather than an error, if the package does not exist.

Common Usage

```
library(package)
return(package)
```

Related Commands

```
search (p. 489)
install.packages (p. 477)
installed.packages (p. 486)
detach (p. 486)
```

Command Parameters

package   The name of the package to load. This can be a character string or the name of the package without quotation marks.

Examples

```
  ## Examine the search path (shows the packages loaded)
> search()
 [1] ".GlobalEnv"        "tools:RGUI"        "package:stats"
 [4] "package:graphics"  "package:grDevices" "package:utils"
 [7] "package:datasets"  "package:methods"   "Autoloads"
[10] "package:base"

  ## Load the "MASS" package
> library(MASS)

Attaching package: 'MASS'
Warning message:
package 'MASS' was built under R version 2.12.2

  ## Turn off warning messages
> options("warn" = -1)

  ## Attempt to load a non-existent package
> library(zzz)
Error in library(zzz) : there is no package called 'zzz'

  ## Attempt to load a non-existent package
> require(zzz)
Loading required package: zzz
```

```
## Examine search path, zzz package not loaded!
> search()
 [1] ".GlobalEnv"         "package:MASS"       "tools:RGUI"
 [4] "package:stats"      "package:graphics"   "package:grDevices"
 [7] "package:utils"      "package:datasets"   "package:methods"
[10] "Autoloads"          "package:base"


 ## Reset warnings
> options("warn" = 0)
```

COMMAND NAME

search
searchpaths

These commands show the search path. Essentially, this lists the packages that are currently loaded and any data frames (or other objects) that have been added to the path using the attach command. The search command shows a simple list of names and the searchpaths command shows the library locations in addition to the names.

Common Usage

search()

searchpaths()

Related Commands

attach (p. 61)
ls (p. 67)
rm (p. 68)
library (p. 487)

Command Parameters

() No parameters are required.

Examples

```
 ## Examine the current search path
> search()
 [1] ".GlobalEnv"         "tools:RGUI"         "package:stats"
 [4] "package:graphics"   "package:grDevices"  "package:utils"
 [7] "package:datasets"   "package:methods"    "Autoloads"
[10] "package:base"
```

```
  ## Load the MASS library
> library(MASS)

Attaching package: 'MASS'
Warning message:
package 'MASS' was built under R version 2.12.2

  ## Make a simple data frame
> dat = data.frame(col1 = 1:3, col2 = 4:6)

  ## Attach the dat data object
> attach(dat)

  ## Look at the search path again
> search()
 [1] ".GlobalEnv"        "dat"               "package:MASS"      "tools:RGUI"
 [5] "package:stats"     "package:graphics"  "package:grDevices" "package:utils"
 [9] "package:datasets"  "package:methods"   "Autoloads"         "package:base"

## An alternative view of the search path
> searchpaths()
 [1] ".GlobalEnv"
 [2] "pw"
 [3] "/Library/Frameworks/R.framework/Versions/2.12/Resources/library/MASS"
 [4] "tools:RGUI"
 [5] "/Library/Frameworks/R.framework/Versions/2.12/Resources/library/stats"
 [6] "/Library/Frameworks/R.framework/Versions/2.12/Resources/library/graphics"
 [7] "/Library/Frameworks/R.framework/Versions/2.12/Resources/library/grDevices"
 [8] "/Library/Frameworks/R.framework/Versions/2.12/Resources/library/utils"
 [9] "/Library/Frameworks/R.framework/Versions/2.12/Resources/library/datasets"
[10] "/Library/Frameworks/R.framework/Versions/2.12/Resources/library/methods"
[11] "Autoloads"
[12] "/Library/Frameworks/R.framework/Resources/library/base"

  ## Tidy up – remove items from search path
> detach(dat)
> detach("package:MASS")
```

Programming

Programming R yourself can be especially useful because in doing so you can prepare scripts that undertake complex or repetitive tasks, which can be brought into operation at any time. Indeed, R is built along these (modular) lines and you can think of R as a bundle of scripts; by making your own you are simply increasing the usefulness of R and bending it to meet your own specific requirements.

This topic contains commands that are especially connected with the production of scripts—you are more likely to encounter the commands in this context than in any other.

MANAGING FUNCTIONS

R provides various commands that help you to manage the functions that you create, enabling you to list the custom functions or to see the required arguments, for example.

COMMAND NAME

`args`

This command displays the arguments required for a named function. Any default values are also displayed.

Common Usage

`args(name)`

Related Commands

`function` (p. 495)
`body` (p. 492)
`formals` (p. 494)
`lsf.str` (p. 496)

Command Parameters

`name`   The name of the function or command. Usually you can simply give the name, but a character string is also accepted.

```
## Make a 1-line function (there are 3 arguments, one has a default value)
> manning = function(radius, grad, coef = 0.1125) (radius^(2/3)*grad^0.5/coef)

## Make a multi-line function (returns the running median of a vector, x)
> cummedian = function(x) {
  tmp = seq_along(x)
  for(i in 1:length(tmp)) tmp[i] = median(x[1:i])
  print(tmp)
}

## Look at arguments (user input)
> args(manning)
function (radius, grad, coef = 0.1125)
NULL

> args(cummedian)
function (x)
NULL

## Show arguments for a built-in function/command, bxp
> args("bxp")
function (z, notch = FALSE, width = NULL, varwidth = FALSE, outline = TRUE,
    notch.frac = 0.5, log = "", border = par("fg"), pars = NULL,
    frame.plot = axes, horizontal = FALSE, add = FALSE, at = NULL,
    show.names = NULL, ...)
NULL
```

COMMAND NAME

body

This command shows the body of a function; that is, "how it works." You can also alter the function, but this is sensible only for fairly short code snippets.

Common Usage

```
body(fun)
body(fun) <- value
```

Related Commands

function (p. 495)
formals (p. 494)
args (p. 491)
lsf.str (p. 496)

Command Parameters

fun   The name of the function or command. Usually you can simply give the name, but a character string is also accepted.

value The new body for the function. You must be careful that this is not evaluated, so you generally have to use a quote or expression.

Examples

```
  ## Make a multi-line function
  ## (returns the running median of a vector, x)
> cummedian = function(x) {
  tmp = seq_along(x)
  for(i in 1:length(tmp)) tmp[i] = median(x[1:i])
  print(tmp)
 }

## View the main body of the function
> body(cummedian)
{
    tmp = seq_along(x)
    for (i in 1:length(tmp)) tmp[i] = median(x[1:i])
    print(tmp)
}

## A simple trivial function
> f = function(x) x^5

  ## View main body
> body(f)
x^5

> f(2)
[1] 32

  ## Change body, note that quote is used
  ## to prevent x being evaluated as an object
> body(f) <- quote(5^x)

  ## Check the new body
> body(f)
5^x

> f(2)
[1] 25
```

COMMAND NAME

formals

This command allows access to the arguments of a function and permits you to alter the default values.

Common Usage

```
formals(fun)
formals(fun) <- value
```

Related Commands

```
function (p. 495)
args (p. 491)
lsf.str (p. 496)
```

Command Parameters

fun   The name of a function. If you are simply looking at the arguments, you can use a character string.

value   A list giving the arguments and their default values. If no default is to be used, specify NULL. Alternatively, you can use alist (see the following examples).

Examples

```
  ## Make a 1-line function
> manning = function(radius, grad, coef = 0.1125) (radius^(2/3)*grad^0.5/coef)

  ## Examine the formal arguments
> formals(manning)
$radius

$grad

$coef
[1] 0.1125

  ## Alter defaults
> formals(manning) <- list(radius = NULL, grad = NULL, coef = 0.21)

  ## View function
> manning
function(radius, gradient, coef = 0.1125) (radius^(2/3)*gradient^0.5/coef)
```

```
  ## Run function but miss out an argument..
  ## ..no result
> manning(2)
numeric(0)


  ## Alter formals but use alist instead (NULL now not needed)
  ## Note all arguments must be listed
> formals(manning) <- alist(radius = , grad = , coef = 0.21)


  ## Run function, missing value now produces an informative error
> manning(2)
Error in grad^0.5 : 'grad' is missing


  ## Use formals to create a function from a template
> func = function(x) a + b


  ## This function will not work as it is because a and b do not exist
  ## Create default values for function
  ## (a: unspecified, b: default value = 3)
> formals(func) <- alist(a = , b = 3)


  ## View the function
> func
function (a, b = 3)
a + b


  ## Run function
> func(a = 2)
[1] 5
```

COMMAND NAME

`function`

This command creates custom functions. A `function` is a collection of R commands that are bundled together in a named object (a `function` or custom command). You can create simple functions directly from the keyboard. When your functions become more complicated, you are more likely to use a text editor to write the source code.

Common Usage

`function(arglist) expr`

Related Commands

formals (p. 494)
args (p. 491)
body (p. 492)
lsf.str (p. 496)
source (p. 501)

Command Parameters

arglist   A list of named arguments. Default values for arguments are given as arg = value.

expr   The expression(s) to be evaluated as part of the function. Essentially this is a series
          of R commands, using the arguments given in the arglist. If your function is more
          than one line, it is common to enclose the expr in braces (curly brackets). Braces are
          also used to separate sections of code (in conditional statements, for example). Once
          functions become larger than just a few lines, it is generally easier to use a text/script
          editor and use source to read them into R.

Examples

```
  ## A simple function
> func = function(x) x^3

  ## View the function
> func
function(x) x^3

  ## Run the function
> func(3)
[1] 27

  ## Make a 1-line function; one argument has a default value
> manning = function(radius, grad, coef = 0.1125) (radius^(2/3)*grad^0.5/coef)
  ## Run the function (calculate speed of water)
> manning(radius = 1, grad = 0.1)
[1] 2.810913

  ## Make a multi-line function; use {} to allow
  ## multiple lines of code to be typed into the console
> cummedian = function(x) {
    tmp = seq_along(x)
    for(i in 1:length(tmp)) tmp[i] = median(x[1:i])
    print(tmp)
  }

  ## Run the function (cumulative median)
> cummedian(1:10)
 [1] 1.0 1.5 2.0 2.5 3.0 3.5 4.0 4.5 5.0 5.5
```

COMMAND NAME

lsf.str

This command shows the structure of functions at a specified position in the search path.

 SEE also Theme 1, "Viewing Data: Data Object Properties."

Common Usage
```
lsf.str(pos = -1)
```

Related Commands
ls (p. 67)
function (p. 495)
ls.str (p. 87)

Command Parameters

pos = -1 The position of the environment to use for the listing as given by the search command. The default pos = -1 and pos = 1 are equivalent and relate to the global environment (the workspace). Other positions relate to various command packages.

Examples
```
  ## Make some simple functions
> func = function(x) x^3

> manning = function(radius, grad, coef = 0.1125) (radius^(2/3)*grad^0.5/coef)

> cummedian = function(x) {
    tmp = seq_along(x)
    for(i in 1:length(tmp)) tmp[i] = median(x[1:i])
    print(tmp)
  }

  ## View the search path
> search()
 [1] ".GlobalEnv"        "tools:rstudio"      "package:stats"
 [4] "package:graphics"  "package:grDevices"  "package:utils"
 [7] "package:datasets"  "package:methods"    "Autoloads"
[10] "package:base"

  ## View functions in the Global Environment ("user functions")
> lsf.str(pos = -1)
cummedian : function (x)
func : function (x)
manning : function (radius, gradient, coef = 0.1125)

  ## Functions in position 2 (Mac OS X GUI)
> lsf.str(pos = 2)
browse.pkgs : function (repos = getOption("repos"),
    contriburl = contrib.url(repos, type), type = getOption("pkgType"))
data.manager : function ()
main.help.url : function ()
package.manager : function ()
```

```
print.hsearch : function (x, ...)
q : function (save = "default", status = 0, runLast = TRUE)
quartz.save : function (file, type = "png", device = dev.cur(),
    dpi = 100, ...)
quit : function (save = "default", status = 0, runLast = TRUE)
Rapp.updates : function ()
```

SAVING AND RUNNING SCRIPTS

You can create scripts by one of several methods. The simplest is to type the commands that make up the script directly into the console window. This is most useful for simple functions that are only a few lines at most. For longer and more complicated functions/scripts, it is better to use a dedicated text editor. Windows and Mac users have script editors built into the R GUI. Your scripts will be in two forms, plain text or R-encoded binary files:

- Scripts that are plain text can be read into R using the source command.

- Custom functions that you save as binary files using the save command can be read into R using the load command.

COMMAND NAME

dump

This command attempts to write a text representation of R objects to disk. The resulting file can often be opened using the source command. This is not always entirely successful, depending on the nature of the object(s) being handled.

 SEE also dump Theme 1, "Saving Data: Saving Data as a Text File to Disk."

Common Usage

```
dump(list, file = "dumpdata.R", append = FALSE, control = "all")
```

Related Commands

save (p. 500)
source (p. 501)
load (p. 499)

Command Parameters

list	A character vector containing the names of the R objects to be written.
file = "dumpdata.R"	The filename in quotes; if blank, the output goes to current device (usually the screen). Filename defaults to the current working directory unless specified explicitly. Can also link to URL. For Windows and Mac OS the filename can be replaced by file.choose(), which brings up a file browser.

append = FALSE	If the output is a file, `append = TRUE` adds the result to the file; otherwise, the file is overwritten.
control = "all"	Controls the deparsing process. Use `control = "all"` for the most complete deparsing. Other options are "keepNA", "keepInteger", "showAttributes", and "useSource". Use `control = NULL` for the simplest representation.

Examples

```
  ## Make a multi-line function
> cummedian = function(x) {
  tmp = seq_along(x)
  for(i in 1:length(tmp)) tmp[i] = median(x[1:i])
  print(tmp)
}

  ## Write the function to disk as text
  ## .R file extension is associated with R scripts
> dump(ls(pattern = "cummedian"), file = "My_Function.R")

  ## Remove function from R
> rm(cummedian)

  ## Restore function from disk
> source(file = "My_Function.R")
```

COMMAND NAME

load

This command reloads data that was saved from R in binary format (usually via the save command). The save command creates a binary file containing named R objects, which may be data, results, or custom functions. The load command reinstates the named objects, overwriting any identically named objects with no warning.

 SEE also load in Theme 1, "Importing Data: Importing Data from Data Files."

Common Usage

load(file)

Related Commands

save (p. 500)
dump (p. 498)
source (p. 501)

file   The filename in quotes. Defaults to the current working directory unless speci-
        fied explicitly. Can also link to URL. For Windows and Mac OS the filename can be
        replaced by file.choose(), which brings up a file browser.

Examples

```
  ## Make a function
> cummedian
function(x) {
  tmp = seq_along(x)
  for(i in 1:length(tmp)) tmp[i] = median(x[1:i])
  print(tmp)
}

  ## Save function to disk as binary file
  ## .RData file is associated with R binary files
> save(cummedian, file = "My_Function_Save.RData")

  ## Remove original from console
> rm(cummedian)

  ## Load function from binary disk file
> load("My_Function_Save.RData")
```

COMMAND NAME

save

This command saves R objects to disk as binary encoded files (that is, not plain text). The objects
saved with the save command can be loaded using the load command.

 SEE also save in Theme 1, "Saving Data: Saving Data as a Data File to Disk."

Common Usage

```
save(..., list = character(0L), file = stop("'file' must be specified"),
    ascii = FALSE)
```

Related Commands

source (p. 501)
load (p. 499)
save.image (p. 485)

Command Parameters

`...`	Names of R objects (separated by commas) to be saved.
`list =`	A list can be given instead of explicit names; this allows the `ls` command to be used, for example.
`file =`	The filename in quotes; defaults to the current working directory unless specified explicitly. Can also link to URL. For Windows and Mac OS the filename can be replaced by `file.choose()`, which brings up a file browser.
`ascii = FALSE`	If set to `TRUE`, an ASCII representation is written to disk. This is not the same as "saving a text file," but rather uses ASCII encoding instead of a binary code. The resulting file can still be opened using the `load` command.

Examples

```
  ## Make a function
> cummedian
function(x) {
  tmp = seq_along(x)
  for(i in 1:length(tmp)) tmp[i] = median(x[1:i])
  print(tmp)
}

  ## Save function to disk as binary file
  ## .RData file is associated with R binary files
> save(cummedian, file = "My_Function_Save.RData")

  ## Remove original from console
> rm(cummedian)

  ## Load function from binary disk file
> load("My_Function_Save.RData")
```

COMMAND NAME

source

Reads a text file and treats it as commands typed from the keyboard. Commonly used to run saved scripts; that is, lines of R commands.

 SEE also source in Theme 1, "Importing Data: Importing Data from Text Files."

Common Usage

source(file)

Related Commands

save (p. 485)
function (p. 495)
dump (p. 498)
load (p. 499)

Command Parameters

file   The filename in quotes. Defaults to the current working directory unless specified explicitly. Can also link to URL. For Windows and Mac OS the filename can be replaced by file.choose(), which brings up a file browser.

Examples

```
  ## Make a custom function/script
> myfunc = function(x) {
  tmp = seq_along(x)
  for(i in 1:length(tmp)) tmp[i] = median(x[1:i])
  print(tmp)
  }

  ## Write to disk and delete original
> dump(ls(pattern = "myfunc"), file = "myfunc.R")
> rm(myfunc)

  ## recall the script
> source("myfunc.R")
```

CONDITIONAL CONTROL

Larger and more complicated scripts are likely to require some decision-making processes. These decisions control the flow of the script and enable you to carry out different tasks according to the result of the decision(s). The R programming language has several commands that allow conditional control, including loops.

COMMAND NAME

all

This command produces a logical result TRUE, if all the conditions are met.

Common Usage

all(..., na.rm = FALSE)

Related Commands

any (p. 503)

Command Parameters

...	Logical vectors or statements that produce a logical result.
na.rm = FALSE	If na.rm = TRUE, NA items are omitted before the result is evaluated.

Examples

```
  ## Set random number generator
> set.seed(7)

  ## Make some numbers from normal distribution
> x = rnorm(n = 10, mean = -1.2, sd = 1)

  ## View range of values
> range(x)
[1] -2.396772  1.087247


  ## Are all values negative?
> all(x < 0)
[1] FALSE

> ## Use conditional statement
> if(all(x < 0)) cat("All are negative") else cat("Some are positive")
Some are positive

  ## Repeat with different random numbers
> set.seed(8)
> x = rnorm(n = 10, mean = -1.2, sd = 1)
> range(x)
[1] -4.2110517 -0.3595999

> all(x < 0)
[1] TRUE

> if(all(x < 0)) cat("All are negative") else cat("Some are positive")
All are negative
```

COMMAND NAME

any

This produces a logical TRUE, if any of the conditions are met.

Common Usage

any(..., na.rm = FALSE)

Related Commands

all (p. 502)

Command Parameters

  ...   Logical vectors or statements that produce a logical result.

`na.rm = FALSE`   If `na.rm = TRUE`, `NA` items are omitted before the result is evaluated.

Examples

```
  ## Set random number generator
> set.seed(7)

  ## Make some numbers from normal distribution
> x = rnorm(n = 10, mean = -1.2, sd = 1)

  ## View range of values
> range(x)
[1] -2.396772  1.087247

  ## Are any values positive?
> any(x > 0)
[1] TRUE

> if(any(x > 0)) cat("There are positive values") else
 cat("None are positive")
There are positive values

  ## Repeat with different random numbers
> set.seed(8)
> x = rnorm(n = 10, mean = -1.2, sd = 1)
> range(x)
[1] -4.2110517 -0.3595999

> any(x > 0)
[1] FALSE

> if(any(x > 0)) cat("There are positive values") else
 cat("None are positive")
None are positive
```

COMMAND NAME

`for`

This creates loops, enabling you to carry out a process repeatedly while some condition applies.

Common Usage

```
for(var in seq) expr
```

Related Commands

if (p. 505)

Command Parameters

var A name of a variable. This is used in the expr part of the command.

seq A vector or, more usually, an expression that evaluates to a vector. This essentially sets how long the loop lasts.

expr An expression to carry out for each step in the loop. If this is more than one line in length, you should enclose the entire expr in braces.

Examples

```
## Simple loop showing number and corresponding LETTER
> for(i in 1:10) cat(paste(i, ":", LETTERS[i], sep = ""), " ")
1:A  2:B  3:C  4:D  5:E  6:F  7:G  8:H  9:I  10:J

## Make a multi-line function to determine running median of a vector
> cummedian = function(x) {
tmp = seq_along(x) # Creates an index for x
for(i in 1:length(tmp)) tmp[i] = median(x[1:i])
print(tmp)
}
```

COMMAND NAME

```
if
else
```

These commands form the basis for conditional control over your scripts. The if command evaluates a condition and then carries out a series of commands if that condition is TRUE. The else command is optional and used only in conjunction with an if command. The else command allows you to specify two expressions to evaluate, one for a TRUE result and one for a FALSE.

Common Usage

```
if(cond) expr
if(cond) expr else alt.expr
```

Related Commands

for (p. 504)

Command Parameters

cond   A condition that produces a logical result. If this is TRUE, the expr is evaluated. If FALSE, control passes to the next line (or after the closing curly bracket) unless the else command is used, when the alt.expr is evaluated.

expr   An expression to evaluate, that is, a series of R commands. It is generally good practice to enclose the expr in curly brackets. This is necessary for multiple lines (everything inside the brackets is evaluated as if it were one line). When the if statement produces a FALSE result, the control passes over the expr to the following line (or curly bracket) unless else was used.

else   When else is used an alternative expression can be supplied; this is evaluated when the if statement returns FALSE.

alt.expr   An alternative expression to evaluate following an else command. This is evaluated only when the if condition returns a FALSE result.

Examples

```
  ## Simple: two options so else is used
> x = 0
> if(x == 0) cat("YES") else cat("NO")
YES


> x = -1
> if(x == 0) cat("YES") else cat("NO")
NO


  ## Multiple options {} not needed as each if() is on single line
  ## But entire "set" is enclosed in {} so multiple lines
  ## can be typed from keyboard into console
> x = 1

> { # Use curly brackets so multiple lines can be typed
    if(x == 0)  cat("Zero")
    if(x > 0)   cat("Positive")
    if(x < 0)   cat("Negative")
  } # This ends the "set" and the result is returned
Positive


  ## Individual if() inside {} as each is > 1-line
> x = -1

> { # Use curly brackets so multiple lines can be typed
    if(x == 0) { cat("Zero\n")
                 cat("Neither +ve or -ve")} # If FALSE goes to next line
    if(x > 0)  { cat("Positive\n")
                 cat("Greater than 0")} # If FALSE goes to next line
```

```
  if(x < 0)  { cat("Negative\n")
               cat("Less than 0")} # If FALSE goes to next line
 } # This ends the "set" and the result is returned
Negative
Less than 0
```

RETURNING RESULTS

At the end of your script you will usually want to handle the result. This may involve creating a named object containing your result or producing a graphic or printed display on the computer screen. Various R commands deal with the returning of results and associated handling of text items.

COMMAND NAME

```
#
```

Anything following the # character is ignored (until the next command line). This provides a mechanism for including annotations (that is, comments) in scripts.

Common Usage

```
# annotations
```

Related Commands

function (p. 495)

Command Parameters

annotations   Any characters that you can type from the keyboard can be used to form annotations, because anything following the # is ignored until a new line is encountered.

Examples

```
  ## Example of annotations
> x = 1:6 # Some numbers
> y = 1:12 # A vector the same length as x
  ## Any √™€π character that you can type is accepted
  ## all are ignored by R!
```

COMMAND NAME

abbreviate

This command takes a series of character strings and shortens them to form unique abbreviations.

Common Usage

```
abbreviate(names.arg, minlength = 4, dot = FALSE,
          strict = FALSE, method = "left.kept")
```

Related Commands

nchar (p. 513)

Command Parameters

names.arg	A character vector of names that are to be abbreviated.
minlength = 4	The minimum length to make the abbreviations. The results can be made longer than the set value to make each one unique (unless strict = TRUE).
dot = FALSE	If TRUE, a dot is appended to the end of each abbreviation.
strict = FALSE	If TRUE, the length of the abbreviation is kept strictly to minlength. This can result in non-unique abbreviations.
method	An algorithm describing how to carry out the abbreviation. The options are "left.kept" (the default) and "both.sides".

Examples

```
  ## Use state.name from R datasets
> data(state.name) # Make sure data is ready

  ## Abbreviate each name to length of 1 if possible
> abbreviate(state.name, minlength = 1)
       Alabama          Alaska         Arizona        Arkansas      California
         "Alb"           "Als"           "Arz"           "Ark"           "Clf"
      Colorado     Connecticut        Delaware         Florida         Georgia
         "Clr"            "Cn"             "D"             "F"             "G"
        Hawaii           Idaho        Illinois         Indiana            Iowa
           "H"            "Id"            "Il"            "In"            "Iw"
        Kansas        Kentucky       Louisiana           Maine        Maryland
         "Kns"           "Knt"             "L"           "Man"            "Mr"
 Massachusetts        Michigan       Minnesota     Mississippi        Missouri
        "Mssc"            "Mc"           "Mnn"          "Msss"          "Mssr"
       Montana        Nebraska          Nevada   New Hampshire      New Jersey
         "Mnt"            "Nb"            "Nv"            "NH"            "NJ"
    New Mexico        New York  North Carolina    North Dakota            Ohio
          "NM"            "NY"            "NC"            "ND"            "Oh"
      Oklahoma          Oregon    Pennsylvania    Rhode Island  South Carolina
          "Ok"            "Or"             "P"            "RI"            "SC"
  South Dakota       Tennessee           Texas            Utah         Vermont
          "SD"            "Tn"            "Tx"             "U"           "Vrm"
      Virginia      Washington   West Virginia       Wisconsin         Wyoming
         "Vrg"           "Wsh"            "WV"           "Wsc"            "Wy"
```

```
  ## Tabulate the result to show
  ## how many states abbreviated to what length
> table(nchar(abbreviate(state.name, minlength = 1)))

 1  2  3  4
 7 25 15  3
```

COMMAND NAME

cat

This command concatenates objects and then prints them; the default output goes to the screen. You can also think of this command as short for "catalog." It is useful for presenting results and messages to screen.

Common Usage

```
cat(... , file = "", sep = " ", fill = FALSE, labels = NULL,
    append = FALSE)
```

Related Commands

print (p. 515)
as.character (p. 16)

Command Parameters

...	R objects to output. Generally, these should be vectors.
file = ""	The default output usually goes to the screen. You can specify a file as a character string (including the path).
sep = " "	The separator character to use between elements. The default is a single space.
fill = FALSE	Specifies how the output is split into new lines. The default uses the current console screen width. You can specify a set width using a numeric value. In any event, using "\n" creates a newline character.
labels = NULL	If fill is not FALSE, you can specify a character vector of labels to use for the beginning of lines.
append = FALSE	If append = TRUE, the output is appended to the specified file. This is really only applicable to off-screen output.

Examples

```
  ## Use US state name abbreviations from R datasets
> data(state.abb) # Make sure data is ready
```

```
  ## Catalog state abbreviations to a width of 75. Separate using comma
  ## Note that labels must be coerced into a character vector
> cat(state.abb, fill = 75, sep = ", ", labels = as.character(1:3))
1 AL, AK, AZ, AR, CA, CO, CT, DE, FL, GA, HI, ID, IL, IN, IA, KS, KY, LA,
2 ME, MD, MA, MI, MN, MS, MO, MT, NE, NV, NH, NJ, NM, NY, NC, ND, OH, OK,
3 OR, PA, RI, SC, SD, TN, TX, UT, VT, VA, WA, WV, WI, WY


  ## Mixed items. Note that break causes incorrect indentation
> cat("US State names in abbreviation:\n", state.abb,
 fill = 75, sep = ", ")

US State names in abbreviation:
, AL, AK, AZ, AR, CA, CO, CT, DE, FL, GA,
HI, ID, IL, IN, IA, KS, KY, LA, ME, MD, MA, MI, MN, MS, MO, MT, NE, NV,
NH, NJ, NM, NY, NC, ND, OH, OK, OR, PA, RI, SC, SD, TN, TX, UT, VT, VA,
WA, WV, WI, WY


  ## Use separate cat statements to ensure correct alignment
> {
    cat("US State names in abbreviation..\n")
    cat(state.abb, sep = ", ", fill = 75)
  }

US State names in abbreviation..
AL, AK, AZ, AR, CA, CO, CT, DE, FL, GA, HI, ID, IL, IN, IA, KS, KY, LA,
ME, MD, MA, MI, MN, MS, MO, MT, NE, NV, NH, NJ, NM, NY, NC, ND, OH, OK,
OR, PA, RI, SC, SD, TN, TX, UT, VT, VA, WA, WV, WI, WY
```

COMMAND NAME

deparse

This command converts R commands and objects into character strings. One use is in conjunction with the substitute command to create labels from user input, which can be used in producing informative labels for the output.

Common Usage

```
deparse(expr, width.cutoff = 60L, backtick, nlines = -1L)
```

Related Commands

substitute (p. 521)
expression (p. 422)

Command Parameters

`expr`	Any R command. The command is unevaluated and a representation written as a character string.
`width.cutoff = 60L`	Sets the width of the output display for line-breaking; this is in bytes.
`backtick`	If `backtick` = `TRUE`, non-standard syntax names are enclosed in backticks.
`control = "keepInteger"`	Controls the deparsing process. Use `control` = "all" for the most complete deparsing. Other options are "keepNA", "keepInteger", "showAttributes", and "useSource". Use `control` = `NULL` for the simplest representation.
`nlines = -1L`	Sets the maximum number of lines of output to produce. A negative value (default) indicates no limit.

Examples

```
  ## Make a 1-line function
> manning = function(radius, grad, coef = 0.1125) (radius^(2/3)*grad^0.5/coef)

  ## Use args command but deparse to get result as character
> deparse(args(manning))
[1] "function (radius, grad, coef = 0.1125) "
[2] "NULL"

  ## Make a function that shows result from user input objects
> function(x, fun = median, ...) { # Start body of function
   tmp = seq_along(x)
   for(i in 1:length(tmp)) tmp[i] = fun(x[1:i], ...)

cat('\n',                      # A newline character
deparse(substitute(fun)),      # Displays name of fun (median by default)
'of',                          # Some text
deparse(substitute(x)),        # Displays name of input data object
'\n')                          # A newline character
print(tmp)                     # Displays tmp object (the cumulative median)
 }                             # End of the function

  ## Make data and run function
> mydat = c(3, 4, 6, 6, 4, 3, 7, 8, 9)
> cum.fun(mydat, fun = median)

 median of mydat
[1] 3.0 3.5 4.0 5.0 4.0 4.0 4.0 5.0 6.0
```

COMMAND NAME

`invisible`

This command stores the result of a function but does not print it; that is, it does not show the result to screen.

Common Usage

`invisible(x)`

Related Commands

`print` (p. 515)
`function` (p. 495)
`return` (p. 520)

Command Parameters

x   An R object. Usually this is the result of a script/function.

Examples

```
  ## A simple function: print() displays result
> f1 = function(x, y = 2) print(x^y)

  ## A simple function: invisible() stores the result
> f2 = function(x, y = 2) invisible(x^y)

  ## Run function and get result
> f1(2, 3)
[1] 8

  ## Run function but result not shown
> f2(2, 3)

  ## Assign object to "hold" result
> fr = f2(2, 3)

  ## Result now held in named object
> fr
[1] 8

  ## A function:  Dedicated results object created but
  ## only saved if function is assigned to an object
> func = function(x, y = 2) { # Set arguments, one has a default value
    powr = x^y                # Calculation 1 (a power)
    root = x^(1/y)            # Calculation 2 (a root)
    temp = c(powr, root)      # Object created to hold power and root
    print(temp)               # Result is displayed
  }                           # End of the function
```

```
   ## Run function to display result
> func(2)
[1] 4.000000 1.414214

   ## Result is stored and displayed if function is assigned to object
> fr = func(2)
[1] 4.000000 1.414214
```

COMMAND NAME

nchar
nzchar

The nchar command counts the number of characters in strings. The nzchar command returns a logical TRUE if a string is non-empty or FALSE if empty.

Common Usage

```
nchar(x, type = "chars")

nzchar(x)
```

Related Commands

abbreviate (p. 507)
paste (p. 514)
cat (p. 509)
print (p. 515)

Command Parameters

x	A character vector, or object that can be coerced into a character vector.
type = "chars"	The type of result. The default is "chars"; e.g., characters. Other options are "bytes" and "width". The former counts the number of bytes required to hold the item, and the latter is the number of columns the cat command would use to display the result. Mostly the three will produce the same result.

Examples

```
   ## Give the number of characters in the month names
> nchar(month.name, type = "chars")
 [1] 7 8 5 5 3 4 4 6 9 7 8 8

   ## Make a character vector
> mychar = c("a", "abc", "", "hello")

   ## Count the characters
> nchar(mychar)
[1] 1 3 0 5
```

```
  ## Are all items in vector non-empty?
> nzchar(mychar)
[1]  TRUE  TRUE FALSE  TRUE
```

COMMAND NAME

paste

This command converts objects to characters and then concatenates them. The result can be represented either as multiple character strings (as many as there are objects) or as one single character string (the objects being joined). This is often used to create labels.

Common Usage

```
paste(..., sep = " ", collapse = NULL)
```

Related Commands

cat (p. 509)
print (p. 515)

Command Parameters

...	One or more R objects. These will be converted to character vectors.
sep = " "	The separator character(s) to use between objects. The default is a single space.
collapse = NULL	If collapse is not NULL, a single character string is the result. The characters specified by collapse will separate the original objects.

Examples

```
  ## Simple labels
> paste("A", 1:6, sep = "")
[1] "A1" "A2" "A3" "A4" "A5" "A6"

  ## Change separator
> paste("A", 1:6, sep = ":")
[1] "A:1" "A:2" "A:3" "A:4" "A:5" "A:6"

  ## Two character strings and numbers
> paste("A", "B", 1:6, sep = ":")
[1] "A:B:1" "A:B:2" "A:B:3" "A:B:4" "A:B:5" "A:B:6"

  ## Simple label
> paste("AB", 1:6, sep = ":")
[1] "AB:1" "AB:2" "AB:3" "AB:4" "AB:5" "AB:6"

  ## Collapse to single string
> paste("AB", 1:6, sep = "-", collapse = "+")
[1] "AB-1+AB-2+AB-3+AB-4+AB-5+AB-6"
```

COMMAND NAME

```
print
print.xxxx
```

The `print` command prints its argument, usually to the screen. It also returns the argument via `invisible`, meaning that if used within a `function`, the argument (usually a result) can be saved. The command is generic and you can write your own dedicated `print` functions to deal with objects that hold a specific `class` attribute. You name your function `print.xxxx`, where xxxx corresponds to the `class` attribute of the object you want to print. Many `print.xxxx` commands are already built into R to deal with various classes of objects.

 SEE also source in Theme 1, "Importing Data: Importing Data from Text Files."

PRINT METHODS

You can check to see if there is a built-in `print.xxxx` command by using the following command:

```
methods(class = "xxxx")
```

where xxxx is the name of the `class` attribute you want to use. The result shows you all the methods associated with that `class`.

Common Usage

```
print(x, ...)

print(x, digits = NULL, quote = TRUE,
    na.print = NULL, print.gap = NULL, right = FALSE,
    max = NULL, useSource = TRUE, ...)
```

Related Commands

```
invisible (p. 512)
class (p. 18, 79)
```

Command Parameters

x	An object. The `class` attribute is used to determine which print method to use.
print.gap	A value that specifies the spacing between adjacent columns for vectors and arrays (including matrix objects). This should be in the range of 1 to 1024 and the default, `NULL`, equates to 1.
right = FALSE	If `right = TRUE`, the output is right justified. The default is left justified.
max	Sets the approximate maximum number of entries to display. The default, `NULL`, reads the value from `option("max.print")`, which is in the region of 10,000.

`...`	Additional arguments can be used. Different print methods can have different defaults. The common usage defaults for this command are for the `print.default` method. Some arguments work only with specific classes.
`quote`	If `quote = FALSE` (the usual default), character strings are shown without quotes.
`max.levels`	Sets how the levels of a `factor` object are shown. If `max.levels = 0`, no additional line labeled "Levels" is printed. An integer value sets how many levels are shown in the "Levels" line. The default, `NULL`, displays as many as can fit on one line set by `width`.
`width`	If `max.levels = NULL`, this sets the width of the "Levels" line that is displayed (see the following examples). The default reads the value in `options("width")`.
`digits`	The minimum number of significant digits to display. The default reads the value in `options("digits")`.
`na.print`	Controls how `NA` items are handled. The default is to display `NA` unless this is a character `NA` and `quote = FALSE`, when `<NA>` is displayed. You can specify a character string to appear instead of `NA`.
`zero.print`	A character that specifies how zero values should be presented in `table` objects. This can be useful in tables where 0 values might dominate.
`justify`	A character string controlling justification. Options are `"left"`, `"right"`, and `"none"` (the usual default).
`useSource`	If `useSource = TRUE`, the default, any attribute that the printed object holds is used.

Examples

```
  ## Simple print
> print(log2(2:8)) # Default print
[1] 1.000000 1.584963 2.000000 2.321928 2.584963 2.807355 3.000000

> print(log2(2:8), digits = 3) # Fewer digits
[1] 1.00 1.58 2.00 2.32 2.58 2.81 3.00

  ## Create some data items
  ## Some numeric data with NA items
> mydat = c(2, 0, 5, NA, NA, 3, 4, NA, 7)

  ## Simple character data (upper case letters)
> mychar = LETTERS[1:12]

  ## A table: you will need the pw data from the download
> mytab = table(pw$water, pw$height)

  ## A factor: you will need the pw data from the download
> myfac = pw$water
```

```
  ## Print items
> print(mydat) # Default for numeric data
[1]  2  0  5 NA NA  3  4 NA  7

> print(mydat, na.print = "-") # Change NA display
[1] 2 0 5 - - 3 4 - 7

> print(mychar) # Default for characters
 [1] "A" "B" "C" "D" "E" "F" "G" "H" "I" "J" "K" "L"

> print(mychar, quote = FALSE) # Do not display quotes
 [1] A B C D E F G H I J K L

> print(mytab, zero.print = ".") # Display 0 in table as .

     5 6 7 9 11 14 15 17 19 28 31 32 37 38 44
 hi  . . . .  .  .  .  .  .  1  1  1  1  1  1
 lo  1 2 1 1  1  .  .  .  .  .  .  .  .  .  .
 mid . . . .  .  2  1  2  1  .  .  .  .  .  .

> print(myfac, max.levels = NULL) # Default for factor
 [1] lo  lo  lo  mid mid mid hi  hi  hi  lo  lo  lo  mid mid mid hi hi hi
Levels: hi lo mid

> print(myfac, max.levels = 0) # Do not display "Levels" line
 [1] lo  lo  lo  mid mid mid hi hi hi  lo  lo  lo  mid mid mid hi hi hi

  ## Make your own dedicated print method
  ## A function
> func = function(x, y = 2) { # Set arguments, one has a default value
    powr = x^y               # Calculation 1 (a power)
    root = x^(1/y)           # Calculation 2 (a root)
    result = list(power = powr, root = root)  # Make a result object
    class(result) <- "pwrrt"    # Make a dedicated class for this result
    invisible(result)           # Result is stored
  }                             # End of the function

  ## Make a function to print the pwrt class object
> print.pwrrt = function(x, digits = 3, ...) {
    # Set inputs and defaults, ... allows additional arguments to be used
    # but not actually needed here

    cat("My own print method\n")      # A simple message and newline
    print(x$power, digits = digits)   # Print power result
    print(x$root, digits = digits)    # Print root result
  }                                    # End of print function

  ## Use the functions to calculate and display (print)
> func(2,3) # Result is calculated but not shown
> fr = func(2,3) # Result stored to fr object
```

```
> class(fr) # View class attribute
[1] "pwrrt"

> print(fr) # Result printed using print.pwrrt command
My own print method
[1] 8
[1] 1.26
```

COMMAND NAME

quote

This command returns its argument as plain text (without quotes). The argument is not evaluated in any way and is simply returned "as is."

Common Usage

quote(expr)

Related Commands

print (p. 515)
deparse (p. 510)
substitute (p. 521)

Command Parameters

expr   Anything can be used. Typically this is an R command of some sort. It is unevaluated, but note that spaces are stripped out.

Examples

```
  ## Make a character vector
> mychar = LETTERS[1:12]
> mychar
 [1] "A" "B" "C" "D" "E" "F" "G" "H" "I" "J" "K" "L"

  ## Print the vector
> print(mychar, quote = FALSE)
 [1] A B C D E F G H I J K L

  ## Use quote
> quote(mychar)
mychar

  ## A function
> func = function(x, y) {      # Start function
    result = x^y               # Simple calculation
```

```
    print(quote(x^y : done.)) # Simple message printed
    invisible(result)          # Actual result stored and not displayed
  }                            # End of function

  ## Use the function
> func(2, 3)       # Message is printed, note spaces stripped out
x^y:done.

> fr = func(2, 3) # Save result to named object
x^y:done.

> fr               # Result is stored in this object
[1] 8
```

COMMAND NAME

readline

This command waits for input from the user. An optional message can be displayed as a prompt.

Common Usage

readline(prompt = "")

Related Commands

function (p. 495)

Command Parameters

prompt = ""   A character string. This is displayed and acts as a prompt for the user.

Examples

```
## Simple function that accepts single value
> func = function(x) {
  #   x = a numeric value
  y = readline(prompt = "Enter a numeric value: ") # User prompted
  y = as.numeric(y) # Force input to be numeric
  result = x^y      # Calculate
  print(result)     # Display result
}

  ## Run the function
> func(2)
Enter a numeric value: 3
[1] 8
```

```
  ## Function that accepts alternatives
> func = function(x, y) {
    # x, y = numeric values
    pr = readline(prompt = "Enter P for Power or R for root: ") # Prompt
    pr = tolower(pr)      # Force input to lower case
    if(pr == "p")         # What to do if input is "p" (or "P")
      result = x^y        # Calculate the power function, otherwise
      else                # do something else if input is not "p"
      result = x^(1/y)    # Calculate the root
    print(result)         # Show the result
    }

  ## Run the function
> func(3, 2)
Enter P for Power or R for root: p
[1] 9

> func(3, 2)
Enter P for Power or R for root: R
[1] 1.732051
```

COMMAND NAME

`return`

This command is used to return results from a `function`. It ends the `function` as soon as it is called. Generally, you would use this as the last line in the `function`.

Common Usage

`return(value)`

Related Commands

`print` (p. 515)
`invisible` (p. 512)

Command Parameters

`value`   A result to return. Usually this is a calculated named object from within a `function`, but you can also use a math expression.

Examples

```
  ## A simple function
> func = function(x, y) {          # Start function body
    powr = x^y                     # Calculate power
    root = x^(1/y)                 # Calculate root
```

```
    result = list(power = powr, root = root) # Make result list object
       print(x+y)          # Print x + y right now
       return(result)      # Return result (ends function)
    cat("Completed:\n") # Does not execute as
                           # return() ends function in previous line
  }                        # End of function body

  ## Run the function
> func(2,3)
[1] 5
$power
[1] 8

$root
[1] 1.259921
```

COMMAND NAME

substitute

This command returns R expressions unevaluated. It is similar to quote but you are able to substitute any variables in the expression with values held in an environment. One use of the command is in conjunction with deparse, for making labels from user input in functions.

Common Usage

substitute(expr, env)

Related Commands

deparse (p. 510)
quote (p. 518)

Command Parameters

expr   An expression of some kind. This is usually a named object or R command.

env   An environment. The default is the current evaluation environment. You can also specify a list object.

Examples

```
  ## Simple substitute is similar to quote()
> substitute(x + y)
x + y

  ## Make a list holding items for substitution
> mylist = list(x = 23, y = 46)
```

```
  ## Use list to substitute
> substitute(x + y, env = mylist)
23 + 46


  ## Make a function that shows result
> cum.fun = function(x, fun = median, ...) {
  tmp = seq_along(x)
  for(i in 1:length(tmp)) tmp[i] = fun(x[1:i], ...)
  cat('\n', deparse(substitute(fun)), # Substitute in name of function
      'of',
             deparse(substitute(x)),    # Substitute in name of data
      '\n')
  print(tmp)
 } # END


  ## Make some data then run the function
> mydat = c(3, 4, 6, 6, 4, 3, 7, 8, 9)


> cum.fun(mydat, fun = median)

 median of mydat
[1] 3.0 3.5 4.0 5.0 4.0 4.0 4.0 5.0 6.0
```

COMMAND NAME

```
summary
summary.xxxx
```

The summary command produces summaries of objects. Often, these objects are the results of your scripts or functions. The summary command is very generic and you can write your own dedicated summary functions to deal with objects that hold a specific class attribute. You name your function summary.xxxx, where xxxx corresponds to the class attribute of the object you want to summarize. Several summary.xxxx commands are already built into R to deal with various classes of objects.

SUMMARY METHODS

You can check to see if there is a built-in summary.xxxx command by using the following command:

```
 methods(class = "xxxx")
```

where xxxx is the name of the class attribute you want to use. The result shows you all the methods associated with that class.

Common Usage

```
summary(object, ...)
summary(object, digits, maxsum, ...)
```

Related Commands

print (p. 515)
cat (p. 509)
invisible (p. 512)

Command Parameters

object	An R object for which you require a summary.
...	Additional arguments can be given.
digits	The number of significant figures to display.
maxsum	The maximum number of levels that should be shown when summarizing a factor object.

Examples

```
## Make some data to summarize
## You will need the pw data from the download
> mydat = c(2, 3, 4, 2, 3, 6, 7, 6, 3, NA) # A vector

## Use summary
> summary(mydat)
   Min. 1st Qu.  Median    Mean 3rd Qu.    Max.    NA's
      2       3       3       4       6       7       1

> summary(pw$water)
 hi  lo mid
  6   6   6

> summary(pw)
     height              plant    water
 Min.   : 5.00   sativa  :9   hi :6
 1st Qu.: 9.50   vulgaris:9   lo :6
 Median :16.00                mid:6
 Mean   :19.44
 3rd Qu.:30.25
 Max.   :44.00

  ## A simple function
> func = function(x, y) {                    # Start function body
    powr = x^y                               # Calculate power
    root = x^(1/y)                           # Calculate root
    result = list(power = powr, root = root) # Make result list object
    class(result) <- "pwrrt"                 # Make a dedicated class
    print(result)                            # Show result
  }                                          # End of function body
```

```
                    ## A dedicated summary for class "pwrrt"
                 >  summary.pwrrt = function(result, digits = 4) { # Start function body
                    rm = rbind(result$power, result$root)         # Make a matrix of results
                    colnames(rm) = "Results"                      # A name for the column
                    rownames(rm) = c("Power", "Root")             # Row names
                    print(rm, digits = digits)                    # Display results
                    }                                             # End of function body

                    ## Run function (produces immediate result)
                 > fr = func(3,2)
                 $power
                 [1] 9

                 $root
                 [1] 1.732051

                 attr(,"class")
                 [1] "pwrrt"

                 ## Use summary (uses summary.pwrt)
                 > summary(fr)
                        Results
                 Power    9.000
                 Root     1.732

                 ## Default summary!
                 > summary.default(fr)
                        Length Class   Mode
                 power  1       -none- numeric
                 root   1       -none- numeric
```

COMMAND NAME

```
tolower
toupper
```

These commands change the case of characters. Useful for converting user input into a particular case so that your script only has to deal with lower- or uppercase.

Common Usage

```
tolower(x)
toupper(x)
```

Related Commands

readline (p. 519)
cat (p. 509)
print (p. 515)

x   A character vector, or an object that can be coerced into one by as.character.

Examples

```
## Make some character data with mixed case letters
> mcl = c("MixEd", "CAse", "leTters")

## Force all to lower case
> tolower(mcl)
[1] "mixed"   "case"    "letters"

## Force to upper case
> toupper(mcl)
[1] "MIXED"   "CASE"    "LETTERS"
```

ERROR TRAPPING

When you write functions and scripts you hope that users will enter the appropriate arguments. If they do not, it is likely that your function will produce an error. The R-generated error message may not be entirely helpful, so it can be useful to incorporate your own error checking into your scripts.

COMMAND NAME

```
missing
```

This command is used to check for missing arguments in functions. This means that it is not usually typed into the keyboard as a regular command, but is found only in custom functions and scripts. You can include commands that substitute in values to replace missing arguments, or use the stop command and display a (helpful) message to the user.

Common Usage

```
missing(x)
```

Related Commands

```
stop (p. 526)
substitute (p. 521)
```

Command Parameters

x   An argument to a function.

Examples

```
  ## A function with error checking
> func = function(x, y) {            # Start of function body
   if(missing(x)) {                  # Check to see if x is supplied...
   stop("You need to supply an x value") } # ...stop & message if not
   if(missing(y)) y = x              # If y is not given make y = x
   powr = x^y
   root = x^(1/y)
   result = list(power = powr, root = root)  # Make result object
   return(result)                   # Show result now
  }                                  # End function body


  ## Run the function
> func(2) # y is missing and will be set equal to x
$power
[1] 4

$root
[1] 1.414214

> func() # both x and y are missing
Error in func() : You need to supply an x value

> func(y = 4) # x is missing
Error in func(y = 4) : You need to supply an x value
```

COMMAND NAME

stop

This command halts the execution of a function and displays an error message.

Common Usage

```
stop(..., call. = TRUE)
```

Related Commands

missing (p. 525)
cat (p. 509)

Command Parameters

...	Character string(s), which is used as an error message. Objects that are not characters are coerced into such.
call. = TRUE	By default the R error message is shown before your own message.

Examples

```
  ## A trivial function
> func = function(x, y, z) {
  if(missing(x)) stop("x is missing") # Default: R error & message
  if(missing(y)) stop("y is missing", call. = TRUE)  # R error & message
  if(missing(z)) stop("z is missing", call. = FALSE) # Don't show R error
  return(x + y + z) # The result displayed immediately
 } # End of function

  ## Run the function
> func() # All missing, first error trap posts R error and message
Error in func() : x is missing

> func(2) # Only x is supplied, 2nd error trap posts R error and message
Error in func(2) : y is missing

> func(x = 1, y = 4) # z is missing, 3rd error trap posts message
Error: z is missing

> func(4, 5, 3) # All arguments supplied: function runs normally
[1] 12
```

CONSTANTS

Several constants are built into R. These are useful for various purposes.

COMMAND NAME

```
letters
LETTERS
month.name
month.abb
pi
```

These commands access the built-in constants for the base package of R. The basic constants are:

- letters: Lowercase alphabetical characters (a–z)

- LETTERS: Uppercase alphabetical characters (A–Z)

- month.name: Months of the year (January–December)

- month.abb: Months of the year abbreviated (Jan–Dec)

- pi: The value of Pi (π), which is approximately 3.142.

Common Usage

```
letters[n]
LETTERS[n]
month.name[n]
month.abb[n]
pi
```

Related Commands

data (p. 46)

Command Parameters

n   A number or range of numbers that form a subset of the constant. If missing, the entire
    constant is returned.

Examples

```
  ## All lower case letters
> letters
 [1] "a" "b" "c" "d" "e" "f" "g" "h" "i" "j" "k" "l" "m" "n" "o" "p" "q" "r"
[19] "s" "t" "u" "v" "w" "x" "y" "z"

  ## 12 upper case letters (A-L)
> LETTERS[1:12]
 [1] "A" "B" "C" "D" "E" "F" "G" "H" "I" "J" "K" "L"

## All the abbreviated month names
> month.abb
 [1] "Jan" "Feb" "Mar" "Apr" "May" "Jun" "Jul" "Aug" "Sep" "Oct" "Nov" "Dec"

  ## Full month names for "odd" months
> month.name[c(1, 3, 5, 7, 9, 11)]
[1] "January"   "March"     "May"       "July"      "September" "November"

  ## The value of Pi
> pi
[1] 3.141593
```

INDEX

SYMBOLS

|| (OR) operator, Logic command, 192–193

! (NOT) operator, Logic command, 192–193

command, ignoring what follows, 507

$ (dollar sign)
  accessing named elements, 29–30
  selecting or adding to object
    elements, 109–110

? (question mark), as helper function of help
  command, 482–483

[] (square brackets)
  enabling sub-settings for extracting or
    adding elements, 30–32
  selecting/extracting object parts, 107–109

A

abbreviate command, for shortening character
  strings, 507–509

abline command, adding straight lines to plots,
  300–301, 404–406

abs command, returns absolute magnitude of
  numeric value, 169–170

acos command, calculating arc-cosine, 202

acosh command, calculating hyperbolic arc-
  cosine, 202

add1 command, adding all possible single terms
  to linear model, 301–303

addmargins command
  applying summary command to tables,
    arrays, or matrices, 121
  carrying out summary command on tables,
    arrays, or matrices, 136–138

aggregate command, computing summary
  statistics based on grouping
  variables, 122–123

all command, returns TRUE value if all values
  are TRUE, 188, 502–503

all.equal command, testing equality of two
  objects, 188–189

altering data types (as.xxxx), 16–17

AND (&) operator, Logic command, 192–193

annotations, ignoring what follows #
  command, 507

ANOVA (Analysis of Variance)
  anova command, 284
  aov command, 285–286
  contrasts command, 286–289
  effects command, 289–290
  formula command, 290–291
  interaction.plot command, 291
  manova command, 292–294
  model.tables command, 294–295
  overview of, 283–284
  power.anova.test command, 295–296
  replications command, 297–298
  TukeyHSD command, 298–300

anova command, computing analysis of
  variance (or deviation), 284, 303–304

Ansari-Bradley two-sample tests, 252–253

ansari.test command, 252–253

any command, returning TRUE value if any
  values are TRUE, 189–190, 503–504

aov command
  computing analysis of variance, 285–286
  computing results from aov model fits
    (model.tables command), 294–295

apply command, applying functions to arrays
  or matrices, 123–124

apropos command, finding objects by partial
  name matching, 480–481

arc-cosine, calculating (acos and acosh
  commands), 202

arc-sine, calculating (asin and asinh
  commands), 203–204

arc-tangent, calculating (atan and atahn
  commands), 204–205

drop command, for removing dimension with only single entry, 212–213

drop1 command, removing terms from fitted-model object, 306–307

droplevels command, dropping unused factor levels, 111–112

dump command, creating text representations of objects, 53–54, 498–499

dxxxx command, density/mass functions for probability distributions, 148–152

E

ecdf command, creating cumulative distribution, 152–153

effects command, returning orthogonal effects from fitted-model object, 289–290

eigen command, computing eigenvalues and eigenvectors for matrix objects, 213–215

else command, for conditional control of scripts, 505–507

erase.screen command, clearing graph screens, 469–473

error trapping
   missing command, 525–526
   overview of, 525
   stop command, 526–527

exclusive OR (XOR) operator, Logic command, 192–193

exp command, computing exponential function, 175

expression command, adding text and math symbols to graphs, 422–425

F

F distribution
   calculating quantiles for various probability distributions (qxxxx command), 160
   cumulative probability for probability distributions (pxxxx command), 157
   density/mass functions for probability distributions (dxxxx command), 150

factorial command, computing factorial, 176

factors
   creating contingency tables based on (ftable command), 138–139
   creating frequency tables for (tabulate command), 144
   creating new factor variable (interaction command), 24–25
   data types, 7–8
   dropping unused factor levels (droplevels command), 111–112
   generating factor levels (gl command), 23–24
   graphing interaction factors (interaction.plot command), 291
   levels attribute, 86–87
   plotting summary statistics for factor interactions (interaction.plot command), 372–373
   reording factor levels (reorder command), 95–98
   replacing or reordering levels (relevel command), 94–95
   returning numbers of object levels (nlevels command), 93–94
   setting contrast options for factors in linear modeling (contrasts command), 286–289

FALSE. *see* TRUE/FALSE values

family command, querying/specifying distribution model parameters, 307–308

file.choose command, for interactive selection of files, 40–43

files
   interactive selection of, 40–43
   viewing (dir command), 64–65

find command, showing object location in search environment, 480–481

Fisher test, of exactness of association, 278–280

fisher.test command, 278–280

fitted/fitted.values command, extracting model fitted values, 309–310

fivenum command, producing Tukey's five-number summary, 126

K

Kendall's Tau Rank correleation
    carrying out correlations, 267
    correlation significance tests, 269
keyboard
    importing data from, 43–45
    reading data from (scan command), 28–29
    reading text files as typed from (source command), 45
keyboard, creating data from
    c command, 22–23
    cbind command, 23
    gl command, 23–24
    interaction command, 24–25
    rbind command, 26–27
    rep command, 25–26
    seq command, 27–28
kmeans command, carrying out k-means clustering, 322–324
Kolmogorov-Smirnov tests, 237–238
kruskal.test command, 258–259
Kruskal-Wallis rank sum test, 258–259
ks.test command, for Kolmogorov-Smirnov tests, 237–238

L

labels, adding to graphs (title command), 430–432
lagged differences
    computing inverse function of (invdiff command), 174–175
    returning (diff command), 173–174
lapply command, applying functions to list elements, 126–127
layout command, managing graph window, 462–464
layout.show command, managing graph window, 462–464
lcm command, managing graph window, 462–464
legend command, adding legend to graphs, 425, 432–436

legends, adding to graphs (legend command), 425, 432–436
length command
    determining number of elements in objects, 127–128, 226
    getting/setting number of items in an object, 86
letters constant, for lower case alphabectical characters, 527–528
LETTERS constant, for upper case alphabectical characters, 527–528
levels
    applying summary function to vector based on levels of another vector (tapply command), 135–136
    dropping unused factor levels (droplevels command), 111–112
    factor command, 7
    generating factor levels (gl command), 23–24
    getting/setting object values (levels command), 86–87
    reording factor levels (reorder command), 95–98
    replacing or reordering (relevel command), 94–95
    returning number of object levels (nlevels command), 93–94
levels command, getting/setting object values, 86–87
library command, for loading packages, 487–489
linear equations
    backsolve command, 206–207
    forwardsolve command, 215
linear modeling
    abline command, 300–301
    add1 command, 301–303
    anova command, 303–304
    coef and coefficients commands, 304–305
    confint command, 305–306
    drop1 command, 306–307
    family command, 307–308

M

Macintosh OS, opening blank windows (quartz command) in, 395–397

mad command, determining median absolute deviation for numeric vector, 128

Mann-Whitney U-test, 265–266

manova command, carrying out multivariate ANOVA, 292–294

margin areas of graphs
  adding text to, 425–427
  setting, 459–461

margin.table command, producing sums for margins of contingency tables, 129, 140–141

mass. *see* density functions

math commands
  abs command, 169–170
  Arith command, 170–171
  ceiling command, 171–172
  cummax, cummin, cumprod, cumsum, 172–173
  diff command, 173–174
  diffinv command, 174–175
  exp command, 175
  factorial command, 176
  floor command, 176–177
  log command, 177–178
  max and pmax commands, 178–179
  min and pmin commands, 179–180
  overview of, 169
  prod command, 180–181
  range command, 181–182
  round command, 182–183
  sign command, 183–184
  signif command, 184–185
  sqrt command, 185
  sum command, 186–187
  trunc command, 187

math expressions, adding math symbols to graphs, 423

mathematics
  complex numbers. *see* complex number commands
  logic. *see* logic commands
  math operations. *see* math commands

matrix math. *see* matrix math commands

trigonometry. *see* trigonometry commands

matlines command, adding lines to graphs, 374–376, 377, 401, 411

matmult command, for matrix multiplication, 216–217

matplot command
  adding lines and points to matplot, 401
  creating multiple series graphs, 374–376

matpoints command, adding points to graphs, 374–376, 377, 401, 411

matrices
  adding columns to (cbind command), 23
  applying functions to (apply command), 123–124
  applying summary command to (addmargins command), 121
  biplot from two matrix objects, 356
  calculating row sums (rowSums command), 131
  carrying out summary commands on (addmargins command), 136–138
  computing Cholesky factorization of (chol command), 207–208
  computing distance matrices (dist command), 319–320
  computing inverse function of lagged differences, 174–175
  creating or adding to (cbind command), 33–34
  creating or adding to (matrix command), 35–36
  extracting subsets of (subset command), 114–116
  producing correlation matrix from covariance matrix, 272–273
  producing sums for margins of contingency tables, arrays, or matrices (margin.table command), 140–141
  producing sums for margins of (margin.table command), 129
  returning lagged differences (diff command), 173–174

sign command, indicating positive, negative, or nil values, 183–184

signif command, returning value rounded to specified number of significant figures, 184–185

sine, calculating (sin and sinh commands), 203–204

solve command, solving a system of equations, 220–221

sort command, rearranging data, 120

sorting and rearranging data
 order command, 117–118
 overview of, 117
 rank command, 119
 sort command, 120
 which command, 120

source command, for reading text files as typed from keyboard, 45

source command, running saved scripts with, 501–502

Spearman's Rho Rank correlation, 267, 269

spline command, for spline interpretation of series of coordinate data, 414–416

split.screen command, splitting graph screens, 469–473

SPSS files, reading (read.spss command), 48

square root, returning (sqrt command), 185

SSlogis command, creating self-starting nonlinear models, 343–344

stacked bar chart, 352

standard deviation, calculating (sd command), 132, 231–232, 234–235

statistics. *see* summary statistics

stem-and-leaf plots, creating (stem command), 388–389

step command, conducting stepwise model building, 315–317

stop command, halting execution of a function, 526–527

storage.mode command, getting/setting object storage attributes, 101–102

str command, viewing object structure, 102–103

Studentized range
 calculating quartiles for (qtukey command), 158
 cumulative distribution of (Q statistic), 154

Student's t distribution
 calculating quantiles for various probability distributions (qxxxx command), 161
 carrying out Student's t-test, 248–251
 cumulative probability for probability distributions (pxxxx command), 157
 density/mass functions for probability distributions (dxxxx command), 152

subscript, adding text to graphs, 422

subset command, extracting subsets of data objects, 114–116

substitute command, returning R expressions without evaluating, 521–522

sum command, returning sums, 132, 186–187, 232–233

summary command, for summarizing objects, 132–133, 233–234, 522–524

summary statistics
 aggregate command, 122–123
 apply command, 123–124
 colMeans command, 124–125
 colSums command, 125
 cummax, cummin, cumprod, and cumsum commands, 126, 223–224
 fivenum command, 126, 224–225
 IQR command, 126, 225–226
 lapply command, 126–127
 length command, 127–128, 226
 mad command, 128, 226–227
 margin.table command, 129
 max and pmax commands, 227
 mean command, 129, 227–228
 median command, 129, 228–229
 min and pmin commands, 229

ts command, 13–14. *see also* time-series
data (`ts`)
t-tests
carrying out multiple t-tests
(`pairwise.t.test` command), 245–247
carrying out Student's t-test (`t.test`
command), 248–251
computing power of (`power.t.test`
command), 247–248
Tukey
producing Tukey's five-number summary
(`fivenum` command),
126, 224–225
Tukey's Honest Significant Difference
(`TukeyHSD` command), 153, 298–300
`typeof` command, determining object
type, 103–104

U

`unclass` command, removing class
attribute, 104–105
uniform distribution
generating random numbers for various
probability distributions (`rxxxx`
command), 165
QQ plot comparing with Gaussian
distribution, 388
`uniroot` command, carrying out one-
dimensional root (zero) finding, 344–345
`unlist` command, converting list into vector
object, 105–106
`upper.tri` command, returning TRUE value for
upper triangle of a matrix, 222–223
user input, `readline` command and, 519–520

V

value, in HSV color, 440
`var` command, calculating variance of numeric
vectors, 136, 273–274
`variable.names` command, showing variable
names, 106–107

variables
computing summary statistics based on
grouping (`aggregate` command), 122–123
creating contingency tables based on (`table`
command), 142–143
quantile-quantile plot of two
variables, 387–388
showing names of (`variable.names`
command), 106–107
variance
analysis of. *see* ANOVA (Analysis of
Variance)
Bartlett test of homogeneity of, 241–242
calculating variance of numeric vectors (`var`
command), 136, 235
Fligner-Kileen tests of homogeneity
of, 254–255
`var.test` command, carrying out
F-tests, 251–252
`vector` command, data types, 15
vectors
applying functions to (`sapply`
command), 131–132
applying summary function to vector
based on levels of another vector (`tapply`
command), 135–136
calculating variance of numeric vectors (`var`
command), 136, 235, 273–274
computing eigenvectors for matrix objects
(`eigen` command), 213–215
computing inverse function of lagged
differences, 174–175
converting list into vector object (`unlist`
command), 105–106
creating arrays from, 4
creating complex (`complex`
command), 195–196
creating frequency tables for (`tabulate`
command), 144
determining median absolute deviation for
numeric vector (`mad` command),
128, 226–227